INTRODUCTION TO REFERENCE WORK

VOLUME I *Basic Information Sources*

McGRAW-HILL SERIES IN LIBRARY EDUCATION
Jean Key Gates, Consulting Editor
University of South Florida

Boll   INTRODUCTION TO CATALOGING, VOL. I:
DESCRIPTIVE CATALOGING
Boll   INTRODUCTION TO CATALOGING, VOL. II:
ENTRY HEADINGS
Chan   CATALOGING AND CLASSIFICATION:
AN INTRODUCTION
Gardner   LIBRARY COLLECTIONS:
THEIR ORIGIN, SELECTION, AND DEVELOPMENT
Gates   INTRODUCTION TO LIBRARIANSHIP
Jackson   LIBRARIES AND LIBRARIANSHIP IN THE WEST:
A BRIEF HISTORY
Katz   INTRODUCTION TO REFERENCE WORK, VOL. I:
BASIC INFORMATION SOURCES
Katz   INTRODUCTION TO REFERENCE WORK, VOL. II:
REFERENCE SERVICES AND REFERENCE PROCESSES

INTRODUCTION
TO REFERENCE WORK

Volume I **Basic Information Sources**

Fifth Edition

William A. Katz
Professor, School of Library and Information Science
State University of New York at Albany

McGraw-Hill Book Company

New York   St. Louis   San Francisco   Auckland   Bogotá
Hamburg   London   Madrid   Mexico   Milan
Montreal   New Delhi   Panama   Paris   São Paulo
Singapore   Sydney   Tokyo   Toronto

INTRODUCTION TO REFERENCE WORK, Volume I
Basic Information Sources

4 5 6 7 8 9 0 D O C D O C 8 9 8

ISBN 0-07-033537-0

This book was set in Baskerville by Black Dot, Inc.
The editor was Emily G. Barrosse;
the cover was designed by Laura
Stover; the production supervisors
were Leroy A. Young and Friederich
Schulte.
Project supervision was done by The Total Book.
R. R. Donnelley & Sons Company was printer and binder.

Library of Congress Cataloging-in-Publication Data

Katz, William A.,
    Introduction to reference work.

    Includes bibliographies and index.
    Contents: v. 1. Basic information sources—
v. 2 Reference services and reference processes.
    1. Reference services (Libraries)   2. Reference
books.   I. Title.
Z711.K32   1987   025.5'2   86-10247
ISBN 0-07-033537-0 (v. 1)
ISBN 0-07-033538-9 (v. 2)

For Emily Rose Chesser

CONTENTS

PREFACE

The purpose of this text is to acquaint librarians, students, and library users with various information sources. Although written with the student and reference librarian in mind, the chapters introduce basic sources which will help the layperson to use the library effectively.

Basic Information Sources is the first volume in the two-volume set, *Introduction to Reference Work.* In this fifth edition, revision is extensive and all material is updated. The organizational pattern remains the same as in the fourth edition. A chapter has been added to provide a brief, nontechnical description of computer-assisted reference services. For a more thorough overview, the reader should turn to the second volume. Throughout the text, basic reference sources now available online are indicated.

Only foundation, or basic, reference works are considered here. The vast and growing area of subject specialization and bibliography is left to other texts and other courses. Notes of some major subject forms are primarily illustrative and not intended to be exhaustive.

After an introduction to reference work and services, the text is divided into chapters on traditional forms, such as bibliographies, indexes, and encyclopedias. Each chapter considers various common aspects of one of the forms and how they relate to answering questions.

The introductory chapter on computers and reference work is just that, and the intention is to give the student a quick, but well grounded overview of the most important development of current reference work. The second volume of this text goes into considerably more detail about online reference services and related matters.

It is pointless for students to memorize details about specific reference sources, but they should grasp the essential areas of agreement and difference among the various forms. To this end, every effort is made to compare rather than to detail. Not all so-called basic titles are included or annotated, because (1) there is no consensus on what constitutes "basic"; (2) more important, the objective of this text is to discuss various forms, and the titles used are those which best illustrate those forms; and finally, (3) the annotations for a specific title are duplicated over and over again in Sheehy's *Guide to Reference Books* and Walford's *Guide to Reference Materials*, which list the numerous subject bibliographies.

Suggested readings are found at the end of each chapter and in the footnotes. When a publication is cited in a footnote, the reference is rarely duplicated in the "Suggested Reading." For the most part, the readings are limited to publications issued since 1982; thus the citations in the fourth edition have been updated, and it is easier for the student to find the readings. A number of the suggested reading items will be found in the author's *Library Lit: The Best of . . .* and in *Reference and Information Sources, A Reader*, 3d ed. Both are published by Scarecrow Press: the former from 1970 to date (annual), the latter in 1986. A critic wisely points out that the readings need not be current, that many older articles and books are as useful today as they were when first published. This is beyond argument. Still, thanks to many teachers' retaining earlier editions of this text and the aforementioned Scarecrow titles, it is possible to have a bibliography of previous readings.

Prices are noted for most of the major basic titles, as has been done since the first edition. This seems particularly useful today, when the librarian must look more and more to budgetary considerations when selecting reference titles. If a particular work is available online, the gross hourly rate as charged by Lockheed is given for its use. Both this rate and the book prices are as of 1986 and are useful in determining relative costs, though increases may occur to quickly outdate what is given here.

Bibliographic data are based on publishers' catalogs, *Books in Print*, and examination of the titles. The information is applicable as of mid-1986 and, like prices, is subject to change.

I am grateful to many teachers of reference and bibliography for their advice and help. My thanks also go to the students who so kindly made suggestions. Special thanks are due to the instructors who reviewed the manuscript: Professor Larry D. Benson, Brigham Young University, and Professor Marilyn White, University of Maryland. Praise for Professor Jean Key Gates, University of Florida, who acted as consulting editor, and Emily Barrosse, my editor at McGraw-Hill. In addition, I am grateful to Annette Bodzin and Keith Herrmann at McGraw-Hill who helped bring this project to fruition.

William A. Katz

INTRODUCTION TO REFERENCE WORK

VOLUME I *Basic Information Sources*

INTRODUCTION

CHAPTER ONE

The Reference Process

There is no more rewarding library work than being a reference librarian.[1] It offers the marvelous opportunity of dealing with people of almost every social, economic, and educational level.[2] It is a constant challenge to find precisely the right book, the right computer printout, or the right article to solve an immediate problem. While there is more to reference service than answering questions, essentially that is the primary goal. Someone wants to know the number of television sets in New York State. Someone else is seeking the meaning of life. Finding the answer, or indicating the various century-old approaches to the answer, is what reference service is all about.

Depending on the type of question, one may imagine reference service as a tremendous bore or a source of considerable intellectual

---

[1]Some now use other titles to mark the reference librarian. These range from information specialist, to search analyst, information broker, or what happens to appeal to the spirit of the day.

[2]Precisely how to refer to the person who uses a library is a mystery. Some say the "user," others the "patron," still others "client" or "borrower." For a discussion of this perplexing problem see Michael Gorman, "A Borrower is a Client is a Patron is a User is a Reader," *American Libraries,* October 1983, p. 597; and the letters about the article in the same magazine, December 1983, p. 702.

pleasure.[3] In most libraries, reference librarians face both situations. After they have told the 101st person where the telephone is located or how to use the card catalog, after they have decided reference service is more pain than pleasure, along comes someone with a challenging query which requires effort, imagination, and knowledge of possible sources of answers. Some days are up, some days are down, but on the average it is a fascinating and exciting profession.

After a year of daily work as a reference librarian, a library school teacher asked the rhetorical question: "What is it about reference librarianship that can make it such a satisfying and rewarding pursuit?"[4] The answer: (1) One has the opportunity to meet and serve people. (2) In helping others to learn, the librarian continually learns about reference sources and the world. (3) Thanks to computers and networks, one has the potential advantage of being able to draw upon all of the world's information, not just that in the individual library.

What do librarians think about reference work? According to one survey: "Among the librarians, those working in reference departments reported the highest levels of satisfaction. Among the nonprofessional employees, those working in reference departments reported the highest levels of satisfaction. Reference service is considered by some to have more esteem than other aspects of library work."[5]

There are, to be sure, wide gaps between the theory of excellent reference service and the realities of that service when the library is understaffed, underfinanced, and badly administered. One or all of these conditions often conspire against the joys of working at the

---

[3]The term "reference service" means much more and that "more" is explored here and in the second volume of the text. Vavrek, in asking rural librarians what the term meant, concluded that it was divided into Answering questions (34%); Locating information (30%); Service (17%); Providing materials (7%); Aiding readers (4%). Bernard Vavrek, "The Meaning of Reference Service—From the Field." *Catholic Library World,* February 1983, pp. 261–265. In a much broader context the able English writer and teacher (Donald Davinson *Reference Service.* London: Bingley, 1980) devotes two chapters in his book to what is essentially a definition. This formulation is by far the best introduction to the subject. For an overview, see almost any issue of *The Reference Librarian, RQ,* or *Reference Services Review*—all journals dedicated to explaining and defining reference work.

[4]Charles Bunge, "Potential and Reality at the Reference Desk: Reflections on a 'Return to the Field'," *Journal of Academic Librarianship,* July 1984, p. 128. Bunge points out the dark side of the picture, too. This is primarily due to lack of proper support by the library.

[5]Beverly P. Lynch and Jo Ann Verdin, "Job Satisfaction in Libraries . . .," *Library Quarterly,* vol. 53, no. 4, 1983, p. 445.

reference desk. Some librarians simply cope, others change jobs, and the majority use various strategies to make their professional lives more interesting. On the whole, though, it is a rewarding and enriching profession.

REFERENCE SERVICE GUIDELINES

The Reference and Adult Services Division of the American Library Association offers reference librarians a set of guidelines which help both to define their work and to chart, if only in a tentative way, a philosophy of service. The guidelines are called "A Commitment to Information Services."[6] Directed "to all those who have any responsibility for providing reference and information services," the guidelines' most valuable contribution is a succinct description of a reference librarian's duties. Defined by function, reference services can be divided into two categories: direct and indirect.

1. The direct category includes:
   a. *Reference or information services.* This is the "personal assistance provided to users in pursuit of information." The depth and character of such service vary with the type of library and the kinds of users it is designed to serve. This service may range from answering an apparently simple query to supplying information based on a bibliographical search combining the librarian/information specialist's competence in research and the subject under investigation.
   b. *Formal and informal instruction in the use of the library or information center and its resources.* This direct service may consist of various activities ranging from helping the user to understand the card catalog to "interpretative tours and lectures" on how to use the library. In most libraries, "instruction" means showing the user how to find an article, book, or other item by "interpreting" the mysteries of an index, reference work, and so on.

[6]"A Commitment to Information Services: Developmental Guidelines," *RQ,* Spring 1979, pp. 275–278. First adopted in 1976, and a section "Ethics of Service" adopted in 1979. "Our Competencies Defined: A Progress Report and Sampling," *American Libraries,* January 1984, pp. 43–45. Quotations which follow are from the guidelines. See, also: Charles Bunge, "Planning, Goals, and Objectives for the Reference Department," *RQ,* Spring 1984, pp. 306–315. A discussion which points up the various avenues for developing reference services in a library.

2. Indirect services may be summarized thus: Indirect services reflect user access to a wide range of informational sources (e.g., bibliographies, indexes, information databases), and may be the extension of the library's information-service potential through cooperation with other library or information centers. This type of service recognizes the key role of interlibrary and interagency cooperation to provide adequate information service to users.

The average reference librarian is likely to perform many indirect services:

Selection of Materials This service requires the recognition of the various types of materials needed for adequate reference service —not only books, but periodicals, manuscripts, newspapers, and anything else which can conceivably assist the librarian in giving direct service. Another aspect of selection is the weeding of book collections and files.

Reference Administration The organization and administration of reference services will not involve everyone, but will be a major consideration for small-to-medium libraries with only one or two librarians.

Interlibrary Loan With the increasing emphasis on networks and the recognition that the whole world of information should be literally at the command of the user, interlibrary loan may be categorized as an access activity. It is a major element in reference service. Administratively, some libraries now divorce it from reference and maintain it as a separate division; others consider it a function of the circulation section.

Evaluation of Reference Section How well is the reference section serving the public? What has been done and what can be done to improve service? This analysis presupposes a method of evaluating not only the collection, but the organization of the reference section and the library as a whole.

Miscellaneous Tasks There are a variety of "housekeeping" duties, including assisting with photocopying, filing, checking in materials, keeping a wary eye on reading rooms, maintaining records, plus all the chores that are the responsibility of any library department— from budgeting to preparing reports and publicity releases. Other services may include creating reference sources, local indexes, and information and referral sources. The extent of this kind of activity depends to a great degree on the size of the library and the philosophy and the financial support of the reference section.

In a 1983–1984 survey of representative large research libraries, it was found that the average academic research librarian "puts in an average of 13.3 hours each week at the reference desk."[7] Looking back at the previous list of reference librarian duties, it is easy to appreciate why the librarian is not more often at the desk. Other principal duties include library instruction, collection development, bibliography work, interlibrary loan, and vertical file maintenance.[8] Add to this the necessity for relief from the tension of answering questions and dealing with people, and it is understandable why relatively so little time is devoted to actual reference queries.

Competencies

The 1976 guidelines were updated in 1979 with an additional section on ethics. This includes the obvious, i.e., the librarian should provide all people with accurate information when it is requested; and the librarian should do this as part of professional duty, not for additional personal payment. Beyond that one should consider the not-so-obvious. A major consideration in terms of ethics is the attitude of the librarian. All people should be given equal service. All people should be treated with courtesy and respect. All people should be treated so that their confidence is respected. Confidentiality is an absolute requirement. And in no case should the librarian's individual attitudes be reflected in the type of service given, or not given. (More attention to ethics will be given in the second volume of this text, as well as throughout both volumes. It's a major consideration, and one each individual must carefully weigh.)

In 1984 the guidelines were examined from another viewpoint. If the original document describes what is done in a library, or what should be done, the second document, "Our Competencies Defined"

---

[7]Paula D. Watson, "Organization and Management of Reference Services in Academic Research Libraries; A Survey," *RQ,* Summer 1984, p. 408.

[8]Nancy Emmick and Luella Davis, "A Survey of Academic Library Reference Service Practices: Preliminary Results," *RQ,* Fall 1984, pp. 67–81. The authors surveyed 367 U.S. and Canadian college and university libraries. Other information is concerned with promotion criteria, status in relation to teaching faculty, etc. Of course, the number of hours spent at the desk varies from library to library, and it is quite possible that in smaller libraries (public, school, or academic) the reference librarian would be spending more than half the time answering questions.

(*American Libraries,* January 1984, pp. 43–45) explores the components of an individual's competency in reference services. "For the purpose of this project," (p. 84) "competencies were defined as comprising these major components: knowledge, skills, and attitudes."

There are to be several lists for various types of librarians in equally varied work situations. Experience is a major factor. A listing of competency for a senior level reference librarian (over 10 years' experience) in a special library is divided into the three parts (skills, knowledge and attitudes).

The list is much too long to quote in full, but from the point of view of an ethical attitude, of the degree to which he or she has "ethical skills," the senior reference librarian should be competent and able to: (1) establish rapport with users, (2) negotiate a reference interview, and (3) evaluate and advise patrons as to the currency, accuracy, and sufficiency of information retrieved or received so that patrons can evaluate the usefulness of that information.

In terms of attitudes, the librarian should demonstrate (1) a positive attitude toward the profession, the organization served, the library, and its users. Parenthetically, this is a two-way street, as any experienced librarian knows, and it has to be assumed that the administration has the same positive attitude toward the librarians. In any case, both should demonstrate a respect for the user. (2) A sense of responsibility. (3) A willingness to help people. (4) A willingness to fail. And so it goes. While the complete list describes a cross between a robot and a saint, it is a list which deserves thought. If nothing else, it is a grand point of departure for discussion.

REFERENCE SERVICE AND THE LIBRARY

The reference librarian does not function alone in a library but is part of a larger unit. Briefly, how do reference services fit into the library?

The specific purpose of any library is to obtain, preserve, and make available the recorded knowledge of human beings. The system for doing so can be as intricate and involved as the table of organization for the Library of Congress or General Motors or as simple as that used in the one-man small-town library or the corner barbershop.

Regardless of organizational patterns or complexities, the parts of the system are interrelated and common to all sizes and types of libraries. They consist of administrative work, technical services (acquisition and cataloging), and reader's services (circulation and reference). These broad categories cover multiple subsections. They are not independent units but parts of larger units; all are closely related. They form a unity essential for library service in general and reference in particular. Let one fail and the whole system will suffer.

Administrative work

The administration is concerned with library organization and communication. The better the administration functions, the less obvious it appears—at least to the user. The reference librarian must be aware of, and often participate in, administrative decisions ranging from budget to automation. Precisely how an administration functions effectively is the subject of countless texts and coffee conversations. It is not the topic of this text, although specific administration of reference sections and departments is discussed later.

Technical services: Acquisitions

The selection and acquisition of materials are governed by the type of library and its users. Policies vary, of course, but the rallying cry of the nineteenth-century activist librarians, "The right book for the right reader at the right time," is still applicable to any library. It presents many challenges. For the general collection, it presupposes a knowledge of the clientele as well as of the material acquired and its applicability to the reader. The librarian must cope with publishers, sources, and reviews and must cooperate with other libraries. The unparalleled production of library materials over the past 50 years makes the process of selection and acquisition a primary intellectual responsibility.

Reference librarians are responsible for the reference collection, but their responsibility extends to the development of the library's entire collection—a collection which serves to help them answer questions.

Technical services: Cataloging

Once a piece of information is acquired, the primary problem is how to retrieve it from the hundreds, thousands, or millions of bits of information in the library. There are a number of avenues open, from oral communication to abstracts; but for dealing with larger information units such as books, recordings, films, periodicals, or reports, the normal finding device is the card catalog. The catalog is the library's main bibliographical instrument. When properly used, it

(1) enables persons to find books for which they have the author, the title, or the subject area; (2) shows what the library has by any given author, on a given subject, and in a given kind of literature; (3) assists in the choice of a book by its form (e.g., handbook, literature, or text) or edition; (4) assists in finding other materials, from government documents to films; and, often most important, (5) specifically locates the item in the library. It is a primary resource for reference librarians, and it is essential they understand not only the general aspects of the card catalog but also its many peculiarities.

Thanks to rapid developments in computer-assisted cataloging, many libraries now have replaced or augmented the familiar card catalog with an online catalog. Here the librarian, or user, sits down before a computer terminal and a screen, types in a few key letters or parts of words, and is given immediate access on the screen to the holdings of the library. Other terminals open up the holdings of national and international libraries. While not everyone is enthusiastic about the gradual replacement of the standard card catalog, it is a safe prediction that "by the end of the decade, the majority of American libraries of all kinds will be involved in, or affected in a major way by, online catalog systems."[9]

Reader's services: Circulation

Circulation is one of the two primary public service points in the library. The other is reference.

After the book has been acquired and prepared for easy access, the circulation department is concerned with (1) checking out the material to the reader, (2) receiving it on return, and (3) returning it to its proper location. Other activities of the circulation department include registering prospective borrowers, keeping records of the number of books and patrons, and maintaining other statistics pertinent to charting the operation of the library. In small libraries, more than 50 percent of the reference work may be centered at the circulation desk. Such a library normally has one or two professionals who must pinch-hit in almost every capacity from administering to cataloging. Also, there may be no space for a separate reference desk,

[9]Michael Gorman, "Thinking the Thinkable: Synergetic Profession, Online Catalogs Go Beyond Bibliographic Control," *American Libraries,* July/August 1982, p. 473. See the second volume of this text for further discussion of online catalogs, as well as Chapter Three of this book. For an overview, see Emily Fayen's *The Era of Online Public Access Catalogs* (White Plains, New York: Knowledge Industry, 1983).

and the circulation point is a logical center where people come not only to check out books but also to ask questions.

Adult services: Reference

An important aspect of reference service in the 1980s is adult services, often used as a synonym for "adult education." This is a specialized area, although in daily work the average reference librarian will be involved in a range of adult services such as giving assistance with job and occupational information and providing service for the handicapped.

REFERENCE QUESTIONS

There are various methods of categorizing reference questions. By way of an introduction to a complex topic, queries may be divided into two general types:

1. *The user asks for a known item.* The request is usually for a specific document, book, article, film, or other item, which can be identified by citing certain features such as an author, title, or source. The librarian only has to locate the needed item through the card catalog, an index, a bibliography, or a similar source.
2. *The user asks for information without any knowledge of a specific source.* Such a query triggers the usual reference interview. Most reference questions are of this type, particularly in school and public libraries where the average user has little or no knowledge of the reference services available.

Handling the two broad types of questions may not be as easy as it seems. For example, the person who asks for a specific book by author may (1) have the wrong author, (2) actually want a different book by that author, (3) discover the wanted book is not the one required (for either information or pleasure), or (4) ask the librarian to obtain the book on interlibrary loan and then fail to appear when the book is received. All of this leads most experienced reference librarians to qualify the "known-item" type of question. The assumption, which is usually correct, is that the user really needs more information or help than indicated. Therefore, librarians tend to ask enough questions to bring out the real needs of the user as opposed to what may be only a weak signal for help. There are other variables which may turn the first type of question into the second type.

A more finely drawn categorization of reference questions is the division into four types:[10]

(1) *Direction.* "Where is the catalog?" "Where are the indexes?" "Where is the telephone?" The general information or directional question is of the information booth variety, and the answer rarely requires more than a geographical knowledge of key locations. The time required to answer such questions is negligible, but directional queries may account for 30 to 50 percent or more of the questions put to a librarian in any day. (It should be stressed that the percentages—here and in what follows—are relative and may vary from library to library.)

(2) *Ready reference.* "What is the name of the governor of Alaska?" "How long is the Amazon River?" "Who is the world's tallest person?" Here is the typical ready-reference or data query which requires only a single, usually uncomplicated, answer. The requested information is normally found without difficulty in standard reference works, ranging from encyclopedias to almanacs and indexes.

Ready reference queries may be divided and subdivided in many ways. Crossing almost all subject lines, one might construct a classification scheme similar to the reporter's five W's. These are (1) Who? Who is . . .; Who said . . .; Who won . . ., etc. (2) What? What is the speed of sound? What are the qualities of a good swimmer? What does coreopsis look like? (3) Where? Where is the center of the United States? Where is the earth's core? (4) Why? Why does water boil? Why, why, why . . . almost anything. This, the favored of all children's queries, continues with most of us through life. (5) When? When was *Coriolanus* written? When was the automobile invented? Most of these require only a specific piece of data. Also, many might be modified or rephrased in such a way as to get a yes or no answer. Is aspirin harmful? Was America discovered in 1492?

The time it takes to answer this type of question is usually no more than a minute or two. The catch is that while 90 percent of such queries are simple to answer, another 5 to 10 percent may take hours of research because no standard reference source in the library will yield the necessary data. Apparently simple questions are sometimes complicated, such as, "What are the dates of National Cat Week?" (Answer: Flexible, but usually in early November.) "When was

[10]There are many methods of analyzing types of reference questions. For a good overview of the literature, as well as typical types of queries, see: G. Rohan James, "Reference: Analysis, Management and Training," *Library Review,* Summer 1982, pp. 93–103.

Russian roulette first played?" (Answer: Cambridge University in 1801. Lord Byron describes the incident in his memoirs.) Difficult questions of this type are often printed in a regular column in *RQ*, the official journal of reference librarians.[11]

The percentage of ready-reference questions will differ from library to library, although they constitute a large proportion (30 to 40 percent) of all queries other than directional questions in public libraries. In one study it was found that about 60 percent of the questions asked in a public library were of the ready-reference type. Requests for background information make up the other 40 to 60 percent or so of the queries. Public libraries, which have a well-developed phone service for reference questions as well as a high percentage of adult users, tend to attract the ready-reference question. In academic, school, and special libraries, search questions may account for 30 to 60 percent of the total.

(3) *Specific search.* "Where can I find information on sexism in business?" "What is the difference between the conservative and the liberal view on inflation and unemployment?" "Do you have anything on the history of atomic energy?" "I have to write a paper on penguins for my science class. What do you have?" The essential difference between the specific search and the ready-reference questions is twofold. Ready-reference queries usually can be answered with data, normally short answers from reference books. Specific search answers almost always take the form of giving the user a document, e.g., a list of citations, a book, or a report.

More information is required if the user is writing a school paper, is preparing a speech, or is simply interested in learning as much about a subject as necessary for his or her needs. This query often is called a "bibliographic inquiry," because the questioner is referred to a bibliographic aid such as the card catalog, an index, or a bibliography. The user then scans available materials and determines how much and what type of them are needed.

One can hardly suggest that all specific search questions involve bibliographies. At a less-sophisticated level, the librarian may merely direct the user to an encyclopedia article, a given section of the book collection, or a newspaper index. If directional queries are discounted, specific search questions constitute the greatest proportion of

---

reference questions in school and academic libraries as well as in many special libraries.

The time taken to answer the question depends not only on what is available in the library (or through interlibrary loan) but also on the attitude of the librarian. If the librarian offers a considerable amount of help, the search may take from 10 minutes to an hour or more. Conversely, the librarian may turn the question into a directional one by simply pointing the user in the direction of the card catalog.

Another variable in determining the degree of service satisfaction is the librarian's knowledge of the sources available in the library. A concerted effort must be made not only to master the basic works, but to keep up with new and useful titles as they are acquired. Also helpful are experience and knowledge of the research process.

Some types of specific search questions are treated by librarians as reader advisory problems. These are the types of questions that, in essence, ask, "What is the best source of information for my needs?" Some questioners are seeking everything from fiction and poetry to hobby magazines. Depending on the size and the organizational pattern of the library, their queries may be handled by subject or reader advisory librarians or by reference librarians.

(4) *Research.* Almost any of the types of questions described in the "Specific Search" section may be turned into research questions. A research query is usually identified as coming from an adult specialist who is seeking detailed information to assist in specific work. The request may be from a professor, a business executive, a scientist, or anyone else who wishes data for a decision or for additional information about a problem. With the exception of some academic and special libraries, this type of inquiry is a negligible part of the total reference pattern.[12]

Ready-reference and specific search queries presuppose specific answers and specific sources, which, with practice, the librarian usually is able to locate quickly. Research questions differ in that most involve trial-and-error searching or browsing, primarily because (1) the average researcher may have a vague notion of the question but usually cannot be specific and (2) the answer to the yet-to-be-completely-formulated question depends on what the researcher is able to find (or not find). The researcher recognizes a problem,

[12]Stephen Stoan, "Research and Library Skills: An Analysis and Interpretation," *College & Research Libraries,* March 1984, pp. 99–109. This is a clear definition of what research is about. The author shows the differences in understanding of research by scholars and librarians.

identifies the area that is likely to cover the problem, and then attempts to find what has been written about the problem.

The complete library, as well as resources outside the library, may be used to assist the researcher. There is no way of measuring the difficulty or the average amount of time spent on such questions. Research queries are usually more interesting for the reference librarian because of the intellectual challenge they present, and they certainly enable the librarian to be more than a directional signal. Fortunately, reference work of the future seems to be turning toward research-oriented situations.

The reader will note another useful method of distinguishing types of queries. The first two types of queries (directional and ready-reference) may be classified as *data retrieval*, i.e., individuals have specific questions and expect answers in the form of data. The specific search and research questions might be classified as *document retrieval* in that the users want information, not just simple answers, and the information is usually in the form of some type of document, i.e., book, report, article, and so on.

Questions can rarely be easily classified into the four types in terms of effort, sources employed, or ease of determining search strategies. A directional query may become a ready-reference question or a specific search problem. And under some circumstances it may even change to a research question. The point is worth stressing that categorization of queries is no more certain than the type of question likely to be asked at this or that library at any given moment.

The type of question may be analyzed in various ways as may the motives of those who make the inquiries. One is often the mirror image of the other. The individual with a research question is usually motivated by a need to know or acquire information to develop a thesis, carry on an experiment, or some other practical or esoteric purpose. Not only is this person willing to spend time with the theme, but wants as much information as possible about the central and related issues. Even those with less rigorous needs for data (such as a search query) are intent on at least gathering enough information to write a paper, deliver a talk, or to help analyze and resolve a problem. The majority of these questions are motivated by employment or school requirements, often with a dash of just pure intellectual delight.

Conversely, many (and these are really the majority in the public library) are intent upon other expeditions. Here they are motivated for almost as many reasons as there are ready reference questions. It may be memory failure, pure curiosity, the desire to be right, the wish to win a bet, or simply the wish to clarify a particular point about a person, place, or thing. Most of this may be classified as personal need, or leisure activity.

Who is to answer?

The fascinating result of analyses of types of questions is that (1) the majority of queries are directional or ready-reference pure and simple; (2) generally, the queries and sources used are basic and easy to understand; (3) most questions, therefore, could be answered by a well-trained person with a bachelor's degree.

Not everyone agrees that the trained nonprofessional can or should replace the professional librarian for the purpose of answering directional and ready-reference queries. As indicated, oftentimes the simple questions develop into complex ones requiring professional aid. There is also the practical consideration of employment opportunities. With fewer professional library positions, it is questionable that many librarians (this side of administrators) will be pushing to replace themselves, even if there is real promise of doing more fulfilling reference work at a higher level.

Even where nonprofessionals are used sparingly, the average library at least depends on nonreference librarians to help at the reference desk. Technical services librarians, for example, may take a turn at answering questions. In a survey of research libraries, it was found that almost 70 percent of respondents rely on the assistance of librarians not formally assigned to the reference department.

The reason for dividing the duties is not so much the ease of answering queries as the fact that there is a maximum number of hours "during which any professional can provide effective direct patron service. Then the use of nonprofessionals and borrowed staff is undoubtedly due to an effort to keep individual work load within acceptable tolerance."[13]

Reference interview

The most common complaint heard among reference librarians about their work is that few people know how to ask reference questions. There are numerous reasons for the public's failure to appreciate the need for clarity at the reference desk, and these are

[13]Paula D. Watson, "Organization and Management of Reference Services in Academic Research Libraries; A Survey," *RQ*, Summer 1984, p. 408.

considered throughout this text. Suffice it to say here that the dialogue between the user and the librarian is called the reference interview and has several objectives. The first is to find out what is required and how much data is needed. This is simplicity itself— except that most people do not know how to frame questions. The child looking for horses may be interested in pictures, an encyclopedia article, or possibly a book on riding. No matter what the scope of the query, it probably will come out as "Do you have anything on horses?"

Searching for answers

Once the actual needs of the library patron are understood, the next step is to formulate a search strategy of possible sources. This requires translating the terms of the question into the language of the reference system. If a basic book on gardening is required, the librarian will find it readily enough in the card catalog under a suitable subject heading. At the other specific extreme, the question may involve searching indexes, such as the *Biological & Agricultural Index,* to find the latest information on elm blight or perhaps checking out various bibliographies, such as *Subject Guide to Books in Print* or a union catalog, to find what may be available on elm blight in general and in other libraries. Once the information is found, it has to be evaluated. That is, the librarian must determine whether it is really the kind and at the level that the patron wants. Is it too technical or too simple? Is it applicable in this geographic area?

Evaluation

A major contribution to the reference search is the evaluation of the search results by the librarian. The user has some notion of what is wanted, both in terms of quantity and quality. Yet, that same person may be vague about whether or not an article should be used from X journal or Y journal. The qualifications of the author and publisher are better known to the librarian than the average user. For example, in a string of 10 citations about solar energy, would a high school senior, a college senior, or a layperson be happier with citations from *Time, Reader's Digest,* and *Newsweek,* or from the *Monthly Energy Review, EPRI Journal,* and *Solar Energy?* These are fundamental decisions which will be of great help to the average user.

Here a distinction should be made between consulting (where the librarian actually chooses the four or five best articles) and counseling (where a recommendation is made). In most cases, the librarian will wish to discuss and consult with the user, not dictate the solution.

INFORMATION SOURCES

In day-to-day activities in most reference libraries, the librarian relies on reference books which are carefully marked and segregated in a special section of the library. The reference book is well known to most people, and the dictionary and the encyclopedia are found in many homes.

A question of interest for reference librarians concerns how many titles the new librarian should be familiar with when taking over a reference position. Some would argue that specific knowledge of individual titles is not very important; but that debate aside, several studies at least indicate the degree of disagreement about how many and which titles every reference librarian should know.

Larsen polled 31 library schools and found only seven titles were listed by all: *New Encyclopaedia Britannica, World Book, Current Biography, Dictionary of American Biography, The New York Times Index, The Readers' Guide to Periodical Literature,* and the *World Almanac.* The lack of agreement among schools is striking but not unusual.[14]

There is no end of select lists, which indicate some consensus but do not dictate "basic" reference collections. Much the same is true when one turns to lists of other reference forms, from databases to video. Ultimately the working, basic collection is the one which is best for the individual librarian and the audience served—and determining this type of list is one of the joys of active reference service.

Another point of view about "basic" will be found in a series of columns, "If I Had to Choose," where experts are asked what 10 sources they would take to a desert island. Although the column ran for at least two years, there was little or no consensus other than the probable need for a dictionary.[15]

Information chain

If the ideal reference service, to paraphrase André Malraux, is "reference service without walls," the nature of information does

---

[14]John C. Larsen, "Information Sources Currently Studied in General Reference Courses," *RQ*, Summer 1979, pp. 341–348.

[15]"If I Had To Choose," ed. by Jim Rettig. *Reference Services Review,* Fall 1982–1985. The columns appear in each quarterly issue, with the first by Charles Bunge, a noted reference book reviewer.

impose certain limitations on that service. Aside from asking experts in the community for "firsthand" information, the library generally must rely on published data—data which, by the nature of publishing, may be weeks, months, or even years out of date. A rough way of measuring the usual timeliness of materials is to classify them as primary, secondary, or tertiary.

(1) *Primary Sources* These are original materials which have not been filtered through interpretation, condensation, or, often, even evaluation by a second party. The materials tend to be the most current in the library, normally taking the form of a journal article, monograph, report, patent, dissertation, or reprint of an article. Some primary sources for information are not published, as, for example, the offering of firsthand information ("I was there," or "I discovered," or "I interpreted. . . .") orally by one person to one or more other people at a meeting or seminar, or in a letter which may be destroyed. Where primary sources are available in a library, the controls to call them up for reference work are usually secondary sources, such as indexes, abstracts, and bibliographies.

(2) *Secondary Sources* If an index is used to locate primary sources, the index itself is a secondary source. A secondary source is information about primary or original information which usually has been modified, selected, or rearranged for a purpose or an audience. The neat distinction between primary and secondary sources is not always apparent. For example, a person at a meeting may not be stating original views, but may simply be repeating what he or she has read or heard from someone else. A journal article is usually a primary source if it represents original thinking or a report on a discovery; but the same journal may include secondary materials which are reports or summaries of the findings of others.

(3) *Tertiary Sources* These consist of information which is a distillation and collection of primary and secondary sources. Twice removed from the original, they include almost all the source types of reference, works such as encyclopedias, reviews, biographical sources, fact books, and almanacs.

The definitions of primary, secondary, and tertiary sources are useful only in that they indicate (1) relative currency (primary sources tend to be more current than secondary sources) and (2) relative accuracy of materials (primary sources will generally be more accurate than secondary sources, only because they represent unfiltered, original ideas; conversely, a secondary source may correct errors in the primary source).

Whenever a reference source has become part of our experience, it requires little thought to match a question with a probable answer form. Those forms may be divided into two large categories: the control-access-directional type and the source type.

The control-access-directional type of source

The first broad class or form of reference sources is the bibliography. This form is variously defined, but in its most general sense it is a systematically produced descriptive list of records.

Control The bibliography serves as a control device—a kind of checklist. It inventories what is produced from day to day and year to year in such a way as to enable both the compiler and the user to feel they have a control, through organization, of the steady flow of knowledge. The bibliography is prepared through research (finding the specific source), identification, description, and classification.

Access Once the items are controlled, the individual items are organized for easy access to facilitate intellectual work. All the access types of reference works can be broadly defined as bibliographies; but they may be subdivided as follows:

1. Bibliographies of reference sources and the literature of a field, of either a general or a subject nature. Example: Sheehy's *Guide to Reference Books* or *The Information Sources of Political Science*. Another type of bibliography includes the bibliography of bibliographies and the index to bibliographies.
2. The library card catalog or the catalogs of numerous libraries arranged for easy access through a union list. Technically, these are not bibliographies but are often used in the same manner.
3. General systematic enumerative bibliography which includes various forms of bibliography. Example: *The National Union Catalog*.
4. Indexes and abstracts, which are usually treated separately from bibliographies, but are considered a bibliographical aid. They are systematic listings which help to identify and trace materials. Indexes to the contents of magazines and newspapers are the most frequently used types in the reference situation. Examples: *The Readers' Guide to Periodical Literature* and *The New York Times Index*.

Direction Bibliographies themselves normally do not give definitive answers, but serve to direct users to the sources of answers. For their effective use, the items listed must be either in the library or available from another library system.

Source type

Works of the source type usually suffice in themselves to give the answers. Unlike the access type of reference work, they are synoptic.

Encyclopedias The single most-used sources are encyclopedias; they may be defined as works containing informational articles on subjects in every field of knowledge, usually arranged in alphabetical order. They are used to answer specific questions about X topic or Y person or general queries which may begin with "I want something about Z." Examples: *Encyclopaedia Britannica; World Book Encyclopedia.*

Fact Sources Yearbooks, almanacs, handbooks, manuals, and directories are included in this category. All the types have different qualities, but they share one common element: They are used to look up factual material for quick reference. Together, they cover many facets of human knowledge. Examples: *World Almanac; Statesman's Year-Book.*

Dictionaries Sources which deal primarily with all aspects of words, from proper definitions to spelling, are classified as dictionaries. Examples: *Webster's Third New International Dictionary; Dictionary of American Slang.*

Biographical Sources The self-evident sources of information on people distinguished in some particular field of interest are known as biographical sources. Examples: *Who's Who; Current Biography.*

Geographical Sources The best-known forms are the atlases, which not only show given countries but may illustrate themes such as historical development, social development, and scientific centers. Geographical sources also include gazetteers, dictionaries of place names, and guidebooks. Example: *The Times Atlas of the World.*

Government documents

Government documents are official publications ordered and normally published by the federal, state, and local governments. Since they may include directional and source works, their separation into a particular unit is more for convenience and organization than for different reference use. Examples: *Monthly Catalog of United States*

Government Publications (access type); *United States Government Manual* (source type).

The neat categorization of reference types by access and by source is not always so distinct in an actual situation. A bibliography may be the only source required if the question is merely one of verification or of trying to complete a bibliographical citation. Conversely, the bibliography at the end of an encyclopedia article or a statement in that article may direct the patron to another source. In general, the two main categories—access and source—serve to differentiate between the principal types of reference works.

Unconventional reference sources

A term frequently seen in connection with reference service at the public library level is "information and referral," or simply "I&R." There are other terms used to describe this service, such as "community information center." Essentially, the purpose of this special reference service is to offer the users access to resources that will help them with health, rent, consumer, legal, and similar problems. The economic situation has caused many people to look for jobs if they are laid off. Libraries often provide free information on sources of employment. While I&R is discussed in the second volume of this text, the beginner should realize that in even the most traditional library, it is now common to (1) call individual experts, including anyone from a local professor to a leader in a local special-interest group, for assistance; (2) provide files, pamphlets, booklists, and so on, which give users information on topics ranging from occupations to local housing regulations; and (3) provide a place which active groups in the community may identify as an information clearinghouse for their needs.

Enter the Computer

Today, as in the past, a convenient method of mastering reference sources is to divide them into the aforementioned categories. The development of computers has begun to change all this. Information may now be stored in such a way that divisions between encyclopedias, biographies and government documents no longer are needed. A vast electronic database of reference material includes all these. Sitting at a computer one is able to search not just an index, not just a bibliography, but all forms of reference works at one time. This may effectively dissolve the present organizational scheme. Still, for now, the traditional divisions, the traditional printed works dominate. This is likely to be the situation for a good many years to come.

EVALUATING REFERENCE SOURCES

A thorough understanding of the day-to-day sources of answers requires some evaluation of those sources. How does the librarian know whether a reference source is good, bad, or indifferent? A detailed answer will be found throughout each of the chapters in this volume. However, in rather simple terms, a good reference source is one that answers questions, and a poor reference source is one that fails to answer questions. Constant and practical use will quickly place any source (whether a book or a database) in one of these two categories.

What follows is primarily concerned with traditional reference books, but much of it is applicable to other reference forms, including machine-readable records. Evaluation of databases is considered in the second volume of this text.

Because of the expense of most reference sources, the typical practice is to read one or more book reviews before deciding whether or not to buy them. Large libraries usually request or automatically receive examination copies before purchase. Smaller libraries may have no choice but to accept the word of the reviewer and order or not order the work. Ideally, the reference source should be examined by a trained reference librarian before it is incorporated into the collection. No review or review medium is infallible.

The librarian must ask at least four basic questions about a reference work: What is its purpose? Its authority? Its scope? Its proposed audience? Finally, the format of the work must be considered.

(1) *Purpose* The purpose of a reference work should be evident from the title or form. The evaluative question: Has the author or compiler fulfilled the purpose? must be posed. An encyclopedia of dance, for example, has the purpose of capturing essential information about dance in encyclopedic form. But immediately the librarian must ask such questions as: What kind of dance and for what period? For what age group or experience or sophistication in dance? For what countries? Is the emphasis on history, biography, practical application, or some other element?

The clues to purpose are found in the (a) table of contents; (b) introduction or preface, which should give details of what the author or compiler expects this work to accomplish; and (c) index, the sampling of which will tell what subjects are covered. A reference book without an index is usually of little or no value. Exceptions are dictionaries, indexes, directories, and other titles where the index is built into an alphabetical arrangement. This system is suitable for the data type of reference work, but not for running prose; then an index is absolutely essential.

Other hints of the purpose of a specific work are often given in the publisher's catalog, in advance notices received in the mails, and in the copy on the jacket of the book. Such descriptions may help to indicate purpose and even relative usefulness, but are understandably less than objective.

(2) *Authority* The question of purpose brings us close to a whole series of questions which relate to the author:

(a) What are the author's qualifications for the fulfillment of his or her purpose? If the writer is a known scholar, there is no problem with authority. Where the difficulty arises is with the other 95 percent of reference works that are prepared by experts but not those who make the best-seller list. Here the librarian must rely on (1) the qualifications of the author given in the book; (2) the librarian's own understanding and depth of knowledge of the subject; and (3) a check of the author in standard biographical works such as *Who's Who* or *American Men and Women of Science.*

(b) What were the sources of the author's knowledge? This question, properly answered, may also serve to answer the query about the author's qualifications. Did he or she go to primary source material—or rely on secondary material? If new sources were explored, were they well chosen and sufficient? Answers to these questions may be found by looking for footnotes, citations to sources, and bibliographies. Many reference works are secondary material (encyclopedias, almanacs, yearbooks, and so on) but draw heavily on primary sources. A book based on derivative material is often useful, but the authority is highly suspect if the primary sources are not cited. In collective works, such as encyclopedias and many handbooks, the articles should be signed or some indication given of who is responsible for the work.

(c) The imprint of the publisher may indicate the relative worth of a book. Some publishers have excellent reputations for issuing reference works; others are known for their fair-to-untrustworthy titles. In a few cases, for example, encyclopedias and dictionaries, the cost of publishing is so high that the field is narrowed down to three or four firms. Even at best, publishers are generally less interested in the progress of learning than in making money; a given group of publishers may have a well-deserved reputation for excellent reference books, but they, too, can slip. A reputable publisher may issue a half-dozen fine reference works, but the seventh may be a "bomb," possibly initiated for commercial purposes; or even if written by a knowledgeable author and fairly informative, it may be superfluous.

(d) Objectivity and fairness are important considerations, particularly in reference works which rely on prose rather than simple statistics or collection of facts. Does the author have a bias about politics, religion, race, sex, or the proper type of color to paint a study? No one is totally objective, but those who write reference books must indicate both sides when there is a matter of controversy. As will be noted in the chapter on encyclopedias, there is always some question about this or that article, not to mention the overall tone of the set. For example, Engle and Futas charge many adult encyclopedias with showing definite signs of sexism.

Authority, then, is a matter of the author and the publishers. But neither is infallible, particularly when money is involved. Today there are numerous pseudo-reference books published, which "aim to be collections of trivia and are designed to read mainly for fun, not for knowledge."[16] Some of these are published by reputable houses, and the authors may be talented. The problem is that a book on the *World's Greatest Snobs,* or *The Yearbook of Frisbee* may be less than in demand for reference work, although a good deal of fun to read. To buy or not to buy such works depends more upon audience use and the sense of humor of the librarian. At any rate, most of these books belong in the general collection, not in reference.

Authority can be measured, finally, only by careful scrutiny of the book by the knowledgeable librarian.

Although writing style is not usually a major consideration in reference works, there is no excuse for poor writing. In fact, a poor presentation is often indicative of muddled thinking or, even worse, lack of impartiality.

(3) *Scope* The first question of major importance in selecting a reference work is, Will this book be a real addition to our collection, and if so, what exactly will it add? The publisher usually will state the scope of the book in the publicity blurb or in the preface, but the librarian should be cautious. The author may or may not have achieved the scope claimed. For example, the publisher may claim that a historical atlas covers all nations and all periods. The librarian

[16]Kenneth Whittaker, "The Pseudo-Reference Book," *New Library World,* August 1982, p. 109.

may check the scope of the new historical atlas by comparing it against standard works. Does the new work actually include *all* nations and *all* periods, or does it exclude material found in the standard works? If an index claims to cover all major articles in X and Y periodicals, a simple check of the periodicals' articles against the index will reveal the actual scope of the index.

(a) What has the author contributed that cannot be found in other bibliographies, indexes, handbooks, almanacs, atlases, dictionaries, and so on? If the work is comprehensive within a narrow subject field, one may easily check it against other sources. For example, a who's who of education which limits itself to educators in the major colleges and universities in the Northeast may easily be checked for scope by comparing the current college catalog of P & Q University against the new who's who. If a number of faculty members are missing from the new work, one may safely conclude the scope is not what is claimed.

Most reference works are selective, and in this case the publisher and author should clearly state what is and is not included. What methods were employed for selection or rejection? And does the selection plan fit the audience claimed by the reference work. An encyclopedia of detection, for example, may or may not include fictional detectives, but if it claims to list the masterminds of detection from novels, are they *all* included? Are the detectives included in keeping with the purpose and the audience of the work?

Other general questions involving scope are almost as numerous as are reference works. One might ask the national or political scope of a work; the scope of the bibliographies in terms of numbers, length, language, timeliness, and so on; the inclusion or lack of guides, indexes, illustrations, and so on; the number of this or that actually covered or considered, for example, the number of entries in a dictionary. Beyond these important general considerations are others a bit easier to pinpoint.

(b) Currency is one of the most important features of any reference work, particularly one used for ready reference. Data change so quickly that last year's almanac may be historically important but of little value in answering today's queries.

Except for current indexes, such as *Facts on File* and *The Readers' Guide to Periodical Literature,* most published reference works are dated before they are even off the presses. The time

between the publisher's receipt of a manuscript and its publication may vary from six months to two years. Thus, in determining the recency of a work, some consideration must be given to
the problems of production. Normally, a timely reference book
will be one that contains information dating from six months to
a year prior to the copyright date.

There are times when revisionist attitudes will turn around
the point of view of even a basic reference work. See, for
example, almost any encyclopedia before and after the advent
of women's liberation. When a country, too, emerges as an
independent nation, it may wish to change reference works, e.g.,
in 1982, Zimbabwe (the former Rhodesia dominated by whites)
developed reference books to show that black people have been
shapers of history and not just bystanders.[17]

The copyright date in itself may be only a relative indication
of timeliness. Is this a new work, or is it based on a previous
publication? In these days of reprints, this is a particularly
important question. A standard reference work may be reissued
with the date of publication shown on the title page as, say, 1985
but on the verso of the same title page, the original copyright
date may be 1976. If the work has been revised and updated, the
copyright date will usually correspond to the date on the title
page. A marked discrepancy should be sufficient warning that
content must be carefully checked for currency.

Few reference works, unless entirely new, will not contain
some dated information. The best method of ascertaining
whether the dated material is of value and checking the recency
factor is to sample the work. This is a matter of looking for
names currently in the news, population figures, geographical
boundaries, records of achievement, new events, and almost any
other recent fact which is consistent with the purpose and scope
of the work. Needless to add, no reference work should be
accepted or rejected on a sampling of one or two items.

If the work purports to be a new edition, the extent of
claimed revisions should be carefully noted. This can easily be
done by checking it against the earlier edition or by noting any
great discrepancy between the dates of the cited materials and
the date of publication. For example, when an encyclopedia
purports to be up to date but has no bibliographies dated within

[17]Joseph Lelyveld, "In Zimbabwe, Blacks Make History Anew," *The New York Times,*
October 17, 1982, p. 11.

two or three years of the date on the title page, something a bit odd is certainly indicated.

(c) Within the work itself, the scope should be consistent for comparable entries. For example, in a biographical dictionary the reader should be certain to find the same general type of information for each entry: birth date, place of birth, address, achievements, and so on.

(d) Can the reference work be used alone, or must it be supplemented by another work? For example, the scope of *Contemporary Authors* is considerably greater than that of *World Authors*. The emphasis on many little-known authors in the former work makes it a valuable finding aid, but the latter is much more useful for detailed biographical sketches. Where a choice must be made, the librarian will have to consider carefully the potential users.

(4) *Audience* With the exception of juvenile encyclopedias, most reference works are prepared for adults. When considering the question of audience, the librarian must ask one major question: Is this for the scholar or student of the subject, or is it for the layperson with little or no knowledge? For example, in the field of organic chemistry, Beilstein's *Handbuch der Organischen Chemie* is as well known to chemists as the "top 10" tunes are to music fans. It is decidedly for the student with some basic knowledge of chemistry. Often the distinction in terms of audience is not so clear-cut.

A useful method of checking the reading level of a given reference work is for the librarian to examine a subject well known to him or her and then turn to one that is not so well understood. If both are comprehended, if the language is equally free of jargon and technical terminology, if the style is informative yet lively, the librarian can be reasonably certain the work is for the layperson. Of course, if the total book is beyond the subject competency of the librarian, advice should be sought from a subject expert. Still, this is an unlikely situation, since reference librarians tend to be experts in fields within which they operate.

(5) *Cost* is a major factor of frustration in the evaluation and purchase of reference works. There is much talk about the countless new reference sources and resources, but many libraries cannot afford expensive printed works. Budget, rather than client need, may determine whether or not X or Y work is purchased.

Reference service, even on a minimum scale, can be a luxury. Vavrek reminds us that 82 percent of the public libraries in the United States serve populations under 25,000. While not all rural communities are financially starved, the majority are in a bad way. Most, with or without state or federal aid, suffer from a lack of reference materials, and 75 percent lack any user education in reference services.[18]

(6) *Format* The questions which have been discussed are essential, but one of the most meaningful questions of all concerns arrangement, treated here as part of the format. Arrangement is of major importance. There must be a handy form of access to the material.

Ease of use is important. Too many reference works (e.g., the citation indexes and online databases) are complicated and difficult to use. The result is that some librarians avoid them. This may result in poor service for the user as well as a feeling of incompetence on the part of the librarian.

There are some general rules for arrangement which are significant guides to the relative worth of a particular work as a tool in answering questions. Briefly:

(a) Wherever possible, information should be arranged alphabetically in dictionary form. The advantage is that there is no need to learn a scheme of organization.

(b) Where alphabetical arrangement is not used, there should be an author, subject, and title index or an index covering aspects of content. Even with alphabetical order, it is usually advisable to have an index, particularly where bits of information must be extracted from long articles.

(c) Where needed (in either the text, the index, or both), there should be sufficient cross-references that lead to other material and not merely to blind entries. For example, a book which refers readers to "archives" when they look up "manuscripts" should have an entry for "archives." This is a simple rule; but too frequently, in the process of editing and revising, the entry for the cross-reference is deleted.

(d) In some works another method must be employed, particularly in scientific sources. The classification should be as simple as possible; certainly it should be consistent and logical throughout. If it is difficult to comprehend, this may be a warning about the merits of the work as a whole.

The arrangement can be either hindered or helped by the physical format. Even the best-arranged work can be a nuisance if it is bound so that the pages do not lie flat, or if there is no clear distinction between headings on a page and subheads within the page.

[18]Bernard Vavrek, "A Struggle for Survival: Reference Services in the Small Public Library," *Library Journal*, May 15, 1983, pp. 966–969.

The apparatuses of abbreviation, typography, symbols, and indication of cross-references must be clear and in keeping with what the user is likely to recognize. The use of offset printing from computerized materials has resulted in some disturbing complexities of format. For example, it may be impossible to tell West Virginia, when abbreviated, from western Virginia. Uniform lower-case letters will be equally confusing. Lack of spacing between lines, poor paper, little or no margins, and other hindrances to reading are all too evident in even some standard reference works.

A word regarding illustrations: When photographs, charts, tables, and diagrams are used, they should be current, clear, and related to the text. They should be adjacent to the material under discussion or at least clearly identified.[19]

The last word on the subject may sound as cynical or as simplistic as the reader cares to interpret it, but it is this: Trust no one. The reviewer, the publisher, and the author do make mistakes, sometimes of horrendous proportions. The librarian who evaluates reference sources with the constant suspicion of the worst is less likely to be the victim of those mistakes.

THE REFERENCE LIBRARIAN

By now it is obvious that information and reference service involves something more than helping the stereotyped little old soul in tennis shoes stumbling around the library looking for last year's almanac. Today's librarian must know reference sources and, for that matter, any other sources in or outside the library likely to yield answers, which, in turn, requires a basic familiarity with methods of acquiring and organizing information sources, from books to microform to computer databases.

On these assets depends what is referred to as collection development. The librarian must be able to separate the worthwhile from the worthless in terms of probable information value. It is one thing to locate 5 or 50 articles on women painters, quite another to be able to tell which of the 5 or 50 are likely to be of use to the person with the question. To avoid an information failure, the librarian must

---

[19]Illustrations are increasingly important in reference works. The importance of illustrations is discussed in a thoughtful article by Charles Bunge, "Illustrated Reference Books: Technological, Intellectual and Economic Developments," *Reference Services Review*, Spring, 1983 pp. 89–98.

be able to translate a question into terms which can be met by the information sources. If someone, for example, asks for information on nuclear waste, the librarian must know, at a rudimentary level, the subject headings under which articles, reports, and books about nuclear waste are listed. And the librarian must be able to search for answers quickly and efficiently.

Every librarian should try to develop the following skills: (1) the ability to organize data and information for people to use; (2) awareness of the totality of information resources and the probabilities of success for strategies of information searches in any specific situation; (3) awareness of and ability to use the range of information technologies, from print to sound and image to computing; (4) sensitivity to use, uses, and users of information, and a strong tradition of service, which demands attention to client satisfaction. The latter requires a knowledge and mastery of communication, question negotiation and, above all, an empathy with the needs of the person who requires assistance.

Reference librarians are analyzed, psychoanalyzed, and quantified. Usually some additional, more personalized, traits are suggested for the perfect librarian. They include *imagination,* which helps the librarian interpret the question and find precisely the right data or documents to answer it; *perseverence,* which keeps the librarian going when the logical source yields nothing; *judgment,* to know when to ask for more information from the user, when to stop, and when to go on; and *accuracy, thoroughness,* and *orderliness,* which are necessary particularly when the librarian is being counted on for the correct answer. Unfortunately, many studies and surveys indicate that too many librarians often give wrong answers, or none at all, to questions.

Librarian as evaluator

A familiar, even hackneyed phrase in library work is the "information explosion." This refers to the ever-increasing amount of information produced at almost every level. Typical statistics are quoted to show the size of the explosion: (1) There are now about 100,000 scientific and technical periodicals, which publish over 2 million articles each year. (2) Book titles in America have increased from about 4000 in 1960 to over 40,000 in the 1980s. (3) There are about 300 billion pieces of information reported to the federal government by states, local government, individuals, and corporations each year. It costs about $125 billion a year or $500 per person to collect, review, and store that information. (4) Academic library holdings have increased over 100 percent in the past decade or so.

All these distant figures may be reduced to the reader's practical world by simply consulting the index of this text, where can be found only a few of the 10,000-plus reference titles suggested as "basic" for larger libraries—too many for any single person to use, much less remember. Yet some 1500 to 2000 reference works (or new editions) are published in America each year. This compares with almost the total annual production of *all* books a few decades ago.

Given the vast amount of material, the average individual is much in the same position as the person looking for a needle in a haystack. The librarian can help by using an educated magnet and by limiting the size of the haystack (i.e., the size of the collection of materials) to some size relevant for the users. The obvious questions: What retrieval devices are best for locating the needed information? What processes should be employed to separate the good from the worthless in the acquisition of materials? These, by the way, lead to scores of other queries which take up a good deal of the time of so-called information scientists, who are as much concerned with the future implications of the growth of information as with the daily activities of the library. The different formats of information add to the confusion.

As each year goes by, it becomes increasingly evident that the librarian is more than someone who acquires and processes materials and delivers them to storage. The librarian must be a guide, a gatekeeper between the mass of undifferentiated information and the specific needs of the individual.

In the average medium-to-large library there may be twenty, thirty, or several hundred different indexes and abstracting services. Which one should be used by the reader who knows little or nothing about the library or (more likely) uses the library often but has never needed an index in a particular subject area? This individual should ask the librarian who, as gatekeeper, will recommend indexes which are best for the particular service. Going a step further, the librarian will go on to explain the use of the service, or help the individual find articles and other materials. Beyond that, the librarian may, again in the role of gatekeeper, suggest periodicals which are likely to be best for the user's need; actively help the user find the periodicals; and, where necessary, mention substitutes.

This approach represents the *liberal* philosophy of reference service, in which the librarian is convinced it is a professional duty to be an active gatekeeper and to produce information as needed. Not all librarians, by any means, agree with this philosophy. At the other extreme is the *conservative*, who believes the individual should not depend on the librarian for active assistance. The conservative thinks it is enough to acquire and process materials, and perhaps show someone how to find or use an index, but certainly not help that person decide which article to use or where to find the article. Between the two is the *moderate* who sometimes gives total service, other times points rather than assists.

In this text the emphasis is on the liberal attitude, that is, that the librarian should give the greatest amount of help to people. The primary function of a reference librarian is to answer questions, and that, essentially, is what the liberal gatekeeper is about.

The fulfillment of this role as gatekeeper is not always possible or even desirable. Some people, after all, want to search through the information to find what they need without any help from anyone. Still, the role of the librarian as gatekeeper or interpreter of available data is a valuable, increasingly important one.

Librarian as intermediary

With the ever-increasing mass of information, the role of the reference librarian has taken on a new meaning. It is no longer enough to simply locate information; one must make value judgments about how much is needed for a particular individual. That, in turn, involves other decisions about the quality of what is retrieved. The latter decision can be made easier by careful selection of materials.

The important role of the reference librarian as an intermediary or gatekeeper between the user and the flood of information is summarized by Asheim: "The librarians' expertise lies, not in their superior knowledge of every subject area as such, but rather in their knowledge of sources and search strategies and in their willingness to put themselves in the user's place. Since overload can be an inhibiting factor in the search for information, control of the flow, not just of the nature of the content, is the librarian's responsibility."[20]

SUGGESTED READING

Arnold, Stephen, "Marketing Information Products," *Online,* January, 1986, pp. 6–11. Although discussing the expanding market for computer-based information, the author considers the parallel concerns of anyone involved with information. In

---

[20]Lester Asheim, "Ortega Revisited," *Library Quarterly,* July 1982, pp. 215–226.

so doing he explains how information is created and how it develops particular problems.

Bunge, Charles, "Strategies for Updating Knowledge of Reference Resources and Techniques," *RQ*, Spring 1982, pp. 228–232. About 81 different libraries were contacted to find out how librarians keep up with their profession. In giving the results, the author suggests basic sources for all reference librarians.

"Current Trends in Reference Services," *Library Trends*, Winter 1983. This issue, ably edited by Bernard Vavrek, offers a solid overview of current reference trends. It touches all major concerns of reference librarians today.

Hendrick, Clyde, "The University Library in the Twenty-First Century," *College & Research Libraries*, March 1986, pp. 127–131. This is a practical, not overly "pie-in-the-sky" look at what the library in the next century is likely to be in terms of technology and use. The author sees the basic mission and objectives of the library as much the same, but drastically changed by both new approaches and new social and financial considerations.

Katz, Bill, *Reference and Information Sources*, 3d ed. Metuchen, NJ: Scarecrow Press, 1986. This is a collection of readings which covers various aspects of reference services. It is edited specifically for students, and particularly for those seeking an introduction to the subject. The articles are selected for their good style and overview of reference services. Most selections are footnoted and/or found in the "Suggested Reading" section of this two volume text.

Lancaster, F. W., "Future Librarianship: Preparing for an Unconventional Career," *Wilson Library Bulletin*, May 1983, pp. 747–753. The author is well known for his prediction that "libraries as we know them seem likely to disappear." What is to take their place he describes in some detail.

McArthur, Tom, *Worlds of Reference*. New York: Cambridge University Press, 1986. The author considers reference works central to an understanding of the history of writing, printing and literature. He draws upon the historical development of reference works from the thematic to the adoption of alphabetization as a standard ordering convention. A scholarly overview with numerous examples from Roget to the latest edition of the *Encyclopaedia Britannica*.

Miller, Constance and James Rettig, "Reference Obsolescence," *RQ*, Fall 1985, pp. 52–58. A historical overview of how little and how much reference services have changed since 1876. The authors cry for change, or for the very good chance the library will cease to function as a center of information.

Murfin, Marjorie and L. R. Wynar, *Reference Service: An Annotated Bibliographic Guide 1976–1981*. Littleton, Colorado: Libraries Unlimited, Inc., 1982. Under 14 subject headings, the compilers offer a massive amount of reading on everything from the theory of reference services to online catalogs. Each item has a full citation and a brief abstract. Note: In 1984, a separate supplement volume (same title) was issued which takes the readings through 1982.

Orgren, Carl F. and James Rice, "The Current Trends and Controversies in the Literature of Reference Services and Their Implications for the Practice of Reference Work," *The Reference Librarian*, no. 14, 1986, pp. 1–15. In this overview of the "primary issues that have been prominent in the literature and in the field during the last 10–15 years," the authors discuss the major topics of interest to both beginning and experienced reference librarians. The article is an excellent introduction to the real and daily questions and problems of reference services in all types and sizes of libraries.

Purcell, Gary and Gail Schlacter, *Reference Sources in Library and Information Services: A Guide to the Literature.* Santa Barbara, California: American Bibliographic Center-Clio, 1984. While this covers the literature of all of library science, there is a good section related to reference services and automation. The list is primarily an annotated guide to English language library-related sources.

"Reference Services and Technical Services: Interactions in Library Practice," *The Reference Librarian,* Fall/Winter 1983. The sometimes uneasy relationship between reference services and technical services (from cataloging to interlibrary loan) is considered here by experienced authors. The discussion offers a valuable introduction for both beginners and experienced reference librarians. The entire issue is devoted to this single subject.

"Reference Services for Children and Young Adults," *The Reference Librarian,* Spring/Summer 1983. The entire issue is devoted to an important, too often overlooked aspect of reference service. Some two dozen experts consider everything from reference materials to serving this audience in both public and school libraries.

Rettig, James, "The Crisis in Academic Reference Work," *Reference Services Review,* Fall 1984, pp. 13–14. In describing the plight of the average reference librarian's burnout, the author addresses several things which might make reference services more rewarding. See, too: Jeannean Elliott and Nathan M. Smith, "Burnout: A Look at Coping With Stress," *School Library Media Quarterly,* Winter 1984, pp. 136–145.

CHAPTER TWO

Computerized Online Reference Service

C onsider two types of searches. The first is a traditional, manual search. The second employs a computer. The librarian is asked to find material on UFOs (unidentified flying objects). There are many ways of progressing towards an answer, but the librarian is likely to consult several indexes and bibliographies looking for pertinent articles and books. This type of searching, which involves going from place to place in the library, consulting different volumes, and writing down the primary sources, is the traditional method.

Now, sit down at a computer terminal with that same question. One enters the key words and there appear citations to the necessary articles, books and other types of source material. Furthermore, it is all printed out and no copying is required.

The computer terminal in the library usually is linked by telephone to a large mainframe computer in a city which can be 20 to 3000 or more miles away. In this mainframe computer is stored the needed information in a database. By employing basic search commands, the librarian is able to get the information out of the database. Instead of referring to an index or a table of contents in a printed volume, the librarian simply commands the mainline computer to show what is available on (for example) UFOs, solar heating, or dog houses. The computer searches its storage unit (database) and shows on a screen, or prints out, the needed information. These days, there is a drift, if not a drive, toward putting the data on disks which the library may access independently of the mainframe computer and a vendor. This is considered in the second volume of the text.

While the technology of the process is mind-boggling, the actual search and the end result are much the same as those carried on in a traditional way at the reference desk. The two essential differences are that one is getting information not from a printed source, but from print consigned to a computer's memory; and that it calls on electronics, rather than a hand turning a page, to find the necessary data. Also, it requires mastering searching skills which, while much the same in principle to manual searches, differ in the command structures.

A computer search is neither as complicated or as difficult as many novices believe. Anyone can learn the mechanics. True, it takes longer to become a skilled searcher, but this is the value of being a reference librarian. It is this precise skill which makes the librarian so necessary in the search process. In the manual search, after all, too many laypersons believe they can use the library effectively without help. That is not true at the computer terminal, at least for more than simple searches.

Computer searching continues to change the image and the duties of the reference librarian. Almost all searches must be done by an intermediary, i.e., the reference librarian, because the average user has neither the skill nor the time to search. Furthermore, searching is expensive and only an experienced search analyst can do it quickly enough to make it economically feasible. Then, too, "online specialists have a whole realm of special . . . language which to the general librarian trained only a few years ago is nearly foreign."[1] All of this, and particularly the mystery and mystique of the computer, has added to the prestige of the reference librarian.

TERMINOLOGY

There are several terms commonly used in speaking of computer-aided reference service in the library.

Online (sometimes hyphenated as "on-line") simply means that the librarian is directly in communication with the computer, just as

[1]Brian Nielsen, "Online Reference and the Great Change," in *Online Catalogs/Online Reference: Converging Trends.* Proceedings of a LITA Preconference Institute. (Chicago: American Library Association, 1984), p. 77. The employment of a reference librarian as an intermediary in the online search may change. This is discussed in the second volume of the text.

one would be when talking to someone on the telephone. One may talk directly to the computer, pose questions, ask for answers, make corrections, and so on.

With that, two points must be made about the online search. First, there is a concerted effort by publishers and almost all those involved with online databases to make searching much easier. The object is to widen the number of users, to make online searching, if not a popular skill, at least one within the grasp of the average library user. So-called "front-end software" takes the inexperienced searcher step by step through the search process, as well as clarifying the search before the user is connected to an expensive online system. An example of this, to be considered later, is WILSEARCH, which makes it possible for beginners to search the various H. W. Wilson indexes, including *The Readers' Guide to Periodical Literature,* online.

Second, while in-depth searches are expensive, if only because they take considerable time, the ready-reference search can be quite inexpensive. Many may be conducted in a matter of seconds, and offer a rapid, accurate answer. It is for this reason that the online search is likely to spread to more and more libraries, and particularly public libraries with a large group of ready-reference, i.e., quick fact queries.

Database is a synonym today for a collection of printed or numeric records which have been transformed and stored in a computer. A database may range from everything from a standard index, such as *Public Affairs Information Service Bulletin,* to an encyclopedia such as the *Encyclopaedia Britannica,* to a statistical collection such as the *U.S. Census.*

The information in a database normally is available in print as well, although not always. There are, for example, some indexes which are only databases and are not in printed form. If anything, the dual approach (database and print) is likely to give way in the future to only the database, which completely bypasses the original printed reference work.

Many divide databases into two large categories: (1) reference, which includes indexes and bibliographies; (2) source, which includes the full text database, as well as a) numeric and b) numeric and text combined. Obviously, these are not exclusive categories in that a bibliographic database may be thought of as an index or abstract and a full text database may include numeric data.

An increasing number of databases offer not only the key to where an article or piece may be found, but the whole article. One finds, for example, a desired article from *The New York Times Index* on third world mineral resources. Normally, one copies down the citation (i.e., where the article is located in the newspaper) and then goes to the newspaper itself to find the article. With a full text search available, one simply calls up the article on the video display screen and/or has it printed out in full or in part. The amount of time, energy, and pure frustration saved by this simple procedure indicates that it will revolutionize much of reference work with indexes and abstracting services.

How many databases are there? The number varies depending on who is doing the counting and what is counted. The number, as of 1986, is somewhere between 500 and 3200. The smaller figure represents primarily bibliographic databases (indexes and abstracts for the most part), while the latter would include numeric and full text databases.

Today almost all major indexes and abstracting services are available as databases, and an increasing number of basic reference works, from encyclopedias to directories, are now in this form. In the not-too-distant future it will be exceptional not to find at least the more frequently used reference sources available as databases.[2]

Online charges   Unlike a reference work, the library does not buy a database. It accesses the database through a vendor or a publisher who charges the library for each minute the database or system is being used. The pricing system is as various as it is confusing, but essentially one may pay from a few dollars to well over several hundred dollars for a single search. Given this type of fee structure, it is imperative that searches be done with dispatch. One cannot dawdle online without costing the user money. The problem of just who pays for what is considered in the second volume of this text, as is the latest development of bypassing the vendor by using disks with the information which can be accessed by the library on a microcomputer.

Database Publishers and Vendors   The form of a database may differ from the standard reference book form, but the publisher for both is usually the same. The publisher simply makes arrangements with a middleperson (a vendor) to distribute the database version of the printed work to users via the computer. In some cases the publisher may furnish the database directly to the library (as, for example, MARC tapes). The vendor, in turn, pays the publisher a set fee or royalty for the use of the printed form on the computer. The revenues normally are based on how often the database is used.

[2]Specific databases are considered in detail in the second volume of this text.

The vendor is the equivalent of the book or periodical jobber. However, the vendor does not sell individual copies of the index, bibliography, encyclopedia, etc., but only sells access to the database.

There are three basic types of vendors:

(1) A commercial service which offers access to numerous databases. There are three primary bibliographic commercial database vendors in the United States. By far the largest, with over 200 databases available, is Lockheed's DIALOG. Bibliographic Retrieval Services (BRS) of Latham, New York, offers close to 70 databases, as does Systems Development Corporation (SDC) of Santa Monica, California. Each of these vendors has developed its own character, or as one writer puts it: "DIALOG continues to lead the online industry as the database supermarket in the sky. BRS is moving closer to being a specialist in two database areas: education and biomedicine. SDC has developed a fast, sophisticated software especially designed for searching complex scientific databases."[3]

(2) A government agency, such as the National Library of Medicine, which offers the user direct access to a file, in this case the well-known MEDLINE (an acronym for MEDLARS On Line; MEDLARS is an acronym for Medical Literature Analysis and Retrieval System). The agency probably makes the same database available to the vendor who, in turn, may distribute it to users.

(3) A commercial publisher or service which does not use a vendor, but sells the use of the database(s) directly to the user. An example of this is Mead Data Central's NEXIS where news and business information is purchased, via the databases, directly from the main source.

While Lockheed, BRS, and Systems Development Corporation are the leading vendors of bibliographic databases to libraries, there are many more. In fact, by early 1986 the estimate is that worldwide there are at least 486 vendors. Unfortunately, each of them tends to have a separate method of use.

Another example of the independent publisher serving the library with the databases and eliminating the vendor is The H. W. Wilson Company. Many of the most heavily used indexes in the library are those published by this company. Of the some 26 services, by far the most familiar is *The Readers' Guide to Periodical Literature*. Until 1985 none of these indexes was available online, and as a result,

---

[3]Lucinda Conger, "The Friendly User," *Database*, June 1984, p. 92. For an example of user friendly software see Barbara Quint, "Menlo Corporation's Pro-Search . . ." *Online*, January, 1986, pp. 17–25.

many librarians seeking a general online index turned to *Magazine Index* or one of the other more specialized online services. By 1985, Wilson finally joined the online groups. It serves libraries directly, not through a vendor.

The five vendors listed here (i.e., Dialog, BRS, SDC, Medline, Mead Data Central) dominate the field, and "account for 98 percent of the revenue and 96.5 percent of the use" of the 250 most-used databases. Actually, only two (Dialog and Mead Data) account for 81.8 percent of the revenue and 68.56 percent of the usage.[4]

Technically, one might say that the so-called bibliographic utilities (OCLC, RLIN, WLN and UTLAS) are vendors. Actually, they do make databases available for bibliographic searching, but are not generally considered as database vendors. A detailed discussion of the utilities' role appears in the second volume of this text.

CD-ROM: Direct Access   It is possible for the librarian to access the material directly and eliminate the middleperson or vendor. Here the database is in the form of a disk, which contains up to 250,000 pages. This is known as a CD-ROM disk, the abbreviation for "compact disk read only memory." Using a microcomputer or other form of player, the librarian may read the disk much as one accesses a phonograph record or microcomputer software. Catalogs are now available in this form, as will eventually be many reference works. For example, the *Academic American Encyclopedia* offers a CD-ROM which stores the entire 21 volumes, 9 million words. All of this is on a 4.72 inch diameter disk.

A similar approach is available from BiblioFile, and numerous other firms. BiblioFile sells compact disks with over three million cataloging records from the Library of Congress. These, too, are CD-ROM and can be loaded into most personal computers. Eventually, one may see the virtual elimination of the vendor, and, instead, witness publishers selling massive sets of books to libraries, as well as offering frequent updates on some form of disks.

Hardware to Software. The basic components of the average online reference system consist of the machinery, i.e., hardware, and the commands, i.e., software.

The hardware is both visible and invisible. The invisible is, at

---

[4]Carol Tenopir, "The Database Industry Today: Some Vendors' Perspectives," *Library Journal*, February 1, 1984, p. 156. She points out that there are 15 vendors leading the industry who share in the $129 million per year that is spent on online databases. However, in terms of revenue, there are other leaders in the estimated $1.5 billion industry. One of the largest is Dow Jones News/Retrieval which sells to individuals. For a chart showing approximate size and type of vendors, see Steven Sieck, "Information Storage and Retrieval," *Publishers Weekly*, November 23, 1984, p. 40.

least in most cases, the giant mainframe computer. It has the information the librarian needs stored in databases, probably on magnetic disk. The visible hardware, usually a computer terminal, which resembles the keyboard of a typewriter, communicates electronically with the mainframe computer. This is done by using a modem, a cable, and a telephone (or directly connecting the phone to the computer).

Some terminals have a printout, and others have a CRT (cathode ray tube) viewer whereby one may see what is sent and what is received. Even where there is only a viewer, most terminals have a separate printer which allows one to print out the data sent from the mainframe computer.

Telecommunications   The connecting link between the computer in the library and the databases loaded on mainframe computers is the telephone line. The primary services in the United States are Tymnet and Telenet, with others appearing. The availability of these networks allows the long distance connection, but at rates considerably less than a typical long distance phone call.

Transmission speed is important, because the faster the message is sent the less expensive it is to receive. This speed is measured in *bauds*. The greater the baud rate, the faster the message. This is relatively simple, because most terminals are either 300 baud (slow) or 1200 baud (fast).[5]

Computer Centers   Today almost all medium to large academic centers have computer centers, and school, public, and special libraries often have access to similar equipment used by other local and state agencies. The typical center has a mainframe computer and serves the data processing needs of the whole community. It may serve, too, as a memory and processing system for microcomputers used throughout the library and by other groups and individuals. Also, it can link the community unit with a larger regional or national network.

There may develop a quiet struggle between the library and the computer center for control of software, microcomputers, and even online information retrieval. The center argues that it is the logical place to house such information resources, but the librarian may rightfully reply: "While the staffs of the computer centers are

[5]Vendors usually charge more for using 1200 baud, and if one is reading the message on a CRT, it often is too fast for comfort. The 1200 baud is preferable for speed, and while one may pay a vendor twice as much to use a database with a 1200 baud, the message comes in four times as fast as on a 300 baud. Speeds up to 3600 baud are available and will surely bring about other rate changes by vendors.

sophisticated about the technology itself, the orientation of most computer center professionals is to the use of hardware. . . . Such individuals are not concerned with training or practice in information dissemination and use."[6]

In most cases, the computer center will be a distinctive aid to the library, particularly in automation efforts which require fast processing and huge memory stores. Obviously, no librarian should proceed with computer development without first consulting the local center.

Computer Networks The placement of the vendor, database, telecommunications, computer terminal, user, and center constitutes a network, or, more properly, an electronic network. Some visionaries see this as eliminating the notion of the library. Why, they ask, is there any reason for printed materials when everything can be consigned to an electronic form? There are many answers to this, from the high cost of the electronic network, to its dependence upon technology (sometimes quite complicated) to relay information. Yet, this misses the point. Libraries will continue to exist because they are convenient sources of information, which is, for the most part, free. Furthermore, the library is a necessary adjunct of the educational process. Even the most devoted computer hack must learn to read, must become literate—albeit, one might argue even this may not be necessary when voice takes over completely, if we return to a totally oral culture. The chances of that happening are about as slim as the demise of the library. Computer networks and libraries will continue to develop and grow together.

Computer Literacy[7] Computer literacy is the catchphrase of the 1980s, but what is it and what does it mean for reference librarians? It is quickly defined as a type of consciousness-raising which makes the individual feel comfortable with the technology of the computer. It has to do "with increasing our understanding of what the machine can and cannot do. There are two major components of computer literacy: hardware and software."[8] One needs to have enough understanding of both to use the computer in a constructive way. This does not mean, however, that computer literacy requires one to be the

[6]Alan Guskin et al., "Library Future Shock: The Microcomputer Revolution and the New Role of the Library," *College & Research Libraries*, May, 1984, p. 182. For another view, see: Charles Anderson, "The Myth of the Expert Searcher," *Library Journal*, February 1, 1986, pp. 37–39.

[7]For a less than optimistic view of computer literacy, see the three articles on the subject which appeared in *The New York Times*, beginning on December 9, 1984, p. 1, p. 80, and continuing through the next two days on various pages.

[8]Forest Horton, "Information Literacy vs. Computer Literacy," *ASIS Bulletin*, April 1983, p. 14.

Shakespeare of the keyboard. Actually, it is quite a simple learning experience which may or may not be necessary for most people. It certainly is required for today's librarian, who also needs something more.

The librarian needs what is known as "information literacy." This may be defined as an awareness of how "machine-aided handling systems can help identify, access, and obtain data, documents and literature needed for problem-solving and decision making."[9] Information literacy goes beyond computer literacy. It requires a knowledge of many factors beyond hardware and software, such as databases; indexing and abstracting; networking; interview and search techniques; and, in short, a complete background in traditional reference work as well as computers.

Programming The software is made operative by what is known as programming, by now a common term which can be thought of as the imaginative use of the language of the computer. A fear many librarians have is that they have to learn to program in order to use the computer. This is not true; in fact, it isn't even desirable except for those who are professionals in such matters.

> *"The professed need to learn programming has become an adjunct of that now all-too-familiar term 'computer literacy.' Somehow the idea of being computer illiterate has been foisted upon the public as a handicap and horror that in today's world of high technology may be even worse than being illiterate in the traditional sense of the word. But the analogy is a false one that has gained acceptance because of fear of the unknown or paying too much heed to 'authorities' who are either recent converts to computerdom or its purveyors.*
>
> *True, computers are part and parcel of our daily lives now. . . . And, true, a computer without programs is as useful as a rusty fishhook in the middle of the Gobi. But does this mean that whoever wants to use a computer must also write the software for it? Would someone purchasing an automobile for a cross-country trip first study cartography, then proceed to obtain aerial and satellite photographs of the proposed route, and finally draw a detailed map for the whole journey? Hardly. It is far easier to go to the A.A.A. and get standard maps or that organization's special trip sheets."[10]*

[9]Horton, *op. cit.,* p. 16.

[10]Erik Sandberg-Diment, "Does Everyone Need to Learn Programming?," *The New York Times,* January 17, 1984, p. C3. Douglas Noble, "The Underside of Computer Literacy," *Raritan,* Spring, 1984, pp. 37–64. The author, writing in this Rutgers University quarterly, is a former computer programmer and educator. He asks for a balanced view of the place of the computer in society.

In other words, there is more than enough software around to make it unnecessary for the librarian to master programming. Go on to the more important aspects of mastering searching.

ONLINE SEARCHING

An online search begins with the librarian, or user, sitting down at a terminal which is connected by phone to the database in a large mainframe computer. In order to get information from the databases, the librarian must know a series of commands which make the specific database available for search and allow one to find citations. The commands are usually typed, and primarily consist of key subject terms and/or author names. There are subtle variations, however, and the actual search can be a complicated procedure. When one finds what is needed, an order is given to have the citations printed out, usually at the same terminal. If the sample printout is satisfactory, one may then ask for more citations; if it is not satisfactory, one may switch tactics and try a new search pattern.

There are numerous problems with this type of search, not the least of which may be getting the search started. The so-called "log-on" procedures can be frustrating. At the same time, there is a concerted effort to make searching much easier through automatic logging-on and specific, standardized search patterns. The earlier-mentioned "front-end software" is a menu-driven package which makes "log-on" procedures, as well as basic searching, relatively simple, even for beginners. The ideal is the computer which will react to a spoken command, thus eliminating typing and most of the complicated search patterns.[11]

Basic search

The basics of searching online are quite simple. Given the equipment, the dialing which connects one to the database vendor, and the log-on procedures, one is prepared to search. Much of the log-on can now be done automatically.

Once the searcher is connected to the vendor, the database must be indicated. This varies with different vendors. For BRS it means typing in an acronym such as Psyc for *Psychological Abstracts*. Wilson-

---

[11]Despite years of research on computer speech recognition, fair estimates are that it will be another 20 to 25 years before such computers are in general use. See Andrew Pollack's "Computers Mastering Speech Recognition," *The New York Times*, September 6, 1983, p. 1 and p. 7.

line uses letters such as RDG for *Readers' Guide to Periodical Literature,* and DIALOG employs numbers such as "1" for *Eric.* The rest of the example is based on DIALOG.

Let's say the database is *Eric,* and the search is on DIALOG.

One types in "b1". The "1" is the symbol for *Eric.* The "b" is the standard code which signifies database and is used before each number of a database.

The computer responds with a "?" which is an invitation to enter the key words in the search.

One then enters "s" for "select" and then the key word or words, e.g., "s academic libraries"

The response is "1" which labels this as the first search, then "220" which indicates the number of citations for which this is a subject heading.

On paper or on the computer screen the search would look like this:

? s academic libraries
   1   220 academic libraries

The select command may be used for a free text search, i.e., to find out how many times one or more words (not subject headings) appear in the title, abstract, descriptive matter, etc. For example, one might enter "s academic" and the response would be "1,450 academic". This could be followed by "s libraries" and the response would be "2,500 libraries." There are more entries for the two words because the search is not limited to subject headings.

On paper or on the computer screen these searches would look like this:

? s academic
   2   1,450 academic
? s libraries
   3   2,500 libraries

If one wants to examine two or three sample citations, one gives a command which asks the computer to search for (usually) the latest entries in the system. These are then printed out in full or in part, depending upon the command expressed.

There are countless methods of making the search broader when there are not enough citations evident, or making it much more narrow when there are too many citations. This so-called proximity searching or "qualifiers" allow one to pinpoint searching. It is the knowledge of how to use these methods that is an indication of an experienced searcher.

A major benefit of online searching is that it offers numerous entry routes other than author, title, and subject. In one system (Wilsonline), there are at least 40 access points to find a single item.

All of this may take no more than two to five minutes online, cost no more than $4 or $5, and save rummaging through volumes of indexes. Of course, many searches require considerably more sophisticated approaches, take more time, employ more expensive databases, and can be quite costly. Still, the basic approach is not difficult.

If such is the case, why bother with a librarian? For now, suffice it to say that anyone can be taught the rules of Ping-Pong in a few minutes, as anyone can be taught the basics of online searching. Still, there is some difference between an expert Ping-Pong player and a beginner, so much that one is willing to pay money to see experts. The analogy holds true for online searching. Where speed, accuracy, skill, and downright amazing results are required, one needs—and will continue to need for many decades—a first-rate searcher.

The Searcher

Using the computer to search databases for information is an acquired skill, but it is a skill built upon traditional reference principles of the interview and search. If one appreciates (1) how to isolate a question in terms of probable sources where answers are found and (2) how to use key words to find the precise answer, one knows what is necessary for either a manual or an online search. There are some fascinating differences when one uses a computer, but none of these require any particular knowledge of technology. They do require mastering more sophisticated interview and search techniques.

Most important is an ability to use logic in problem solving. The online search requires specific appreciation of component parts. Information has to be approached from several different paths, if only in terms of synonyms. At the same time, one should have an appreciation for detail, particularly where more than one vendor or database is employed.

These and other traits are considered in the second volume of this text and summarized in the work, *Effective Online Searching*. The authors draw the profile of a good searcher and include these points: good communication skills and a people-orientation; self confidence; patience and perseverance; logical and flexible approach to problem solving; memory for details; spelling, grammar, and typing skills; subject area knowledge; good organization and efficient work habits; motivation for additional training; willingness to share knowledge with others. "This profile . . . may make it appear that only perfect individuals can become searchers. Alas, searchers are far from perfect, but they are people with a variety of talents and interests who enjoy the challenge of gaining new knowledge and ideas."[12] Online, as at the reference desk, information services are only as effective as the reference librarian.

ADVANTAGES OF THE ONLINE SEARCH

Practical experience with computer-aided searches indicates certain basic advantages over the manual search as well as some disadvantages. The only absolute certainty in this discussion is that there are times when one type of search is better than the other, but there is no situation in which one type is always better than the other.

Among the most often cited reasons for using the computer in a search are:

(1) *Speed of searching* A computer-aided search may take only a fraction of the time needed for a manual search, particularly when it is retrospective and requires searching several years of material. Various studies indicate that in general a computer search may be performed in 5 to 10 percent of the time required for a manual search. A considerable amount of time and effort is saved in not having to look up the same term in each volume of the printed service. Another reduction in time is made possible by the printing out of the citations, which sidesteps the need to photocopy or laboriously write out the citations.

The combination of convenience and time saved is the greatest benefit for the user. In one study, users were asked to rank the advantages of a computer search. Time saved was ranked highest by 82 percent. The next benefit, introduction to new areas, was ranked highest by only 47 percent of the users.

The response time to reference questions using books and regular sources will vary from a few minutes to days. Much depends upon the complexity of the query and the ability of the librarian. When one turns to online searches the time factor decreases noticeably. There are hundreds of examples, but take only one in a public library: "Our response time to research requests varied from an hour to several days. . . . As a result of careful preparation of search strategies, 98 percent of all DIALOG searches (i.e., via a computer)

[12]Christine Borgman, Dineh Moghdam, and Patti Corbett, *Effective Online Searching, A Basic Text,* (New York: Marcel Dekker, 1984), pp. 14–18. See, too, Robert Jack, "Meatball Searching," *Database,* December 1985, pp. 45–52.

were completed within the 15-minute free allocation of online time."[13]

(2) *Convenience* A terminal is all that is needed, and one need not go from reference work to reference work, volume to volume, on different floors and in different places in the library. More important, the terminal opens up the resources of countless indexes and abstracting services heretofore too costly for all but the largest of research libraries. Terminals may be located almost anywhere and searchers are not limited to the indexes or abstracts they may find in the library.

As most searches end with a printed out list of citations, the computer eliminates the necessity for painful and time-consuming copying of information from printed sources. It even cancels out the necessity of xeroxing or otherwise automatically copying data.

(3) *In-depth searching* The primary benefit for the librarian is the qualitative advantage of enhanced information-delivery capability. There is a higher level of subject specificity than is possible with most printed indexes. This is so because the user is not limited to assigned subject categories which are often too broad or narrow. Almost the whole of a citation online becomes a searchable element. One may search by author, by address, by words in the title, by journal title, by type of article, and by words in the abstract. Also, a document can be retrieved through searches on many different category "tags" in logical combinations, rather than on just one. For example, one may search by such tags as date, language, publication type, and so on. Each tag either expands or limits what may be retrieved.

A related benefit is that new areas (often new subjects and authors) are turned up. Also, the online search is particularly useful for finding difficult bits of information when only minor clues are available. For example, someone may want an article by Smith in the midwestern United States. The user does not know the initials of Smith but does remember that the term "archways" appears in a book or article about sparrows that he wrote. Given one or all of these clues, the search analyst may be able to locate the item by employing multiple coordinates in the search.

The computer search is useful when the librarian is faced with a somewhat complicated question, or those that include multiple concepts.

> With questions that include multiple concepts (we were once asked to
> search for material on the effects of the Taft-Hartley Act on labor

---

[13]Katherine Golomb and Sydelle Reisman, "Using DIALOG for Ready Reference," *Library Journal,* April 15, 1984, p. 786. See, too, Tina Roose, "Online Searching—Easier Than You May Think," *Library Journal,* November 1, 1985, pp. 38–39.

negotiations among coal miners in the southern U.S., especially Tennes-see), a manual search on that topic would probably require separate searches of each concept in many different volumes of a printed index. The searcher would then have to cull out the possible articles that combine all the desired concepts. With the computerized indexes, all those concepts can be combined into one search statement and searched almost instantly, with the results including only those items that include all the desired concepts. The computer search has the advantage of searching many different indexes at the same time. People have estimated that computer searches often take as little as one tenth of the time needed for a manual search, a saving of 1000 percent.[14]

(4) *Currency* Because the printed volumes are usually produced from a modified machine-readable database, the actual database may be ready for delivery weeks or months before the printed version. The time elapsed between indexing and the published index is a constant problem, which can be overcome with the database. For example, *The New York Times Index,* which in printed form is two to three months behind, may be updated daily and weekly online. However, some databases are still quite late compared to their printed counterparts. The actual speed of the printed or the online form depends on the individual publisher and the technology employed, as well as how material is compiled, indexed, and so on.

Who uses the service?

No one is certain how many libraries are active in computer-assisted reference service. By the mid-1980s, a fair estimate is that about 70 to 80 percent of large academic and public libraries offer online search-es.[15] In medium-sized and smaller libraries, it is almost nonexistent, although some have access to online searching through regional and state networks.

Even where the service is available, only about three percent of the questions answered in an academic or public library employ a computer search. The percentage goes up to as much as 20 percent when one considers medical libraries and other types of better-financed special and government libraries.

[14]Tina Roose, "Computer Searches for Kids," *Library Journal,* November 1, 1984, p. 2011.

[15]See Eileen Hitchingham et al., "A Survey of Database Use at the Reference Desk," *Online,* March 1984, p. 46; James B. Woy, "Surveys of Online Information Service in Large Public Libraries," *Drexel Library Quarterly,* Fall 1983, p. 79; and Tina Roose, "Online Database Searching in Smaller Public Libraries," *Library Journal,* September 15, 1983, pp. 1769–70.

Most academic and special library users are (1) specialists in private and public universities and research centers, often faculty; (2) specialists in government agencies and departments; (3) technologists and business people in the private sector; or (4) students, normally at the university graduate level.

Who uses the available public library services? Business people predominate, followed by students, teachers, university administrators, and local government agencies and individuals. In the study of public library use it was found that "business topics represent 36 percent, science and technology was 30 percent, and other topics were 34 percent."[16]

The amount of use of computer searches increases each day and with more sophisticated technology and additional searching experience by librarians, it is quite likely to be a normal reference function within the next few years. The primary problem now is cost. Searches can run from a few cents to well over $100.[17] Most libraries absorb at least some of these expenses, but fees charged to individuals are more common than exceptional. Whether to charge, how much to charge, etc., are questions still to be resolved.

SUGGESTED READING

Anderson, Charles, "The Myth of the Expert Searcher," *Library Journal*, February 1, 1986, pp. 37–39. A public librarian believes there are numerous myths about the online search, and that it is really fairly simple to perform at a moderate cost. The conclusions are based upon experience over a period of six years. Anderson believes online searching should be a major part of all public library reference services.

Anderson, Verl, "Simultaneous Remote Searching," *Library Journal*, November 1, 1985, pp. 167–169. An easy-to-understand explanation of a type of search online which is likely to become more popular. See in the same issue, pp. 38–39, Tina Roose, "Online Searching—Easier Than You May Think."

Boss, Richard, "Technology and the Modern Library," *Library Journal*, June 15, 1984, pp. 1183–1189. A well-written, easy to follow survey of automation in the library from 1979 to mid-1984. Covers both online searching and networks and other electronic developments. For another view see Kevin Hegarty, "Myths of Library Automation," *Library Journal*, October 1, 1985, pp. 43–49. Other related titles:

---

[16]Woy, *op, cit.*, p. 84.

[17]See an ongoing series by Tina Roose, "Online or Print: Comparing Costs," which appear in the *Library Journal* (March 1, May 1, July and September 15, 1985 for example). In one large public library, it was found the cost per online search per question was $15.75 vs. $22.50 for manual searches. (September 15, 1985, pp. 54–55). There are so many variables the specific difference is difficult to calculate.

Dennis Reynolds, *Library Automation* (New York: R. R. Bowker, 1985), and the *Bowker Annual of Library and Book Trade Information* which includes developments in this area.

"Computer Literacy: A Core Collection," *Choice,* January, 1986, pp. 709–716. "The goal of this bibliography is to suggest a core collection: books, periodicals, and reference materials that will provide an introduction to the history and philosophy" . . . of computers. The select, briefly annotated list is a good beginning point for librarians, as well as laypersons involved with computer literacy.

"Computers", *Consumer Reports,* September, October, 1983. Various pages. There are two lengthy sections in this well-known magazine on the home computer. In addition to making recommendations for purchase, the articles explain simply and well the various components of the home systems. Particularly good for a clear analysis of what the computer can and can't do for the average person. Since this initial study, individual issues now feature reports on different systems. The index should be checked for the years from 1983 to date. See, too, numerous guides to individual microcomputers, e.g. N. W. Cain, *Hard Disk Management* (Englewood Cliffs, New Jersey: Prentice Hall, 1986); R. W. Haigh, *Macintosh Logo* (New York, Wiley, 1986).

Crichton, Michael, *Electronic Life: How to Think About Computers.* New York: Knopf, 1983. One of the better books on the social and philosophical aspects of the computer age. At the same time there is clear advice on practical guidelines for buying a computer for everything from word processing to games.

Daily, Jay, *Staff Personality Problems in the Library Automation Process: A Case In Point.* Littleton, CO: Libraries Unlimited, 1985. A master of the good prose style turns his skills to a telling, and extremely well thought out, discussion of automated technical services and the interpersonal problems they may cause. There are five case histories with excellent introductions on the history of a particular phase of automation.

Dowlin, Kenneth, *The Electronic Library: The Promise and the Process.* New York: Neal-Schuman Publishers, Inc., 1984. A librarian indicates how the new technology is used, and will be used, in libraries. Of particular interest: the section on how individuals access databases from their micros at home. Among books of this type, it is one of the best and a first choice for its good overview. To keep current on computer books see the subject index to any up-to-date issue of *Book Review Digest;* and for an ongoing nonevaluative bibliography use *Computer Books and Serials in Print* (New York: R. R. Bowker, 1985 to date, annual.)

Grossman, George, "The Totally Online Library: Northwestern's Integrated Library System," *Law Library Journal,* vol. 77, no. 1, 1984–85, pp. 47–57. One of the few libraries in the United States with a total online system, Northwestern University offers an excellent example of what it means to be automated. The history and present operating procedures of the system is explained. (Despite the source of the article, little of it is involved with law. Focus is on the total system).

Hawkins, Donald T., "Online Information Retrieval Bibliography," *Online Review,* 1977 to date, annual. Divided by broad subject headings, this offers close to 1000 references each year to the literature. A first place to turn for retrospective materials.

Mason, Robert, "Woodstock in Seattle? CD-ROM & CD-I," *Library Journal,* May 15, 1986, pp. 50–51. A report on the first international CD-ROM conference, and a clear explanation about the new marvel for storage. Both the pros and cons of the system are given, as well as variations for library use. For a layperson's explanation of CD-ROM see: "A Library on a Disc," *Newsweek,* April 21, 1983, p. 73.

Reference Books Bulletin, "Wilsonline," *The Booklist,* March 1, 1986, pp. 950–952. The H. W. Wilson Co. system of databases is reviewed. In the process the detailed review serves as an excellent introduction not only to Wilsonline, but to the joys and problems of online searching and databases.

Rice, James, *Introduction to Library Automation.* Littleton, Colorado: Libraries Unlimited, Inc., 1984. While this covers the whole of library automation, there are several good sections on computers, as well as networks and turnkey systems. The text is well written and the explanations are as topical as they are easy to follow. It should be used with more explicit titles, i.e., those which go into more details about databases, vendors, etc.

Turkle, Sherry, *The Second Self: Computers and the Human Spirit.* New York: Simon & Schuster, 1984. The results of a six-year study of 400 computer users (about half children), this offers a vivid account of the way the computer has changed, and is likely to change, human conduct. Children, for example, seem to think of the machine as something between the living and the inanimate, and adults may become addicted to programming.

Winner, Langdon, "Mythinformation," *Whole Earth Review,* January 1985, pp. 22–28. The author points out the fallacies in the notion that "computer literacy" is necessarily more useful than any other skill. In fact, he demonstrates it is a far cry from real knowledge or mastering the information available.

INFORMATION: CONTROL AND ACCESS

CHAPTER THREE

Bibliographies: Introduction and Selection of Reference Works

B ibliography is one of the most common terms used by reference librarians. As a listing of data and documents, a bibliography is the primary tool in the three-step service of the reference librarian. Given a good bibliography the librarian is able to (1) identify what someone requests by title, by author, or by subject (common questions answered this way: What do you have by Kurt Vonnegut? Do you have the novel *Eyes and Nose Together?* Where can I find a book on small rockets?); (2) locate the items either in the library or in another library by using the card catalog or a catalog which shows the holdings of other libraries; (3) deliver the items to the user.

In a broader sense, the bibliography brings order out of chaos. The frightening thing about many libraries is that there appears to be too much of everything. How can one person even imagine the contents of a small portion of this mass of information, delight, and frustration? A partial answer to the query, as well as a method of at least controlling the fear of abundance, is the bibliography.

There are numerous definitions of bibliography, but no single definition is suitable for all situations. For most people, it is a list of books, but for experts it has a different meaning—the critical and historical study of printed books. In France, particularly during the late eighteenth century, the term emerged as a form of library science, i.e., the knowledge and the theory of book lists. The Americans and English now tend to divide it into critical, analytical, and historical, as differentiated from a simple listing. The central problem of definition is not likely to be solved, but for most purposes it is enough to say that when Americans are talking about bibliography they are concerned with the study of books, and lists of books or other materials.

SYSTEMATIC ENUMERATIVE BIBLIOGRAPHY

The average librarian, when speaking of bibliography, is probably referring to systematic enumerative bibliography, i.e., a list of books, films, or recordings. If a bibliography is adequately to meet the need for control and access, several elements are required.

Completeness Through either a single bibliography or a combination of bibliographies, the librarian should have access to the complete records of all areas of interest; not only what is now available but also what has been published in the past and what is being published today or is proposed for publication tomorrow. Also, the net should be broad enough to include the world, not only one nation's works.

Access to a Part Normally the librarian is apt to think of bibliographies in terms of the whole unit—book, periodical, manuscript, or the like, but an ideal bibliography should also be analytical, allowing the librarian to approach the specific unit in terms of the smallest part of a work.

Various Forms Books are considered the main element of most bibliographies, but a comprehensive bibliographical tool will include all forms of published communication from reports and documents to phonograph records and databases.

These three elements are usually referred to as parts of bibliographical control or organization, that is, of effective access to sources of information. No bibliography or set of bibliographies has yet met all these needs. At best, a bibliography is a compromise between completeness, access to parts, and various forms.

With the bibliography ready at hand, how does the librarian use it on a day-to-day basis? Regardless of form, a bibliography is used primarily for three basic purposes: (1) to identify and verify, (2) to locate, and (3) to select.

Identification and Verification The usual bibliography gives standard information similar to that found on most catalog cards: author, title, edition (if other than a first edition), place of publication, publisher, date of publication, a collation (i.e., number of pages, illustrations, size), and price. Another element added to many bibliographies is the International Standard Book Number, abbreviated as ISBN or simply SBN, which is employed by publishers to distinguish one title from another. The ISBN number usually is on the verso of the title page. A similar system, the International Standard Serial Number (ISSN) is employed to identify serials. In seeking to identify or verify any of these elements, a librarian will turn to the proper bibliography, usually beginning with the general, such as *Books in Print* or *The National Union Catalog,* and moving to the particular, such as a bibliography in a narrow subject area.

Location Location may be in terms of where the book is published, where it can be found in a library, or where it can be purchased. However, from the point of view of the patron's needs, the location is more apt to be in terms of subject. What is available in this subject area, in a book, periodical, article, report, or some other form of communication?

Selection The primary aim of a library is to build a useful collection to serve users. This objective presupposes selection from a vast number of possibilities. In order to assist the librarian, certain bibliographies indicate what is available in a given subject area, by a given author, in a given form, or for certain groups of readers. A bibliography may give an estimate of the value of the particular work for a certain type of reader.

Forms of systematic enumerative bibliography: Universal bibliography

A true universal bibliography would include everything published, issued, or pressed in the field of communications from the beginning through the present to the future. Such universality is now an impossible dream. In practice, the term is employed in a narrower sense. It generally means a bibliography that is not necessarily limited by time, territory, language, subject, or form. National library catalogs, some book dealers' catalogs, and auction catalogs are the nearest thing to a universal bibliography now available.

Online capture of not only national but also international materials may come close to realization of a type of universal bibliography. The computer's memory is so vast that given the proper entry form, it is able to hold as many works as published. The main problem remains, though, and that is how to discover the elusive works from equally elusive sources. One may claim universal bibliography, only to be frustrated by a country, region, or individual who refuses to methodically list what is issued.

National and trade bibliographies[1]

These kinds of works are limited to materials published within a given country. They may be limited in scope to a section of the country, a city, or even a hamlet. For ease of use and convenience, national bibliographies normally are divided into even finer parts.

Time This is a matter of listing works previously published, works being published, or works to be published. Such bibliographies are normally labeled as either retrospective or current.

Form This classification may be in terms of bibliographical form: collections of works, monographs, components (e.g., essays, periodical articles, poems); physical form: books, recordings, pamphlets, microfilm; or published and unpublished works (manuscripts, dissertations).

A typical national bibliography will set itself limits of time, form, and, obviously, origin. For example, *Books in Print* is limited to books available for purchase (time); it includes only printed books, both hardbound and paperback, and some monographs and series (form); and it is a trade bibliography, i.e., issued by a commercial organization (origin).

There is no limit to the possible subdivisions of national bibliography. For example, within the overall area appear bibliographies (works by and about a given author) and anonymous and pseudonymous listings.

A distinction must be made between national bibliography and national library catalogs. A national bibliography often is the product of the government and is an effort to include everything published within the boundaries of that nation. An example is the *British National Bibliography*, which, since 1950, weekly lists and describes every new work published in Great Britain, with some exceptions. A national library catalog, such as our *National Union Catalog*, not only

---

[1]The term "trade" bibliography is often used synonymously with "national." Trade bibliography refers to a bibliography issued for and usually by the booksellers and publishers of a particular nation. The emphasis of a trade bibliography is on basic purchasing data. A national bibliography includes basic data plus much other information used primarily by bibliographers.

includes books published in the country of origin, but contains material in many languages from around the world.

Subject bibliography

The universal and the national bibliographies are the base for any subject bibliography. While the two major forms tend to be used almost exclusively by generalists such as the book dealer, the librarian, and the publisher, the subject bibliography is intended for the research worker and for others in special areas.

Once a subject is chosen, the divisions common to national bibliographies may be employed—time, form, origin, and others. However, unlike most national bibliographies, a subject work may use all the divisions. For example, a definitive bibliography on railroad engines may be retrospective, current (at least at date of publishing), inclusive of all forms from individual monographs to government publications, and reflective of various sources or origins.

Guides to reference materials

Theoretically, lists which include the "best" works for a given situation or audience are not bibliographies in the accepted definition of the term. In practice, however, they are normally so considered. They include guides to reference books, special reading lists issued by a library, and books devoted to the "best" works for children, adults, students, business people, and others.

Bibliography of bibliographies

There are a few of this type of bibliography, but they guide the user to other helpful bibliographies, normally by subject, by place, or by individual.

This description of five types of bibliography does not exhaust the innumerable possibilities for methods of organizing and describing bibliographies. It barely touches on the various combinations. There is no universally accepted method of even approaching parts and divisions of a bibliography. The problem is to bring order out of this chaotic, primarily free-wheeling approach to listing materials.

Analytical and textual bibliography

Analytical bibliography is concerned with the physical description of the book. Textual bibliography goes a step further and highlights certain textual variations between a manuscript and the printed book or between various editions. Often the two are combined into one scientific or art form. This type of research is designed to discover everything possible about the author's ultimate intentions. The goal is to recover the exact words that the author intended to constitute his or her work. In driving toward this goal, one group of bibliographers may be experts, for example, in nineteenth-century printing practices and bookbinding, another group in paper watermarks or title pages.

There are differences between analytical and textual bibliographies—the most basic being that analytical bibliography is more concerned with the physical aspects of the book, and textual bibliography with the author's words, i.e., the exact text as the author meant it to appear in printed form.

Daily use

Returning to the standard enumerative bibliography, how is this form used in a library? Normally it directs the individual to an item, and it is employed primarily to find X book or Y article. There are two basic approaches for looking in the bibliography for X or for Y.

Most people (as high as 70 percent in some surveys) look up X or Y by its title or by the author's name. If, for example, Tom Smith wants a book on automobiles, he is likely to approach the card catalog, a periodical index, or a librarian with the name or the title of the book.

About 50 percent of the searches of bibliographies in a library are by subject. Here, Mr. Smith does not know the author or the title but turns to a subject heading to help him find what is needed.

The more sophisticated and knowledgeable a person is in any field (whether it be automobiles or psychology), the more likely the individual is to try to search a bibliography by author or by title. This is not only more precise but much easier, because one does not have to guess the subject headings in the bibliography. For example, is automobile under automobiles or cars or transportation or (you fill in your own guess)? The most complex search is a subject search.

EVALUATION OF A BIBLIOGRAPHY

When considering the relative merits of a bibliography, one applies the general criteria used for evaluation of all reference works, e.g., see the discussion on "Evaluating Reference Sources" in Chapter 1. Beyond this, the Reference and Adult Services Division Bibliography

Committee offers specific steps one may use in considering the quality and character of the elements included in a bibliography.[2]

(1) *Purpose* It is important that the bibliography fill a real need, and that it is not a repetition of another work, or so esoteric that it is of little or no value. The subject is stated clearly in the title and well defined in the preface.

(2) *Scope* The bibliography should be as complete as possible within its stated purpose. For example, a bibliography of books and periodical articles about nineteenth-century American railroads will include contemporary magazine reports about the construction of railroads. Where there are different forms, such as magazines and books, these must be clearly identified.

(3) *Methodology* The method of compiling the bibliography is clear, and the compiler has examined all material listed. The items are described in a standard bibliographic style, and include the basic elements of a bibliographical entry.

(4) *Organization* The bibliography is organized in a clear, easy-to-use fashion and indexes (from subject and author to geographical location) are included where multiple access is desirable. At the same time the material is arranged in a logical fashion so it is not always necessary to use the index, e.g., alphabetical by author, by date, by subject, etc. The author offers a clear explanation of how to use the work as well as definitions, key to abbreviations and the like.

(5) *Annotations-Abstracts* Where descriptive and/or critical notes are used for entries, these are clear, succinct, and informative.

(6) *Bibliographic Form* This is a standard entry with the information one needs to identify and locate the item.

(7) *Current* The material is current, at least where this is the purpose of the bibliography. It is conceivable one would only list eighteenth- or nineteenth-century publications, and timeliness as such would not be a factor.

(8) *Accuracy* It goes without saying that the material must be accurate. Some arrangement for corrections to be made after publication, should the need arise, is desirable.

Other elements such as format and distribution are important, although these may be more in the hands of the publisher than the compiler. Distribution may be the most important element of all, and one which, unfortunately, is often overlooked. Consider, for example, the horror story of the first discovery of penicillin:

[2]"Guidelines for the Preparation of a Bibliography," *RQ*, Fall 1982, pp. 31–32. The wording used in the summary is a paraphrase of the much longer "Guidelines".

In 1896 at a French university medical school, after fulfilling classroom and laboratory requirements, students were obligated to submit theses of quality sufficient for the awarding of the M.D. degree. The theses were subsequently (and routinely) filed away in the university's archives to gather dust. One thesis, however (in a nation during a period when no medical bibliographical announcement service existed), apparently escaped the eyes of the faculty charged with approving theses, for it contained the information requisite for the manufacture of penicillin. As a result, the world was forced to wait until 1929, when Dr. Alexander Fleming "reinvented the wheel" and announced what was actually the rediscovery of penicillin. Between 1897 and 1929, countless millions of people worldwide died of pneumonia and other diseases, who might have lived, had the 1896 French medical thesis been identified and announced bibliographically. The foregoing indicates the significance of bibliography and of bibliographic services: without such tools, the discovery of penicillin did not become a reality until 1929.[3]

GUIDES TO REFERENCE BOOKS

The basic purpose of a bibliographical guide to reference material is to introduce the user to (1) general reference sources which will be of assistance in research in all fields and (2) specific reference sources which will help in research in particular fields. These guides take a number of forms, but primarily are either (1) annotated lists of titles with brief introductory remarks before each section or chapter or (2) handbooks which not only list and annotate basic sources, but also introduce the user to investigative tools by a discursive, almost textbook-like, approach.

There are numerous research guides of this latter type, but the most widely useful one is Jacques Barzun and Henry Graff's *The Modern Researcher* (3rd ed. New York: Harcourt Brace Jovanovich, 1977, 378 pp.). While written for history students, the advice on the research and preparation of a paper is useful for anyone in almost any field. It is particularly useful for the clear presentation of how to use reference works.

The general bibliographical guide to reference materials is the starting point to answer many questions. There are several guides which are helpful in the selection and use of reference books.

[3]Martin Sable, "Systematic Bibliography," *International Library Review,* January 1981, p. 21.

Sheehy, Eugene P. *Guide to Reference Books,* 10th ed. Chicago: American Library Association, 1986. $50.

Walford, Albert John. *Guide to Reference Materials,* 4th ed. London: The Library Association, 1980–in progress, 3 vols. $67.50 each. (Distributed in the United States by Oryx Press, Phoenix, Arizona)

Wynar, Bohdan. *American Reference Books Annual.* Littleton, Colorado: Libraries Unlimited, Inc., 1970 to date, annual. $70.

Ryder, Dorothy E. *Canadian Reference Sources: A Selective Guide,* 2d ed. Ottawa: Canadian Library Association, 1981. 311 pp. $20.

The two basic guides which tell a reference librarian what reference books are basic in all fields are those by Sheehy and Walford. Most librarians refer to them as "Sheehy" and "Walford." (Prior to Sheehy's ninth edition of *Guide to Reference Books,* the work was compiled by Constance Winchell. Many librarians still refer to the guide as "Winchell.")

The guides list and annotate the major titles used in reference service. Sheehy includes some 14,000 entries, Walford about the same. Complete bibliographical information is given for each entry, and most of the entries are annotated.

Their arrangements differ. Sheehy has five main sections in a single volume. Walford, using the Universal Decimal Classification System, divides his work into three separate volumes: science and technology; social sciences; and generalities, languages, the arts, and literature.

Both works begin with a large subject and then subdivide by smaller subjects and by forms. For example, Sheehy has a section on economics under the social sciences. This is subdivided by forms: guides, bibliographies, periodicals, dissertations, indexes and abstract journals, dictionaries and encyclopedias, atlases, handbooks, and so on. The economics section is later broken down into smaller subjects and often, within the subject, a further division is made by country, as, for example, in political science. Walford subdivides economics by bibliographies, thesauruses, encyclopedias and dictionaries, dissertations, and so on, generally following the Sheehy pattern. In practice, the arrangement is not really important. Each volume has an excellent title, author, and subject index.

Sheehy concentrates on American, Canadian, and English titles, and Walford is stronger on English and European titles. In the second volume of Walford, about 13 percent of the listings are from

American publishers, 31 percent from Great Britain, and over 50 percent from European and Commonwealth nations.

The problem with Sheehy is currency. Supplements are issued about every four years but also have a history of being behind. The primary editions seem to be on a ten-year schedule, i.e., the 9th edition was issued in 1976, the tenth in 1986. The ten-year gap between editions is much too long.

Walford is more current. The complete three-volume revision is carried out over six years, and then begins again.[4] A useful, condensed version of the three-volume set will be found in the one-volume *Concise Guide to Reference Material* (London: Library Association, 1981, 440 pp.) This follows the same organizational pattern of the large work and is valuable primarily for the excellent annotations and the focus on English and European reference works.

A partial answer to the time-lapse problems of Sheehy and Walford is offered by the *American Reference Books Annual* (usually cited as ARBA). It differs from both Sheehy and Walford in three important respects: (1) It is limited to reference titles published or distributed in the United States; (2) it is comprehensive for a given year and makes no effort to be selective; (3) the annotations are written by more than 320 subject experts and are both more critical and more expository than those found in Sheehy or Walford. Depending on the extent of American publishing, the annual volume usually available in March or April of the year following the year covered in the text analyzes some 1600 to 1800 separate reference titles. (Since its inception, the service has examined over 27,000 reference sources.) The work is well-organized and well-indexed. Every five years the publisher issues a cumulative index to the set, e.g., *Index to American Reference Books Annual 1980–1984* (1984); 1975–1979; 1970–1974. Each indexes about 8000 reference works by author, title, and subject for a total of 25,349 reviews covered in the three indexes.

With the 1985 volume, ARBA changed its format and arrangement so it is now divided into four main sections and the text is in two columns per page. (A 1985 spinoff of this volume is *Library Science Annual,* which includes reviews of library science monographs, essays, dissertations, etc. It is of considerably less general value than ARBA.)

The Canadian cousin to Sheehy and Walford is arranged in much the same way and has the same type of descriptive annotations.

---

[4]The publisher of *Guide to Reference Books* in late 1986 announced tentative plans for a quarterly or semi-annual method of updating the *Guide.*

If anything, the compiler is more sensitive to changes in interests. In the second edition she adds sections on the history of women, children's literature, ethnic groups, and labor. The titles are limited to those published in Canada, and/or reference works about Canada. There is an author, title, and selected subject index. The work is updated every four or five years, but is supplemented annually via a list of Canadian reference sources in the August number of the *Canadian Library Journal*.[5]

A related title: Diane Henderson, *Guide to Basic Reference Materials for Canadian Libraries*. Toronto: University of Toronto Press, various editions. This is a looseleaf work which is primarily for library school students, but may be used by libraries. The primary focus is on directory and statistical types of information sources.

Guides for smaller libraries[6]

There are scores of listings, guides, and catalogs of reference works which are either smaller, larger, or more specialized than Sheehy or Walford. But this one is the most often used in smaller libraries:

Reference Sources for Small- and Medium-Sized Libraries. (4th ed. Chicago: American Library Association, 1984, 252 pp.) A standard guide, this consists of about 1800 basic reference books for children, young adults and adults, as well as reference works in other formats. Each title is briefly described, and where reference material is available online, this is so noted. Arrangement is by 22 broad subject headings, with an author and title index. The selection represents careful judgement, and this is a fine guide for the smaller library where one may wish to evaluate holdings, or locate a specific reference title for an equally specific topic.

CURRENT SELECTION AIDS

Librarians who want to build collections in given subjects need only consult their preferred guides for basic titles. Beyond that, they run

---

[5]Edith Jarvi and Diane Henderson, "Canadian Reference Books; or Benevolent Ignorance Dispelled," *Reference Services Review*, Fall 1983, pp. 87–95. Here is a well-written, annotated listing of basic Canadian works which should be found in most libraries, including those in America.

[6]Edgar C. Bailey, "Library Guides and Handbooks," *Reference Services Review*, Spring 1983, pp. 47–52. This is an analysis of books which help the beginner discover the delights of the library. Most include some help in the question/answer field.

into the problem of currency. The reference librarian with an interest in current titles must study reviews in periodicals. Most of the periodicals to be discussed review books ranging from fiction to technical publications.

The selection of reference sources is a highly individualized process. The character and the distribution of the elements which constitute the needs of users differ from library to library. Consequently, the first and most important rule when considering the selection of reference materials, or anything else for the library, is to recognize the needs, both known and anticipated, of the users. ①

How is a satisfactory selection policy arrived at? First and foremost, there must be a librarian who has some subject competence; that is, one who knows the basic literature of a field, or several fields, including not only the reference works but also the philosophy, jargon, ideas, ideals, and problems that make up that field. There is no substitute for substantive knowledge. Second, the librarian must be aware in some depth of the type of writing and publishing done in that special field. Where is there likely to be the best review? Who are the outstanding authors, publishers, and editors in this field? What can and cannot be answered readily?

Selection is charted, rather than dictated, by the following:

1. Knowing as much as possible about the needs of those who use the reference collection.
2. Calling upon expert advice. In a school situation the expert may be the teacher who is knowledgeable in a certain area. In a public library it may be the layperson, skilled practitioner, or subject specialist who uses the library. Most people are flattered by a request that draws upon their experience and knowledge, and one of the best resources for wise selection of reference materials is the informed user.
3. Keeping a record of questions. This is done to determine not only what materials the library has but what it does not have. Most important, a record of *unanswered* queries will often be the basis for an evaluation of the reference collection.
4. Knowing what other libraries have, and what resources are available. For example, the small library contemplating the purchase of an expensive run of periodicals or a bibliography would certainly first check to see whether the same materials may be readily available in a nearby library.

These four points only begin to suggest the complexity of selection. Many libraries have detailed selection policy statements which consider the necessary administrative steps only hinted at here.

Reference Book Reviews

Choice. Chicago: American Library Association, 1964 to date, monthly. $85.

Library Journal. New York: R. R. Bowker Company, 1876 to date, semimonthly. $59.

RQ. Chicago: American Library Association, 1960 to date, quarterly. $20.

"Reference Books Bulletin," in *The Booklist.* Chicago: American Library Association, 1905 to date, semimonthly. $40.

Reference Services Review. Ann Arbor, Michigan: Pierian Press, 1972 to date, quarterly. $42.50.

Wilson Library Bulletin. New York: The H. W. Wilson Company, 1914 to date, monthly. $35.

The most exhaustive essay-reviews appear as the "Reference Books Bulletin," a center section in the twice-a-month issue of *The Booklist.* (Until mid-1983 this was known as "Reference and Subscription Books Reviews.") Each section is prefaced by a series of notes about publishing, reference services, and new works. This is followed by unsigned reviews. The names of the members who write the reviews and serve on the committee (librarians and teachers) are given in each issue.

In the course of a year, the service will review about 100 to 150 major works, and about double that number of more conventional, less expensive titles. From time to time a whole issue, or a good part of an issue, will be dedicated to an overview of encyclopedias, dictionaries, children's reference works, and the like. The reviews are cumulated in a separate publication each year, and librarians often refer laypersons to these for information on encyclopedias.

Reviews appear no more than six months after publication of the reviewed book, and sometimes even sooner. Although hardly timely, this is an improvement over the ten-month to even three-year gap of earlier times. Almost all reviews in other media are late, but the average time lapse is normally no more than a few weeks or months after publication of the title.

Other current sources are:

1. *Choice* While specifically geared to college libraries, this professional journal evaluates a number of reference titles of value to all libraries. The reference books lead off the main section of general reviews. Also, from time to time bibliographical essays in the front of the magazine highlight

reference titles. There are approximately 6000 reviews a
year, of which about 500 are of reference books. The reviews
are usually 120 to 500 words in length and are signed. Almost
all reviewers make an effort to compare the title under review
with previously published titles in the same subject area, a
feature which is particularly useful but rarely found in the
other reviews. When budgets are tight, when choices must be
made, it is of considerable importance that comparisons are
available.

2. *Library Journal* Again, the general book review section leads
off with "Reference." (To be more precise, it follows "The
Contemporary Scene" section.) There are about 450 reference reviews each year. These are 100 to 150 words long,
usually written by librarians or teachers, and all are signed.
Approximately the same number of reviews appear annually
in *Library Journal* (LJ) as in *Choice*. Also, *School Library Journal*
includes reviews of reference titles.

3. *RQ* The last section of this quarterly is given over entirely to
the review of reference books. A few other related titles are
considered, but, unlike *Library Journal* and *Choice*, *RQ* makes
no effort to review general books. About 140 to 150 reference titles are considered each year. Reviews average about
200 words each.

4. *Wilson Library Bulletin* One section is devoted to "Current
Reference Books," and has the distinction of being the only
series of reviews by an individual. James Rettig, head reference librarian, University of Illinois at Chicago, covers about
20 to 30 current titles each month. Most of these are suitable
for the general reference collection in public, academic, and
school libraries. They are both descriptive and evaluative,
although Rettig tends to select only books he can recommend. The reviews are current, and help the librarian to
decide immediately whether or not to purchase the work.

5. *Reference Services Review* This is a quarterly which differs from
the other titles in that it is more discursive, and each number
not only includes individual reviews, but has essays on various
aspects of reference publishing and reference services. It
covers all areas from government documents to individual
publishers, and is particularly valuable for the intelligent
overview of the field. It is hard to imagine any reference
librarian who does not read this regularly, as much for the
reviews as for the excellent articles. Beginning with the

Spring 1985 issue, there is a special section for reviews, "Recent Reference Books" arranged by broad subject area. These are both descriptive and evaluative, and there are from 150 to 200 per issue.

American Libraries, the monthly magazine of the American Library Association, does not regularly review reference books, but it does have an annual feature of interest. This is "Outstanding Reference Sources of 19—." Appearing in the May issue, it is a compilation of the best reference titles of the year selected by the Reference Sources Committee of the ALA. (Note: Until 1984 this was in the *Library Journal,* but switched over to *American Libraries* that year.) *Library Journal* now offers a competitor, "Reference Books of 198—" which are selected by its book review editors. This appears in the April 15 issue which is devoted almost entirely to reference services.

INDEXES TO REVIEWS

Book Review Digest. New York: The H. W. Wilson Company, 1905 to date, monthly. Service. Author/title index, 1905–1974, 4 vols. $275; 1975–1984. 900pp. Inquire. (Wilsonline, $25 to $45 per hour.)[7]

Book Review Index. Detroit: Gale Research Company, 1965 to date, bimonthly. $150. Cumulation, 1965–1984 10 vols. $1,250. (DIALOG file 137, $55 per hour.)

For reference questions involving reviews not only of reference titles, but of general trade books, the answer can usually be found in any of the H. W. Wilson indexes, where reviews are listed separately. (For a discussion of these indexes see Chapter 5.)

The *Magazine Index* offers a handy book review listing, differing from those in other indexes in that with each review is a grade from A to F. This began in 1978, and, although limited to opinions in about 370 magazines, it is useful in many ways.

All the titles considered here are considered specialized because their sole purpose is to list reviews. They are used by students and

[7]Here and throughout the two volumes of this text, online reference services are noted by giving the name of a primary vendor and the price per hour of usage. Almost all vendors include other charges, but these vary. The hourly rate gives an approximate notion of cost as compared with the printed version. No effort is made to indicate that databases are available from many vendors.

others seeking background material on a given work as well as by the reference librarian on the lookout for notices about specific reference books.

The major indexes in this field—*Book Review Index* and *The Book Review Digest*—rely on author or title entries. In addition, the librarian must know the approximate date that the book was published. The fastest method is simply to search *The Book Review Digest Author/Title Index, 1905–1974*. For reviews published after 1974, one needs to go to the annual index volumes or other services. If the date cannot be found in these indexes, the librarian should turn to the card catalog where the title may be entered, or to one of the national or trade bibliographies such as *Books in Print*. Another possibility is to search for a title by using the online bibliographic service, such as OCLC. (For a discussion of OCLC, see the second volume of this text and the chapters on bibliography.)

Book Review Index seeks out reviews in about 450 periodicals, and is published every two months. There are annual cumulations. The reviews are listed in two parts. The first section is by author, and the second section by title. Unfortunately, there is no subject approach. On an average, about 45,000 to 50,000 books are covered each year, with about one to two reviews per title. This contrasts sharply with the other basic key to reviews, *The Book Review Digest*. Here one finds only about 6,000 titles considered.

The Book Review Digest, however, has a distinct advantage and one which makes it preferable to *Book Review Index*. Not only does it list where a review may be located, but it excerpts enough from the review to give the reader a notion of content and whether or not the book is favored by the reviewer. With this, the user does not have to consult the reviews but can make judgments about a title by merely reading *BRD*. Found in almost every library, the *BRD*, going back to 1905, often serves the scholar as an invaluable key to contemporary reviews.

The catch is in the limitations exercised by the *BRD*. It analyzes only 80 periodicals, and, even more unfortunately, it includes reviews of nonfiction only when there have been a minimum of two reviews, and of fiction only when four or more reviews have appeared. The result is that the *BRD* is a bastion of conservatism and is almost the last place anyone might hope to find a review of a book by a beginning author.

Both of the book review services are available online. Wilsonline offers its own *Book Review Digest*, but this only goes back to 1983 and is of limited value, except for the annotations. *Book Review Index* is online from 1969.

Another H. W. Wilson index to reviews ceased publication. This is *Current Book Review Citations* which was published from 1976 to 1982 and can be used for those years to check for reviews from about 1000 periodicals.

Of considerably more value are several standard indexes to specialized reviews. Among these: (1) *Combined Retrospective Index to Book Reviews in Scholarly Journals 1886–1974.* 15 vols; and *Combined Retrospective Reviews in Humanities Journals 1802–1974.* 10 vols. Both were published in 1983 by Research Publications of Woodbridge, Connecticut. The first lists reviews from about 450 journals in political science, history and sociology; the second records reviews from 150 journals. (2) *Index to Book Reviews in the Humanities* (Detroit Thomas, 1960 to date, annual) lists reviews in almost all of the humanities.

WEEDING

Weeding is the process of eliminating certain materials from the reference collection. It is a delicate process. Conceivably, any book, pamphlet, magazine, newspaper, or other written material can have reference value, particularly for the historian or anyone else concerned with social mores and records of the past. To discard such a work is little short of destroying the past. For example, one of the most difficult research problems is to locate materials in local newspapers of the nineteenth century.

Anyone who has sought contemporary opinion or a biography of a little-known figure or statistical data knows that there is no limit to the material that may be found in older reference works, certainly in books from both the general and the specific reference collections. Many, such as the early editions of the *Encyclopaedia Britannica,* are now classics, invaluable sources of material found nowhere else.

Given these warnings, there is a need for judicious weeding. Libraries are always short of space, and this is particularly true in the reference section. Weeding clears the shelves of little-used, or sometimes never-used, materials. Actually, few works are discarded in larger libraries. They are sent off to storage. Smaller libraries cannot afford this luxury, and the material normally is systematically removed.

Guidelines for discarding

Each library must establish its own general and specific guidelines for discarding materials. As with acquisitions, each library has its own peculiar needs, its own type of users, which makes it important to weed materials to meet the needs of those users, not the standards established in a text or at another library.

With that word of caution, some general criteria may be suggested.

Currency Most of the reference books that are used for ready reference have to be up to date. Older ones may be helpful historically, but are of little value for current material.

Reliability Data and viewpoints change, and the changes must be reflected in the reference collection. Yesterday's reliable explanation of a given event or phenomenon may no longer be applicable.

Use Needs change from generation to generation, and yesterday's valued reference work may no longer be used by today's reference librarian or the public.

Physical Condition Some books wear out and must be either discarded or replaced with new editions.

Later Editions Most popular reference works go into several editions, and it normally is pointless to maintain earlier editions of a standard work. Another linked consideration: duplication of materials. Perhaps a title four or five years ago was unique, but today there are more recent, even better titles in the field. In that case the older title may be discarded.

Language Sometimes a foreign language work may be discarded because no one is using it. It was purchased at a time when the particular language was important to the library.

To select discards wisely requires:

Thorough Knowledge of the Collection The librarian should know how it is used and by whom. Should X work be totally eliminated, or should a new edition be purchased, or should a similar work be considered? These are all questions that vary from situation to situation and can be answered only by the librarian working closely with the collection and the public.

Knowledge of Other Resources An understanding of the collections of regional and national libraries is needed. Is at least one copy of what you propose to discard in a local or national collection for use at some later date? Obviously a much-used work, such as a 10-year-old copy of the *World Almanac,* need not be checked. But any material that is purely local (particularly pamphlets and ephemera) or anything more than 50 years old or any items about which there is any question at all regarding use or value, should first be cleared with the larger libraries in the region. Such an item may appear shabby and of little use, but may prove to be a unique copy.

Older Works Worth Keeping One should appreciate that age does not necessarily dictate discarding. No worthwhile reference collection lacks, for example, the dated *Encyclopedia of the Social Sciences* or the mass of bibliographies and other guides that were published a number of years ago and are still basic works.

Some general guidelines for reference works may be suggested, but specific rules for discarding depend on use, not on any arbitrary set of rules.

Encyclopedias Maintain as many older editions as possible, *but* a new edition is needed at least every five years, and preferably every year.

Almanacs, Yearbooks, Manuals These are usually superseded by the next edition or the succeeding volume. Nevertheless, as the information in each is rarely duplicated exactly (new material is added, old material deleted), it is wise to keep old editions for at least 5 years, preferably 10.

Dictionaries In a sense, these are never dated and should never be discarded unless replaced by the same editions. An exception might be the abridged desk-type dictionaries. The unabridged works and those devoted to special areas are of constant value.

Biographical Sources Again, the more of these and the more retrospective the sources, the better. Only in a few select cases should any be discarded.

Directories Like yearbooks, almanacs, and other such works, these are frequently updated, and the older ones (5 to 10 years) can generally be discarded safely.

Geographical Sources Inexpensive atlases may be safely discarded after 5 to 10 years. More expansive, expensive works are invaluable. In fact, many gain in both research and monetary value over the years.

Government Documents Never discard these if they are part of a permanent collection. Discards should be considered where material is used only peripherally for pamphlet files. However, be particularly careful to check local and state materials before discarding.

In the subject areas, it is relatively safe to assume that except for botany and natural history, science books are generally dated within five years. The recurrent yearbooks, manuals, and encyclopedias may be discarded as new editions are obtained. In the humanities, discarding should rarely take place unless the material is quite obviously totally dated and of no historical or research value. In the social sciences, timely or topical materials may be considered for discard after 10 to 15 years.

SUGGESTED READING

Bain, Anne Lee and John Rutledge, "Editing and Publishing Scholarly Book Reviews: A Dialogue," *The Journal of Academic Librarianship,* No. 6, 1986. A former editor of the scholarly *American Historical Review* explains the basics of how books are selected for review and what a good review should consider. Most of the points are applicable for reference work.

Cave, Roderick, "Historical Bibliographical Work: Its Role in Library Education," *Journal of Education for Librarianship* Fall 1980, pp. 109–121. Although this is an argument for inclusion of the history of the book courses in library science, it explains, too, the meaning of analytical bibliography and its importance.

Cleland, Nancy, "Comparison of Sports Coverage in Book Review Digest and Book Review Index," *RQ,* Summer 1984, pp. 451–459. While this is a study of only sports books, the methodology is applicable to other areas. The results are as expected: *BRI* indexed 36 percent of the new titles; 8 percent were reviewed by both; and only 0.2 percent were reviewed exclusively by *BRD*.

Davison, Peter, "Editing Orwell: Eight Problems," *The Library,* September 1984, pp. 217–228. A brilliant discussion of analytical bibliography and its application to the actual editing and publishing of a series of works by Orwell. The numerous questions (and answers) the bibliographer must put are given here in great detail.

Engeldinger, Eugene, "Weeding of Academic Library Reference Collections: A Survey of Current Practices," *RQ,* Spring 1986, pp. 366–371. An extensive survey (over 500 libraries) reveals most librarians pay more lip service than action to the weeding of reference collections. The author concludes that "reference collections often are not being managed as well as they might be." The article is useful, too, in that it indicates various approaches to weeding, at least where it is done.

Krummel, D. W., *Bibliographies: Their Aims and Methods,* New York: Mansell, 1984. A well-known teacher and music bibliographer, the author offers an excellent explanation of different approaches to bibliography. While the introduction is a good beginning for the student, the other chapters are even better in that they give specific instructions on how to compile bibliographies in various subject areas. See, too, the concluding section, "Major writings on the compiling of bibliographies 1883–1983."

Wilkerson, Isabel, "Scholars, Who Point to Points in Text, End Meeting," *The New York Times,* April 29, 1985, p. B2. Experts in analytical and textual bibliography meet in New York, and a reporter gives a full explanation of their "exacting discipline, where rewards stem largely from the inner satisfaction that one contributes to a better understanding of one's author." The point of contention at one session: the size of the period at the end of the seventeenth chapter of Joyce's *Ulysses.*

CHAPTER FOUR

Bibliographies: National Library Catalogs and Trade Bibliographies

 fairly common problem concerns the person who wants to know just how much is available on a given subject, such as eighteenth-century gardens or nuclear-waste dumping facilities. One searches the library and may even tap other resources by computer, the telephone, or reference works, but even the most refined search inevitably ends with the question: Yes, but is that all? Furthermore, is what was found the best available information for the query? We would not have these puzzling questions if we knew that everything available had been considered; but this simply is not possible—at least today.

There is no single place a reader can go to find what materials are available from all parts of the world or from the United States or another country. The lack of a universal finding tool, called "universal bibliography," has frustrated librarians for centuries, and while the computer and its ability to store massive amounts of information suggests the technological possibility of listing everything in one gigantic bibliography, the numerous problems associated with the dream of universal control have yet to be solved. Still, the effort continues to fascinate, and inevitably the time will come when UBC (universal bibliographic control) is realized. One can conceivably see the time when every piece of material, printed or otherwise, will be dutifully entered into a computer's memory for eventual access online. The problems at that stage one can only imagine. It won't be "Where is X or Y book?" but "How can I tell which of these hundreds of titles is useful?"

The dream of universal bibliography could be a nightmare. The notion of indiscriminate registering of all the world's publications is an invitation to the garbage dump. If one must build a mountain of material, these critics plead for selective bibliography to eliminate the rubbish from the worthwhile.

Meanwhile, there is a type of coordination—some would say fitting together of different pieces of a puzzle—which allows at least a fairly good overview of what is available from many parts of the world. The procedure is to consult various national library catalogs. This does not work well for bits of information (say in periodicals or reports) or in all catalogs for different forms (from recordings to films), but it is quite sophisticated for specific books. For example, if the reader wants to locate a copy of a 1934 autobiography, *I Remember*, by J. Henry Harper, the search is facilitated by the use of one of a number of national catalogs. One simply turns to the catalog, looks up Harper, Henry, and locates the book as well as a full bibliographical description and probably where it may be found in a number of libraries. The same procedure might be exercised in London, Paris, or communities in any of the numerous Western countries which have national catalogs.

Since a national library catalog is not limited by time, territory, language, subject, or forms of communication, it does come close to the ideal universal bibliography. And although none of the national library catalogs claims to be universal in scope, collectively they do offer a relatively comprehensive record of international publishing. The Library of Congress, for example, catalogs materials from around the world, and a good proportion of its holdings are books, magazines, music, and the like from international publishers. Numerically, an idea of the scope of the Library of Congress holdings may be gathered from the fact that the Library contains more than 100 million discrete items and, on the average, adds from 5 to 6 million new items each year. Comparatively speaking, the average number of books published in America each year hovers around 40,000 to 50,000 titles, a small part of the overall annual acquisitions of the Library's net, which sweeps in titles of books as well as other published items from around the world. Quite similar figures apply to the British Library.

UNION CATALOGS

A term associated with national catalogs is "union catalog," for example, the Library of Congress's *National Union Catalog* and *Union List of Serials*. Interlibrary cooperation on local, regional, and international scale makes a union list of particular importance. In fact, wherever two or more libraries band together, there is apt to be a by-product of that cooperation—a union list. The use of the union list and bibliography is considered in Chapter 3, "Interview and Search" in the second volume of this text; but because the term appears through this volume, it is well to define it clearly, if only briefly, at this point.

A union catalog indicates who has what. A fuller, often-repeated definition is this: an inventory common to several libraries and listing some or all of their publications maintained in one or more orders of arrangement. The user turns to a union list to locate a given book, periodical, or newspaper in another library, which may be in the same city or thousands of miles away. Given the location and the operation of an interlibrary loan or copying process, the user can then have the particular book or item borrowed from the holding library.

When each library in the bibliographical network or bibliographic center knows what fellow members have purchased, a union list can be helpful in acquisitions. Expensive and little-used items, for example, need be purchased by only one or two of the cooperating libraries, because those items are always on call for members.

Some, although not all, of the union lists will give pertinent bibliographical information to help the library trace and identify a given item. When the sole purpose of the union catalog is location, the descriptive entry is normally kept to a minimum, e.g., *New Serial Titles*. However, when it serves numerous other purposes as well (e.g., *The National Union Catalog*), the description will be relatively complete. In most cases, arrangement is alphabetical by title or author.

National library catalogs

U.S. Library of Congress. *The National Union Catalog: A Cumulative Author List*. Washington: Library of Congress, Card Division, 1956 to 1983. Nine monthly issues and three quarterly cumulations. Ten- and four-year cumulations from 1956.

————.*Library of Congress Catalogs: Subject Catalog*. Washington: Library of Congress, 1950 to 1983. Three quarterly issues with annual cumulations. Four-year cumulations from 1950.

————.*The National Union Catalogs in Microfiche*. Washington: Library of Congress, January 1983 to date. Monthly issues and quarterly cumulations.

a) NUC Books. $350.
b) NUC U.S. Books. $195.

c) NUC Audiovisual Materials. (Quarterly) $23.
d) NUC Cartographic Materials. (Quarterly) $105.
e) NUC Register of Additional Locations. (Quarterly) $150.

[Note: The National Union Catalog in part is available online from 1968 to date as MARC (Machine Readable Cataloging) from the Library of Congress and other sources. Dialog file 426 is $45 per online hour.]

————.*The National Union Catalog: Pre-1956 Imprints.* London: Mansell, 1968–1981, 754 vols. $35,000. Microform: $11,750.
[Note: Part of the Pre-1956 Imprints is available online as REMARC (Retrospective Machine Readable Cataloging). Eventually, it all may be online.]

What is the scope of *The National Union Catalog?* One will note that each page photographically reproduces catalog cards—the same familiar cards found in most libraries. Each card represents an item cataloged by the Library of Congress or by one of more than 1500 libraries in the United States and Canada. This feature makes it a union catalog in that it shows the holdings of more than one library.

What is cataloged? Almost every communication medium. In this case, the entries are primarily for books; maps; atlases; pamphlets; and serials, including periodicals. The magazines are listed by title, and only those cataloged by the Library of Congress are included. The various forms are in separate sets; i.e., books in one set, music and recordings in another set, and so on.

The ongoing book catalogs of the Library of Congress are essentially no different from the familiar catalog found in the local library. This is important to recognize. Sometimes the imposing sets, as well as the microfiche, confuse the novice. Before turning to the microfiche format, which replaced the book format in January, 1983, consider the general scope, purpose and use of the service.

The printed volumes are arranged alphabetically by author or main entry. Generally, the heading of a main entry is an author's name, but lacking such information, it may be a title. It is never both author and title. There is no subject approach in the main *National Union Catalog* and cross-references are minimal. (A subject approach is offered but in another set to be discussed.)

The reproduced card varies in quantity and type of information given, but in almost all cases it includes the typical bibliographical description in this order: full name of author, dates of birth and death; full title; place, publisher, and date; collation (e.g., paging, illustrations, maps); series; edition; notes on contents, history; tracing for subject headings and added entries; the Library of Congress and, usually, the Dewey classifications; and The International Standard Book Numbers.

How is *The National Union Catalog* used in reference work?

1. Since this is a union catalog, showing not only the holdings of the Library of Congress but also titles in over 1500 other libraries, it allows the reference librarian to locate a given title quickly. Hence users who need a work not in their library may find the nearest location in *The National Union Catalog*. For example, the first edition of *I Remember,* by J. Henry Harper, is identified as being in eight other libraries. Location symbols for the eight are: OOxM, TxU, OCU, OCL, MnU, NIC, ViBibV, and WU. The initials stand for libraries in various parts of the country and are explained in the front of cumulative volumes. Depending on the policy of the holding library, the librarian may or may not be able to borrow the title on interlibrary loan. Failing a loan, it may be possible to get sections copied. All titles without indication of a contributing library are held by the Library of Congress. (The symbol of the Library is DLC.) After 1973, the bulk of location reports are not found in the NUC main set. One must turn to the *National Union Catalog–Register of Additional Locations* for such information. Books are listed chronologically by the Library of Congress catalog card number.

2. *The National Union Catalog* amounts to virtually a basic, full author bibliography. Anyone wanting to know everything (magazine articles and other such items aside) that author X has published has only to consult the author's name under the full *National Union Catalog* set.

3. The full cataloging not only gives details on a book (e.g., when it was published, by whom, and where), but helps the reference librarian to verify that it exists—an important matter when there is a question on whether X actually did publish this or that. Verification, however, is even more important when the reference librarian is attempting to straighten out the misspelling of a title or an author's name. In other words, *The National Union Catalog* sets the record straight when there is doubt about the validity of a given bit of information.

4. In terms of acquisitions, particularly of expensive or rare items, *The National Union Catalog* permits a library to concentrate in subject areas with the assurance that the less-

developed areas may be augmented by interlibrary loan from other libraries.

5. In terms of cataloging (which is basic to reference service), *The National Union Catalog* offers a number of advantages (and headaches). The primary asset is central cataloging, which should limit the amount of original cataloging necessary.

6. The sixth advantage of *The National Union Catalog* is as much psychological as real. Its very existence gives the librarian (and more-involved users) a sense of order and control which would otherwise be lacking in a world that cries for some type of order.

The National Union Catalog is primarily an approach by author. What does one do when one wants to find books in a given subject area? The user turns to the *Library of Congress Catalogs: Subject Catalog*. Here *The National Union Catalog* entries are rearranged by subject. There is one important catch. The subject approach can be used only for material published since 1945. (The set begins in 1950, but cataloging goes back to books published in 1945.) Prior to that date, there is no subject avenue to *The National Union Catalog* titles.[1]

So far, the discussion has concerned only ongoing issues of *The National Union Catalog,* i.e., those published monthly and cumulated annually. But how does one locate a title published, say, in 1950 or, for that matter, any one of 10 million retrospective entries not in the current *National Union Catalog?* The answer requires a brief historical sketch of a monumental undertaking.

The National Union Catalog began in card form in 1901. By 1926, the *NUC* had over 2 million cards, physically located in the Library of Congress. Anyone who wanted to consult the *NUC* had to query the Library of Congress or go there in person. The problem was solved, or so it was thought, by sending duplicate cards of the *NUC* to key research libraries throughout the United States. This procedure proved as costly as it was inefficient. Therefore, beginning in the early 1940s, work started on the printed book catalog; the individual cards were reproduced in the familiar *NUC* book form instead of being sent to libraries card by card. However, it was not until January 1, 1956,

---

[1]An online search of REMARC (REtrospective MARC) does enable a limited subject approach in that one may search for key words in the title of a book. Also, K. G. Saur offers *The Main Catalog of the Library of Congress 1898–1980* on fiche. One may search the 7.5 million items by subject as well as author. There is also a title and series approach. Unfortunately, this is not the NUC, but only a holding of the Library, and it costs from $14,900 to $15,900.

that it was decided that the book catalogs should be expanded to include not only Library of Congress holdings but also the imprints of other libraries.

What was to be done with *The National Union Catalog* prior to 1956, that is, with the card catalog in the Library of Congress which was not in book form? The answer came in 1968 when *The National Union Catalog: Pre-1956 Imprints* began to be published.

The *Pre-1956 Imprints* is a cumulative *National Union Catalog* up to 1956. The over 11 million entries represent the *NUC* holdings prior to 1956 and take the place of other sets.

The rapid development of technology, from microfiche to online catalogs, makes it unlikely that there will ever be another printed bibliography of this size.[2] (Balanced one upon the other, the 13.6 inch tall volumes in a single set would be higher than the Pan American Building in New York, although less suitable as a helicopter pad.) Future catalogs, if there are any of this size, will be in another form—probably on the order of the microfiche edition of the NUC.

Microform

When one speaks of microfiche, one refers to a type of microform. Microform is used more and more in libraries to preserve space, to keep bibliographies and other reference aids relatively current, and to provide easy access for users. Before going on with the latest development of the NUC, one should have at least an elementary understanding of microform.

Microform exists in two formats: the roll and the flat transparency or card. The familiar 35mm reel or roll has been in libraries for so long that many librarians and users think only of this form when microform is mentioned. In the flat microform there are several basic varieties or types: (1) Microfiche, or fiche, is available in different sizes, but the favored is the standard 4 by 6 inches, with an average of 98 pages per sheet. Various reductions may either increase or decrease the number of pages. (2) Ultrafiche, as the name implies, is an ultrafine reduction, usually on a 4- by 6-inch transparency. One card may contain 3000 to 5000 pages. (3) Micropoint is a 6- by 9-inch card which contains up to 100 pages of text in 10 rows and 10 columns.

---

[2]William J. Welsh, "Last of the Monumental Book Catalogs," *American Libraries*, September 1981, p. 467. This is an excellent, imaginative history of the development of the set.

NUC in Microfiche

The ongoing *National Union Catalog*'s familiar printed book form gave way to microfiche in 1983, and is now issued only in this format. The reasons for the change are multiple, but primarily they involved cutting costs, e.g., the printed version was over $1200 while the microform is under $500. Also, the microfiche tends to be current and saves a tremendous amount of space.

Essentially, this version has the same information as the book form, but it is in a different order. The main set, *NUC Books* averages about 340 fiche a year. (*NUC U.S. Books* is limited to American publications, has 128 fiche a year, but follows the same procedures as the larger set.) It is subdivided, each on a separate series of microfiche, by: author, title, subject and series. This allows a new title and a new series entry into the holdings, but it has some drawbacks in terms of rapid use.

In order to locate the full Library of Congress entry one must have the Register Number—found in the lower righthand corner of the author or title or subject or series entry, right after the Library of Congress catalog card number. One then turns to another sheet of microfiche (*NUC Books Register*) where the numbers are in order. When the number is located (in the upper lefthand section of the main entry) one has the complete cataloging information. Actually, the author, title, or subject entry may be enough in that each gives the author, title, publisher, date, and Library of Congress Classification. Conversely, if one wants to know the pages in the book, its size, or find tracings or the Dewey Decimal Classification, one must turn to the *NUC Books Register*. This two-step process can be confusing, particularly if one needs data on a series of books.

The same process is followed when one is looking up audiovisual materials in the *NUC Audiovisual Materials,* or is seeking information from the *NUC Cartographic Materials.*

There is even a third step involved. If the user wants to find what other libraries may have a copy of *The Journey of a Librarian,* it is necessary to a) locate the Library of Congress catalog card number at the bottom of the author, title, subject, or series card; then b) locate that number in the *NUC Register of Additional Locations.* Here additional libraries holding the book are noted as NUC symbols.

Another drawback to the microfiche system is that a mechanical viewer must be employed, and that can break down. Also, only one person at a time may search each microfiche. None of this is a major barrier to use, but it will be inconvenient for those accustomed to the printed form—or, for that matter, the rapid location of bibliographic information via the terminal online.

NUC Online

Online it is possible to interrogate a file of over 18 million bibliographical records, or, for that matter, only what is in the user's library, or in the group of libraries in a regional network. Furthermore, the records include not only books, but other materials and formats from maps and manuscripts to audiovisual items and periodicals. As one writer puts it: "For the first time in the history of bibliography the truly curious have an opportunity to be gratified. The computer has replaced the drudgery of the multiple index; made possible the relational index. We can now ask questions we could never answer before."[3] If nothing else, the terminal makes it possible to query files which heretofore may have required identifying, locating and searching numerous volumes.

The National Union Catalog at a computer terminal is known as MARC, an acronym for Machine-Readable Cataloging. MARC is usually accessed through a national bibliographic networking system such as OCLC or RLIN or a commercial database vendor system such as DIALOG. The catalog is on a magnetic tape which is sent to the various networks, or, for that matter, to large individual libraries.[4] Coverage is from 1968 to the present, and one enters the name of the author or title to find the desired bibliographic information, which usually appears on a screen or can be printed out.[5]

Using three compact discs, which are updated and republished every month, *BiblioFile* (Washington, D.C.: Library Corporation, 1985 to date) the entire MARC record may now be accessed at a personal computer. One-time purchase price of the compact laser disc drive and BiblioFile software is about $3000. The delivery of the monthly updated disks is about $1500 per year.

Given the alternative of the discs, online searching, etc., it is unlikely that the microfiche edition of the NUC will be employed by anyone but the smallest of libraries. It's simply too time-consuming and difficult to use.

[3]R. C. Alston, "ESTC Six Years On," *The Times Literary Supplement,* July 2, 1982, p. 726.

[4]While tape is the most prevalent form, there is no reason that MARC records can't be included, say, on individual floppy disks or on laser optical disks. They are available from several firms, including Library Systems of Rockville, Maryland.

[5]Before 1968 one uses REMARC (REtrospective MARC), but this is only for English titles before 1968. Other languages have different cut-off dates.

If MARC is at the heart of national and international online bibliographical searches, there are numerous other bibliographies now available, or soon to be available, at a terminal. These are mentioned throughout this text. One example is the familiar *Books in Print,* discussed in the next section, which allows the reference librarian to verify the most recent publication's date, price, author, etc.

National Bibliography in Canada

Canadiana. Ottawa: National Library of Canada, 1950 to date, monthly with annual cumulations. $100. Microfiche, $96.

Canada's national bibliography, the *Canadiana,* has varied in scope, arrangement, and publication period. Today it is arranged by Dewey and classifies material published in Canada or of Canadian interest. It does not include everything received by the National Library of Canada, but is selective. It does list books, pamphlets, government publications, dissertations and theses, and report literature, in this respect differing from many national catalogs. There are five indexes: author; title; series; English subject headings and French subject headings; and ISBN and ISSN. There is enough information given for most of the entries to permit verification without returning to the main entry.

As with the NUC, there is now a microfiche edition of *Canadiana.* It is arranged much like the NUC in that there is a Register where the primary information about a title is found and there are various indexes which refer the user to the Register. The indexes are the same as found in the printed version.

Canadiana may be searched online through the National Library's machine-readable bibliographic file, CAN/MARC, which is on the CAN/OLE (Canadian On-Line-Enquiry) system. The system includes locations of scientific serials as well. Most large Canadian libraries have access to MARC tapes of the Library of Congress and the *British National Bibliography* through this or other online systems.

National Bibliography in Great Britain

British Library. Department of Printed Books. *General Catalogue of Printed Books.* London: Trustees of the British Museum, 1959–1966, 263 vols. *Ten-Year Supplement,* 1956–1965, 1968, 50 vols. *Five-Year Supplement,* 1966–1970, 1971–1972, 26 vols.; 1971–1975, 1978–1980, 13 vols. Prices on request.

————.*The British Library General Catalogue of Printed Books to 1975.* London/New York: K. G. Saur, 1979 to 1983. Supplement, 1976–1982, 256 vols + 50 vols. Price on request.

The British Library is roughly equivalent to our Library of Congress, and its various catalogs are similar in purpose (if not in scope) to *The National Union Catalog.* The essential differences are:

1. The British Library is much older than the Library of Congress and has a considerably larger collection of titles dating from the fifteenth century up to the 1960s when the Library of Congress moved to embrace all world publications.
2. The British Library's catalog is not a union catalog and shows holdings only of the British Library.
3. The data for titles are somewhat briefer than those in *The National Union Catalog.*
4. Larger amounts of analytical material and cross references are included. For example, considerable attention is given to the analysis of series, and there are numerous cross-references from names of editors, translators, and other names connected with a title.
5. Keyword title entries are used; and in some ways this approach is useful because of the lack of a satisfactory subject catalog. The problem, of course, is that the title must reveal something of the contents.
6. Whereas *The National Union Catalog* can be considered very much a current bibliographical aid, the *General Catalogue,* because of its approach and infrequent publication, is more retrospective.

How much duplication is there between the massive British catalog and *The National Union Catalog?* Walford did a sampling and found that 75 to 80 percent of the titles in the British work are not in the American equivalent, and for titles published before 1800, 90 percent. Some estimate there are from 900,000 to over 1,000,000 titles in the British Library catalog not found in other national bibliographies. With increased interest in capturing worldwide titles in *The National Union Catalog,* the amount of duplication is bound to increase in the years ahead. Meanwhile, no large research library can afford to be without the British Library's *General Catalogue.*

Just as *NUC* has its massive *Pre-1956 Imprints,* so the British Library has an equivalent in the *British Library General Catalogue.* The set incorporates in a single alphabet the *General Catalogue* plus the supplements.

NATIONAL AND TRADE BIBLIOGRAPHY

Most of the enumerative bibliographies found in libraries can be classified as national and trade bibliographies. The distinction between the types is not always clear, if indeed there is a distinction. There are numerous types and possible combinations. The important consideration is not so much where the bibliography falls in the sometimes esoteric reference scheme but, rather, how it is used.

The pragmatic function of a national bibliography is to tell the librarian what was, what is, and what will be available either by purchase or by possible loan from another library. The bibliographies give necessary bibliographical information (e.g., publisher, price, author, subject area, Library of Congress or Dewey numbers), which is used for a number of purposes ranging from clarifying proper spelling to locating an item by subject area. Also, the national bibliography is a primary control device for bringing some order to the 40,000 or more books published in the United States each year, not to mention similarly staggering figures for pamphlets, reports, recordings, films, and other items.

The process of compiling national bibliographies differs from country to country, but there is a basic pattern. An effort is made first to give a current listing of titles published the previous week, month, or quarter. These data are then cumulated for the annual breakdown of titles published and beyond that, those that are in print, out of print, and going to be published. (The same process applies to forms other than books.)

United States national and trade bibliography: Weekly and monthly

Weekly Record. New York: R. R. Bowker Company, 1974 to date, weekly. $75.

American Book Publishing Record. New York: R. R. Bowker Company, 1961 to date, monthly. $65 (Annual cumulation, $110). Cumulations: 1876–1949, 15 vols.; 1950–1977, 15 vols.; 1980–1984, 5 vols.; Microfiche edition, 1876–1981; Annual cumulations.

Cumulative Book Index. New York: The H. W. Wilson Company, 1898 to date, monthly, with three-month, annual, and two- and five-year cumulations. Service. (Wilsonline, $37 to $50 per hour).

Forthcoming Books. New York: R. R. Bowker Company, 1966 to date, bimonthly $95. *Subject Guide to Forthcoming Books,* 1967 to date, bimonthly $65.

United States: Annual and biannual

(All titles listed below published by the R. R. Bowker Company)

Publisher's Trade List Annual, 1973 to date, annual, 5 vols. $124.95.

Books in Print, 1948 to date, annual, 6 vols. $199.95.

Supplement, 1973 to date, 2 vols., annual. $110 (DIALOG file 234, $65 per hour includes *Books in Print* and *Supplement*).

Books Out-of-Print, 1980 to date, 2 vols., annual. $89.

Subject Guide to Books in Print, 1957 to date, annual, 4 vols. $142.93.

Paperbound Books in Print, 1955 to date, bi-annual, 3 vols. $220.

International Books in Print, New York: K. G. Saur Inc., 1979 to date, 2 vols. $225.

Booksellers call the national and trade bibliographies listed here "the tools of the trade." Librarians also regard them as such, and their purpose is evident from the titles. Essentially, the bibliographies list the books that can be purchased from American publishers (i.e., are in print), in what forms (hardbound, paperback), and at what prices. Depending on the individual trade bibliography, additional information is given as to the date of publication, the number of pages, the subjects covered, and other data necessary for proper and easy use of the bibliography.

The most frequently consulted titles are *Books in Print (BIP)* and *Subject Guide to Books in Print.* More than 692,000 in-print books of all kinds (hardbounds, paperbacks, trade books, textbooks, adult titles, juveniles) are indexed by author and by title in *Books in Print.* ("In print" is a term which indicates the book is still available from a publisher. If not available, it is called "out-of-print.") Besides telling the user whether the book can be purchased, from whom, and at what price, the trade bibliography also answers such questions as: What books by William Faulkner are in print, including both hardbound and paperbound editions at various prices? Who is the publisher of *The Old Patagonian Express?* Is John Irving's first novel still in print?

(The fact that sometimes the inquiry cannot be answered is not always the fault of the questioner's spelling of the title or because the author's name is not correct or even close. *Books in Print,* through either filing errors or misinformation from the publishers, may fail to guide users to a title which they know to be correct.)

Almost every entry in *BIP* includes the author, coauthor (if any), editor, price, publisher, year of publication, number of volumes, Library of Congress card number and the International Standard Book Numbers (ISBN). The names and addresses of the nearly 17,000 U.S. publishers represented in *BIP* are included. The listings provide answers to queries about publishers, although the librarian who needs more details should consult reference works specifically intended for information about publishers, e.g., *American Book Trade Directory,* discussed later.

Issued in October of each year, *Books in Print* is supplemented by two volumes in April of the following year. Here publishers list some 175,000 titles newly published or with price changes and not included in the basic *BIP,* as well as titles which are out of print or which they plan to issue before the next annual *BIP* volumes. These listings are arranged by author and by title as well as by subject; thus the *Books in Print Supplement* is also a supplement to *Subject Guide to Books in Print.* The *Supplement* includes an updated list of all publishers, with any address changes. For normal purposes, *BIP* is enough for most questions. When the original publishing date is more than one or two years old, when there has been a spurt of inflation, or when the librarian cannot find a title, a double-check in the *Books in Print Supplement* is wise.

The majority of titles listed in *BIP* are similarly found in *Subject Guide to Books in Print.* In the subject approach, no entries are made for fiction, poetry, or bibles. (Note, though, that the guide does list books *about* fiction under the name of the author of the fiction; criticism of Henry James, for example, is found under James.) The use of the subject guide, which virtually rearranges *BIP* under 65,000 Library of Congress subject headings, is self-evident.[6] It not only helps in locating books about a given subject but may also be used to help expand the library's collection in given areas. If, for example, books about veterinarians are in great demand, the guide gives a complete list of those available from American publishers. An important point: The list is inclusive, not selective. No warning sign

---

[6]LC subject cataloging is used only as a guide, and Bowker or the publisher frequently assigns modified LC headings. This, coupled with only about 1.1 subject headings per book, results in less-than-satisfactory retrieval. Often, too, a vast number of titles may be assigned under a broad heading—so broad that a search is almost impossible.

differentiates the world's most misleading book about veterinarians from the best among, say, 20 titles listed. The librarian must turn to other bibliographies and reviews for judgments and evaluations of titles in any subject area.

A constant problem is the out-of-print or out-of-stock book. The former means the book is no longer being published; the latter, that the publisher has not yet decided whether or not to continue publishing the work. At any rate, it is a great help to know the status of a book, and here *Books Out-of-Print* is an invaluable aid. The first author section gives a page number to the complete listing in the title section. There is information, too, on remainder dealers and on-demand publishers where the librarian might locate one or more of the o.p. (out-of-print) titles.

International Books in Print is a listing of English language titles published outside the United States and the United Kingdom, i.e., primarily in Western Europe, Australia, Canada and where the English language is important, such as India. The main work follows the standard author–title listing. A second set of two volumes offers a subject guide to the set.

The massive *Publishers' Trade List Annual (PTLA)*, while less frequently used by reference librarians, fits in here because it is part of the bibliographical apparatus for tracing books in print. The *PTLA,* usually published in September, is a collection of U.S. publishers' catalogs in book form. The catalogs conform to a certain physical cut size but may be in hundreds of various typefaces, arrangements, and lengths. For convenience, the catalogs are bound in alphabetical order in six volumes. The set will vary in number of volumes from year to year. The first volume contains the index and a section reserved for small publishers who do not have enough titles to warrant a separate bound catalog. *PTLA* is the listings or catalogs of publishers represented in *Books in Print.* It is not complete, as some 17,000 publishers have titles in *BIP* but only about 1800 in *PTLA.*

PTLA, beginning with the 1979 edition, includes a brief subject approach to the publishers' catalogs. There are about 70 subject and form categories which lead the reader to a publisher who concentrates on, say, reprints or textbooks or journalism and writing or law.

In terms of reference work, the subject index helps to give a broad picture of the publishers of certain types of materials. Other information which can be found in the *PTLA* includes (1) location of titles when the user knows only the name of the publisher (e.g., I know X publisher is famous for cookbooks, but what cookbooks?); (2) all titles in a publisher's series, such as a series on rivers of America or librarians I have known and loved; (3) the prices of various titles by one publisher of, say, dictionaries; (4) sometimes, although not always, a brief description of a book or books; and (5) added information about a publisher. The "Publishers Index" includes imprints, subsidiaries, affiliations, and so on.

The lack of completeness of the PTLA can be upsetting, especially when one is looking for the catalog of a publisher which may not be included because that publisher did not wish to pay for inclusion. Here the *Publishers' Catalogs Annual* (Westport, Connecticut: Meckler Publishing, 1984 to date, annual, 300 microfiche with paper index, $147.50) is a tremendous help. It includes a greater number of complete catalogs than in PTLA, possibly because the service is free to publishers. It reproduces over 2000 catalogs, and often much more complete ones than in PTLA. Arrangement is alphabetical by name of publisher, and there is a subject index.

Published since 1898, the familiar brown-covered *CBI (Cumulative Book Index)* is to be found in almost all libraries, as are the monthly and annual cumulations. It has the advantage of being well known, accurate, and easy to use. Annually about 50,000 to 60,000 books are listed in one alphabet by author, title, and subject. The author, or main, entry includes pertinent bibliographic information, as well as useful data for catalogers and acquisitions librarians. The subject headings, which follow those established by the Library of Congress, are exhaustive. Although fiction is not included as a subject, one does find headings on science fiction, short stories, mystery and detective stories, and so on. There is also a good directory of publishers.

The publisher of *CBI* is able to list new titles monthly because "most publishers in the United States and Canada send copies of their books to the H. W. Wilson Company promptly," to quote a Wilson Company brochure, "and these are processed quickly and appear in the earliest possible issue of *CBI*. Therefore books are frequently listed in *CBI* before they appear in any other major bibliography." There is an understandable "sales pitch" here which is of interest because *CBI*'s rival does much the same thing in terms of listing new titles each month. One would not want to argue that *CBI* is faster to the mark with new titles than the *ABPR (American Book Publishing Record)*, but only that the librarian who cannot find a title in one has the advantage of being able to check the other.

ABPR covers much the same ground as CBI, but differs in that (1) it limits listings to titles published in the United States and includes from 38,000 to 42,000 entries, the number depending on how many books are published or distributed in the United States the previous year; (2) it is arranged by the Dewey Decimal System, that is, by subject, and has an author and title index; and (3) it includes separate sections on juvenile and adult fiction and paperbacks.

There are three cumulations (one on microfiche) which cover the years 1876–1981. The publisher says the microfiche set has about 1.7 million author/title and subject entries of books published in the United States.

The monthly issues of ABPR lead back to another service, the *Weekly Record*. Although more important to catalogers and acquisitions librarians, the *Weekly Record* is interesting to reference librarians because it records, on a weekly basis, what is published in the United States. About 700 to 800 new titles are listed each week by author. Full bibliographic information is given for each, including Dewey and Library of Congress classifications and, often, descriptive cataloging notes. Most of the data is furnished by the Library of Congress and supplemented by the staff at Bowker. In advertising for the APBR, the publisher claims that "approximately 80% of all entries have been significantly supplemented with revised and updated publication information, verified prices, and other essential data *not* included in the MARC tapes." One suspects this is much the case with the publishers of the CBI.

The author arrangement limits the use for most reference purposes. However, every four weeks the contents of *Weekly Record* are rearranged by subject and cumulated as the aforementioned *ABPR*.

As a running record of what is going on in publishing, *Publishers Weekly* (New York: R. R. Bowker Company, 1872 to date) is required reading for reference librarians. This is the trade magazine of American publishers and, in addition, often contains articles, features, and news items of value to librarians. It is difficult to imagine an involved reference librarian not at least thumbing through the weekly issues, if only for the "PW Forecasts." Here the critical annotations on some 50 to 100 titles give the reader a notion of what to expect in popular fiction and nonfiction to be published in the next month or so.

A more definitive approach to what is going to be published is found in *Forthcoming Books*. Again, this periodical is likely to be of more value to acquisitions and cataloging than to reference, but it does answer queries about a new book or possibly about a book which the patron may have heard discussed on a radio or television program before it is actually published. The bimonthly lists by author and by title (not by subject) books due to be published in the next five months. For a subject approach, one must consult the bimonthly *Subject Guide to Forthcoming Books*. One need not be an expert to realize that the two works would be much easier and faster to use were they combined.

While *Books in Print* lists paperbound titles, *Paperbound Books in*

Print rearranges these same listings in three volumes: title, author, and subject. The 1985 compilation includes more than 242,000 books, with full bibliographical information about each. As a guide to a particular form, *Paperbound Books in Print* is invaluable in bookshops but is of more limited use in libraries. Librarians tend to use it as a double-check against *BIP,* particularly as not all new paperbound titles are in *BIP.*

Books in Print Online & Microfiche

A pressing problem with *Books in Print* and related volumes is that they soon are dated. In an effort to keep the information current, the publisher now makes the services available online and on microfiche. The online version includes *Books in Print, Subject Guide to Books in Print, Books in Print Supplement, Paperbound Books in Print, Forthcoming Books, Subject Guide to Forthcoming Books,* and several specialized titles such as *Children's Books in Print.* The database is updated monthly, or even more often. As of 1985 it is available through two commercial vendors, BRS and Lockheed.

Less extensive, though even less expensive is the microfiche edition of *Books in Print.* Published quarterly for $445, each quarterly edition is a complete revised version of the basic set. Not only does it record new prices, o.p. books, and other changes, but it includes forthcoming titles for the next six months. There are separate author and title indexes for each entry, albeit no subject approach. While primarily used in acquisitions, the microfiche can be a useful ready reference aid. The frequent updating makes it an exemplary work for information currency.

There are two separate microfiche editions of *Paperbound Books in Print,* both of which have the advantage of being updated each month, rather than the semi-annual schedule of the printed work. The first set of microfiches consists of approximately 27,000 to 30,000 mass market paperbound titles. This is $50 per year. The second is the all-inclusive version and includes all titles found in the printed format; its cost is $295 per year. Both sets offer complete author and title entries, but do not have a subject approach.

Other national trade bibliographies

While the preceding discussion has been limited to two American publishers, the bibliographical apparatus for recording published titles and those still to be published is much the same throughout the United States and the rest of the world. Differences exist in scope and in emphasis, but essentially the purpose is the same, as one finds when one explores the current and retrospective bibliographies of other countries.

For Canada there is *Canadian Books in Print* (Downsview, Ontario: University of Toronto Press, 1967 to date, annual). This is in two volumes. The first covers author and title; the second, subjects. A microfiche edition of the author-title volume is issued each quarter.

British Books in Print (London: J. Whitaker & Sons Ltd., 1974 to date, annual, 4 vols. Distributed in the United States by R. R. Bowker) lists about 400,000 titles from almost 10,000 publishers. The author, title, and subjects are interfiled in one alphabet, and subjects are primarily those which surface when there is a keyword in the title. The subject approach is somewhat less than satisfactory. This is part of a chain which begins with the weekly *Bookseller* and the *British National Bibliography* (a national, not a trade bibliography, but somewhat equivalent to the *Weekly Record* and the *Cumulative Book Index*), the monthly *Whitaker's Books of the Month,* and the quarterly *Whitaker's Cumulative Book List* (again, somewhat equivalent to the *American Book Publishing Record* and the *CBI*).

UNITED STATES RETROSPECTIVE BIBLIOGRAPHY

Most daily reference work is carried on with relatively current national and trade bibliographies. There are times, however, when one or more retrospective bibliographies are needed, i.e., bibliographies which list titles published not last week, month, or year, but from 10 to over 100 years ago. These bibliographies may be used to answer such questions as: Who is the author of *The Ballad of the Abolition Blunder-buss,* published in 1861? What is the correct title of a work on rattlesnakes by S. W. Mitchell, published in 1860? The person asking this type of question is likely to be a historian, literary scholar, librarian, or anyone else deeply involved in research of a given subject, place, or person.

In trying to fathom a retrospective bibliography, which is not always easy to do because of erratic arrangement, coverage, and purpose, the librarian is apt to overlook other approaches which are somewhat simpler. By far the easiest approach is to use one of the bibliographic utilities, such as OCLC where many (although far from all) of the references may be available online. Even here, though, the online entry is not likely to be as full as that found in a standard retrospective bibliography. The *National Union Catalog,* and particularly the pre-1956 imprint volumes is another handy source.

Retrospective bibliography is not limited to the United States. In fact, it has reached scholarly, awesome proportions in England and on the Continent. Examples of the basic foreign retrospective bibliographies will be found in Sheehy and Walford. Regardless of national origin, retrospective bibliographies tell what was published where and by whom. They are a source of information about national, state, and local history and thus trace the cultural and scientific development of people in a given place and time.

In chronological order, the leading American retrospective bibliographies are (original publishers given, but most reprinted and a number available on microform):

1500–1892   Sabin, Joseph. *Bibliotheca Americana. Dictionary of Books Relating to America from Its Discovery to the Present Time*. New York: Sabin, 1869–1892; Bibliographical Society of America, 1928–1936, 29 vols.

Molnar, John. *Author-Title Index to Joseph Sabin's Dictionary of Books Relating to America*. Metuchen, New Jersey: Scarecrow Press, 1974, 3 vols.

1639–1800   Evans, Charles. *American Bibliography: A Chronological Dictionary of All Books, Pamphlets and Periodical Publications Printed in the United States of America From the Genesis of Printing in 1639 Down to and Including the Year 1800*. Chicago: Printed for the author, 1903–1959, 14 vols. (Vols. 13 and 14 published by the American Antiquarian Society.)

Shipton, Clifford. *National Index of American Imprints Through 1800; The Short Title Evans*. Worcester, Massachusetts: American Antiquarian Society, 1969, 2 vols.

1801–1819   Shaw, Ralph, and Richard Shoemaker. *American Bibliography: A Preliminary Checklist*. Metuchen, New Jersey: Scarecrow Press, 1958–1963, 22 vols.

1820–1861   Roorbach, Orville. *Bibliotheca Americana*. New York: O. A. Roorbach, 1852–1861, 4 vols.

1820–1875   Shoemaker, Richard H., and others. *A Checklist of American Imprints, 1820 +*, Metuchen, New Jersey: Scarecrow Press, 1964 to date.

1861–1870   Kelly, James. *American Catalogue of Books, Published in the United States from January 1861 to January 1871, with Date of Publication, Size, Price, and Publisher's Name*. New York: John Wiley & Sons, Inc., 1866–1871, 2 vols.

1876–1910   *American Catalogue of Books, 1876–1910*. New York: Publishers' Weekly, 1880–1911, 15 vols.

1899–1927   *United States Catalog: Books in Print*. 4th ed. New York: The H. W. Wilson Company, 1928, 3164 pp.

The following titles are still being published and are discussed elsewhere. They are listed here by their beginning publishing date as an indication of what can be used for retrospective searching from 1928 to the present.

1872– *Publishers' Weekly*
1873– *Publishers' Trade List Annual*
1898– *Cumulative Book Index*
1948– *Books in Print*
1957– *Subject Guide to Books in Print*

Sabin differs from all the other bibliographies listed here in that he includes books, pamphlets, and periodicals printed in the United States *and* works printed about American in other countries. The others are limited to titles published in the United States. An Oxford scholar, Sabin was an authority on rare books about America. He began his ambitious project (often called *Bibliotheca Americana*) in the early 1860s and lived long enough to see 13 volumes published by 1881. The next seven volumes were by Wilberforce Eames. R. W. G. Vail ultimately called a halt to the proceedings with the final volumes in 1936. Arrangement is by author, with some title entries and other entries by names of places. Entries include collation, usually the location of a copy, and a note on contents. There is no subject index. Each volume contains entries for one section of the alphabet up to the date of publication; hence, it is uneven in chronological coverage, particularly since cutoff dates of acceptable publications moved further and further back as the work continued. There is no guarantee that a work published in 1870, say, is listed here. The author must be known or the set is virtually worthless. However, once the author is identified, the information found is enough to warrant searching. Thanks to Molnar's index, it is now a relatively simple thing to consult the otherwise badly organized Sabin. The massive author-title index includes 270,000 entries.

Sabin is alphabetically arranged by author and has no chronologically logical approach. It thus tends to obscure the interrelationships between books and pamphlets printed at about the same time. Some improvement will come with the expected 45,000 separate listings of books or printed materials to supplement Sabin. Prepared by the John Carter Brown Library staff, this will be a chronological guide to materials published in Europe about America from the period 1493 to 1800 which are not listed in Sabin. The work is expected to be completed in the mid-1980s.

A work of love and considerable hardship for Charles Evans, his

American Bibliography is a classic. It is considered the keystone upon which all retrospective American bibliography is built and is basic to any large collection. Arrangement is not alphabetical by author. It is chronological by dates of publication. If one does not know the date, or approximate date, there is an author, subject, and printer and publisher index to help. For each entry, there is the author's full name with birth and death dates, a full title, place, publisher, date, paging, size, and usually the location of one or more copies in American libraries.

The *National Index* is a required addition for anyone using Evans. It serves to eliminate nonexistent titles, or "ghosts" which Evans recorded without seeing a copy of the actual item. Furthermore, it adds over 10,000 titles discovered since Evans's set was published. The 49,197 entries are arranged alphabetically by author and short title, and there is reference to the original entry in Evans—if it is listed there. (The *National Index* is particularly valuable for use with the microcard reproduction of all nonserial titles listed in Evans and elsewhere and published in America before 1801. It is virtually an index to the tremendous set of nearly 50,000 individual books on microform.)

Shaw and Shoemaker continued Evans's initial efforts to 1820, and the gap between Evans and Roorbach is filled only partially. Each volume covers one year and gives the briefest author citation, along with a location for some copies. Addenda volumes include a title and author index for the full series.

Another set in the same series is *A Checklist of American Imprints,* which was to carry the same type of listing down to 1875 and the beginning of Kelly. From the 1821 volume on, this series differs from the 1801–1819 set in that locations are given for most of the copies and the compiler did check out the books listed. (In the earlier compilation, titles were primarily from secondary sources, with little attention given to checking the accuracy of those sources.) Since Shoemaker's death in 1970, the series has been carried on by Scott Bruntjen and Carol Rinderknecht and the publisher. There is a title and author index to the 1820–1829 series.

Until the *Checklist of American Imprints* is taken down through 1875, the Roorbach and Kelly bibliographies must be used. Roorbach is a contemporary bibliography similar in its intent to *Books in Print* but done with considerably less care. The arrangement is alphabetical by author and title, with information on the publisher; size; and usually, but not always, the price and date. Entries are frequently incomplete. From 1861 to 1870, Kelly serves the same purpose as Roorbach and gives the same type of incomplete information. Both

Roorbach and Kelly, for example, list less than one-half as many titles per year as Evans, who was recording a much less productive period in American publishing. Although inaccurate and incomplete, the two bibliographies are the only reference aids of their kind.

In terms of retrospective searching, then, there is something more than a blank period from the time of the last Shoemaker volume to the beginning of the *American Catalog of Books* in 1876, i.e., from 1830 to 1876. Begun by Frederick Leypoldt as a trade bibliography of books in print, the *American Catalog* was published annually and later cumulated. Arrangement is by author and title with subject supplements. The information is generally reliable and comprehensive—but no more so than the publisher's catalogs from which the information came.

Competition from The H. W. Wilson Company's *United States Catalog* caused cessation of the *American Catalog* in 1910, and it did not begin publishing again until 1948 as *Books in Print*. The *United States Catalog* is really a cumulation of the *Cumulative Book Index* which began in 1898 as a type of *Books in Print* in competition with the *American Catalog*. There are four editions of the *United States Catalog*, but the most often used is the last, which lists all the books published in English in the United States and Canada in print in 1928. (Earlier volumes must be consulted for finding books out of print by 1928 and for fuller information on other titles.) By 1928, the increase in the number of titles published forced Wilson to abandon the *United States Catalog* in favor of cumulative issues of the *CBI*.

Book prices

American Book Prices Current. New York: Bancroft Parkman, 1895 to date, annual. $90.

Book Auction Records. Folkestone, England: Wm. Dawson & Sons, 1903 to date, annual. Publisher and price vary (approximately $150).

Bookman's Price Index. Detroit: Gale Research Company, 1965 to date, annual. $155.

The average layperson's contact with retrospective bibliography is indirect, usually taking the form of trying to find a long-out-of-print book or, more likely, the answer to a question about the value of a book printed years ago. "What is my book, map, or broadside worth?" is a familiar question in many libraries. The three guides listed here are the most often used for an answer. The larger library will have them, not only to help the user but to assist in acquisitions when a question about a used-book dealer's asking price arises.

Should the library pay X dollars for a title which last year cost Y dollars less at an auction? There are many variables for both the user and the library, but the guides indicate the logical parameters of pricing.

American Book Prices Current and *Book Auction Records* are collections of book prices paid at various auctions. The third, *Bookman's Price Index,* is based on prices garnered from antiquarian dealers' catalogs. The two first titles are frequently indexed over a period of a number of years. Hence, it is not always necessary to search each volume for a given title.

The American work lists items sold for $20 or more and includes books, serials, autographs, manuscripts, broadsides, and maps. Arrangement is alphabetical by main entry with cross-references. Each of the forms is treated in its own section. Sales run from the fall to the spring, hence each volume is usually numbered with two years, e.g., 1987–1988. Some 14 major auction firms, from Parke-Bernet Galleries to Christie, Manson & Woods Ltd., are included, as are a number of large individual sales of private libraries. The entries are cumulated about every five years.

Book Auction Records is the English equivalent of the American title, and while it duplicates some of the information found in that work, it includes a number of European auctions not covered elsewhere. Arrangement and form are similar to the *American Book Prices Current,* and there are periodic cumulations. Both titles suffer a time lag and normally are at least one year, and usually two years, behind the sales reported.

Bookman's Price Index differs from the other two titles in that it includes prices in catalogs of some 60 booksellers. Entries are listed in a standard main-entry form. Volume 30, issued in 1985, includes over 45,000 titles—almost twice the number found in the auction price lists. It also has the advantage of representing retail prices which may be somewhat higher than those at an auction where book dealers themselves are bidding.

The guides give only relative indications of price. The price requested by a book dealer or at an auction often represents the maximum. Someone selling the same copy of the book to a dealer must expect a lower price in order for the dealer to realize a profit. Other variables, such as condition and the demands of the current market, enter into pricing. On the whole, a librarian should refer such matters of pricing to an antiquarian book dealer. The most the librarian should do is show the price lists to inquirers, who can then reach their own conclusions.

Frequently the price of a book will turn on whether or not it is a first edition or has some other peculiar feature which sets it apart from the thousands of copies printed over the years. There are numerous guides, as well as detailed explanations of what constitutes a first edition, although the most valuable are the individual author bibliographies which give detailed information on such matters. These bibliographies are listed in the standard guides, from Sheehy to the *American Reference Books Annual.*

READER'S ADVISORY SERVICES

Reader's advisory services are common in public libraries, and often a part of reference services. They are defined succinctly by the Free Library of Philadelphia as "reading guidance, selection of materials to meet a particular interest or need, aid in identifying the best sources of information for a given purpose, instruction in the use of the library or a particular book, seeking an answer from or referral to other agencies or information sources outside the library".[7] Actually, most libraries are somewhat more limited in their definition, and equate the descriptive phrase with helping people find books they wish to read, as well as assisting in the purchase of those books.

In one sense, the reference librarian is constantly serving as a guide to readers in the choice of materials, either specific or general. This is particularly true as an adjunct to the search-and-research type of question. Here the librarian may assist the reader in finding a considerable amount of material outside the reference collection or may suggest the right book in that collection as an aid in searching.

At an informal stage, particularly in smaller and medium-sized libraries with limited staff, the reference librarian may help a patron to select a title. For example, someone may wander into the reference room looking for a good historical novel or a nonfiction work on the siege of Troy. The staff member will assist in finding the desired material, usually in the general collection.

Reader's advisory aids

> *Fiction Catalog*, 11th ed. New York: The H. W. Wilson Company, with four annual supplements, 1986–1990. $80.
>
> *Public Library Catalog*, 8th ed. New York: The H. W. Wilson Company, with four annual supplements, 1984–1987. $140.
>
> *The Reader's Adviser*, 13th ed. New York: R. R. Bowker Company, 3 vols, 1986. $195.

[7]The Free Library of Philadelphia, "Policies & Procedures" 40B (Revised), September 15, 1979 (processed), p. 5.

Of lists there is no end, and one of the more popular types centers on "best" books for a given library situation. The lists, despite certain definite drawbacks, are useful for the following:

1. Evaluating a collection. A normal method of evaluating the relative worth of a library collection is to check the collection at random or in depth by the lists noted here.
2. Building a collection. Where a library begins without a book but with a reasonable budget, many of these lists serve as the key to purchasing the core collection.
3. Helping a patron find a particular work in a subject area. Most of the lists are arranged by some type of subject approach, and as the "best" of their kind, they frequently serve to help the user find material on a desired topic.

The advantage of a list is that it is compiled by a group of experts. Usually there is an editor and an authority or several authorities assisting in each of the major subject fields. However, one disadvantage of this committee approach is that mediocrity tends to rule, and the book exceptional for a daring stand, in either content or style, is not likely to be included.

Used wisely, a "best" bibliography is a guide; it should be no more than that. The librarian has to form the necessary conclusions about what should or should not be included in the collection. If unable to do this, the librarian had better turn in his or her library school degree and call it quits before ruining a library. When any group of librarians discuss the pros and cons of best-book lists, the opinion is always expressed that such lists are nice but highly dubious crutches.

Another obvious flaw, in even the finest special list, is that it is normally tailored for a particular audience. Finally, despite efforts to keep the lists current (and here Wilson's policy of issuing frequent supplements is a great aid), many of them simply cannot keep up with the rate of book production. No sooner is the list of "best" books in anthropology out when a scholar publishes the definitive work in one area that makes the others historically interesting but not particularly pertinent for current needs.

For a number of years the Wilson Company, with the aid of qualified consultants, has been providing lists of selected books for the school and public library. The consultants who determine which titles will be included are normally drawn from various divisions of the American Library Association. Consequently, from the point of view of authority and reliability, the Wilson lists are considered basic for most library collection purposes.

There are five titles in what has come to be known as the Wilson "Standard Catalog Series." They follow more or less the same organization, differing primarily in the scope evident from the title, e.g., *Children's Catalog, Junior High School Library Catalog, Senior High School Library Catalog,* and *Public Library Catalog.* The *Fiction Catalog* crosses almost all age groups, although it essentially supplements the *Public Library Catalog,* which does not list fiction. All the other catalogs have fiction entries.

Typical of the group, the *Public Library Catalog* begins with a classified arrangement of 8000 nonfiction works. Each title is listed under the author's name. Complete bibliographical information is given plus an informative annotation. Except for an occasional few words of description added by the compilers, the majority of the annotations are quotes from one or more reviews. The reviews are noted by name, i.e., *Choice, Library Journal,* etc., but there is no further citation to year, month, or page. Quotes are selected to indicate both content and value, albeit the latter is expected in that only the "best" books are chosen for inclusion.

From the point of view of partial reference work, the librarian may make a selection of a title by reading the annotation, or invite the inquisitive reader to glance at the description. Further access is provided by a detailed title, author and subject index.

In order to keep the service updated, a soft-cover annual volume of new selections is published each year until the next edition is issued—in this case, in 1988. This method of updating is employed by Wilson in all of the standard catalog series.

The *Fiction Catalog* follows the same format as the public library aid. In it there are 5056 titles with critical annotations. An additional 2000 titles will be included in the supplements. It is particularly useful for the detailed subject index which lists books under not just one area but numerous related subject areas. Furthermore, broad subjects are subdivided by geographical and historical area, and novelettes and composite works are analyzed by each distinctive part. Most of the titles are in print. Anyone who has tried to advise a user about the "best," or even any, title in a given subject area will find this work of extreme value.

The Reader's Adviser is among the best known of scores of general listings of "best" books. Planned originally for the bookseller seeking to build a basic stock, the three-volume set is now used extensively in libraries. There are close to 40,000 titles listed. The first volume concentrates on literature, biography, bibliography, and reference; the second concerns drama and world literature in English translation; and the third is really a subject guide to reference books in that it includes a wide range of titles on many subjects, which might be used for reference. However, "reference" is used in its broadest context, which means there are standard biographies, science and history titles, travel books, and so on. Arrangement differs from volume to volume, although either subject or chronological order is followed, with titles listed and usually annotated. Particularly useful are the listings of major books of criticism, which are included for most authors. With the publication of the revised three-volume edition in late 1986, the publisher announced plans for another two volumes, covering world literature and related aspects of selection, in 1987 or 1988.

Since most of these titles are treated as both reference books and selection aids, it may be argued that the reference librarian should know them as well as the other bibliographies and guides. The answer to that is to turn to Sheehy, Walford, and the current reference-book review sources. Inevitably they examine and list the major bibliographies in the area of selection. Beyond knowing where to find such titles, the reference librarian is into another field, that of book selection.

BIBLIOGRAPHIES: PERIODICALS AND NEWSPAPERS

To this point, the primary focus has been on books, but national and trade bibliographies are also concerned with other physical forms of information. Library materials include not only books but periodicals, recordings, films, databases, etc.

> Titus, Edna Brown (ed.), *Union List of Serials in Libraries of the United States and Canada,* 3d ed. New York: The H. W. Wilson Company, 1965, 5 vols. $175.
>
> *New Serial Titles.* Washington: Library of Congress, 1961 to date, eight issues per year, cumulated quarterly and annually. $225.
>
> *The Standard Periodical Directory.* New York: Oxbridge Communications, Inc., 1964 to date, biennial. $225.
>
> *Ulrich's International Periodicals Directory.* New York: R. R. Bowker, 1932 to date, annual. 2 vols. $149.95. *Bowker's International Serials Database Update* (Formerly *Ulrich's Quarterly*). 1977 to date, quarterly. $60. (DIALOG file 480, $65 per hour).

A "serial" may be defined in numerous ways, but at its most basic it is a publication issued in parts (e.g., a magazine which comes out weekly) over an indefinite period (i.e., the magazine will be published as long as possible; there is no cutoff date). Serials may be divided in several ways, for example: (1) Irregular Serials; many types of these. (2) Periodicals: (*a*) Journals, from the scholarly and scientific to the professional; (*b*) Magazines, such as found on most newstands; and (*c*) Newspapers. Some would not subdivide journals and magazines, while others would offer more esoteric subdivisions.

The approximate equivalent of *The National Union Catalog* for periodicals is the *Union List of Serials* and its continuation in *New Serial Titles*. *The National Union Catalog* lists serials, including periodicals, but only those acquired by the Library of Congress. The series for serials is a better guide, if only because more than one source is indicated for location and, more important, the serials, bibliographies, and union lists are limited solely to that form.

The base of the American series of union lists is the *Union List of Serials in Libraries of the United States and Canada,* which includes titles published before 1950. It is continued by *New Serial Titles* on an eight-times-a-year basis. *New Serial Titles* is cumulated not only annually, but every 21 years, e.g., *New Serial Titles, 1950–1970.* Given the basic volumes and the almost monthly updating, the librarian is able to (1) locate in one or more libraries almost any periodical published from its beginning until today; (2) learn the name and location of the publisher; (3) discover the name, and various changes in the name, of a magazine; (4) check the beginning date of publication and, where applicable, the date it ceased publication and possibly the date it began publication again. This information is valuable for interlibrary loan purposes and for determining whether a library has a complete run of a magazine, whether the magazine is still being published, whether it has changed its name, and so on.

When someone finds an article through one of the library indexes in a journal or magazine which the library does not have, the librarian turns to one of the union lists to find the closest library where the magazine may be borrowed or the article copied. However, not all locations are given for a magazine. This has led to the development of regional, state, and even citywide periodical union lists. A regional list is composed of holdings of libraries in the immediate vicinity. Borrowing is easier and faster from a neighbor than from a distant library located through *New Serial Titles.* Ongoing and older local and regional union lists are found in Sheehy, Walford, and the *American Reference Books Annual.* The most frequently used lists are those published at the local, regional, or state level. These are known to any librarian who is in the least involved with periodicals.

The librarian searching for a periodical published before 1950 will turn to the basic unit in the periodical union lists, the *Union List of Serials in Libraries of the United States and Canada.* Here, alphabetically listed by title, are 156,499 serial titles held by 956 libraries in the

United States and Canada. As defined by the compilers of this reference work, as with *New Serial Titles,* the primary meaning of "serial" is a periodical. Newspapers are not included nor are government publications, except for some periodicals and monographic series. As many serials change name, numerous cross-references to the main entry give complete bibliographical information on the title. Serials published in all countries are included. This sometimes confuses beginners. The list shows *holdings* of only American and Canadian libraries, but it includes titles *published* in all countries.

If a serial has been issued after 1950 but before 1971, the next place to look is *New Serial Titles, 1950–1970.* The twenty-one-year cumulation contains the same type of basic bibliographic data found in the basic *Union List.* The number of serials listed for only 21 years is almost half again the number of the basic list—220,000 titles held by 800 United States and Canadian libraries, with the addition of International Standard Serial Numbers (ISSN) and country codes. There is also a separate listing of cessation.

For information after 1970, the librarian should turn to the monthly, quarterly, and annual *New Serial Titles.* Here one finds full bibliographical information for serials cataloged by the Library of Congress or one of the cooperating libraries. Serials are added regardless of the date of publication, and this means even eighteenth- or nineteenth-century titles may appear. Still, the majority fit the description "new" and information is usually given for a title which began publication one to three years ago. Holdings are given for libraries at the bottom of each entry.

With the development of computerized support, *New Serials Titles* expanded its entry form in 1981. It now offers full cataloging information, including tracings, for each entry. The traditional catalog card format makes it much easier to use.

The majority of entries are available online, via vendors from OCLC to DIALOG. The library with online facilities finds it much easier to trace a title in this fashion, particularly when little is known about date of publication.

Standard Guides

The basic periodical guide is *Ulrich's International Periodical Directory.* (Beginning in 1985 the title is prefaced with *Bowker's International Serials Database* which, one suspects, will replace *Ulrich's* as a title.) Revised and updated every year, it provides bibliographical information for close to 67,000 periodicals. Unlike *Books in Print,* it is not limited to American publishers but includes works from around the world. The titles are arranged alphabetically under about 550 broad subject headings, and there is a title index in the second volume. The second volume includes a cessations list which gives, in as much detail as possible, information on which works are no longer published, but were included in the previous edition. This is followed by an "Index to Publications of International Organizations," as well as a title index.

Reference librarians use *Ulrich's* to locate such basic information about a periodical as the address of the publisher, frequency of issue, year first published, and price. The primary abstracting and indexing services for each subject area are included in the subject section. The problem is that information is dated almost as soon as the volume is published—a fault which, of course, cannot be overcome as long as periodical publishers change prices, names, locations, and so on, with alarming frequency.

Here *Bowker's International Serials Database Update* is of help. The supplement follows the same organization as the main volume; it reports on new titles, changes in titles, cessations, and the like. There are some 1500 listings in each issue.

For current data on periodicals, the best place to turn is the online version of *Ulrich's* which is updated as changes occur. Equally, if not even more current, is the online service offered by the serials and periodicals jobber, F. W. Faxon. This is DataLinx, available directly from the jobber, which, among other things, provides access to continuously updated information on thousands of serials.

The large vendors of periodicals (i.e., those firms from which the librarian usually purchased periodical subscriptions) issue annual catalogs with basic price and frequency information. Usually these are free. In 1986 the vendor Ebsco expanded its catalog to three volumes. Each entry now includes numerous additional pieces of information such as major classifications for each title. The annual *Serials Directory* is $249 from Ebsco (P.O. Box 1943, Birmingham, AL).

The Standard Periodical Directory (beginning in 1986, distributed by Gale) is another aid in that it lists and sometimes briefly annotates thousands of house organs, newsletters, reports, and so on, not found in *Ulrich's*. The ninth edition (1985–1986) lists some 25,000 magazines (less than half found in Ulrich's), but has 5000 newsletters, 4000 house organs, 7000 directories, and 20,000 bulletins, association publications, and other types of ephemeral materials. Here, however, the titles listed are limited to those published in the United States and Canada—about 70,000 in total. Entries give somewhat different types of information from that found in *Ulrich's* and include advertising rates, trim size, print methods, and so on. The availability of the title on microform is indicated. The directory is a useful backup for *Ulrich's*, particularly as it includes types of work not found in the other directory.

In addition to using *Ulrich's* for bibliographical data about a title or *New Serial Titles* for location of a serial, these and other serial aids can answer reference questions such as the following:

(1) What are the *basic* periodicals in chemistry, geography, art, needlework, and so on? Since *Ulrich's* and *New Serial Titles* have a subject approach, one can at least isolate old and new titles in subject areas. However, in both cases the lists are no more selective than *Subject Guide to Books in Print* and therefore are questionable selection aids, particularly as neither has annotations.

For more specific results, the librarian should turn to selection tools such as *Magazines for Libraries* by W. A. Katz (5th ed. New York: R. R. Bowker Company, 1986). This is a selected annotated list of some 6,500 periodicals under more than 100 subject headings. The descriptive and critical annotations are by experts. The guide is employed for basic acquisitions and selection. The annotations point out the strengths and weaknesses of each title for different readers.

(2) Where is *Time,* or *Ocean Engineering,* or *Indiana Slavic Studies* indexed? Such a question may be asked when the librarian or the user knows that a particular periodical title is likely to give an answer to a query. The traditional source is *Ulrich's,* which lists one to four indexes or abstracting services for many, although not all, titles. However, *Ulrich's* analyzes only the basic services, and then not always well. More extensive indexing information is found in the new *Serials Directory* issued by Ebsco, but this is not likely to be found in as many libraries as *Ulrich's.*

(3) What does this abbreviation mean? Often the user and the librarian may be confused by an author or editor employing different abbreviations for the same journal. The best source to check to solve the problem: *Periodical Title Abbreviations* (4th ed. Detroit: Gale Research Company, 1983). This and the annual supplements cover some 55,000 abbreviations.

While irregular serials offer a major challenge to librarians, space does not permit more than a cursory glance at the subject. The basic guide: *Irregular Serials and Annuals* (New York: R. R. Bowker Company, 1972 to date, biennial). Following much the same pattern as *Ulrich's,* some 35,000 entries are arranged under 560 subjects with a detailed index. An irregular serial is a promise by a publisher to keep issuing such things as transactions, almanacs, proceedings of meetings, and the like, from time to time for an unspecified period. The publisher fails, or is unable, to state when the material is to be published—hence "irregular."

Serials: Newspapers

American Newspapers, 1821–1936 . . . reprint. Millwood, New York: Kraus Reprint Company, 1970, 791 pp. $130.

The IMS 198( ) Directory of Publications (Formerly *Ayer Directory of Publications*). Fort Washington, Pennsylvania: IMS Press, 1880 to date, annual. $80.

How does one locate American newspapers in a given library? For those before 1936, the answer is *American Newspapers*. After 1936, and assuming the wanted newspaper is still being published, one may turn to the *IMS Directory* to locate the city or town likely to have a run of the newspapers, usually in the local library.

The lack of a national union list may be accounted for as follows:

1. In the United States at least, the number of newspapers has decreased. There were 2461 dailies in 1916; today there are fewer than 1600 and the number is shrinking. The control problem, therefore, is nowhere near the control problem for magazines which, worldwide, now number over 150,000.[8]
2. Current newspapers are filed, often indexed, and microformed by the state and by larger cities; therefore locating them, or parts of them, for interlibrary loan is usually a simple matter.
3. Lacking indexes to all but the largest newspapers, access is limited and demand is small for given newspapers of a given date on any national or international scale. (The local newspapers may be indexed and used locally or regionally, but seldom nationally.) For these and other reasons, the need for an up-to-date newspaper union list has never been pressing.

The location of American newspapers prior to 1821 is found in Clarence S. Brigham's *History and Bibliography of American Newspapers, 1690–1820* (Worcester, Massachusetts: American Antiquarian Society, 1947, 2 vols.). The list is not chronologically complete; where research is being done in a given geographical area, it is wise to check with libraries for local union lists of holdings of newspapers not included in the two major union lists.

As the online records increase, most newspapers can now be found at the terminal. For example, one network (OCLC) gives

---

[8]The 1984 issue of *IMS Ayer Directory of Publications* (p. viii) says the total number of dailies for the United States in 1983 was 1708; but dropped to 1687 in 1984. They list only about 11,000 periodicals, but their listing is far from complete.

information on 25,000 titles from all periods, although at this writing it is limited to holdings in 15 states. This is the "United States Newspaper Program National Union List." It is designed to identify newspapers published in all fifty states; identify libraries where the newpapers are located; and list the issues held by each of the libraries. Coverage is from *Public Occurrences* (published in 1690) to *The New York Times*. The U.S. Library of Congress offers the printed *Newspapers in Microform* which now lists close to 40,000 titles reported by over 1000 libraries. The arrangement is by state and city, with a full title index.

Published each year since 1880, the *IMS '8( ) Directory of Publications* is roughly the equivalent of *Ulrich's* for newspapers. It covers newspapers, and other media published in the United States, Canada, Puerto Rico, Virgin Islands, Bahamas, Bermuda, and the Philippines. While it previously included detailed information on newspapers, this was dropped in the early 1980s. Now it is a simple listing of newspapers and periodicals with basic information on price, editor's names, etc. Arrangement is first by state or province and then alphabetically by city or town.

The guide is filled with much ready reference material which is only incidentally related to publications. For example, there is a large map reference section in the front of the guide; after each town and city name there are coordinates which help the user to locate the town or city on a map. Census figures are given as well as background information on the state, province, etc. Each state or province section opens with a brief description of the state, as well as vital statistics.

Basic guides for newspapers (and some periodicals) outside the United States are: *Newspaper Press Directory, Benn's Guide to Newspapers and Periodicals of the World* (London: Benn Brothers, 1846 to date, annual), and *Willing's Press Guide* (London: Willing, 1874 to date, annual). In America, one can keep up with the annual activities of the foreign press via *Editor and Publisher International Yearbook* (New York: Editor and Publisher, 1920 to date). This lists all major international newspapers with details on markets, personnel, etc. There are, also, special press directories covering everything from black newspapers to alternative newspapers listed in Sheehy, *American Reference Books Annual,* and so on.

BIBLIOGRAPHIES: MICROFORM

Guide to Microforms in Print: Author-Title. Weston, Connecticut: Meckler Publishing, 1961 to date, annual, 2 vols. $84.50.

Books on Demand. Ann Arbor, Michigan: University Microfilms, 1975 to date, irregular. 1983 ed. 1013 pp. Price upon request.

For purposes of storage and convenience, most libraries with substantial holdings in periodicals and newspapers have them on microform. Books, particularly those hard to locate or out of print, are on microform as are various other printed works, from reports to government documents. Most of the aids for locating these forms are employed in acquisitions, but there are times when the reference librarian should know at least the basic microform bibliographies.

The equivalent of *Books in Print* for microform is the ever-expanding *Guide to Microforms in Print.* It alphabetically lists over 100,000 titles from some 500 publishers, including international firms. Arranged by title and author in one alphabet, the guide lists books, journals, newspapers, government publications, and related materials. Sixteen different types of microform are considered and the types, with explanation, are listed in the preface. Not all microforms are listed, for example, theses and dissertations. Another approach by the same company is *Guide to Microforms in Print: Subject* which lists the material under 135 broad Library of Congress headings. Certain types are classified by form; i.e., government documents, manuscripts, and so on.

Microform is employed in a library for many reasons, one of the most frequent being its use as a substitute for books or other forms of printed material which are no longer in print, no longer available from a used-book dealer, or so prohibitive in cost as to make microform preferable. It would require a whole chapter to explain how librarians find out-of-print materials, but one approach is suggested by *Books on Demand.* This is a multivolume author, title, and subject catalog of about 100,000 out-of-print titles which may be purchased literally "on demand." The titles are available on microfilm or as hard-copy xerographic prints on the microform at an average cost of $15 to $20, depending on the number of pages. Other companies offer similar services as well as standard reprints of titles which the publisher thinks will be in sufficient demand. The reprints usually are listed in *Books in Print* as well as in a number of specialized guides.

PAMPHLETS

Vertical File Index. New York: The H. W. Wilson Company, 1935 to date, monthly. $30.

A pamphlet is understood to be a publication of a few printed leaves, normally bound in paper. *The Weekly Record* does not list pamphlets under 49 pages, and such works are rarely included in the standard trade bibliographies. Individual libraries classify pamphlets as important to rebind and catalog separately or ephemeral enough to warrant no more than placement in a vertical file under an appropriate subject.

Recognizing the failure of most general trade bibliographies to list pamphlets, the Wilson Company has a bibliography devoted solely to this form. Issued monthly except in August, *Vertical File Index* is a subject approach to a select group of pamphlets. Selection is based on their probable use for the general library, not for the special, technical library.

Each entry includes the standard bibliographical information and a short descriptive note of content. A title index follows the subject list. Wilson does not recommend any of the works, many of which are distributed by companies and organizations for advertising and propaganda.

One of the headaches of ordering pamphlets is that they must be purchased from the publisher. No general book jobber will bother handling them. A free pamphlet may involve many dollars' worth of paperwork and time on the part of a librarian or clerk.

BIBLIOGRAPHIES: NONPRINT MATERIALS

"Nonprint" is not a precise description. It has come to mean any communication material other than the traditional book, periodical, and newspaper. Nonprint is closely linked with terms such as the "new media," "audiovisual," "multimedia," "nonbook," and other expressions which indicate new approaches to reference work in particular and library services in general. Nonprint materials are an essential part of reference service, particularly in school libraries or, as they are called, "school media centers" or "learning centers."

When working with resources other than books, the reference librarian functions much as she would when working with the traditional media:

1. In schools, universities, and colleges, the librarian will be called upon by the teacher for information on media not only available in the library, but also that may be ordered, or even borrowed from other libraries.
2. The students will want information and advice about multimedia for the primary learning process.

3. The layperson's needs will be somewhat similar, although here most of the emphasis is likely to be on advice about films, recordings, and so on, within the library which may extend knowledge (or recreational interests) beyond the traditional book.

The reference librarian should be conversant with at least the basic bibliographies and control devices for the new media. Knowledge of bibliographies and sources is important for answering questions directly dealing with audiovisual materials: "Where can I find [such and such] a catalog of films, records, tapes?" "Do you have anything on film that will illustrate this or that?" "What do you have pertaining to local history on recordings or film?" In large libraries, such questions might be referred to the proper department, but in small- and medium-sized libraries, the questions usually will have to be answered by the reference librarian.

Guides and bibliographies

Sive, Mary R. *Selecting Instructional Media: A Guide to Audio-Visual and Other Instructional Media Lists*, 3d ed. Littleton, Colorado: Libraries Unlimited, Inc., 1983, 330 pp. $22.50.

National Information Center for Educational Media. *NICEM Media Indexes.* Los Angeles: University of Southern California, National Information Center, 1967 to date. Various services, prices. (DIALOG file 40, $70 per hour.)

Audiovisual Market Place. New York: R. R. Bowker Company, 1964 to date, annual. $49.95.

There are no entirely satisfactory bibliographies for all nonprint materials—no *Books in Print,* no *Cumulative Book Index,* no *National Union Catalog.* And even the by-now-standard bibliographies leave much to be desired in organization and coverage. Lacking overall bibliographical control, the materials are difficult to track. The lack of such tools accounts in no small way for the development of media experts who are familiar with the many access routes, routes which the average harassed reference librarian has neither the time nor the inclination to follow.

Sive's book offers a guide to 400 selected lists of audiovisual and related types of material. The listings are limited to those of interest to the elementary and secondary grades. Arrangement is by subject and there are numerous indexes. The book is noteworthy for Sive's evaluative and descriptive annotations. A related work: *A Multimedia Approach to Children's Literature* (Chicago: American Library Association, 1983). The third edition of this basic guide offers annotated entries of books, filmstrips, recordings, etc., suitable for children.

The closest thing to *Books in Print* for audiovisual materials is the *NICEM Media Indexes*. The purpose of these indexes, which are really bibliographies, is to provide noncritical information on what is available in nonprint materials. And, although directed at elementary and secondary school needs, a good deal of the data is applicable to other types of libraries. Hence it can be used to answer such queries as, What transparencies are available for geography? What educational films are there on animals? Environmental studies? And so on.

The *NICEM Indexes* are really a series of 13 individual indexes, *not* a single work. In 1985 the combined indexes included close to one million items. Each item is briefly annotated, but this is only descriptive, not evaluative. Full information is given as to cost, rental (when available), and necessary bibliographical information for identification and order. Almost all types of audiovisual materials are covered from overhead transparencies and films to video cassettes.

Available online, the file is much easier to search because one does not have to go through each of the multiple volumes. The online file goes back to 1964, but suffers from lack of any regular updating.

The *NICEM Indexes,* and especially the volume on producers and distributors, give information on who sells what. A more thorough listing is offered in the annual *Audiovisual Market Place,* which claims some 5000 listings under 625 subject headings. The librarian looking for information on, say, overhead projector manufacturers, distributors of films, or sources of slides will find the needed data under the subject or through a detailed index. A third section is a listing of some 10,000 AV individuals and their firms.

Indexes to reviews

> *Media Review Digest.* Ann Arbor, Michigan: The Pierian Press, 1970 to date, annual. 2 vols. $198.

A type of *Book Review Index* for films, videotapes, filmstrips, records, tapes, and other miscellaneous media. *Media Review Digest* analyzes reviews of the media appearing in over 150 periodicals. The 60,000 or so reviews are then indexed, with full citations, by type of medium. Some excerpts from reviews are given and an evaluative sign shows whether the comments were favorable or not. Its use by a librarian is almost the same as for the indexes to book reviews, i.e., to check reviews, probably for purposes of buying or renting a given item. The information provided is full, and often includes descriptions of the material as well as cataloging information. The service has the major drawback of lack of currency. While one supplement a year is provided, it is late and the time lag is considerable.

BIBLIOGRAPHY OF BIBLIOGRAPHIES

Bibliographic Index: A Cumulative Bibliography of Bibliographies. New York: The H. W. Wilson Company, 1937 to date, triannual with cumulations. Service. (Wilsonline, $38–$40 per hour.)

A bibliography of bibliographies is, as the name suggests, a listing of bibliographies. One may find a bibliography on dogs at the end of a periodical article, an encyclopedia essay, or as part of a book on pets. If one lists these three bibliographies and adds a dozen to a thousand more, one has a bibliography of bibliographies—in this case, a listing of bibliographies, from various sources, about dogs. (In turn, each of the bibliographies constitutes a subject bibliography.)

The primary example of a bibliography of bibliographies is *Bibliographic Index.* Under numerous headings, one may find bibliographies about subjects, persons, and places. The entries represent (1) separate published books and pamphlets which are normally bibliographies in a specific subject area, e.g., *East European and Soviet Economic Affairs: A Bibliography* . . .; (2) bibliographies which are parts of books and pamphlets, such as the bibliography which appears at the end of David Kunzle's book *The Early Comic Strip;* and (3) bibliographies which have been published separately or in articles in some 2200 English and foreign-language periodicals. Emphasis is on American publications, and to be listed, a bibliography must contain more than 50 citations.

The inevitable catch to many reference works is applicable here: (1) the bibliographies are not listed until six months to a year after they are published, and (2) while books, and to a lesser degree pamphlets, are well covered, the index cannot be trusted to include many periodical bibliographies. Why? Because there are over 55,000 periodicals issued, often with bibliographies, and the index includes only 2600.[9] The result is that the *Bibliographic Index* is usually a starting point for the subject expert, or, most likely, a way for the

---

[9]When a bibliography is published separately as a book, it is picked up through Library of Congress copy. If the bibliography is published as part of a periodical index, it may be identified by the various Wilson indexers when they are going through the periodicals for indexing. "If the bibliography is published as part of something else, the author should send a copy of the bibliography to *Bibliographic Index* for possible listing. This is the only way *Bibliographic Index* will know about the bibliography's existence. . . .", *RQ,* Fall 1982, p. 32, "Appendix".

expert to check to see whether anything has been missed in the mining of more detailed sources. General users are likely to find all they need in the way of bibliographies in the card catalog, *Subject Guide to Books in Print*, a subject index such as *Music Index*, or other general sources in the library. For the person between the expert and the generalist, *Bibliographic Index* is useful for finding hard-to-locate materials on less-known personalities and subjects.

The ultimate source for bibliographies is *Guide to Reference Books* and/or *Guide to Reference Materials*. Here one finds bibliographies under almost every main subject entry, as well as bibliographies of bibliographies, guides to the literature, and ongoing sources of current material. This is recommended primarily for the subject expert, and as a mnemonic device for librarians.

A point to remember about any bibliography of bibliographies is that it is twice removed from the subject. Once a bibliography is located in *Bibliographic Index*, the next step is to find the bibliography itself. After that, still another step is required: the location of the particular article or book listed in the bibliography. At any point along the way, the user may be frustrated by not finding what is listed in the index or, if finding it, by not being able to locate the desired information in the bibliography. With these stumbling blocks, it is no wonder that many reference librarians favor more direct sources.

Libraries, including the Library of Congress, are continually compiling bibliographies. One of the most useful groups is the "LC Science Tracer Bullet." These listings, which are periodically updated, expanded, and added to, provide access to a mass of information. Prepared by the Library of Congress, each explores the resources available on a topic and lists texts, handbooks, encyclopedias, dictionaries, bibliographies, government documents, and journal articles. Subjects range from aeronautics to folk medicine and women scientists.[10]

SUGGESTED READING

Alston, Robin, "The Philosophy of Bibliography: Beyond 1800," *The Times Literary Supplement*, April 6, 1984, pp. 381–382. In this review of the *Nineteenth Century Short Title Catalogue* (first volume), the critic examines the criteria of a good bibliography—and, incidentally, finds this compilation lacking.

[10]Ellen P. Conrad, "Who Was That Masked Librarian," *Reference Services Review*, Winter 1983, pp. 75–79. The author briefly explains the bibliographies and then lists them by Superintendent of Documents number. They are all available in government document depository libraries, and may be found in other libraries as well.

Basefsky, Stuart, "Citation Training: Why and How," *Reference Services Review,* Winter 1982, pp. 89–91. While this is a plea to teach citation training in library schools, along the way the author offers a fine explanation of the elements in a citation and necessary standards for bibliographies.

"Bibliographic Services and User Needs," *Information Reports and Bibliographies,* no. 4, 1985. A series of papers on various aspects of bibliographies, and particularly the pragmatic use of them in libraries. The articles are from the conference sponsored by The Council on Library Resources and edited by Paul Peterson.

Conochie, Jean, "Has Serials Union Listing Come of Age?" *The Serials Librarian,* Summer 1985, pp. 67–72. A critical examination of four guidelines for the compilation of union catalogues, this details what one should look for in a good union list.

Line, Maurice, "National Library and Information Planning," *International Library Review,* July 1983, pp. 227–243. While discussing the functions of a national library system, the author shows how such a system functions, particularly in terms of bibliographic control and access.

Nash, Frederick N., "Enumerative Bibliography from Gesner to James," *Library History,* no. 1, 1985. The author traces the development of enumerative, and to a lesser extent universal, bibliography from the latter half of the sixteenth-century through the beginning of the seventeenth-century. The arrangement and wording of early guides is explained, as is the influence on later bibliography.

Salvaggio, Ruth, "Interpreting the MLA Bibliography," *Scholarly Publishing,* July 1983, pp. 363–368. Primarily a discussion of the new subject approach to this standard bibliography, the article suggests the numerous problems associated with subject analysis. Also, the author employs the subject headings for "some interesting commentary on our literary culture." This analysis would be suitable in most subject fields where descriptive headings are evaluated.

"Union Catalogues of Serials," *The Serials Librarian,* Fall 1983. The complete issue is turned over to "guidelines for creation and maintenance, with recommended standards for bibliographic and holdings control" of union catalogs. Anyone interested in the bibliographic control of serials should refer to this outstanding journal.

CHAPTER FIVE

Indexing and Abstracting Services

An index represents an analysis, usually by name and by subject, of a document. As most books, magazines, reports, and other sources are about a number of different things, it is necessary for the indexer to select key terms which are likely to be of most value to the user. The noun "index" is "derived from the stem of the verb 'dicare' which means literally to show, and the prefix 'in', used to indicate the direction from a point outside to one within a limited distance, thus generating the verb 'indicare' which meant to make known, point out, reveal, declare, give essential information. . . ."[1]

In the quest to give the user more entries to information, there is an ever-increasing number of indexes and abstracts in various forms. The contents of many indexes and abstracting publications can now be accessed at a computer terminal. Online indexes offer the advantage of making it easy to search many years of indexing. They, also, offer more current citations, and provide a flexible search strategy.

The future of many printed and online indexes may be in CD-ROM, the optical disk which can store up to 250,000 printed

---

[1]Hans Wellisch, "Index: The Word, Its History, Meaning and Usages," *The Indexer,* April 1983, p. 147. This is a thorough, easy-to-follow, and even entertaining explanation of what the term "index" means. "Derivations and relation to other concepts and their terms are investigated, based on listings of usage in the major English dictionaries."

pages. The H. W. Wilson Company, as of 1986, plans to put its major indexes in this form. The Information Access Corporation (*Magazine Index, Business Index,* etc.) now has available "Infotrac" which is a CD-ROM disk of its indexes which makes it possible to search 900 periodicals in one index. (See more on CD-ROM in the second volume of the text.)

The universe of indexes is large. Some estimate the number at several thousand, but for the average working reference librarian it is more likely to be a) a dozen standard works which cover general materials and b) about the same number of subject indexes. The number of online indexes which can be readily used is closer to 250, or more. Still, even with the wonders of technology available, the librarian is likely to concentrate on only the few which are well known.[2] They are most likely to be concerned with the following types of traditional indexes:

1. Periodicals
   a. General indexes, covering many periodicals in a wide or specific subject field. *The Readers' Guide to Periodical Literature* is the most widely known of this type of index.
   b. Subject indexes, covering not only several periodicals but also other material found in new books, pamphlets, reports, and government documents. The purpose is to index material in a narrow subject field. Examples of this type of index are the *Applied Science & Technology Index* and *Library Literature.*
   c. Indexes to single magazines, either at the end of a volume or as separately published works. *The National Geographic Index* (3 volumes covering 1888 to 1983), and the *Handy Key to Your National Geographics,* published and edited by Charles Underhill of East Aurora, New York. This is a much more detailed index. The sixteenth edition, 1984, covers the years 1915–1983.
2. Newspapers
   There are now numerous newspaper indexes in the United States. The best-known newspaper index is *The New York Times Index.*
3. Serials
   There are indexes to reports both published and unpub-

---

[2]And there are never enough indexes, particularly in the humanities. For example, as of 1985 there is no index devoted specifically to all aspects of dance, e.g., Daniel Clenett, "The Need for a Dance Periodical Index," *no,* Fall 1983, pp. 87–90.

lished, government documents; proceedings of conferences and congresses, continuations; and other materials which can be defined as serials, i.e., any publication issued in parts over an indefinite period. Many of the subject periodical indexes include some of these forms, while other indexes such as *Resources in Education* are limited to indexing only reports.

4. Material in collections

These indexes cover collections of poems, plays, fiction, songs, and so on. The *Speech Index* and *Granger's Index to Poetry* are examples.

5. Other indexes

Here one might include everything from concordances to indexes of various forms, from *Book Review Index,* to collections of quotations, to indexes to patents or music. Scientific searching may include indexes which have specifications, formulas, standards, prospectuses, and so on. And machine-readable databases may deal exclusively with numbers or their equivalent. Usually these indexes are treated by reference librarians in terms of the subject covered rather than as indexes per se.

Abstracting services

Abstracting services are an extension of indexes; they perform the same function in locating and recording the contents of periodicals, books, and various types of documents. They differ from indexes in that (1) by definition, they include a summary of the material indexed; (2) they tend to be confined to relatively narrow subject areas; and (3) the arrangement rarely follows the single author, subject, and sometimes title alphabetical arrangement of indexes. The abstract provides a clue to the relevance of the material and is valuable as a method of determining whether or not the user really wants the article, report, book, and so on. An index only gives a key to where the material is located and rarely indicates relevancy.

Most of the abstracting services aim at relatively complete coverage of a narrow subject area.[3] Coverage tends to be worldwide,

---

[3]Technically, there are two types of abstracts. The "indicative" abstract indicates the type of article and the author's approach and treatment, but does not usually include specific data. The "informative", and most often used in works described in this text, summarizes enough of the data and findings to relieve the reader of the necessity of always reading the article. In neither case does the abstractor make any critical assessment.

with abstracts of foreign-language articles in English. The format varies from abstract to abstract, although normally the issues are arranged under broad subject headings, with appropriate author and some subject indexing.

The arrangement by broad subject classification sometimes confuses beginners. It is a blessing to experts who need only turn to the classification section of interest. The traditional index uses the specific rather than the broad approach, thus often requiring the searcher to go back and forth in the index to run down related subject headings. Most abstracting services have limited author and subject indexes. The librarian unfamiliar with the subject will save time by turning to the annual cumulated index to discover the subject classifications under which this or that specific subject is likely to appear in the monthly abstracts.

A drawback even more severe for most abstracting services than for indexes is the delay time in publication. Whereas an average index may be 1 to 3 months behind the material analyzed, the average abstract has a time lag of 9 to 15 months or more. The exception is the few online newspaper and business services which make a special effort to get certain materials abstracted and available before a week is out. However, for the majority of online abstracting services, the waiting period, while not as great, is still longer than that of the standard index. As of 1985, The H. W. Wilson Company offered abstracts of material indexed in *The Readers' Guide to Periodical Literature* online and in microfiche.

While any reasonably important journal may be covered by two or three different abstracting services in the United States, if time is a factor, the librarian should first consult standard indexes which may include the same titles but analyze them more quickly than the abstracting services.

EVALUATION

With the understanding that online index and abstracting services (i.e., bibliographic databases) should be evaluated as carefully as the traditional printed forms, although such evaluation is outside the scope of this chapter, the reader is asked to move to a consideration of standard printed sources.[4]

---

[4]Database format aside, much of what follows is equally applicable to machine-readable index or abstract services. Notes on evaluation of databases will be found in the second volume of this text.

Read the preface or introductory remarks. This is not always helpful, but at least it should give the reader a notion of what the index is about and, if nothing else, explain arrangement, abbreviations, and type of subject headings employed.

There are eight relative constants in the evaluation of indexes and abstracting services. They are:

1. The publisher

The most frequently used indexes in all but special libraries are issued by The H. W. Wilson Company. The firm has an excellent reputation for producing easy-to-use, accurate indexes. One may argue with what is or is not included in one of these indexes, but the format and the depth of indexing are excellent. At the other extreme are the publishers of time-tested specialized and technical indexes such as *Science Citation Index.* In between are publishers about whom the librarian may know nothing and who seem to be offering (*a*) a duplication of another service or (*b*) a questionable venture into a new area. The librarian should check out the publisher, preferably by talking to subject experts and to other librarians who may have knowledge of the field and by reading reviews. Any or all of these safety checks will quickly reveal whom to trust and whom not to trust.

2. Scope[5]

The most essential evaluative point about an index or an abstract is that of coverage. Neither librarians nor users will consult an index unless they think it adequately covers the periodicals or other materials in the field of interest. Here one must consider obvious points: (*a*) the number and kind of periodicals indexed, especially whether the number is adequate for the field and whether the titles represent the best in the United States and, if necessary, abroad; (*b*) the inclusion of other material, since in some disciplines it will be necessary to consider not only periodicals but reports, books, monographs, and so on.

Few librarians or users are ever content that index or abstract X or Y is totally satisfactory in scope. In general or in large, undivided

---

[5]How can one judge if the index is even close to the right length (i.e., includes enough basic material to be useful) in a book? The American Society of Indexers believe a good index must have at least five pages for every hundred pages of text. The Society also suggests that if one fails to find cross references, the index is as bad as the work which is limited simply to names and places.

disciplines, there is always the nagging doubt that this or that journal (or type of book, or report, or other item) should be indexed rather than P or Q. In narrow, specialized subject areas, the question is usually resolved for the so-called core titles which everyone agrees are necessary, but arguments arise over what should be indexed in the fringe areas or in closely related disciplines.

When considering scope, related areas should be examined: (a) In an effort to include everything with the least amount of effort, the index may be virtually a concordance in that most keywords mentioned in the text are listed. The result is a bulky, often blind-alley, finding aid. A fallout of this type of indexing is the equally frustrating practice of including after each work a number of undifferentiated page references. In a cluster of, say, 20 page numbers after "Ostrich Eggs," the user has no idea which page reference is major, minor, or of absolutely no importance. (b) The text may be indexed, but there is no reference to plates, tables, diagrams, and so on. (c) There may be recurrent use of "see" entries instead of simply listing the place twice; e.g., "American Test Tube Concern, *see* ATTC." It would be much simpler to list the page under both the full name and the acronym, thus saving the reader the bother of flipping back and forth through the index.

3. Duplication and gaps

A decade or so ago users complained of the lack of proper indexes or abstracts, but in the early 1980s the same people are complaining about too many services.

Ideally, index and abstract publishers would divide the disciplines in such a way that duplication of titles covered would be limited. They do not. Therefore the librarian must always ask the key evaluative question: How much duplication exists between X and Y service, and is the difference so much (or so little) that X should be chosen over Y?

Comparing duplication among indexes is a favored and beneficial study for librarians. There are numerous such reports; e.g., Goehlert found that among the 30 basic indexing and abstracting services in the social and political sciences there is a tremendous amount of duplication in what they index. Some 50 percent of the journals were indexed in 6 or more of the services, and 5 indexes would give access to 78 percent of the journals in the field. Knowing this, users tend to avoid esoteric indexes unless absolutely necessary. In fact, in the social sciences the experts turn to only 1 or 2 of the 30, and both are from the 5 which cover most of the journals.

The methods of comparing duplication differ but primarily consist of (*a*) checking what journals and monographs are indexed by both and (*b*) checking the effectiveness of indexing by running the same search in both indexes.

4. Depth of indexing

Indexing thoroughness varies considerably, and the publisher of a periodicals index should explain (but often does not) whether all articles in the relevant periodicals are indexed. Few indexes include short items, notices, announcements, and so on, but reputable ones should cite at least the main articles in terms of subjects covered, authors, and possibly titles. In a survey of 10 political science services, one study found that only 3 of the services actually indexed all possible articles. Depth of indexing for other services ranged from a low of 4.20 percent to a high of 96 percent.

The obvious—some would say deceptively obvious—way of recovering a maximum amount of information from a given document is to index it in considerable depth. This means assigning a maximum number of subject headings to the document (as well, of course, as author and sometimes title labels). The question is, What is the optimal depth of indexing? To put it more precisely, for a given collection of documents and a given population of users of those documents, what is the best number of index terms to assign to those documents on the average and for any single document. Unfortunately there is no consensus on this, even among experts.

5. Currency

The frequency of publication is a fair indication of the currency of the service. This is only a fair yardstick, because there are factors which cancel out publication frequency as a method of evaluation. For example, *The New York Times Index* is always two and sometimes three months behind in indexing the newspaper. The December 29 issue of *The New York Times* will not be in index form and available for library use until at least the following March. Other indexes may be as much as a year or more behind.

In another situation, the index or abstract does reach the library within the calendar period announced on its cover, but the material indexed is several weeks or months behind the date on the cover. The lag between the time a periodical appears and the time it is picked up in the index is easy to check. Compare a few dates of indexed articles with the date on the cover of the index or abstract.

How often, if at all, is the index cumulated? Is there an annual volume which cumulates the weekly, monthly, quarterly, or other issues? Are there five-year, ten-year, or other cumulations? For retrospective searching, the necessity for frequent cumulations is apparent to anyone who has had to search laboriously through, say, the bimonthly issues of *Library Literature* before the annual or the two-year cumulation appears.

6. Format

Employing "format" as a general descriptor, the index or abstract may be evaluated in a number of ways. First, is it easy or difficult to understand? This normally depends upon arrangement. The standard alphabetically arranged index is easy to follow. It may be a different matter if the index is arranged by subject, by class, or is a citation type of indexing. Second, how readable is the index? This can be a real problem when it is a computer printout. Third, the citation should be complete with enough bibliographical information to identify the material which is indexed. Finally, the citations and information in the index should be accurate, particularly in terms of sending one to the proper source, page, book, etc.

In one study it was found that format could make it easy or difficult to use an index. "The typeface of printed indexes was often confusing to patrons. . . . Indexes printed with the same weight lettering for the entire citation were more likely to confuse a patron than those printed with a combination of boldface, italics and light-weight print. . . . Patrons complained about small print, especially in computer printed sources.[6]

7. Subject headings

The type, number, and form of subject headings used in an index or abstract are important. Many standard indexes rely on the Library of Congress subject headings, or Sears. Conversely, indexes for specific disciplines may develop their own subject headings, rely on keywords in the title, or adopt a plan suitable for the material being indexed or abstracted. Regardless of what type of subject-heading system is employed, there should be adequate *see* and *see also* references, a thesaurus of subject terms, or both.

[6]Kevin Carey, "Problems and Patterns of Periodical Literature Searching at an Urban University Research Library" (University of Illinois at Chicago), *RQ*, Winter 1983, pp. 216–217.

The preceding brief paragraph only skims the most vexing problem of indexers, one which has resulted in a considerable body of theoretical and practical literature. (See, for example, any issue of *The Indexer*, the official journal of The American Society of Indexers.)

8. Description

When one turns to abstracts, there is the added dimension of whether the abstract adequately describes the document. The readability factor may be high or low, depending on how the abstracts were prepared (by the author of the indexed item, by the publisher, or by both—in other words, whether the author's abstract has been edited judiciously or by "automatic" methods such as keyword scanning).

In order truly to test an index for inclusion in a library, a considerable amount of time and effort is required, as well as some expertise in comparative analysis. Consequently, the majority of librarians rely on reviews, the advice of experts, or both—particularly when considering a specialized service. The benefit of learning evaluation techniques is as much to show the librarian how indexes or abstracts are (or should be) constructed as it is to reveal points for acceptance or rejection.

INDEXING PRINCIPLES

There are some basic principles which indexers follow, and help to indicate the problems—problems which beset the librarian in using almost any index.

(1) The indexer tries to be as specific as possible by using subject headings which immediately clarify the primary points of the text. The difficulties: a) The text may be muddled and it may not be possible to be any more specific than the author; b) the text may employ new terms which are not yet in the list of subject headings, e.g., "frisbees" is a well-known description of a game, but catalogers must rely on less exact, recorded terms such as Flying Discs (Game); c) conversely the indexer may employ older terms which simply are no longer applicable to describe new events or concepts. This explains· why when one searches a number of years of any index, many of the subject headings change, or are deleted, or seem out of date.

(2) The indexer is usually limited (by considerations of the size of the index, costs of printing and labor, etc.) in the number of assigned subject headings. Where there may be more than the

traditional two to three subject headings assigned, the problem multiplies itself. Instead of being overly specific, there are now too many nonspecific subject headings employed. While the "optimum" number of desired subjects assigned a text has never been determined—despite much research—it is by now agreed that simply adding more and more descriptors to a 10- or 15-page article will not necessarily make it any easier to retrieve in terms of importance. For example, there may be 30 articles about housing, and the subject heading "housing" is employed for all 30. The question now is: Yes, but how many are directly involved with housing, and how many are only addressing it incidentally, and, most important, how can the user tell? Where there is specific, well-done assignment of subject headings, the indexer makes these determinations and out of the 30 articles may decide to use "housing" as a main subject heading with only 5.

(3) The indexer must be consistent in assigning subject headings. This requires not only an understanding of the article being indexed, but of the possible terms to employ. The problem is the human factor. It takes an unusual person to be able to accurately match subject headings with a text consistently and with precision. Either the indexer uses the wrong terms or fails to assign the precise terms.

The reference librarian who is searching an index has to assume the indexer has been specific, consistent and has assigned the reasonable number of subject headings. Even given that, there is the basic problem of trying to match the search with the indexer's approach to the texts analyzed.

ONLINE INDEXES

With The H. W. Wilson Company putting their indexes online, it is now possible to access many of the general indexes at a computer terminal. The number of online indexes is likely to increase. The present problem is that the Wilsonline indexes only go back to 1983. Retrospective searches still must be made in printed volumes. At the same time, the indexes are kept more current than before.

The next step will be the availability, where desired, of the full text of the magazines online. One merely determines whether the whole article or any part of it should be printed out. This will save hours of frustration seeking the articles, not to mention savings for libraries trying to cut back on individual subscriptions. What effect full text searches will have on other aspects of libraries and publishing is still to be determined.

As of 1985, *Magazine Index* now has over 50 periodicals which one may have printed out in full text (the file is identified as Magazine Asap). NEXIS makes available online the full text of major newspapers, including *The New York Times,* and over 100 periodicals.

A tremendous advantage to online searches is that the librarian is able to make a run around the thinking of the indexer. By combining terms online, one can often turn up material which is otherwise lost because the indexer assigned subject headings not apparently relevant to an average search pattern.

> *One example involved a seemingly straightforward search to locate a shrimp recipe in the* New York Times. *The patron was positive the recipe had appeared at the beginning of 1983 and that shrimp shells were an ingredient. The librarian and patron searched the printed, biweekly* New York Times Index *for 1983 and, in frustration, resorted to its 1982 annual. Searching under "Recipes" led them to "Cooking and Cookbooks," but they were unable to locate the article. The librarian then turned to the National Newspaper Index database on DIALOG. Using truncated terms for shrimp shells and recipes, she located the article instantly. Out of curiosity, she went back to the printed index and searched again under "Cooking and Cookbooks." There she found the recipe under the author's name and "flavored butters," a term also found in the title. None of the five recipes included in the article were indexed; nor was a single ingredient, such as shrimp shells. Since the patron had not made a connection between the shrimp shells and "flavored butters," the recipe would have been lost without DIALOG.*
>
> *That search was a simple one, but it illustrates the lack of depth of subject headings in printed indexes. Going online enabled us to use a wider variety of terms and to succeed where we otherwise would have failed.*[7]

There is a major catch to all of this, and that is that one may use key words such as shrimp shells and end up with not one, but perhaps scores of citations, particularly where more than one database is

---

[7]Katherine Golomb and Sydelle Reisman, "Using DIALOG for Ready Reference," *Library Journal,* April 15, 1984, p. 787.

searched. The citations may or may not be relevant to the user's need. Inevitably, it is best to start with an assigned subject heading(s), which gives the online searcher a precise entry. Only when this fails, or when one wishes to expand the number of citations, should the free text approach be employed. There are exceptions to the rule, but for beginners it is a solid point of departure.

SEARCHING AN INDEX

In searching most printed indexes, one has to match the search subject or concept with those used by the indexer. If the indexer, for example, uses the term "dwelling," the user will find nothing if a search is made for "home," albeit in many cases there may be a cross reference from home which says, "see dwelling." If there were enough cross references, there would be no real problem, but there would be a gigantic index. The result is a compromise. The indexer scans the text and then tries to assign subject headings which are most likely to be used by a majority of researchers.

Where do the indexers get these terms? Directly they come from what is known as "controlled" subject heading lists. Indirectly, indexers are influenced by the key words they see in the text, the depth of indexing being used, and the type of subject heading list being employed. The end result may or may not be satisfactory.

Searching for the specific subject, indexers rely upon certain reference works and techniques which, in turn, can be useful to the reference librarian seeking the specific subject term. They are:

(1) *The subject heading list* Most indexes employ some form of *controlled vocabulary*. The subject headings are predetermined and the article is matched against the authority list of subject headings. The indexer selects one to three or even more terms from the list which best describe the article's contents. The result is rigid, which makes it difficult to introduce new concepts, although all systems do have methods of updating the subject list.

The two basic lists of subject headings consulted by reference librarians and catalogers are:

(a) *Library of Congress Subject Headings* (Washington: Library of Congress, various dates) This is the familiar two-volume set, usually bound in red, which lists the standard Library of Congress subject headings in alphabetical order. If one wishes to see how they list the history of England, one turns here, finds England and a reference to see Great Britain–History. That one step gives the user a specific subject heading and saves much time churning about the card catalog looking for nonexistent English history books, at least under that subject heading and covering all of the land area of Great Britain. There are cross references, synonyms, and other bits of advice and help which assist the user in finding the proper subject heading. (See an explanation of symbols, organization, etc., in the front of the first volume.)

(b) *Sears List of Subject Headings* (New York: The H. W. Wilson Company, various dates) This is the rough equivalent of the Library of Congress Subject Headings for smaller libraries. There are fewer of them and Sears represents a much-abridged edition, with changes suitable for smaller collections, of the LC work. The twelfth edition (1982), as with previous editions, reflects the interests of the 1980s in that there are added subject headings which cover current social and political issues, as well as forms of entertainment, and developments in technology. Note: *The Sears List of Subject Headings: Canadian Companion* (2d ed., 1984) includes over 150 pages of subjects which may be of special interest to Canadian public and school librarians. As with the basic set, it is often updated.

(2) *The thesaurus* The thesaurus is similar to the subject heading list in that it is a list of terms used for indexing and for searching. The essential difference is that the terms are drawn from the documents themselves, or from similar documents in the subject area. Typically, then, thesauri are used only in specific subject fields from education to the sciences.

Another important aspect of the thesaurus is that it shows relationships between terms. One may look up what amounts to broader and narrower concepts within a hierarchical tree structure built on one or more basic term categories. A term family in reference services, for example, could be terms for different kinds of services. Here one might find the term "Reference interview" with the Broader Term: Information Search; Narrower Term: Verbal Cues.

There are numerous examples of thesauri, but one of the most often used is the *Thesaurus of ERIC Descriptors* (Phoenix, Arizona: Oryx Press, 1982). This work is essential for any detailed, online search of the educational database; and it can be a tremendous help for searching the printed form, too. (See p. 162 for more on ERIC.)

Primarily, then, the thesaurus is a massive type of cross reference work which, if nothing else, suggests related terms which one may use to search for the necessary information.

(3) *Coordinate indexing* Here original words of the author in the title and the document may be used to generate the index terms. Instead of the indexer having to determine what the article or book is about and assigning subject terms, either from the subject headings

list or the thesaurus, the terms are generated from within the document itself. In fact, no indexer really is needed—although in practice, most systems do employ indexers to check to see if the title is truly descriptive of content, and, if not, to add descriptors as needed.

For example, if one takes the book title *Paperbound Books for Young People,* this can be broken into at least three separate index terms— paperbound, books, young people. In order to find the necessary item the user must coordinate the terms. Hence, one must at least use "young people" and "books", or "paperbound" to locate the work.

Coordinate indexes take many forms, and the methodology is used for online searching of indexes.

This type of indexing, and related varieties, is known as one which uses an *uncontrolled vocabulary,* as contrasted with the *controlled vocabulary* approach of the subject headings and thesauri. Here one may search for the term anywhere, from the title to a key word in the text itself.

A popular printed form of the free selection of keywords is the KWIC index—i.e. keyword in context. Here the keywords are arranged so they appear several times in a single alphabet of all the keywords in the index. Hence, one might find *Paperbound* Books for Young People; or *Books* for Young People, Paperbound; or *Young People,* Paperbound Books for; or even *People,* Paperbound Books for Young. The obvious problem is that the system is limited by how well the title represents the document.

Contrasted with a thesaurus, a subject heading list is a list of the subject terms used in an index. Normally, it is alphabetically arranged. A good subject index includes cross references which indicate relationships among terms. The thesaurus carries this even further in that the relationships are more evident.

Some argue that both the Library of Congress and the Sears lists of subjects are thesauri. This is more a matter of definition and discussion than it is of practical value to the working reference librarian. Still, it is worth noting if only to indicate the vast amount of argument, disagreement, and discussion when it comes to defining, explaining, and exploring the task of finding materials via subject words or terms.

Which Index?

Which index should one turn to for X or Y question?

Being able to answer that quickly is a mark of the professional reference librarian. It is not really all that difficult. At a simple level, one turns to the general indexes for typical student and layperson queries; and for more detailed subject questions, one turns to a subject index. Most indexes indicate their scope in the title (it is not difficult to imagine the contents of *Art Index*, for example). At a more complex level, the librarian becomes familiar with several subject fields and is able to quickly call up names of highly specialized indexes within the subject area.

The computer database makes it all much simpler, particularly at the complex subject level. Each of the major database vendors has a system whereby one need only select a broad subject area or subject grouping, enter key word(s), and a listing of databases with that term is shown. Furthermore, it indicates how many times the term appears in each of the indexes. (See the second volume for additional information on these systems, e.g., BRS/Cross; DIALOG/Dialindex and SDC/Data Base Index.)

While this chapter is concerned with indexes primarily to periodicals and their articles, one should not forget the important individual book index. Many reference questions are answered by consulting the index in the back of a standard work. This can be frustrating, of course, as one may have to search numerous books to find the right item(s).

Ideally, there would be a master index to whole groups of books in a particular subject area. This would eliminate the tedium of searching many volumes. The computer now makes this possible, and in the years to come there is every reason to believe that all major reference book indexes may be available for the person making an online search of a topic.

BRS's Superindex (SUPE) offers a master index to over 2000 technical and science reference works. The process is simple enough. The index in the back of each reference work is put into the computer tape. Full text search of the tape at the computer terminal allows the user to find what books have the required subjects. For example, one may look for "deforestation", and the screen/print-out will indicate three reference works with that term occurring. One may then call up a full bibliographic citation for one or all three of the works which, among other things, will indicate the number of pages, chapters, or sections given over to the term. (Also, one may limit or expand the search. For example if the term "acid rain" turns up too many references, one may limit it by date, another qualifier, etc.)

One can see the time when a reference librarian, given a subject or personal name, may simply enter it into a computer index which will (*a*) indicate the major reference works where the needed information can be located, and (*b*) simultaneously show what periodical articles, reports, studies, etc., are available on the same subject. One, again, might limit the search to one type of material, or one citation, or as many as are available.

A print approach to finding the correct periodical index is *Abstracting and Indexing Services Directory*. Detroit, Michigan: Gale Research Company, 1982–1983, 3 issues. The three paperback issues of this guide include about 1800 indexes and abstracting services arranged by name in alphabetical order. For each entry there is a full bibliographic description as well as a standard abstract which explains what is covered. Information was gathered from publishers and is only as accurate as what was reported. There is no subject approach, although there is an inadequate keyword index which lists in a single alphabet current and variant titles of the publications covered. The subject index may be added later. Still, the guide is a useful, usually detailed summary of individual indexes and abstracting services.[8]

Other sources for information include: *Magazines for Libraries*, 5th ed. (New York: R. R. Bowker Company, 1986). The first section is an annotated listing of over 200 basic indexes and abstracting services, and is useful because here one finds the truly "basic" services. A more ambitious and specialized work is Dolores Owen's excellent *Abstracts and Indexes in Science and Technology* 2d ed. (Metuchen, New Jersey: Scarecrow Press, 1985). Here one finds over 200 titles arranged by broad subject category with full descriptive annotations for each.

GENERAL PERIODICAL INDEXES

Readers' Guide to Periodical Literature. New York: The H. W. Wilson Company, 1900 to date, semimonthly and monthly, 18 issues a year, $100. (Wilsonline $25 to $45 per hour.)

Magazine Index. Los Altos, California: Information Access Corporation, 1977 to date, monthly. $1700. From $900 to $1400 for schools and some libraries depending on budget. (DIALOG File 47, $84 per hour.)

Access. Evanston, Illinois: J. G. Burke, 1975 to date, 3 issues per year. $85.

Popular Periodical Index, Wayne, New Jersey: Popular Periodical Index, 1973 to date, semiannual. $20.

[8]The publication, to a lesser extent, also lists relevant "indexes, digests, serial bibliographies, catalogs, title announcement bulletins."

Today there are two indexes which analyze almost all the magazines likely to be considered popular, that is to say, sold at the corner drugstore or found in many homes. These indexes include the traditional *Readers' Guide to Periodical Literature* and the not-so-traditional *Magazine Index*. On the periphery other publishers cover ground not considered by the *Readers' Guide*. Two such indexes are: *Access, Popular Periodical Index.*

A large proportion of periodical indexes used in small and medium-sized American libraries, as well as in the largest research library on a more limited scale, originate from The H. W. Wilson Company. The Wilson indexes are celebrated for their ease of use and have become a model of the best in indexing. Many of the company's publications are sold on a service basis. Since the larger, better-financed libraries often use more services, they usually pay more than the small libraries for the same index. This service arrangement is explained in any current H. W. Wilson catalog.

The Readers' Guide is by far the most popular periodical index in the United States, Canada, and most of the English-speaking world. Its success is due both to the excellent indexing and the selection of periodicals indexed—a selection which concentrates on relatively high-circulation, well-read magazines. There are now about 186 titles indexed by author and by subject. Book reviews are in a separate section and are arranged alphabetically by author.

The *Readers' Guide* is an excellent source of relatively current materials and is one of the first places a librarian would turn for information on a news event of a month or so ago.

The actual lag between the time an article is published and it is indexed differs from journal to journal, i.e., obviously a late journal will be indexed late. For the *Readers' Guide* the lag seems to be one to two months.

Although the book reviews are clearly set off at the end of each issue, the service includes a number of other reviews which are part of the main index. Each of these is indexed under the heading of the subject, e.g., ballet reviews, dance reviews, etc. Subjects in these categories also include: motion pictures, musicals, opera, phonograph records, radio programs, television, theater, and videodiscs.

Where fiction, poetry, and short stories are included in a magazine, these are indexed under the author's name. For further information, see the "Suggestions for the Use of the Readers' Guide to Periodical Literature" in the front of each cumulation. With variation, this same system is employed in all of the H. W. Wilson indexes. Librarians should remember that the book reviews usually are found in a separate section at the end of each index issue.

In addition to going online in 1984–1985, the publisher offered the *Readers' Guide* with abstracts, to compete favorably with *Magazine Index*. This is by far the most revolutionary action taken in the history of the index, and it is the most important for the average user. Now it is possible to find summaries of all the articles indexed. This will save users many hours of frustration, particularly when a title is not clear about content. Unfortunately, abstracts are now available only in microfiche and will be eventually online as well, but not in the regular printed version. There are plans to extend the abstracting to other Wilson indexes. Meanwhile, the basic snag is a familiar one. The price of the service, to be cumulated and updated every six weeks is, in 1986, $675 per year. This compares to $100 per year for the printed version without the annotations.

An *Abridged Readers' Guide* which indexes only 68 titles is available, but it follows the same general indexing procedures as the senior version. It is published monthly, rather than every two weeks, and is only about one-half the annual price of the larger work. Its use in libraries is questionable, in that it is much better for even the smallest library to have the larger index, which is more frequent and indexes three times as many periodicals.[9]

The great advantage of the indexes for general use is their arrangement. Author and subject entries are in a single alphabet. The subject headings, as in all the Wilson indexes, are consistent and easy to locate. Furthermore, numerous cross references make the indexes a model for rapid use. Each entry contains all the necessary information to find the article. Abbreviations are held to a minimum, and they are clearly explained in the front of the index.

Selection of periodicals for the *Readers' Guide* (and the other Wilson indexes) is determined by a committee and by polling librarians. When asked to consider a title to be added or deleted, the publisher reminds users of the purpose of the service to "index U.S. periodicals of broad, general and popular character." A deciding factor is the determination of whether or not the indexed material will be of any "reference value" to the users. Here "reference" is used to mean a work to assist in ready-reference questions and to a lesser extent specific search queries. The general coverage of essentially

[9]Even the publisher casts doubts on the wisdom of the abridged version. In a 1984 publicity release, The H. W. Wilson Company observes: "If you subscribe to only a few periodicals, you have good reason to subscribe to the unabridged *Readers' Guide* which indexes 128 more magazines, but costs only an additional $32 a year. Increasing use of inter-library loan in your county, school or regional libraries can make many of the 186 periodicals indexed in the unabridged *Readers' Guide* available to your patrons, thus meeting their needs while expanding the reference capabilities of your library."

popular and semipopular magazines makes it of little or no real use for detailed research questions.

The *Readers' Guide* offers a device for selection of periodicals. Many libraries purchase only those titles indexed here, or at least a high percentage of the periodicals budget goes to *Readers' Guide* titles before other magazines are considered. One may argue the merits of such a system, but it does exist. There is rarely a consensus on what is omitted or included in the *Readers' Guide,* and it is a continuing three-way debate among publishers of magazines which are left out, librarians who want something in or out, and the committee and publisher, who try to please everyone. For example in 1983 the committee added 12 popular magazines, to bring the total number to 186. Most of the new additions, as might be expected, were science and computer titles.

Parallel to the acquisitions procedure for periodicals is the question of how long the library should retain titles indexed in the *Readers' Guide.* Research indicates that in most libraries the user is likely to concentrate on using the past five years of the *Readers' Guide,* i.e., seek material in magazines of the past five years. This leads most librarians to agree that in small- and medium-sized libraries, retention of titles indexed in the *Readers' Guide* for more than five years is a waste of space. When people do want earlier issues, there should be a fast and efficient way to find them in larger area libraries or through various other regional and national networks.

The serious challenge to the *Readers' Guide,* particularly online, is *Magazine Index.* Here there is coverage of more than 400 popular magazines, or more than double the number found in *Readers' Guide.* The challenge is muted by cost. Online *Magazine Index* costs two to three times more to scan than *Readers' Guide,* and the microform version is from 10 to almost 20 times more expensive.[10]

The *Magazine Index* is available in most libraries through a microfilm-like reader. Each month the publisher sends the library an updated reel of film which cumulates previous month's listings. The film is mounted in the machine, and when someone wants to look up an item, a simple, motorized system makes it possible to view the wanted area almost immediately.

The *Magazine Index* has several advantages over the *Readers'*

---

[10]Mary Davis and John Riddick, "Readers' Guide to Periodical Literature and Magazine Index: A Comparison," *Reference Services Review,* Winter 1983, pp. 43–54. A detailed analysis of the two indexes, this serves, too, as a model for evaluating and comparing any index or set of indexes. For a comparison of both the online and printed versions, see Carol Tenopir, "General Literature Online: Magazine Index & Readers' Guide, *Library Journal,* May 1, 1986, pp. 92–93.

Guide: (1) It indexes more titles, some 435 as compared to 186. It indexes about 140,000 articles each year as compared with about 56,000 for *RG.* (2) There are short, supplementary annotations for articles the titles of which do not clearly indicate content. In many cases, additional phrases are added to explain a less than descriptive title. (3) There is a built-in consumer feature which makes it possible to check material on specific brands and models. (4) Because it is updated as a complete unit at least once a month, one need only use the reading machine; there is no need to consult various volumes and cumulations. The cumulation will cover five years, and after that, when each new month is added, a month's listing will be dropped. Printed versions of the deleted material are promised. For example, as each month of 1987 indexing is added, that month of 1982 indexing is deleted from the microform edition. (5) The publisher provides full text coverage, via microform, of the majority of periodicals indexed. The full text begins with 1980. A special loading device makes this extremely easy to use, and the film often is found with the reader.

Book reviews are coded in the index by the grades A through F. Each grade represents a reviewer's opinion, and it is a simple matter to count the number of A or C grades to ascertain the probable level of acceptance of a given work by the critics found in the 370-plus magazines indexed. In days past, *The Book Review Digest* used to grade reviews, but the system was dropped. Now it reappears, for better or for worse, in the *Magazine Index.* Note, too, that the same grading system is applied to records, film, theatre, restaurant reviews, and so on.

There are several other indexes which augment the *Readers' Guide.* "Augment" is perhaps the wrong word, as the raison d'être of these indexes is the inclusion of periodicals which for one reason or another have been excluded by the selection committee for the *Readers' Guide.*

The earliest of the indexes of omission is the *Popular Periodical Index,* which includes about 40 titles not found in the Wilson index. Some examples: *Analog, TV Guide, Mother Jones,* and *Playboy.* The librarian-publisher, Robert Bottorff, includes subject headings for reviews, motion pictures, recordings, and so on. Where a title does not describe content, the editor often adds a word or line or two explaining what the article is about. While this is hardly a full abstract, enough information is given to make the index particularly useful.

Access is another general index. It emphasizes works on popular music, travel magazines, science fiction, and arts and crafts titles. It is particularly strong in its coverage of city and regional magazines. Its value to librarians is as a wide net, in the indexing of really popular titles which are not in *Readers' Guide,* e.g., *Playboy, T.V. Guide, Creem,* and so on.

About 150 periodicals are indexed in each issue. The index is divided into two parts. The first section is subject, and the second is author. The index tends to be behind by as much as six months, e.g., the annual cumulation for 1985 was not published until June 1986.

Both *Access* and *Popular Periodical Index* follow a policy of deleting titles which eventually may be indexed by *Readers' Guide.* At the same time, there is some repetition between *Access* and *Popular Periodical Index.* In the *A*'s, for example, both index *American Film, American Spectator,* and *Analog.*

Which of these indexes is best? Thanks as much to its popularity as to its longevity and skill of indexing, the *Readers' Guide* is a must in all libraries. This can be followed by *Popular Periodical Index,* both for its low price and for the excellent selection of titles. Next *Access,* and, if the library has the need and the money, *Popular Magazine Review.*

Magazine Index would be a first choice for any library, but the price is often prohibitive. Online it is a serious rival of *Readers' Guide,* although again, the online search costs are higher.

Canadian and British indexes

Libraries in Canada and England normally use the *Readers' Guide,* although both have rough equivalents to it. Having suffered a division, the *British Humanities Index* is somewhat less ambitious than the *Readers' Guide.* From 1915 on, it was called the *Subject Index to Periodicals,* but after 1962, it omitted titles in the fields of education (taken up by *British Educational Index*) and technology (now in *British Technology Index*). Medical sciences and business were also cut out. What remains is a serviceable and relatively general guide to British journals covering such subjects as politics, economics, history, and literature. Unlike the *Readers' Guide,* it is of limited use in the area of current materials, because it is published only quarterly with annual cumulations. By the time the *British Humanities Index* and the corresponding periodicals reach North America, the timeliness factor is nil.

The *Canadian Periodical Index* is an approximate equivalent to the *Readers' Guide.* It is an author-subject index to about 138 Canadian magazines, including French titles. The book reviews are listed separately as are poems and short stories. The index follows the same meticulous path established by the *Readers' Guide,* and it is an excellent source of added information. One should remember that the periodicals indexed are Canadian, and this makes it an invaluable guide to Canadian activities. There is an annual cumulation. Note, too, the "editorial" comments on indexing which appear often in many issues. For French readers there is RADAR, *Répertoire Analytique des Articles de Revues du Québec* (Montréal, Québec: Bibliotheque Nationale du Québec, 1972 to date, bimonthly.)

Retrospective periodical indexes

Poole's Index to Periodical Literature, 1802–1906. Vol. 1, 1802–1881, Boston: Houghton Mifflin Company, 1981; vols. 2–6 (supplements 1–5), 1882–1907, Boston: Houghton Mifflin Company; 1888–1908 (6 vols. reprinted in 7 vols., Gloucester), Massachusetts: Peter Smith Publisher, 1963.

This was the first general magazine index, and the forerunner of the *Readers' Guide.* It was the imagination of William Frederick Poole, a pioneer in both bibliography and library science, that made the index possible. Recognizing that many older periodicals were not being used for lack of proper indexing, he set out, after one or two preliminary starts, to index 470 American and English periodicals covering the period 1802 to 1881. Having completed this work, he issued five supplements which brought the indexing to the end of 1906.

The modern user is sometimes frustrated upon realizing that the cited journals do not have a date, but are identified only by the volume in which they appear, and by the first page number. For example, the article "Dress and Its Critics" is from *Nation,* 2:10. A "chronological conspectus" in each volume gives an indication of the year.

While names of authors appear frequently after the title of the index, there is no author approach. Indexing is entirely by subject. The author index to some 300,000 references in the main set and the supplements is supplied by C. Edward Wall, *Cumulative Author Index for Poole's Index.* . . . (Ann Arbor, Michigan: Pierian Press, 1971, 488 pp.). The index is computer-produced and not entirely easy to follow, but it is a great help to anyone seeking an author entry in *Poole.*

With all its faults, Poole's work is still a considerable achievement and an invaluable key to nineteenth-century periodicals. The last decade of the century is better treated in *Nineteenth Century Readers' Guide to Periodical Literature,* 1890–1899, with supplementary indexing

1900–1922 (New York: The H. W. Wilson Company, 1944, 2 vols.). Limited to 51 periodicals (in contrast to Poole's 470), this guide thoroughly indexes magazines by author and subject for the years 1890 to 1899. Some 14 magazines are indexed between 1900 and 1922.

INDEXES TO MATERIAL IN COLLECTIONS

Essay and General Literature Index. New York: The H. W. Wilson Company, 1900 to date, semiannual. $70.

Short Story Index. New York: The H. W. Wilson Company, 1953 to date, annual. $44.

Granger's Index to Poetry. 8th ed. New York: Columbia University Press, 1986. 2000 pp. $150.

Play Index. New York: The H. W. Wilson Company, 1953 to date. (Irregular; basic volume, 1953, plus five additional volumes. $15 to $45.)

Anthologies and collections are a peculiar blessing or curse for the reference librarian. Many of them are useless, others are on the borderline, and a few are worthwhile in that they bring the attention of readers to material which otherwise might be missed or over-looked. Regardless of merit, all collections may serve the reference librarian who is seeking a particular speech, essay, poem, play, or other literary form. In reference, the usefulness of anthologies is dependent on adequate indexes.

This type of material is approached by the average user in one of several ways. He or she may know the author and want a play, a poem, or other form by that author. The name of the work may be known, but more than likely it is not. Another approach is to want something about X subject in a play, poem, short story, and so on.

Consequently, the most useful indexes to material in collections are organized so they may be approached by author, subject, and title of a specific work. Failure to find a particular title in an anthology or collection usually means it has been published independently and has still to find its way into a collective form. The card catalog certainly should be checked; if it fails to produce an answer, standard biblio-graphical tools, such as the *Cumulative Book Index* and *Books in Print,* should be consulted.

Indexes to materials in collections serve two other valuable purposes. Most of them cover books or other materials which have been analyzed; and since the analysis tends to be selective, the librarian has a built-in buying guide to the better or outstanding books in the field. For example, the *Essay and General Literature Index* picks up selections from most of the outstanding collections of essays. The library that has a large number of these books in its collection will have a good, representative group of works.

The second benefit, particularly in these days of close cooperation among libraries, is that the indexes can be used to locate books not in the library. Given a specific request for an essay and lacking the title in which the essay appears, the librarian may request the book on interlibrary loan by giving the specific and precise bibliographical information found in the index.

Aside from sharing a similar purpose of locating bits of information from collections, anthologies, and individual books and magazines, this type of reference aid tends to center on the humanities, particularly in literature. There is little need for such assistance in the social sciences and the sciences, and where the need does exist, it is usually met by an abstracting or indexing service. While the titles listed here are the best known, new entries appear each year. They range from guides to science fiction to information on handicrafts, costumes, photographs, and such. Once the form is recognized, the only basic change is in the topics covered and the thoroughness, or lack of it, in arrangement and depth of analysis.

The single most useful work in libraries as an entry into miscellaneous collections of articles is the *Essay and General Literature Index*. It is valuable for general reference questions, in that the analyzed essays cover a wide variety of topics. There are analytical subject entries to the contents of some 300 collected works on every subject from art to medicine. While the indexing emphasis is on subjects, the index is useful for approaching an author's work via his or her name as well as for locating criticism of the author's individual efforts. There are regular four-year cumulations. The one covering 1980-84 covers 20,000 essays which appeared in 1520 collections. The list of books analyzed often is used by librarians as a buying guide.

The elusive short story may be tracked down in the *Short Story Index*. Now published annually, the *Index* lists stories in both book collections and periodicals. A single index identifies the story by author, by title, and by subject. The subject listing is a handy aid for the reference librarian attempting to find a suitable study topic for a student who may not want to read an entire book on the Civil War or life in Alaska. The names of the books and the magazines analyzed are listed. More than 3000 stories are considered each year. A basic volume covers collections published from 1900 to 1949, and there are five-year cumulations, or with the 1979–1983 cumulation, a group of 8 volumes to search. There's also *Short Story Index: Collections Indexed 1900–1978* which lists the 8400 collections analyzed.

The difficulty with these and other ongoing indexes to collections is that one often may have to search numerous volumes to find the needed item. For example, almost any story of Henry James will be reprinted year after year, and it can be found by looking in the latest *Short Story Index,* or, at best, in the five-year cumulation. Conversely, a short story by Joseph Roth may have appeared in only one collection. But which collection, and what year? It is conceivable one will search all 8 volumes before finding what is needed. The same problem presents itself when searching the *Essay and General Literature Index, Play Index,* and all indexes to collections. Unfortunately, laypersons may search only one series and thereby fail to find what is needed. What is desirable, of course, is a cumulative index for all such works. This is most likely to be available when indexes to collections are accessed via a computer terminal, rather than volume by volume.

Indexing both individually published plays and plays in collections, *Play Index* is a standard reference work. The basic part is an author, title, and subject index. The author entry for a play "contains the full name of the author, title of the play, a brief descriptive note, the number of acts and scenes, the size of the cast, and the number of sets required." There are numerous other helpful devices, ranging from symbols for plays suitable for elementary school children to prizes a play has won. A cast analysis, making up the second section, helps the reference librarian locate plays by number of players required. The other sections key the plays to collections from which they have been taken.

The eighth edition of *Granger's Index to Poetry* follows previous editions in arrangement and approach. Close to 405 poetry anthologies are indexed. There are four indexes by first line, author, subject, and title.

There is access here to over 40,000 poems published in anthologies between 1970 and 1981. While there is some carry-over of titles from previous editions, for the most part it is wise to consult earlier editions for poems not found in the latest edition.[11] In fact, each edition is a unique index to poetry collections published for the years covered, beginning in 1904.

---

[11]The 7th edition, for example, includes only 100 anthologies from the previous edition, and adds 128 new titles. Much the same will happen with the 8th edition, and so on. Note, too, that collections especially suitable for smaller libraries are so marked.

Concordances

There is one other form of index which is "basic" in most libraries, and that is the concordance. A concordance is an alphabetical index of the principal words in a book, or more likely, in the total works of a single author, with their contexts. Early concordances were limited to the Bible; a classic of its type, often reprinted, is Alexander Cruden's *Complete Concordance to the Old and New Testament* . . . , first published in 1737.

The laborious task of analyzing the Bible word by word, passage by passage, is matched only by the preparation of early concordances to Shakespeare. Fortunately, the advent of the computer considerably simplified the concordance effort (for both editorial and production purposes). Today there are concordances to not only the Bible and Shakespeare, but almost every major writer. Examples include concordances to F. Scott Fitzgerald's *The Great Gatsby,* James Joyce's *Finnegans Wake,* the complete poetry of Stephen Crane, and the plays of Federico Garcia Lorca.

The Concordance to the Plays, Poems and Translations of Christopher Marlowe (Ithaca, New York: Cornell University Press, 1982, 1681 pp.) is typical. The main part of the text lists each word, with the line or lines in which it appears. The word frequencies are listed in an appendix, as are foreign words and related items. Thoughtfully developed by the compilers (Robert Fehrenbach et al.), the work is a monument to excellent bibliographic planning.

A concordance is used in a library for two basic purposes: (1) to enable students of literature to study the literary style of an author on the basis of use or nonuse of given words; and (2) more often, to run down elusive quotations. With one or two key words, the librarian may often find the exact quotation in the concordance. This approach presupposes some knowledge of the author.

Quotations

Bartlett, John. *Familiar Quotations,* 15th ed. Boston: Little, Brown and Company, 1980, 1540 pp. $24.95.

Stevenson, Burton E. *The Home Book of Quotations, Classical and Modern,* 10th ed. New York: Dodd, Mead & Company, Inc., 1967, 2816 pp. $34.95.

The Oxford Dictionary of Quotations. 3d ed. New York: Oxford University Press, 1979, 907 pp. $39.95.

Quotations are beloved by everyone, and they pop up everywhere. They may salt an after-dinner speaker's delivery, get a laugh on a late television show, or be enshrined in literature. Saul Bellow uses quotations in his fiction, e.g., from a short story, "Persistent fragments, inspired epigrams, or spontaneous expressions of ill will come and go. . . . Disraeli on his deathbed, informed that Queen Victoria has come to see him and is in the anteroom, says to his man servant: 'Her Majesty only wants me to carry a message to dear Albert.' "[12]

If one wished to find the precise source of this quote, it would be necessary to search a book of quotations. The librarian would hope a) that it was an actual quote, and not one made up or slightly changed by the author; b) that the wording was approximately, if not precisely, correct; c) and that the primary actors involved in the quote were the Queen, Albert, and Disraeli, and not the King, Caesar, and Cicero.

Indexing "who said what" is the role of the book of quotations. Actually, these books are not so much indexes as distinctive forms unto themselves, defying ready classification. Having found the quotation, for example, the average user is satisfied and does not want to go to the source, as he or she might do when using the standard index to materials in collections. Be that as it may, a frequent question in any library is either, Who said the following? or What do you have in the way of a quote by or about X subject? Any of the standard books of quotations may provide the answer. "May" is used here advisedly, for frequently the quotation is not found in any of the standard sources, either because it is so unusual or, more than likely, because it is garbled. When the patron is not certain about the actual wording, another approach is by subject.

Still, there are times when nothing seems to work, when no source turns up the quote. It is no accident that *RQ*, the American Library Association's official journal for reference librarians, frequently publishes quotes which stump readers, i.e., librarians. For example: "Let us hear no more of trust in men. Let us bind them down with the chains of the Constitution." It was used in a letter to the editor of one of Atlanta's newspapers (unable to verify) and was (incorrectly?) attributed to Thomas Jefferson or Alexander Hamilton.[13]

---

[12]Saul Bellow, *Him With His Foot in His Mouth* (New York: Harper and Row, Publishers, 1984, pp. 57–58).

[13]"The Exchange," *RQ*, Summer 1984, p. 393. Answers, when found, appear in later issues of *RQ*. At times, however, no answer is published because, as the example suggests, the quote is so garbled and out of context that it can't be found in any book of quotations.

Some quotations are so common that it is difficult to say just who said it first. For example, W. C. Fields is credited by Bartlett's for having said "Anyone who hates children and dogs can't be all bad." This was in 1939. But now it is found that someone else, two years earlier, said much the same thing.[14] Previous citations continue to plague compilers.

By far the most famous book of quotations is Bartlett (as *Familiar Quotations* is often called). A native of Plymouth, Massachusetts, John Bartlett was born in 1820 and at sixteen was employed by the owner of the University Bookstore in Cambridge. By the time he owned the store, he had become famous for his remarkable memory, and the word around Harvard was, "Ask John Bartlett." He began a notebook which expanded into the first edition of his work in 1855. After the Civil War, he joined Little, Brown and Company, and he continued to edit his work through nine editions until his death in December 1905.

The work is updated about every 10 to 12 years, and the fifteenth edition, published in 1980, includes more than 450 new authors. Most of these are contemporary and, thanks to a famous word or two, have made their way to fame in the standard work. A few are historical and represent a new look at history; e.g., the fifteenth edition has several more representatives of the early women's movement than has the fourteenth. The total is now some 2500 individuals including such new figures as Woody Allen, Pope John Paul II, and a late-comer, George Sand. The number of quotes is claimed to be near 23,000, or some 2500 more than the last edition. As with past efforts, the editors favor establishment figures; e.g., Milton Friedman has a solid page of quotes, but there are considerably briefer entries from Dorothy Parker, Mick Jagger, and the Beatles.

Although Bartlett and the other sources contain similar material, many quotation works are needed; often what will be found in one may not be found in the others.

The Oxford Dictionary of Quotations is another popular book of this type found in many libraries. The third edition represents the first substantial revision since the original 1941 publication, and of the three basic books of quotations, the Oxford has the advantage of being the most current. According to the admirably written preface, selection is based on what is most familiar to a majority of people—and in this case, while the bias is English, most of the quotations

[14]William Safire, "On Language," *The New York Times Magazine*, September 30, 1984, p. 14. Apparently, the sentiment was published in *Harper's Magazine* in November 1937 by one Cedric Worth.

represent a considerably more international tone and will be equally well known to educated Americans.

Briefly, the difference between Bartlett, Oxford, and Stevenson (a common identification of *The Home of Quotations, . . .*), aside from content, are:

1. *Arrangement* Stevenson is arranged alphabetically under subject. Bartlett is arranged chronologically by author. In this, Bartlett differs from almost every other anthology of quotations. Oxford is organized alphabetically by author.
2. *Index* All have thorough indexes by subject, author, and key words of the quotation or verses. Stevenson does not repeat the subject words employed in the main text in the index.
3. *Other features* Stevenson has brief biographical data on authors. Bartlett features helpful historical footnotes, sometimes tracing the original quotation normally associated with one individual back to another person or time. The Oxford has a separate Greek Index.

Each year seems to produce more compilations of quotations, most of which disappear without any great loss. Regardless of overall quality, many librarians prefer to collect such works because the quotation query is so popular and no one can ever be sure where a quotation may appear. Note, again, the difficult query section in each issue of *RQ*. A major part of each column consists of elusive quotations, which may be traced to an even more elusive book of quotations.

Examples of relatively new works might include: *The Travellers' Dictionary of Quotations,* (London: Routledge and Kegan Paul, Ltd., 1983, 1022 pp.), a collection of quotations from about the fifteenth century to the present. Arrangement is by country, with an index by author and place. The speaker might wish to turn to Gerald Lieberman's *3,500 Good Quotes for Speakers.* (New York: Doubleday and Company, 1983, 285 pp.), while libraries might want to add *The Oxford Book of Aphorisms* (New York: Oxford University Press, 1983, 383 pp.). Here the compiler, John Gross, divides the book into 58 subjects, but fails to offer a subject index.

SUGGESTED READING

"A Long Look at Quotation Books," *Booklist,* Reference Books Bulletin, November 1, 1985, pp. 383–387. In three parts. The first section gives an invaluable, albeit somewhat too long, evaluative guide for deciding on what book of quotations to purchase. The second part is a critical and descriptive annotated listing of works in the field. The article concludes with a excellent essay on related works, such as concordances and dictionaries.

Berman, Sanford (ed.), *Subject Cataloging: Critiques and Innovations.* New York: The Haworth Press, 1984. (Also published as vol. 2, no. 1 and 2, *Technical Services Quarterly.*) A collection of articles by Berman and others on the vagaries of subject headings and how they affect the access to materials.

Cornog, Martha, "A History of Indexing Techniques," *The Indexer,* April 1983, pp. 152–157. This is an exceptionally clear explanation of the various forms of indexes, as well as a brief history of how they developed. The author moves from fourteenth century subject indexes to citation indexing.

Fischer, Russell, "The Librarian as Entrepreneur," *Library Journal* September 15, 1985, pp. 47–50. The story of how a new index (*Microcomputer Index*) was developed. In the telling, the author touches on the problems of technology, organization and, to say the least, finance.

Hallman, Clark and Jean McGruer, "Local Periodical Indexes Provide Access to Regional Publications," *Reference Services Review,* Summer 1985, pp. 35–39. "Magazines and newsletters focusing on city, county, state, and regional concerns offer a remarkable amount of information." It is with these the authors are concerned. Good, practical advice is given on how to index such reference works.

Intner, Sheila, "Censorship in Indexing," *The Indexer,* October 1984, pp. 105–108. Just how much is hidden in an index due to poor indexing is discussed in terms of the content and structure of the index. The author calls for indexers to be more affirmative in their demands for good indexing.

McPheron, Elaine, "Dictionaries of Quotations: A Comparative Review," *Reference Services Review,* Winter 1984, pp. 21–31. A detailed study of nine basic quotation sources, with particular emphasis on Stevenson and Bartlett. The article is particularly helpful in the discussion of lesser known subject quotation sources and specialized works.

Poyer, Robert, "Time Lag in Four Indexing Services," *Special Libraries,* April 1982, pp. 142–146. In a study of four indexing services, the author explains a method of checking the "time lag between the publication of an article in a journal and its appearance in an (index)". He shows why it is important to understand the time lag in order to establish guidelines in setting up search strategies.

Rowley, Jennifer, "A Future for Printed Indexes?", *Aslib Proceedings,* May 1983, pp. 234–238. The author examines various types of indexes and how they are made available in both printed and online form. She concludes the printed index will continue, "but this does not automatically imply that the art of indexing will be maintained."

Wellisch, Hans, *Indexing and Abstracting 1977–1981,* Santa Barbara, California: American Bibliographical Center Clio, 1984. A listing of more than 1600 items, most of which are abstracted, this is the definitive bibliography for those seeking information on indexing. Coverage is international. See, too, the same author's/ publisher's earlier bibliography (1980) which covers the early literature of indexing through 1976.

CHAPTER SIX

Indexing and Abstracting Services: Various Forms

So far we have considered only the general periodical index, but there are numerous other forms. Let us begin with the more specialized subject index. The natural progression from the general index to the subject index is direct when the user or the librarian has a question which is quickly associated with a particular subject and with an index. Yet it is not quite that simple. A high school student who asks for an article on the American Civil War should be referred to almost any year of *Readers' Guide*. The same student, or, for that matter, the teacher or subject expert, who is doing a detailed paper on the Civil War will require not only more periodicals likely to have such material, but sophisticated approaches. Then one might turn to several indexes, but more likely the one which concentrates on American history, i.e., *America: History and Life*. The subject indexes are of major importance in libraries, and it is with examples of these that the next section is concerned.

SUBJECT INDEXES

All of the following are published by The H. W. Wilson Company:

> *Humanities Index.* 1974 to date, quarterly. Service. (Wilsonline, $37 to $55 per hour.)
> *Social Sciences Index.* 1974 to date, quarterly. Service. (Wilsonline, $34 to $55 per hour.)

General Science Index. 1978 to date, monthly. Service. (Wilsonline, $34 to $55 per hour.)

The H. W. Wilson Company issues three indexes which bridge the general to the specific subject, edited specifically for the student, average public library user, and the nonexpert who wants more depth in a subject than found in the *Readers' Guide* but not as much specialization as in the subject indexes such as *Business Periodicals Index.*

The *Humanities Index* analyzes 294 English-language periodicals. The single index is by subject and author, with the usual section for book reviews. It has several unique features: (1) Opera and film reviews are listed under appropriate subject headings, i.e., "opera reviews" and "motion picture reviews"; (2) poems may be located both by the author's name and under a section, "poems"; (3) the same procedure is followed for short stories; and (4) there is a section for theatre reviews. Given these divisions, the work is valuable for checking current critical thought on a wide variety of subjects in the humanities—here taken to mean archaeology and classical studies, folklore, history, language and literature, literary and political criticism, performing arts, philosophy, religion and theology, and, according to the publisher, "related subjects."

The *Social Sciences Index* covers about 307 English-language periodicals in anthropology, area studies, psychology, public administration, sociology, environmental science, economics, and related areas. There are author and subject entries with a separate section for book reviews.

The *General Science Index* completes The H. W. Wilson Company semi-subject approach to general indexing. It is an effort to be more popular than their *Applied Science and Technology Index,* more specialized than what is found in Readers' Guide. About 111 English-language general science periodicals are indexed by subject. As in the *Applied Science and Technology Index,* there is *no* author approach other than in the citations to book reviews, which are listed by authors of the books. The subject headings are selected for the nonspecialist, and where specialized subjects are employed, there are adequate cross-references. Fields covered range from astronomy to zoology.

Specific subject indexes

All of the following are published by The H. W. Wilson Company. All are available on Wilsonline at various charges ranging from $25 to $65 per hour.

Applied Science and Technology Index. 1958 to date, monthly. Service.

Art Index. 1929 to date, quarterly. Service.

Biological and Agricultural Index. 1964 to date, monthly. Service.

Business Periodicals Index. 1958 to date, monthly. Service.

Education Index. 1929 to date, monthly. Service.

Index to Legal Periodicals. 1908 to date, monthly. $140.

Library Literature. 1934 to date, bimonthly. Service.

The following are non-Wilson Company publications:

Public Affairs Information Service Bulletin. New York: Public Affairs Information Service, 1915 to date, twice each month, including cumulations and annual. Rates on request. (DIALOG File 49, $60 per hour)

Hispanic American Periodicals Index (HAPI). Los Angeles: University of California, 1974 to date, annual, $100.

Index to Periodicals By and About Blacks. Boston: G. K. Hall, 1950 to date, annual $68.

The Business Index. Los Altos, California: Information Access Corporation, 1979 to date, monthly, $1860. (DIALOG file 148, "Trade & Industry Index," $85 per hour)

Canadian Business Index. (CBI) Toronto: Micromedia, 1975 to date, monthly, $850. For smaller libraries, $275–$400. (QL File)

Predicasts F & S Index. Cleveland, Ohio: Predicasts. (DIALOG files 98 (1972–1978); file 18, (1979 +), $90 per hour.)

. . . *United States.* 1960 to date, monthly, quarterly, and annual cumulations. $540.

. . . *Europe.* 1979 to date, monthly, quarterly, and annual cumulations. $540.

. . . *International.* 1967 to date, monthly, quarterly, and annual cumulations. $540.

Canadian Education Index. Toronto: Canadian Education Association, 1965 to date, three issues per year including annual cumulation, $140.

The basic subject indexes found in most American and Canadian libraries are published by The H. W. Wilson Company, and follow much the same format and approach as do Wilson's aforementioned general indexes. There are several hundred subject indexes and abstracting services from other publishers. They concentrate on more specialized areas than those covered in the Wilson entries.

When considering subject indexes, three facts must be kept in mind:

1. Many are broader in coverage than is indicated by such key title words as "Art" or "Education." Related fields are often considered. Therefore, anyone doing a subject analysis in depth often should consult indexes which take in fringe-area topics.
2. Most of the subject indexes are not confined solely to magazines. They often include books, monographs, bulletins, and even government documents.
3. A great number are not parochial but international in scope. True, not many foreign-language works are listed, but anything in English is usually noted, even if issued abroad.

Because of this wider base of coverage, many libraries are doubtful about including such indexes. What good is it to find a particular article in a specialized journal and then be unable to obtain the journal? The library should be in a position either to borrow the journal or to have a copy made of the article. If it is not, it had better look to improving its services. Also, even without the pertinent items indexed, the indexes do serve to give readers a broader view of the topic than they might get from only a general index.

There is little point in describing each of the Wilson subject indexes. For the most part, their titles explain their scope and purpose. The user may be either the specialist or the generalist—journals and periodicals for both are indexed. Most indexed titles are American, but there are representative selections from other countries in other languages. The number of works indexed ranges from 185 to over 300.

The approach in all the Wilson indexes is much the same; that is, the author and subject entries are in a single alphabet and there are the usual excellent cross-references. (Some indexes, such as the *Applied Science and Technology Index,* have only a subject approach.) Subject headings are frequently revised, and in most services, book reviews are listed in a separate section. Each index has its peculiarities, but a reading of the prefatory material in each will clarify the finer points.

Applied Science and Technology Index is complemented by the *General Science Index* and *Biological and Agricultural Index.* The index analyzes about 336 English-language periodicals by subject. In addition to the sciences, it covers such areas as transportation, food, and a wide variety of engineering titles. The *General Science Index* has been considered; the *Biological and Agricultural* work is different in that it is more subject-oriented than either of the others. Here emphasis is on 202 periodicals in biology and more detailed aspects of agriculture. The normal search pattern for anyone but a subject expert would be the *General Science Index* to the *Applied Science and Technology Index* to the last title.

There are several hundred, perhaps even a thousand, indexing and abstracting services in science, and almost every discipline and subsection of a scientific or technological area has its own service(s). The basic ones are considered in the second volume of the text, primarily because most of them are now in machine-readable form for online searches.

Art Index is the only one of its type in the Wilson family, although numerous art titles are covered in the *Humanities Index*. It indexes more than 230 periodicals, yearbooks, and museum publications. The definition of "art" is broad and includes areas from films and photography to architecture and landscape design.

Business Periodicals Index covers 304 titles with indexed items by subject, not by author. Subjects are so all-inclusive as to make this almost a general index, and it is used as such by librarians who cannot find enough material in the basic services. For example, one may be looking for an article on reading and television, only to find that an analysis of the subject (from the point of view of sales of books and television sets) has been indexed in *Business Periodicals Index* although hardly considered in the more likely *Library Literature*. Still, the index is used primarily for finance, business technology, and economics.

Index to Legal Periodicals may be used in connection with a business query. It offers access to material in almost 460 publications. It differs from many of the other indexes in that it analyzes books, yearbooks, annual institutes' publications, and the like. It has the standard subject and author index but adds an index for law cases, and case notes are found at the end of many subject headings. While a good deal of this is technical, the careful librarian will find material here which is equally suitable for the involved layperson, and it can be of considerable help in almost any field which is remotely connected with the law or a legal decision.

Education Index covers material in 354 publications, and while it concentrates on periodicals, it does analyze some books, reports, and the like. All aspects of education are considered, and numerous allied fields are touched upon, such as language and linguistics and library science. It has a strong competitor in *Current Index to Journals in Education,* which is considered in the next section.

Library Literature offers a subject and author entry to articles which have appeared in about 190 library-oriented periodicals. As with other specialized Wilson indexes, the contents of books are analyzed as are reports, pamphlets, etc., which relate to library science. It gives the librarian a fairly complete view of the subject field, albeit because of its publication schedule, *Library Literature* lags at least three months, often up to six months behind, in its indexing.

Of added help, although rarely any more current, are two other services: (1) *Library and Information Science Abstracts* (London: Library Association, 1969 to date, bimonthly). Whereas *Library Literature* is in the traditional alphabetical subject-author arrangement, the abstracting service depends on a classification system for the arrangement of material. Some 400 journals are indexed, and the service abstracts selected reports, theses, and other monographs. The number of abstracts now runs to well over 4000 each year. There is an excellent coverage of U.S. Government Reports, primarily because the National Technical Information Service of the U.S. now allows LISA to reprint its abstracts. There are similar arrangements with other groups which account for the increased number of abstracts each year. The service is available online (DIALOG File 61).

An even more sophisticated approach is offered in (2) *Information Science Abstracts* (Philadelphia: Documentation Abstracts, Inc., 1966 to date, bimonthly). The emphasis is on technical periodicals, books, reports, proceedings, and similar materials. And of the some 4500 abstracts issued each year, a vast proportion deal with aspects of automation, communication, computers, mathematics, artificial intelligence, and so on. It is a service particularly suited to the needs of the researcher and the librarian in a large system. Arranged under broad subject headings, the abstracts are well-written and complete. Each issue has an author index, and there is an annual subject index.

Non-Wilson Indexes

One non-Wilson subject index which is found in most libraries is the *Public Affairs Information Service Bulletin.* This has the advantage of relative currency. The *Bulletin* (or PAIS, as it is usually called) is issued twice each month. Coverage is primarily of material in political science, government, legislation, economics, and sociology. Periodicals, government documents, pamphlets, reports, and some books in such areas as government, public administration, international affairs, and economics are indexed. About 1400 journals and some

6000 other items (from books to reports) are indexed each year. Valuable additions are a "Key to Periodical References" and a list of "Publications Analyzed." Both serve as a handy checklist and buying guide for the library.

While works analyzed are limited to those in English, coverage is international. Arrangement is alphabetical, primarily by subject. A few of the entries have brief descriptive notes on both contents and purpose. Beginning in 1972, PAIS issued a second index, *Foreign Language Index,* which offers much the same service as the *Bulletin.* Here about 400 journals are indexed along with 2000 non-journal items. The essential difference is that the quarterly index considers the same subject areas in a number of foreign-language journals, books, reports, pamphlets, and the like. Online the two are combined and called *PAIS International.*

Indexes directed to geographical areas and ethnic groups are still another form of the ubiquitous subject approach. The *Hispanic American Periodicals Index* examines about 250 periodicals, most of which are published in Latin America, or by Latin American groups in the United States. While popular magazines are not included, the representative group of other titles more than indicates trends and ideas in Latin America and among Hispanics living in the United States.

One problem with annual indexes is that they are at least one year, and sometimes two or even three years behind. For example, the 1981 edition of *Index to Periodical Articles By and About Blacks* did not come out until 1984. Lack of finance accounts for the delay, particularly as most of these indexes must rely on volunteer, or less than well-paid, part-time indexers. At any rate, there are 32 popular and scholarly titles indexed in the service for those serving a black community. Another index in this same area: *The Afro-American Studies Index.* (Chicago: Center for Afro-American Studies, 1982 to date, annual). This covers more periodicals (about 44 to 50), and selectively indexes material of interest from about 200 non-black titles. Unfortunately, it, too, is lagging behind by several years.

The *Business Index* is a specialized version of the *Magazine Index.* It comes with a reader and a monthly update on computer output microfilm. Some 810 periodicals are indexed, as well as major books noted, and there is cover-to-cover indexing of *The Wall Street Journal, Barrons,* and the business section of *The New York Times.* Brief annotations are usually included where needed. It is used just like the *Magazine Index,* but for those who wish to refresh their memories, there is a detailed set of instructions both at the beginning and the end of the file.

As with its companion, *The Magazine Index,* it has the advantage of being updated once a month and allowing the user to search three years of indexing at one place. The disadvantage is that it only goes back three years, and for retrospective materials one must look elsewhere, i.e., in The H. W. Wilson *Business Periodicals Index.*

The *Canadian Business Index* (formerly *The Canadian Business Periodicals Index*) is a monthly analysis of 170 periodicals and newspapers published in Canada. Aside from the usual subject arrangement, there is a personal name and corporate name index. Few of the titles indexed here are found in the American indexes. The service is available online through QUIC Law System (QL) of Canada and DIALOG (as part of Canadian Business and Current Affairs, DIALOG File 262).

The *Predicasts F & S* (Funk & Scott) indexes cover the United States, Europe, and International (i.e., all other countries not found in the first two series). Each work is arranged in a similar fashion and covers the same basic type of data. Here one finds current information on individual corporations, industries and products. Each indexes about 750 different periodicals, newspapers, and reports. (These are designated in the front of the issue.) The basic arrangement and method of use is similar in all of the services.

The first section, "Industries and Products," is a subject-heading approach to a wide variety of topics, from population to energy. Groupings are in a hierarchical system, and automotive brakes, for example, is a subgroup of motor vehicle parts. Fortunately, the major subject divisions are given in alphabetical order in the cumulative alphabetical guide—and each issue has an "Alphabetical Guide to the SIC Code" which allows ready access to the Industry & Product section. Also, there is a "user's guide" which clearly explains the arrangement.

The second part of the index is alphabetical by the name of the company, and where the company is vast, there are subheadings. This is easy to follow and presents no momentary problem as does the first section. There is another related service; this is the F & S *Predicasts Forecasts* which comes out quarterly and indexes journals, newspaper and other sources which publish trends about business and products.

Available both in print and online, the index is timely and about as basic for business information as any index. It is a starting point for a serious query concerning business or economics, and particularly for data on a special industry, corporation, company, and so on.

The *Canadian Education Index* covers both English and French publications and indexes about 230 periodicals. Also books, reports and other materials dealing with education are analyzed. The author/ subject index covers materials only which relate to Canadian educational activities. There is a list of French subject headings with the English language equivalents.

While technically one should classify the *Catholic Periodical and Literature Index* (Haverford, Pennsylvania: Catholic Library Association, 1930 to date, bimonthly. Service.) as a religious index, actually it is much broader in scope. It indexes by author, subject, and title approximately 160 periodicals, most of which are Catholic, although they vary widely as to editorial content. In fact, many of the titles could be classified as general magazines. Also, the index includes analyses of books by and about Catholics. There are sections for book reviews, movie reviews, and theater criticism. Although this is of limited value in many libraries, it should be a consideration for public and college libraries serving a Catholic population.

ABSTRACTING SERVICES

Although subject indexes are much-used, abstracting services are preferable because (1) they include a brief summary of the contents of an article, book, report, and so on, allowing the librarian to decide whether or not to read the entire document; and (2) arrangement is normally more complex and, as such, favors the needs of the subject expert. On the other hand, as they do require abstracts, the services tend to take longer to publish and may be later than the normal index—though this is not always the case.

By the mid-1980s, abstracting seemed to be moving from the specialized to the general, i.e., The H. W. Wilson Company's offer of abstracts for *The Readers' Guide* and the promise of abstracts for additional indexes from the same publisher. The use of computers for indexing now makes it much more feasible to employ abstracts, if only of a limited scope. One may envisage the day, in the not too distant future, when all major indexes will offer abstracts.

Representative abstracting services

Psychological Abstracts. Washington, D.C.: American Psychological Association, Inc., 1927 to date, monthly. $600. (DIALOG file 11, $65 per hour.)

America: History and Life: Part A, Article Abstracts and Citations. Santa Barbara, California: American Bibliographical Center-

Clio Press, 1964. Seven issues per year. Service. (Dialog file 38, $65 per hour.)

Dissertations Abstracts International. Ann Arbor, Michigan, 1938 to date, monthly. $140 per section.

a) *Comprehensive Dissertation Index.* Ann Arbor, Michigan, 1973 to date, annual. Inquire. (The basic set covers 1861–1972. There is a ten-year cumulation (38 vols.) for 1973 to 1982.) (DIALOG file 35, $55 per hour.)

These three abstracting services are representative of what is available in the humanities, science, and the social sciences. More technical scientific abstracts and indexes are considered in the second volume of this text.

Psychological Abstracts is familiar to many people, primarily because, as with a few other subject abstracting services (such as *Resources in Education*), it can be used in related areas of interest. For example, an important section concerns communication which, in turn, includes abstracts on language, speech, literature, and even art. Anyone involved with, say, the personality of an engineer or an artist would turn here, as would the better-educated layperson seeking information on everything from why a companion talks in his or her sleep to learning about why people do or do not read.

The abstracts are arranged under 16 broad subject categories from physiological intervention to personality. This allows the busy user to glance quickly at a subject area of interest without being bothered by unrelated topics. As a guide to the less experienced, there is an author and a brief subject index in each issue. The subject approach is expanded and modified in the cumulative indexes published twice a year. (When in doubt about a subject, turn first to the cumulation, not the individual issues.)

The service indexes over 1000 periodicals, as well as a group of selected books, reports, studies, etc. There are about 2500 abstracts in each monthly issue. As in most services of this type the abstracts are *not* cumulative, only the index.

The online version goes back to records from 1967 to date. In an effort to attract online users, the online service as of 1980 contains more references than the printed version.

America: History and Life, Part A, Article Abstracts and Citations covers articles on U.S. and Canadian history in 2000 scholarly journals throughout the world. Approximately 5000 to 6000 abstracts are published each year, as well as about the same number of brief descriptions from local and specialist historical publications. The classified arrangement ends with a subject and author index. The "subject profile index" expands the subject approach to the classified abstracts in four areas: subject, geography, biography, and chronology. An article on Cornwallis's campaign for Virginia, for example, would be listed as follows: subject: Revolutionary War; biography: Cornwallis; geography: Virginia; chronology: 1781. Under these and other headings, the article analyzed appears in the subject index an average of four or five times, providing insurance against a user's not finding a work.

Part B is *Index to Book Reviews* (covering over 100 scholarly U.S. and Canadian journals of history); Part C is *American History Bibliography (Books, Articles and Dissertations);* Part D is *Annual Index.* The whole series is often simply called *America: History and Life.* All three are available on the online database.

Historical Abstracts has been issued by the same publisher since 1955, and the quarterly follows the same organizational pattern as *America: History and Life.* Here, all aspects of world history are considered, first generally and then by topic, and finally by area of the world and country. About 2000 journals, books and other related materials are abstracted each year.

Most abstracting services not only analyze periodicals and books but often include dissertations. However, only the *Dissertations Abstracts International* concentrates exclusively on the form—a form which covers all disciplines and interests. Dissertations are important for the reference librarian seeking specific, often unpublished, information about a given subject, place, or person. Since most dissertations contain extensive bibliographies and footnotes, they can be used as unofficial bibliographies for some relatively narrow areas. Before a librarian begins a broad search for bibliographies in any area, these lists should be checked. There is a good chance that some student has already completed the bibliography sought or at least has done enough work to indicate other major sources.

A problem with dissertations is that most libraries will not lend them. Policy differs, but the excuse for not lending is that (1) there is only one copy and it cannot be replaced or (2) a microfilm copy may be purchased from University Microfilms, who just happens to publish the index. The second explanation is most often the case, and today a library requiring a dissertation must usually purchase the microfilm or a printout copy at a slight additional cost.

How does one trace the dissertation? The answer is twofold. The first place to go is *Comprehensive Dissertation Index.* The index set is divided into the sciences, social sciences, and humanities, and each of these broad categories has subdivision, for example, biological sciences, chemistry, and engineering. One locates the volume(s) likely to cover the subject and then turns to the finer subject heading where one will find a list of dissertations by full title and name of the author. Entry is possible by author too; i.e., the final volumes of the main set and the supplement are author index volumes.

After each entry there is a citation to *Dissertation Abstracts,* where the librarian then turns for the full abstract. The citation refers one to the volume and page number in *Dissertation Abstracts.* For example, in the index one finds "Defining the Roles of Library/Media Personnel . . ." the author's name, degree-granting university, number of pages, and then: 43/06A, p. 1733. The reference is to vol. 43, no. 06A of *Dissertation Abstracts,* on page 1733. This becomes confusing, because on the spine of the volume there is the notation for the volume/number (43/06) and then numbers (1322A–2135A) which are the inclusive page numbers. Once the number system is understood it is easy enough to use.

Dissertation Abstracts International is a separate set from the index, but is issued by the same publisher. Like the index, it appears in three parts. Until the annual index is issued, the monthly issues of *Dissertation Abstracts* must be searched individually. Each of the three sections has its own index. It is published monthly, and the arrangement by broad subject headings and then by narrow subject areas is similar to that of the index. Each entry includes a full abstract.

ERIC/IR: Specialized information service

U.S. Educational Resources Information Center. *Resources in Education.* Washington: Government Printing Office, 1966 to date, monthly. $70. (DIALOG file 1, $25 per hour.)

Current Index to Journals in Education. Phoenix, Arizona: Oryx Press, 1969 to date, monthly, semiannual cumulations. $115. (DIALOG file 1, $25 per hour.)

Many of the current abstracting and indexing services are only one part of fuller information systems which not only publish indexes and abstracts, but offer other services. This may be illustrated by ERIC/IR, or, in full, Educational Resources Information Center/ (Clearinghouse for) Information Resources. The system includes (1) an index and an abstracting service available both in printed form and on database for online retrieval; (2) an ongoing subject vocabulary, represented in the frequently updated *Thesaurus of ERIC Descriptors;* (3) a dissemination system which depends primarily on reproducing the material indexed on microfiche and distributing that microfiche to libraries; and (4) a decentralized organizational structure for acquiring and processing the documents which are indexed and abstracted.

The first abstract part of ERIC is *Resources in Education,* which lists reports and associated items and includes for each a narrative abstract of 200 or fewer words. The abstracts are written by the authors. Approximately 400 to 500 reports are submitted to ERIC each month, but at least 50 percent are rejected, often as much for lack of typing skills as for content. The reports have to be reproduced on microfiche and if not typed properly cannot be properly reproduced, hence rejection. Selection is made at one of 16 clearinghouses —each considers only a particular subject and has experts able to evaluate the submitted material.

The actual type of material includes research and technical reports (about one-third); published proceedings, dissertations, preprints and papers presented at a conference; and another one-third consists of curriculum guides, educational legislation, lesson plans, and the like. The key to access includes both a subject and an author index as well as an index by institution. The index is cumulated semiannually and annually.

The second method of tapping ERIC is through *Current Index to Journals in Education.* This is an index to some 775 periodicals in education, which results in about 1700 citations each month. Although published by a commercial firm, the indexing is provided by the 16 clearinghouses. The first part of the index is much like *Resources in Education* in form; that is, items are abstracted and arranged numerically by the accession number. The second part is the subject index, which, again, follows the style of *Resources in Education.* There are also an author index and a fourth section in which the indexed journals are arranged alphabetically by title, and the table of contents for each is given, with accession numbers for articles.

One outstanding feature of ERIC, although a usual one among similar documentation systems such as that developed by the National Aeronautics and Space Administration, is that some 80 percent of the documents abstracted in *Resources in Education* are available on microfiche. In most large libraries, the user finds the required citation in *Resources in Education* and then, instead of laboriously looking for the item abstracted, simply turns to the microfiche collection, where the items are arranged by accession number. This, then, is a total information system and not the normal two-step bibliographical reference quest in which one finds the abstract or the indexed item and then must try to find the document, journal, book, or what have you, which the library may or may not have available.

Ideally, the total information system would be offered with the second ERIC finding tool, *Current Index to Journals in Education.* It is not. Why? Because here the index and abstracts are for journal articles, and the journals themselves have to be searched. The cost of putting each article on a microfiche card, not to mention copyright problems with publishers, makes the cost of a total information service prohibitive. This may change as more indexing concerns, such as the publishers of *Magazine Index,* not only make the full text available on microfiche, but online. This is discussed in detail in the second volume of the text.

At the same time, the publishers state "that reprints of articles included in approximately 65 percent of the journals covered in CIJE are available from University Microfilms." One knows whether or not a reprint is available, because "Reprint:UMI" is after each citation where the service may be employed. Ordering information is given in the front of each issue.

Many indexes and abstracting services offer this retrieval of articles, and some of these are discussed in the second volume of this text. For the time being, suffice it to say that in an effort to get around the problem of finding the article after the citation is located, the movement is toward quick document delivery at the computer terminal. (1) The librarian may order the article at the terminal from the publisher or from a representative of the publisher—usually the latter. The publisher can have the article in the mail within 24 hours. (2) Full text of the article may be viewed online, i.e., one can read the article at the computer terminal and have printed out what is needed. This, as indicated, is the trend. (3) Telefacsimile (an old procedure) is another option by which the required article is requested on the computer, and then later sent and printed out where needed. This has numerous problems, from speed of transmission (it has been slow and uneconomical) to quality of the printout.

INDEXES TO CURRENT EVENTS

In any reference library, one of the most time-consuming, sometimes futile, types of search is for current material on recent events. How is one to answer the question concerning a presidential appointment of a week or a month ago, trace current sporting records, or find information on a prominent woman who died only last week?

The first general index source is *The Readers' Guide to Periodical Literature* which is issued every two weeks and may be no more than four to six weeks behind in actually indexing some current news periodicals. A subject rather than a general aid, with somewhat more of a time lag, is the semimonthly *Public Affairs Information Service Bulletin.*

The natural inclination is to turn to a newspaper index. This is of limited use, because the standard print indexes are several months behind. There are two exceptions: (1) the *National Newspaper Index* (to be discussed shortly) is on a microfilm roll and is updated once a month. However, this is so expensive as to be out of the question for most libraries. (2) *The New York Times,* as well as several other indexes, is available for online searches. Here the material is updated once each week, with really current headlines updated every 24 hours. Cost may be prohibitive for all but the largest of libraries.

Of these two answers to the problem of recency, the online service is the most satisfactory. This is the direction in which the long-term solution to data on current events is going. In the library, in private and government organizations, the computer terminal is used more and more to find data which are no more than a few hours or a few days old. One of the great blessings of the new technology is its ability, given enough funding, to short-circuit the long delays associated with printed indexes and abstracting services.

Lacking a computer terminal, how does one locate material published yesterday, or a week or a month ago, if the average index is so far behind or so expensive? There are several approaches: (1) The least satisfactory is simply to go through current issues of magazines related to the subject or to examine the latest issues of newspapers. (2) A somewhat more rewarding step is to consult the weekly summaries of events, such as *Facts on File,* which, if nothing more, give the date of the event. (3) One may consult with the local newspaper, radio, or television news bureau. There is always the "expert" in the community who may have exactly the information needed. (4) The last suggestion, and ultimately the best solution of all, is for the librarian to keep advised of current events by careful reading of at least one newspaper each day and the weekly news magazines, and also to keep an ear open for community events. Obviously the "one" newspaper should include the local publication(s), and, where possible, the closest thing we have to a national newspaper, i.e., *The New York Times.*

Sources for last week's events

Facts on File, A Weekly World News Digest, with Cumulative Index. New York: Facts on File, Inc., 1940 to date, weekly. $385. (DIALOG File 264, $60.)

Keesing's Contemporary Archives. London: Longman Group Ltd., 1931 to date, monthly. $180.

Canadian News Index. Toronto: Micromedia, 1977 to date,

monthly. $850 with lower rates ($275–$400) for smaller librar-
ies. (QL File).
Canadian News Facts. Toronto: Marpep Publishing, 1967 to date,
biweekly, $200.

Essentially, these loose-leaf binder services are objective summaries of the events of the past week or month. They may be used to
quickly locate a fact, a date, or a name. Unfortunately, while at one
time, two were weekly, now only *Facts on File* maintains this schedule.
The result is that the others are at least six weeks or more in arrears of
the actual event.

Of all the services, *Facts on File* is the most prompt (the U.S. mails
permitting), and normally only a few days elapse between the last date
covered and receipt of the publication. Emphasis is on news events in
the United States, with international coverage related for the most
part to American affairs. Material is gathered mainly from 50 major
newspapers and magazines, and condensed into objective, short,
factual reports. The twice-monthly, blue-colored index is arranged
under four primary headings: "U.S. Affairs," "International Affairs,"
"World News" and "Miscellaneous." Then, under these one finds
broad subject headings, such as "Finance," "Economics," and so on.
This a bit confusing, but, fortunately, every two weeks, each month,
and then quarterly and annually, a detailed index is issued which
covers previous issues. There is also a *Five-Year Master News Index,*
published since 1950.

The subject index (which includes numerous names of people in
the news) features the brief tag line name of the item and then
reference to the date of the event, the page in the issue of *Facts on File,*
as well as the margin letter and column number. For example, under
Afghanistan, one finds, "Govt ldrs listed 1–21 (date, January 21, 1984)
177 (page number) B1 (the letter on the margin of p. 177 and the first
column).

The publisher notes a "few ways" the service may be used: Check
dates in the index, skim the weekly issues to prepare for current
affairs tests, read Supreme Court decisions in the Digest, or scan the
"U.S. and World Affairs" column for ideas for short papers. And
there are countless other uses, although the most frequent call is for
specific current data.

In *Keesing's Contemporary Archives,* emphasis differs from *Facts on
File* in two important respects. The scope is primarily the United
Kingdom, Europe, and the British Commonwealth. Detailed subject
reports in certain areas are frequently included (the reports are by
experts and frequently delay the weekly publication by several days),

as are full texts of important speeches and documents. However, *Keesing's* does not cover in any detail many ephemeral events, such as sports, art exhibitions, and movies, which may be included in *Facts on File*. Arrangement is by country, territory, or continent, with some broad subject headings, such as "Religion," "Aviation," and "Fine Arts." Every second week, an index is issued which is cumulated quarterly and annually.

Following much the same procedure and format as *Facts on File*, *Canadian News Facts* differs in its scope and its frequency; it appears every two weeks rather than weekly. The news digests average eight pages, and are concerned almost exclusively with Canada. Arrangement is by large areas (Africa South of the Sahara; Americas—Caribbean, etc.) and then subdivided by country. International developments, and particularly activities of the United Nations, are covered. There are some broad subject headings by topic, such as Fine Arts. There are three indexes each year. Two are published every four months, with the last index cumulating the first. The annual index is published during the first quarter of the following year. Unfortunately, except for the table of contents in the monthly numbers, the monthly index is sparse and not detailed enough for fine reference work, although it is cumulative until a mid-year index is issued.

Newspaper indexes

> *The New York Times Index.* New York: The New York Times, 1851 to date, semimonthly, with quarterly and annual cumulations. $425. (NEXIS, $80 to $100 per hour.)
>
> *The National Newspaper Index.* Los Altos, California: Information Access Corporation, 1979 to date, monthly. $1880. (DIALOG file 111, $75 per hour.)
>
> *Canadian News Index.* Toronto: Micromedia, 1977 to date, monthly. $850, with lower rates ($275–$400) for smaller libraries. (QL File).

Only a decade or so ago there were few national newspaper indexes. Today the number is increasing for two reasons: (1) There is an urgent need and demand for facts which are current (less than a day or two old) and found in national newspapers. (2) The computer has allowed rapid processing and availability of the index at a terminal.

The computer has revolutionized both the number and the types of newspaper indexes. Before the introduction of the computer, there was only one well-known national newspaper index, and that was to *The New York Times.* At the same time there were and are some 500 to 700 local indexes, i.e., those maintained by the local newspaper, or the library. Today, thanks to the speed and the efficiency of computer storage and read-outs, all large newspapers are nationally indexed. In addition, all are available on microfilm.

If anything, there is now an overabundance of indexing, as well as considerable duplication. For example, one may access *The New York Times* via its own printed index, as well as through *The National Newspaper Index,* and online through NEXIS and Dialog. There are at least two to four individual access points as well to *The Wall Street Journal, The Washington Post* and *The Christian Science Monitor.* Each online index service varies—from one offering full text printouts online to another with little more than a brief subject approach to news items.

These multiple access points to newspapers has made it exceedingly easy to find out-of-the-way material on current affairs from every part of the United States, if not the world. The problem, at least for those without access to up-to-date online services, is that most of the newspaper indexes in printed form lag one to three months behind the newspaper which is indexed. Despite improved computer composition and printouts, the time gap is such that none of them really can be used for current reference work. Here one must resort to periodicals and weekly and biweekly indexes. Still, as technology improves there is every reason to believe the majority of newspaper indexes will be issued weekly, and be current. As of now this still has yet to happen.

No matter what its form, the best-known newspaper index in the United States is the one published by *The New York Times.* A distinct advantage of *The New York Times Index* is its wide scope and relative completeness. Although the United States does not have a truly national newspaper, the *Times,* in its effort to cover all major news events, both national and international, comes close to being a daily national newspaper. The *Times Index* provides a wealth of information and frequently is used even without reference to the individual paper of the date cited. Each entry includes a brief abstract of the news story. Consequently, someone seeking a single fact, such as the name of an official, the date of an event, or the title of a play, may often find all that is needed in the index. Also, since all material is dated, the *Times Index* serves as an entry into other, unindexed newspapers and magazines. For example, if the user is uncertain of the day ship X sank and wishes to see how the disaster was covered in another newspaper or in a magazine, the *Times Index* will narrow the search by providing the date the event occurred.

The New York Times Index is arranged in dictionary form with sufficient cross references to names and related topics. Events under each of the main headings are arranged chronologically. Book and theater reviews are listed under those respective headings.

Some libraries subscribe only to the annual cumulated *Index.* This volume serves as an index and guide to the activities of the previous year. Thanks to the rather full abstracts, maps, and charts, one may use the cumulated volume as a reference source in itself. The annual cumulation is fine, but it is late; normally it is published from six to seven months after the end of the year.

Currency is the major difficulty. The twice-a-month issues do not appear in a library for two to three months after the period indexed. The situation is not likely to improve, although the online service for the index offers 24-hour and one-week indexing of the same material.

The modern index dates only from about 1913 to the present. The earlier indexes, which begin on September 18, 1851, present problems in terms of alphabetizing, location of the issue (date not given) by issue number, and there is a great variety on how other material is listed. A guide is badly needed, particularly to the first seven, erratic years of indexing.[1]

The New York Times online version is similar to the printed one, but with three important exceptions: (1) The information is updated daily, and one does not have to wait the usual two to three months for the printed index. (2) The user either may ask for the full entry, which normally includes an abstract, or (3) may call to see the full text of the story on the viewer screen and/or printed out.

The NEXIS system not only includes *The Times,* but selective indexing of ten other national newspapers and over 60 periodicals. (For further discussion of this, see NEXIS in the second volume of this text.)

Using an approach similar to that of the *Magazine Index,* the publishers of the *National Newspaper Index* offer the service on microfilm, which is updated once a month and loaded into a reader. Thanks to this system, it is not necessary to consult various volumes, supplements, and cumulations, as it is for *The New York Times Index.* In

---

[1]Douglas Shepard, "A Corrective Supplement to Morse's Guide to the Incomparable New York Times Index," *Reference Services Review,* October/December 1981, pp. 33–35. This is a detailed discussion of the early indexing.

addition to *The Times,* this service includes *The Wall Street Journal, The Christian Science Monitor, The Washington Post,* and *The Los Angeles Times.* A tremendous advantage is that one may search for one item in five newspapers at the same time, e.g., one can see how train wrecks, Giant Pandas, and sporting and political events are handled in all newspapers, not just a single one. The wide indexing makes it easier to locate hard-to-find items which may appear in only one of the newspapers.

The National Newspaper Index does not include the annotations found in *The New York Times,* but it does give the reader access to product evaluation, book reviews, and the like. The monthly *National Newspaper Index* compares with twice-a-month issues from *The New York Times,* but the important difference is that the monthly index is just that—up to date and not two to three months behind publishing schedule. The result, at least as of this writing, is that the *National Newspaper Index* is considerably more timely than its rival.

As with the *Magazine Index,* the newspaper index is available for search online; in fact, it can be searched in conjunction with the *Magazine Index,* so one looks for a subject not only in a newspaper but in a magazine. This service is called *NewsSearch.* The database gives access to four printed services: *The National Newspaper Index, Magazine Index, Legal Resource Index,* and *Management Contents.*

Most libraries offer access to the national newspapers on microform, although in the decades ahead this may be replaced by full text available online, as is the case today with several publications, including *The New York Times.* At any rate, it obviously is important that the microform or printout edition be the same as the one indexed. All of the indexes indicate which edition of a newspaper is used for indexing.[2] For example, in the instructions in the front of the *National Newspaper Index* there is an explanation of the symbols employed to show whether the edition is national, or late city, or . . .. *The New York Times* has a similar explanation for various regional editions.

It is wise, too, to become familiar with other abbreviations. All are explained in each index. *The New York Times,* for example, indicates the length (and importance) of a story by simply labeling each item with one of three initials: (L) for a long story; (M) for a medium length story; and (S) for a short piece.

[2]This is really not a problem for most libraries as the index and the microfilm are closely linked by the publisher so that to use one is to find ready access to the other. The difficulty may arise when someone wishes to see a story which appeared in one edition, but not in another; or when someone requests a specific edition. Sources of the variable editions will be found in Antoinette Colbert's "Document Delivery," *Online,* January 1984, pp. 85–86.

The Canadian News Index offers access to the contents of seven national newspapers, including the Toronto Star and the Vancouver Sun. Divided into two sections, the index has personal names in one part and subjects in another. There are brief notes for stories where the content is not explained in the title. Published monthly, it tends to be relatively current.

CITATION INDEXING

The following are published by the Institute for Scientific Information, Philadelphia:

Social Sciences Citation Index, 1973 to date, three issues per year, including annual, $2300. (DIALOG File 7, $75 to $110 per hour.)

Science Citation Index, 1961 to date, six issues per year, including annual, $5527. (DIALOG Files 34, 94, and 186, $65 to $165 per hour.)

Arts & Humanities Citation Index, 1977 to date, three per year, including annual, $2200. (BRS File, AHCI)

Citation indexing is unique in that it employs a different approach. The avenue of access is through references cited in articles, hence the name of the service.

Each issue is in three parts:

1. The "Citation Index," which lists alphabetically by author each paper cited. The title(s) of the article(s) appears under the author's name, and beneath each article is a list of those who have cited the author's work. Most of the material is abbreviated.
2. The "Source Index," which gives standard bibliographic information for each of the papers in the "Citation Index."
3. The "Permuterm Subject Index," which indexes the articles by subject, i.e., by significant words in the title.

The uniqueness of this system, as opposed to other retrieval schemes, is that it is a network of connections between authors citing the same papers during a current year. In other words, if, in searching for particular subject matter, one has a key paper or review article in the field, or even in author's name, one consults the "Citation Index" by author. Beneath the author's name will be listed in chronological order *any* of his or her publications cited during a particular year, together with the *citing* authors (source items) who have referred to the particular work. If one continues to check the citing authors in the "Citation Index," a cyclical process takes place, often with mushrooming results. The "Source Index" is then used to establish the full bibliographic reference to the citing author.

Even without a citation index, the basic process of citations is familiar. Students who know, for example, that Collison is an expert on indexing, will look in X paper by Collison. There they find references to books, articles, reports, and the like. These citations, it can be safely assumed, have a certain relationship to indexing, and the searcher then chooses the citations which seem relevant and looks them up. The citations, in turn, cite other works, which the student may follow ad infinitum.

To describe the process in simple, metaphorical terms, friends attract other friends of similar disposition and background. In this case, articles attract other articles (via citations) of similar disposition and background. One friend may introduce you to five friends, who in turn will each introduce you to five friends, etc. One article will introduce you to five similar articles, each of which in turn may introduce you to five related articles, etc. This chain reaction is familiar to everyone.

A citation index has a major production advantage which makes it particularly suited for automation. Indexers do not have to be subject specialists, and there is no need to read the articles for subject headings. All the compiler must do is (1) enter the author, title, and full citation in machine-readable form and (2) list all the citations used in the primary article in order by author, title, and full citation in machine-readable form. As a consequence, a careful clerk may prepare material for the computer. This obviously speeds up indexing and also makes it possible to index considerably more material quickly.

The "Source Index" gives full bibliographic details of items listed. It is arranged by author. The "Permuterm Subject Index" is an alphabetically arranged KWIC-type index. Subjects are derived from words appearing in the titles of the source articles. Each significant word has been precoordinated with other terms to produce all possible permutations of terms.

The heart of the system is the "Citation Index," which lists authors alphabetically. It is assumed that the user (1) either knows the name of an author in the subject area of particular interest or (2) lacking the name of the author, finds the subject(s) in the "Permuterm

Subject Index" and from that finds the name of the author(s) for search in the "Citation Index."

A sample search, using the 1983 cumulative *Arts & Humanities Citation Index,* might go like this: (1) I am looking for someone who cited W. H. Auden's poem, "Age of Anxiety." Turn to Auden, W. H. in the citation index. Here poems and other works by him which are cited, are listed under his name. For the question, one finds a single name, i.e., Lehman D., *Shenandoah,* (volume 33, page 73, for 1982). (2) One then turns to the "Source Index" to find the full entry for Lehman. Under his name one finds numerous articles, but the librarian is looking for the key, i.e., *Shenandoah* magazine. When that is found, then one is given the full entry, including the name of the article, the total pages and how many references were cited. Beneath the title of the piece are the references in alphabetical order, and here we find Auden's "Age of Anxiety." One need now only turn to the article for more on the poem and on Auden.

Let's say the librarian wants something on book auctions, but does not have the name of anyone who might be cited, i.e., any expert's name to check out in the "Citation Index." In this case, one turns to the "Permuterm Subject Index." (1) Here, under "Auctions," one finds "Book" and two names, one of which is C. Sammons. (2) One turns to Sammons in the "Source Index" and finds an article "Book Auctions in the 17th century . . ." with, of course, the full citation to the journal in which the article appeared.

The multiple volumes make this a difficult set to use, which is all the more reason for its value as an online database. Here one may search for the cited author, and who did the citing, as well as the subject. The online result is much quicker than going through one or two or even three volumes. Also, when used only on occasion, the online index may be less expensive than the printed work.

Other disadvantages of the printed volumes are numerous: the high price, the reliance on type so small that it makes classified-ad-size type look gigantic, and confusing abbreviations. The most serious drawback is the lack of controlled vocabulary; where subject is an approach, there is total dependence on words in the title. This may work well enough in science, but it fails in the service of the humanities and the social sciences. Conversely, the great advantage is the trade-off in timeliness. As human indexers are not needed, the material may be entered into the database much faster than normal; citation indexes tend to be months, even years, ahead of other services.

The three sets may be described briefly:

The Social Sciences Citation Index fully indexes about 1400 period-icals, and selectively indexes another 3000. A few (about 250) books are noted. Coverage is of the complete social sciences from anthropol-ogy to urban planning and development. Either the online or printed version may be used to answer questions in almost any area. Note it is particularly useful for business and statistical questions as well as those dealing with community problems.

Science Citation Index is the oldest of the group, and probably the most used, as well as the most expensive. Coverage is from acoustics and aeronautics to surgery and zoology. Not only are scientific topics covered in full, but many related areas are considered, which is to say the index may be used for more than science. Over 3000 journals are indexed in depth, and this is by far the most extensive of the general science indexes. An abridged edition is published monthly for $780.

The Arts & Humanities Citation Index is another multidisciplinary index. Here about 1200 periodicals are indexed in depth, while another 4500 are covered selectively. About 75 to 150 books are noted each year. Coverage is from architecture and art to theater and theology.

Except for the largest of libraries, very few can offer all or even a good number of the periodicals indexed in these services. The solution is interlibrary loan, which is much used, and, eventually, full text of many of the titles will be available online. Meanwhile, the publisher follows by now a normal practice of large index firms—the user may order tear sheets of one or a thousand articles needed from the publisher. Here the system is known as OATS (Original article tear sheet). While service is rapid, from 24 to 48 hours, the problem is cost, with each article running $6 or more.

SUGGESTED READING

Andrews, Charles, "Cooperation at its Best: The Committee on Wilson Indexes at Work," *RQ,* Winter, 1984, pp. 155–161. A well-written and carefully illustrated history of the various approaches Wilson uses to update and revise its indexes. The primary focus is on how the periodical committee functions today.

Cleveland, Donald and Ana Cleveland, *Introduction to Indexing and Abstracting,* Littleton, Colorado: Libraries Unlimited, Inc., 1983. This is an easy-to-understand, basic guide to the fundamentals of indexing and abstracting. It is written for the person who wishes to compile either one, and principles are clearly explained. The step-by-step instructions are excellent.

Cremmins, Edward T., *The Art of Abstracting.* Philadelphia: ISI Press, 1982. A guide to the writing and editing of scientific abstracts, this can be used both by the person who wishes to understand what an abstract is about, and by the individual who wishes to learn the mastery of writing abstracts. The book is as well written as it is thorough. Most of the advice may be applied to writing abstracts in the social sciences and humanities.

Feinberg, Hilda, *Indexing Specialized Formats and Subjects.* Metuchen, New Jersey: Scarecrow Press, 1983. Whereas the Clevelands' work offers a broad overview of indexing, this is a guide for different subject needs. Chapters cover various areas from newspaper indexing to indexing encyclopedias. It is clearly written and well illustrated.

Fisher, Kim, "Film Studies: The Periodical Indexes," *Reference Services Review.* Winter 1982, pp. 29–35. While of value for its study of film journals, the article is even more useful as a model for how to compare various indexes within a given subject field.

Gilzinger, Donald, "Creation of an In-House Newspaper Index," *Community & Junior College Libraries.* Spring 1984, pp. 9–13. The author explains how a community college began indexing the Long Island Newspaper *Newsday* on cards and then moved to online. The nontechnical discussion indicates the problems involved with individual libraries indexing newspapers.

Kauffman, Inge (ed.), "Psychological Abstracts: Past, Present and Future: A Review and Annotated Bibliography," *Behavioral & Social Sciences Librarian,* Fall 1985, pp. 21–42. Although this primarily is an annotated bibliography of material about *Psychological Abstracts,* many of the titles are relevant for other types of abstracting and indexing. The eighteen-item bibliography is preceded by an excellent history of the service as well as "concerns and problems of both the publisher and users."

Sable, Martin, "What Constitutes Minimum Bibliographical Control in New Disciplines?", *International Library Review,* January 1986, pp. 29–32. What are the most important bibliographical controls for a new discipline? The author answers: "My choices would be abstracting service and directory. . . . I would select the abstracting service because it provides continuing current-awareness." Sable then goes on to explore the various facets of abstracting services, and directories which make them useful—not only for new disciplines, but for all disciplines.

Sellen, Mary and Robert Tauber, "Selective Criteria for ERIC: A Survey of Clearinghouse Acquisition Coordinators," *Behavioral & Social Sciences Librarian.* Summer 1984, pp. 25–31. A clear explanation of how documents are selected for indexing by ERIC. The study is based upon questions put to 16 ERIC clearinghouses. Acceptance rate runs 50 to 85 percent. Choice is primarily a matter of screening by experts.

CHAPTER SEVEN

Encyclopedias: General and Subject

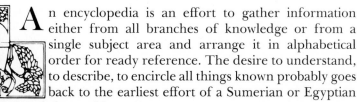

An encyclopedia is an effort to gather information either from all branches of knowledge or from a single subject area and arrange it in alphabetical order for ready reference. The desire to understand, to describe, to encircle all things known probably goes back to the earliest effort of a Sumerian or Egyptian to comprehend the world.

"Encyclopedia" from the Greek "instruction in the circle of knowledge" was first applied to what we conceive of as an encyclopedia by the attractive Pliny the Elder (23–79 A.D.). Pliny, who had a remarkable capacity for work, wrote *Natural History*, of which thirty-one books survive. This vast encyclopedia is shapeless, but in it the Roman deals with everything from the universe and zoology to the fine arts. Most of the material was taken from other works, and Pliny estimated he had gathered about 20,000 facts from 100 authors.

History notes other men and women who followed in Pliny's ambitious footsteps. A classical example, among many, is Isidore of Seville (560–636 A.D.), who wrote a history of the Visigoths and composed the *Etymologies*. It is an effort to gather all human knowledge in twenty volumes. Drawing primarily from Latin authors, he composed what was to be the basic encyclopedia of the Middle Ages. Isidore derived his title for the set from the fact that he gave the origins of names and words he wrote about. In about 1360 the English monk Bartholomew de Glanville repeated the process in 19 books, although John Harris (1667–1719) was the first to produce an English language work.

The eighteenth century was the Age of Enlightenment, when Diderot, eternal optimist, believed it possible to capture all knowledge in his great *Encyclopédie*. The Enlightenment, although a landmark in the history of knowledge, remains, as Hugh Kenner puts it, as "a mystical experience through which the minds of Europe passed." Kenner then goes on to cleverly summarize the content and purpose of an encyclopedia:

> *We carry with us still one piece of baggage from those far off days, and that is the book which nobody wrote and nobody is expected to read, and which is marketed as* The Encyclopaedia: Britannica, Americana, Antarctica *or other. The* Encyclopaedia . . . *takes all that we know apart into little pieces, and then arranges those pieces so that they can be found one at a time. It is produced by a feat of organizing, not a feat of understanding. . . . If the Encyclopaedia means anything as a whole, no one connected with the enterprise can be assumed to know what that meaning is.*[1]

The complaint is common, although in some ways it is to miss the point of the modern encyclopedia. Today the general set serves a variety of purposes, but essentially it is to capsulize and organize the world's accumulated knowledge, or at least that part of it that is of interest to readers. Through detailed articles and brief facts, an effort is made to include a wide variety of information from all fields.

Encyclopedias may be divided into two or three categories: (1) by format—there are the general and subject sets of 4 to 32 volumes (such as the *World Book*) and the smaller works of 1, 2, or 3 volumes (such as the one-volume *New Columbia Encyclopedia*); (2) by scope— here the division is either general (the *World Book*) or by subject (*International Encyclopedia of the Social Sciences*); (3) by audience—the general work may be for a child, teenager, or layperson. If a subject set, it is likely to be directed to an expert or near-expert in that subject field. There are other methods of dividing and subdividing encyclopedias, many of which will be evident as the reader progresses through this chapter.

Purpose

No matter which type of encyclopedia is published, it usually will include detailed survey articles, often with bibliographies, in certain

---

[1]Hugh Kenner, *The Stoic Comedians* (Berkeley, California: University of California Press, 1974), pp. 1, 2.

fields or areas; explanatory material, normally shorter; and brief informational data such as the birth and death dates of famous people, geographical locations, and historical events. This scope makes the encyclopedia ideal for reference work, and the general set is often the first place the librarian will turn for answering questions.

The bibliographies at the end of articles may help the reader to find additional material in a given subject area. The importance of adequate bibliographies is particularly well recognized at the juvenile level (augmented by the use of study aids) and at the specialist's level (by highly developed bibliographies in narrow subject areas). Many encyclopedias now offer a variety of study guides which indicate related articles the student might read so as to put together, with the help of other books, a truly creative paper rather than a carbon copy of an encyclopedia article.

To clear up a common misunderstanding, no general encyclopedia is a proper source for research. (This does not include specialized works.) It is only a springboard. Furthermore, in presenting material with almost no differentiation, the general encyclopedia is not completely accurate or up to date; important facts must be double-checked in another source, if only in a second encyclopedia.

At the child's level, another purpose is often falsely advanced. An encyclopedia, no matter how good, is not a substitute for additional reading or for a collection of supporting reference books. In their natural enthusiasm, some salespeople and advertising copy-writers are carried away with the proposition that an encyclopedia-oriented child is an educated child.

Publishers

How good is any given encyclopedia? Before considering that vital question, as well as considerations of cost, one must ask: Just what choice do I have in the purchase of a set? The real, as opposed to the theoretical, choice among various general encyclopedias is radically limited by the number of publishers.

At one time, there are from 40 to 45 general encyclopedias in print. Of these no more than one-third can be rated acceptable for library or home purchase. And almost all of the passable sets are published by just four firms. With annual sales of over $350 million, these companies control approximately 95 percent of the general encyclopedias published for all age groups in the United States. They are:

(1) Encyclopaedia Britannica Educational Corporation. The Chicago-based publisher, largest of the four, issues *Encyclopaedia Britannica, Compton's Encyclopedia and Fact Index, Britannica Junior*

Encyclopaedia, Compton's Precyclopedia, Young Children's Encyclopedia, Great Books of the Western World, The Annals of America, and so on. Among their other holdings are G. & C. Merriam Company, publisher of Webster's dictionaries; Frederick A. Praeger, Inc.; and the Phaidon Press, Ltd. They also distribute, but do not publish, the *Random House Encyclopedia.*

(2) World Book. This publisher sells more than one-half of all the encyclopedia units in the United States, and its *World Book* is by and large the most popular among children's and young people's sets. The Chicago-based firm also publishes *Childcraft,* a set for beginning readers and not really an encyclopedia, and the excellent *World Book Dictionary.*

(3) Grolier Incorporated. The New York firm publishes *The Encyclopedia Americana, The Encyclopedia International, The New Book of Knowledge, Academic American Encyclopedia,* and *The Catholic Encyclopedia,* and distributes a number of other sets. It also has controlling interest in Scarecrow Press and Franklin Watts. Sales are close to the *Britannica* in volume.

(4) Macmillan Educational Corporation. Although a large publishing house, it is only fourth in sales of encyclopedias. Its only two major sets are *Collier's* and the *Merit Students Encyclopedia.* However, Macmillan publishes a number of related works ranging from the *Encyclopedia of Philosophy* to the *Harvard Classics* and has an interest in Brentano's bookstores, Berlitz language schools, and so on.

(5) Others. Here one might include one or two firms whose sets are passable, in that they have been approved by librarians and, more particularly, the Reference and Subscription Books Review Committee of the American Library Association. For example, Funk & Wagnalls (a division of Standard Reference Library), whose *Funk & Wagnalls New Encyclopedia* is an acceptable set.

Then, too, there are the encyclopedias from England which are quite acceptable, e.g., *New Caxton Encyclopedia* and the *Everyman's Encyclopaedia,* to name only two.

Of the major four, the two leaders are the *Britannica* and *World Book. World Book* leads them all in the actual number of sets sold. Their sales account for from 50 to 65 percent of sets purchased by individuals over the year. The *World Book* may sell from 400,000 to 450,000 sets annually, as compared with slightly over 100,000 of the *Britannica.*

Grolier, at one time a serious challenge to both *Britannica* and *World Book,* has lost ground over the years. While the *Americana* remains one of the most popular of the sets, in usually second or third position in terms of sales, the other Grolier items are less popular. In fact, some have been dropped, e.g., *American People's Encyclopedia*. The smallest of the group, Macmillan, has slow but steady sellers in its two sets.

A reason for lack of competition is the falling market for sets. Selling fewer sets, faced with higher costs, the publishers have generally reacted in the traditional way—by raising prices. Whereas a few years ago the only set approaching $1,000 was the *Britannica,* today this figure is more the rule than the exception. Most sets now hover in the $600 to $800 range as compared to $200 to $400 a decade ago. Whether the sagging market is a result of Americans becoming more cautious, sophisticated and better-educated,[2] or simply being inundated with information from the television set to the newspaper, they have lost some of their previous interest in general encyclopedias. Others claim it is due to the leveling off of the baby boom, the drop in birthrates. Most families, after all, buy sets for their children. Still others see the problem with the bad reputation of encyclopedia salespeople. No matter what the reason, the fact remains that sales are not what they used to be and while certainly good (about 5 to 7 percent of gross sales of books sold in America), they are not large enough to encourage new venture capital.

EVALUATING ENCYCLOPEDIAS

Most librarians and, for that matter, laypersons will turn to one or two sources for objective evaluations of encyclopedias. These are trusted, tried, and true.

The first choice is Kenneth Kister's *Best Encyclopedias: A guide to general and specialized Encyclopedias* (Phoenix, Arizona: Oryx Press, 1986). Updated every three or four years, this last edition is considerably expanded over the 1981 work. An experienced librarian and critic, the author methodically examines some 50 English language sets published in the United States and Canada. He has added an important section on "specialized encyclopedias," and under headings, from architecture to transportation, offers a critical analysis of some 450 subject-oriented sets. (Select foreign language titles also are listed in the appendix.) Librarians should pay particular attention to the first chapter which considers basic questions concerning the

---

[2]Fewer, for example, seem to be buying encyclopedias anymore as a yard of books in a binding to match the interior decoration and to indicate the education level of the family. Also, more people realize that not all of the world's information is in a set.

evaluation and purchase of an encyclopedia. There is an excellent "encyclopedia comparison chart" which at a glance allows one to see the difference in price, number of volumes, illustrations, etc. Each set is considered in terms of history and authority, purpose, reliability, recency, objectivity and all of the major points one would wish to consider in an evaluation of any type of reference work. Of particular value: the "In Comparison" part which compares like sets.

Another useful source of reviews is the well-known "Reference Books Bulletin" in *Booklist*, which is discussed in Chapter 3 of this text. Almost every or every other issue has a lengthy review either of a general set or, more likely, of a subject encyclopedia. These are detailed, objective, and meticulously documented. The reviews of the general sets, if anything, tend to be too long. Inevitably the trained reference librarian skips to the last paragraph to see whether or not the work is recommended. If not, nothing is lost. If it is, then one should go back and discover why it may be required for the library.[3]

The *American Reference Books Annual* is a fine source of brief, yet carefully considered reviews. See, for example, the 1986 edition which has lengthy reviews on *Colliers, Britannica,* and *Merit Student Encyclopedia.* Unlike those in the "Reference Books Bulletin," these are signed by individual reviewers.

Evaluation Points

Librarians tend to make up their own minds about which are the better encyclopedias. The decision is based primarily on daily use of the sets. Still, there are definite points to consider in a systematic evaluation. These are: (1) scope, or subject coverage, emphasis, and the intended audience; (2) authority, which includes accuracy and reliability; (3) writing style; (4) recency, including revision plans, if any, of the publisher; (5) viewpoint and objectivity; (6) arrangement and entry; (7) index with reference to how one gains access to information in the set; (8) format, including the physical format and illustrations; and (9) cost. The presence of bibliographies is considered, too.

[3]In addition to the regular reviews, from time to time there are summaries. See, for example: "Five Multivolume Children's Encyclopedias," *Booklist,* May 15, 1983, pp. 1233–1243. Beginning in 1983, there is an annual summary of the 8 to 12 popular sets, usually in the December issue, e.g., "1984 Annual Encyclopedia Roundup," *Booklist,* December 15, 1984, pp. 565–574.

Scope

The scope of the specialized encyclopedia is evident in its name, and becomes even more obvious with use. The scope of the general encyclopedia is dictated primarily by two considerations.

Age Level   The children's encyclopedias, such as the *World Book,* are tied to curriculum. Consequently, they include more in-depth material on subjects of general interest to grade and high schools than does an adult encyclopedia such as the *Britannica.* Recognizing that the strongest sales appeal is to adults with children, most encyclopedia publishers aim their advertising at them. All the standard sets claim that an audience ranging from grades 6 to 12 can understand and use their respective works. This may be true of the exceptionally bright child, but the librarian is advised to check the real age compatibility of the material before purchase, not merely the advertised age level. For an example of these practices, see "Sales Practices" on p. 190.

A consequence of attempting to be all things to all age levels is twofold: (1) Even in many adult encyclopedias, the material is shortened for easier comprehension by a child; and (2) the effort at clarity frequently results in an oversimplified approach to complex questions.

Emphasis   If age level dictates one approach to scope, the emphasis of the editor accounts for the other. At one time, this varied more than it does today; one set would be especially good for science, another for literature. Today, the emphasis is essentially a matter of deciding what compromise will be made between scholarship and popularity. Why, for example, in most adult encyclopedias, is as much space given to the subject of advertising as to communism? This is not to argue the merit of any particular emphasis, but only to point out that examining emphasis is a method of determining scope.

Authority

The first question to ask about any reference book is its authority. If it is authoritative, it normally follows that it will be up to date, accurate, and relatively objective. Contributors and publishers constitute the authority for encyclopedias.

Authority is evident in the names of the scholars and experts who sign the articles or are listed as contributors somewhere in the set. There are three quick tests for authority: (1) recognition of a prominent name, particularly the author of the best recent book on the subject; (2) recognition of a field known to the reader, and a quick check to see whether leaders in that field are represented in the contributor list; and (3) finally, determination of whether the author's qualifications (as noted by position, degrees, occupation, and so on) are related to the article.

An indication of the encyclopedia's revision policy and age can be ascertained from knowledge about the authors. Some contributors may literally be dead, and while a certain number of deceased authorities is perfectly acceptable, too many in this category indicates either overabundant plagiarism from older sets or lack of any meaningful revision.

Reliability is a part of authority, and here the general encyclopedias are not completely trustworthy. The "Reference Books Bulletin" reviews reveal examples of accuracy failure. An article on Graham Greene in the *Academic American Encyclopedia* states that "Greene started his long career of uninterrupted successes with *The Man Within.* . . ." That book was a success, but his next two were failures. In examining the *Americana,* the committee found that "certain well known organizations are not included." And the *Britannica* often fails to include "contemporary figures."

Any encyclopedia will contain errors and some omissions. Most are quickly corrected when brought to the attention of a publisher. The real test, of course, is the number of such mistakes. The sets considered here, while not perfect, can rarely be faulted for more than a few errors.

Writing style

When the writing style of today's encyclopedia is considered, one notices that none of the general sets is for the expert. As the former editor of the *Britannica* puts it: "Perhaps the most critical editorial policy that was established [was] our absolute certainty that general encyclopaedias are inappropriate source books for specialists in their own areas." Basically, everything should be comprehensible to the person Preece calls "the curious intelligent lay reader." For the *Britannica,* at least, this is an about-face since the time when not only advertising but the articles themselves proclaimed the scholarly and pedantic nature of many of the contributions.

Recognizing that the purchasers are laypersons, who considerably outnumber the scholars, encyclopedia firms tend to operate in a relatively standard fashion. Contributors are given certain topics and outlines of what is needed and expected. Their manuscripts are then submitted to the encyclopedia's editors (editorial staffs of the larger encyclopedias range from 100 to 200 full-time persons), who revise, cut, and query—all for the purpose of making those manuscripts understandable to the average reader. The extent of editing varies with each encyclopedia, from the extreme for the children's works (where word difficulty and length of sentence are almost as important as content) to a limited amount for big-name contributors.

Serving as a bridge between contributor and reader, the editor strives for readability by reducing complicated vocabulary and jargon to terms understandable to the lay reader or young person. The purpose is to rephrase specialized thought into common language without insulting that thought—or, more likely, that eminent contributor. In the humanities and the social sciences, this often works, but only as long as the contributing scholar is willing to have his or her initials appended to something that will not cause a colleague's criticism.

Recency: Continuous revision

As most large encyclopedia companies issue new printings of their sets or individual volumes each year, it is necessary to constantly update the work. This has been made considerably easier through word processing and automation procedures which allow the editors to enter new material, delete, and correct without completely resetting the whole article or section.

No matter what the technological procedures may be for updating new printings of an encyclopedia, the librarian should know: (1) Few general encyclopedias use the "edition" as an indication of the relative currency of the work. For example, the *Britannica's* fourteenth edition was just that from about 1929 until the fifteenth edition in 1974. (2) Most encyclopedias do revise material with each printing, and a printing normally is done at least once or twice, or even more often, each year. The relative date of the printing will be found on the verso of the title page, but this in itself means little. (3) There is no accurate measure of how much of any given encyclopedia is revised with each printing or how often it is done, but most large publishers claim to revise about 5 to 10 percent of the material each year.

Continuous revision is a major sales point for publishers involved with selling sets to libraries. They rightly reason that no library is going to buy a new set of the same encyclopedia (loss or damage aside) unless there has been substantial revision.

One possible solution to more rapid revision is the introduction of the online encyclopedia. At this writing two American sets are now available online—*Academic American* and the *Encyclopaedia Brittanica.* In the case of the former, it was announced in 1985 that there is a quarterly updating of the set. Just how much material is revised each quarter is not reported, but in a general way, the contemporary articles on science, technology, politics, business, and the social sciences are given the most attention. (See p. 203 for further details about online sets.)

The best way to check the degree of revision is to look up a subject, place, individual, or statistic one knows to see if the set has the latest information. For example, in a review of *Compton's* 1982 edition it was found that "population statistics for the U.S. are based on the 1970 U.S. Census, with some later estimates for particular countries." Referring to the *Merit Student Encyclopedia,* the same reviewer notes "The policy toward adding new topics sometimes seems unduly conservative, e.g., articles on Julian Bond . . . acid rain, and vasectomy were not added until this (1982) edition." Turning to the *World Book,* it was found that "many articles remain substantially unchanged from year to year . . . *WB* is scrupulous about recording recent deaths among biographees".[4]

Kister has what he calls "recency tables" throughout his guide, and compares three or more encyclopedias on about a dozen subjects from Afghanistan to Tuberculosis. He ranks each by "Very current," "Fairly current," or "Not current." These charts are supported in the text with specific examples.

Viewpoint and objectivity

As general encyclopedias are profit ventures, they aim to please everyone, and insult or injure no one. Despite sometimes pious claims of objectivity on grounds of justice for all, the real reason often is commercial. For example, it was not until many years of active prodding by women that encyclopedia publishers made a conscious effort to curb sexual bias.

Blatant sexual and racial bias has been eliminated from standard, acceptable encyclopedias. The slate is not completely clean or neutral. Comparing how women are treated in 10 encyclopedias (all of which are considered in this chapter), June Engles and Elizabeth Futas offer a model of how to evaluate viewpoint and objectivity. Briefly, they found that even today: (a) men will be included more

[4]"Five Multivolume Children's Encyclopedias," Reference Books Bulletin, *Booklist,* May 15, 1983, pp. 1238, 1239, and 1242.

frequently than women; (b) more men than women are included by name when discussing a given topic; (c) few encyclopedias use neutral language and many employ terms which are stereotypically sexist; and (d) illustrative matter is primarily male. The authors conclude that "encyclopedias should perhaps be regarded as an important factor in perpetuating sexism in our society."[5]

How is the encyclopedia to be objective when such controversial issues as capitalism and communism, civil rights and segregation, conservatism or liberalism are involved? There are two approaches here. One is to ignore the differences entirely, depending on a chronological, historical approach. The other is an effort to balance an article by presenting two or more sides. The reader should expect at least a consideration of different views, either by the contributor or by the editor.

Another aspect of the question of viewpoint is what the editor chooses to include or to exclude, to emphasize or deemphasize. Nothing dates an encyclopedia faster than antiquated articles about issues and ideas either no longer acceptable or of limited interest. An encyclopedia directed at the Western reader can scarcely be expected to give as much coverage in depth to, let us say, Egypt as to New York State. Yet, to include only a passing mention of Egypt will not be suitable either, particularly in view of ancient history and the emergence of Africa as a new world force. The proportion of one article to another plagues any conscientious encyclopedia editor, and there probably is no entirely satisfactory solution.

Arrangement and entry

The traditional encyclopedic arrangement is the familiar alphabetical approach to material, with numerous cross-references and an index. Most major sets follow this tradition. Average users are accustomed to the alphabetical order of information, or the *specific entry*. Here, the information is broken down into small, specific parts.

Index

Most general encyclopedias are alphabetically arranged, and some publishers have concluded that with suitable *see* and *see also* references, the arrangement should serve to eliminate the index.

[5]June Engle and Elizabeth Futas, "Sexism in Adult Encyclopedias," *RQ,* Fall 1983, pp. 29–39. The final quote is on p. 37, and there are two pages of references. See, too, "Letters" in the Summer 1984 issue of *RQ* for responses to the research project.

The argument for an index is simply that a single article may contain dozens of names and events which cannot be located unless there is a detailed, separate index volume. A good index is an absolute necessity.

Format

A good format considers the size, typeface, illustrations, binding, and total arrangement. Among the components to consider when evaluating format are the following:

Illustrations (photographs, diagrams, charts, maps, etc.)   Nothing will tip off the evaluator faster as to the currency of the encyclopedia than a cursory glance at the illustrations. Even illustrations of the 1980s will not be suitable unless they relate directly to the text and to the interests of the reader. The librarian might ask: Do the illustrations consider the age of the user, or do they depend on figures or drawings totally foreign to, say, a twelve-year-old? Do they emphasize important matters, or are they too general? Are they functional, or simply attractive? Are the captions adequate?

The reproduction process is important. Some illustrations have a displeasing physical quality, perhaps because too little or too much ink was employed, or the paper was a poor grade, or an inadequate cut or halftone screen was used.

Illustrations are particularly useful in children's and young people's encyclopedias. The *World Book,* for example, has a well-deserved reputation for the timeliness and excellence of both its black and white and numerous colored illustrations. At the same time, an abundance of illustrations is a tip-off that an encyclopedia is: (1) primarily for children and young people, or (2) primarily a "popular" set or one-volume work purposely prepared for a wide appeal. Neither objective is to be censured, but the librarian seeking an encyclopedia superior for ready-reference is likely to be more interested in the amount of text (and how it is presented) than in the number of illustrations.

Maps are an important part of any encyclopedia and vary in number from 2300 in *World Book* to 1175 in *Britannica* to slightly over 250 in the one-volume *Columbia.* Many of the maps are prepared by Rand McNally or C. S. Hammond and usually are good to excellent. In the adult sets, the major maps frequently are in a separate volume, often with the index. The young adults' and children's encyclopedias usually have the maps in the text, and if this is the case, there should be reference to them in the index and cross-references as needed.

The librarian should check how many and what types of maps are employed to show major cities of the world, historical development, political changes, land use, weather, and so on. The actual evaluation of the maps is discussed in the chapter on geography.

Size of type The type style is important, as is the spacing between lines and the width of the column. All these factors affect the readability of the work.

Binding Encyclopedias should be bound in a fashion that is suitable for rough use, particularly in a library. Conversely, buyers should be warned that a frequent method of jacking up the price of an encyclopedia is to charge the user for a so-called deluxe binding which often is no better, and in fact may be worse, than the standard library binding.

Volume size Finally, consideration should be given to the physical size of the volume. Is it comfortable to use? Equally important, can it be opened without strain on the binding?

The sheer weight of a single volume, heretofore the concern chiefly of librarians who had to wrestle with giant folios or the prosaic bound volume of newspapers, is worth considering. More and more publishers seem to favor larger and heavier one-volume encyclopedias.

Cost

Reporting on the average discussion of cost by a salesperson, John Cunningham writes: "There is a sort of mythical snob appeal about the cost (of an encyclopedia). It is rather like a posh funeral: you don't ask about the bill. Britannica salesmen are tactful about it, though quite open, rather in the manner of undertakers leading the bereaved through the types of coffins available, starting at the top with a leather binding and gold lettering."[6]

Not only do prices vary dramatically from set to set, but they can go from under $1000 to several multiples of that figure for precisely the same work. One can buy the *Britannica* alone, but this is not likely. The salesperson will try to have the sale include other Britannica items from *Great Books of the Western World* to junior encyclopedias. The end result is that one might pay from $1000 to $7500 for the

[6]John Cunningham, "A Britannica A Day Keeps the Recession at Bay," *The Guardian*, February 17, 1984, p. 15. For a detailed review of the revised *Britannica*, see Reference Books Bulletin, *The Booklist*, November 15, 1985, pp. 472–474.

Britannica, depending on what is purchased along with the basic set—as well as the kind of binding.

Another factor is the library discount. Most publishers grant large discounts to libraries. For example, the $1099 *Merit Students Encyclopedia* is about $500 to libraries. Note: Prices given in this chapter are retail, not the library/school discount figure.

Sales Practices

Although encyclopedias are still sold door-to-door, this practice is dying out. The usual procedure now is to sell the set directly to the consumer via the bookstore, or some other outlet such as a booth in a train station, or at a specific trade show. In the 1960s and early 1970s there was much emphasis on salespersons who used less than desirable tactics to sell sets. Today this still goes on, but on a more limited scale due to the falling away of general set sales and the emphasis of the U.S. Federal Trade Commission on fair sales practices.

The idealized audience for an encyclopedia is often reflected in the idealized advertising. For example, in a November 10, 1985 issue of the much-read *New York Times Book Review* (p. 23), the Britannica had a full page ad which began "Make your child a winner with the new *Encyclopaedia Britannica* . . . now more valuable than ever." Next to this was a line drawing of a six- to ten-year-old boy. No actual age was mentioned, but the set is difficult even for some college graduates. The emphasis on children is understandable. Most sets are purchased for the children in the family.

Who buys encyclopedias? Primarily people from about thirty to fifty years of age, and particularly those with children. It is little wonder that almost all encyclopedia advertisements indicate that the set is ideal for children. Most purchases are made by middle class and lower income middle class families, although the lower income classes with ambition for their children are good customers, too. Most sales are on the installment plan, which allows the companies to charge rather hefty interest rates. People who don't buy encyclopedias are usually the single, and the older.

Consumer advice

The librarian has several ways of meeting the request for information about a given set:

> **1.** Give no advice. Several major public libraries, fearful of repercussions from salespersons and publishers, adamantly

refuse to advise on the purchase of this or that set. Such a refusal is unprofessional and highly questionable.

2. Give limited advice. Normally, the procedure here is to give the inquirer several reviews of the set or sets under question, leaving the final decision to the user. Of particular assistance in this respect is the "Reference Books Bulletin" in *The Booklist* and Kister's *Encyclopedia Buying Guide*.

3. Go all out with an endorsement or a condemnation. Privately, of course, many librarians do just this. Such opinionated statements may have some nasty repercussions, particularly when the question is between sets that are approved by ALA and are more or less even in quality.

Of the three, the second option is best. If the set is not readily recognized by either publisher or reputation, the librarian should not hesitate to point out that the chances are it is a poor buy from the standpoint of both cost and quality. The librarian should be prepared to support this statement with reviews; or lacking reviews (either because the set is too new or such a "dog" as not to have been noticed), there should be no hesitation about standing on one's own professional knowledge of the set. If nothing can be found about it in print (and who is not familiar with many of the works which pass for encyclopedias in supermarkets and in questionable advertisements?), the librarian should explain that the opinion may be personal, but the odds are all against the set being of good quality.

Many public librarians avoid recommending their own favorite titles. Instead they refer the person to one of the standard review compilations and to encyclopedias in the library which can be examined. Actually, the presence of a work in the library is a tacit stamp of approval by the librarian. Asked in a survey if they ever recommended "their favorite encyclopedia," 47 replied "never," 20 said "sometimes," and only 2 replied "always."[7] The reluctance to give advice is not so much a decision taken by the individual reference librarian as it is policy of the library. Many libraries have policy statements which specifically state that the librarian is to give no advice on such matters.

Replacement

Most libraries replace an encyclopedia every two to five years. In practical terms this usually means that the one of the most-used sets

[7]Ken Kister, "Encyclopedias and the Public Library: A National Survey," *Library Journal*, April 15, 1979, p. 893.

(*World Book, Americana, Britannica,* and *Collier's*) is replaced with a revised set every two years, the next most used every three years, the next every four years, and so on. Where the library is medium or large, the two-to-four-year-old sets are sent to the branches, put in the general reading room, or duplicated in heavily used parts of the library, such as the young adults' area. When a set is more than five years old, it should be discarded. Note that the older sets may be quite suitable for home use, but not for libraries, where the reader expects to find the most up-to-date information. Ideally, and where budgets allow, all the four to five basic sets should be replaced every one to two years; but these days that is rarely possible.

Replacement depends upon whether the publisher actually revises the set from year to year. Where this apparently is not done, or done at a rate of less than 5 percent revision annually (such as the case of the current *Britannica*), it is pointless to replace the set unless it is worn. Therefore the amount of continuous revision carried on by the publisher should be checked carefully.

ADULT ENCYCLOPEDIAS

> *The New Encyclopaedia Britannica,* 15th ed. Chicago: Encyclopaedia Britannica Inc., 32 vols. $1,249.
>
> *The Encyclopedia Americana.* Danbury, Connecticut: Grolier Incorporated, 30 vols. $960.

There are few multivolume adult encyclopedias; therefore, the choice is limited. The basic sets found in most public, secondary school, and college and university libraries include (1) *The New Encyclopaedia Britannica,* (2) *The Encyclopedia Americana,* and (3) possibly an English or Canadian set, such as the *New Caxton Encyclopaedia* or *The Canadian Encyclopedia.*

Some librarians will include *Collier's* as an adult set, although it is probably more suitable for teenagers, and others will constantly use the young adult and children's *World Book* for ready-reference work with adults.

In homes, the choices are about the same, although many adults will wisely settle for the *Funk & Wagnalls New Encyclopedia* for under $200 (compared with over $1000 for the *Britannica*), or use the multipurpose *World Book,* or purchase a second-hand set at a large discount. Another·good choice is a one- or two-volume work, which is a "best buy" in terms of comparative cost.

Which of the sets is best? Public librarians believe that of the some 50 general sets, as described by Kister in *Best Encyclopedias,* the *World Book* is the most in demand—certainly the most effective for reference work in the library. Close behind is the *Americana,* and much lower on the usability ladder are the *Britannica, Collier's* and *Compton's.* The *World Book* has always been a favorite among librarians, even though book reviewers and encyclopedia critics have praised the *Britannica* more—at least for adult use. Working librarians find that the *World Book* can be used for adults better than the *Britannica* in many situations.[8]

The Britannica

The best-known encyclopedia in the Western world is the *Britannica.* First published in 1768, it underwent many revisions and changes until the triumphant Ninth edition in 1889. This was the "scholar's edition," with long articles from such contributors as Arnold, Swinburne, Huxley, and other major English minds of the nineteenth century. The Ninth was followed, after a lackluster Tenth, by the equally famous Eleventh. (Note: Both of these are discussed in considerable detail in a *New Yorker* article. See "Suggested Reading," Koning, Hans.)

After several changes caused by economic difficulties, the set came to the United States and by 1929 appeared as the Fourteenth edition. By that time, the long essays had been reduced and divided, although the set continued to be sold (as it is even today) on the reputation built with the Ninth and Eleventh editions. The first total revision of the Fourteenth edition of the *Britannica* appeared in 1974. Complaints about lack of a proper index brought about another change in 1985 when the number of volumes was increased by two, and an index added.

The set includes (1) the *Micropaedia,* 12 volumes containing some 60,000 short entries from a few words to 3000 words in length in alphabetical order; (2) the *Macropaedia,* 17 volumes of 681 essay-length articles; and (3) the *Propaedia,* a single-volume so-called outline of knowledge. There is a two-volume index (with some 410,000 references), and the publishers claim the *Propaedia* serves as a topical index to 15,000 items in the other two parts. What all this comes down to is two distinct, although related, encyclopedias. The *Micropaedia* is a ready-reference work, whereas the *Macropaedia* is the typical, time-tested topical set. The *Propaedia* is so difficult to use that it tends to

---

[8]Kister, *op. cit.* The study compiles the results of replies from 77 public libraries of various types and sizes throughout the United States.

gather dust in libraries. It is a single volume arranged by broad subjects. The idea is to outline human knowledge, to show relationships between ideas, persons, and events.

The current set, as just described, represents a radical revision of the 1974 version. The *Micropaedia* was expanded from 10 to 12 volumes and many of the shorter articles were made longer, up to 3000 words. Bibliographies were added, and the type size increased for easier reading. The *Macropaedia,* reduced by two volumes, and cut back to long, scholarly articles, is a major effort to construct an old-fashioned approach to knowledge. There are now 681 articles as contrasted with over 4000 before the revision. The focus is on giving the reader a clear, detailed overview of larger issues and concerns. There are only about 100 biographies retained, and most of the geographical pieces have been transferred to the *Micropaedia.* The index, in the best tradition of older sets, contains about 200,000 main entries, as well as 250,000 subentries.

The publisher promises, too, to make more of an effort to keep the set current. It had lagged behind badly in terms of revision. The need for revision may be more apparent if and when the online version of the set is made available to more people. Presently, it is limited so that it cannot be accessed by librarians.

The Americana

The Encyclopedia Americana is based on the seventh edition of the German encyclopedia *Brockhaus Konversations Lexikon.* In fact, the first published set (1829 to 1833) was little more than pirated, translated articles from the German work. It was asserted in 1903 that the *Americana* was a wholly new work, but still many of the articles were carried over from *Brockhaus.* The set was reissued in 1918 with changes and additions, although still with material from *Brockhaus.* It claims to be the oldest "all-American" encyclopedia in existence.

As the title implies, the strength of this work is the emphasis on American history, geography, and biography. This encyclopedia unquestionably places greater emphasis on this area than any of the other sets, and it is particularly useful for finding out-of-the-way, little-known material about the United States. However, general coverage of the United States is matched in other major encyclopedias.

The writing style is clear, the arrangement admirable, the index good, and the general format (including illustrations and type size) adequate. A helpful feature is the insertion of summaries, resembling a table of contents, at the beginning of multiple-page articles. The set is edited for the adult with a high school education. It is not suitable (despite zealous copywriters) for grade school children.

The illustrations in the set are outstanding—some 24,000 of which about 10 percent are in color. Most are closely associated with the text. The maps are detailed and easy to follow, although they are not always best when it comes to detailed city plans. Still, on balance, the graphics of the set are much above average and at least equal to what is found in the *Britannica.*

While the articles on science and technology have improved considerably over the past few years, the set still can be faulted for failure to revise thoroughly. There is a definite need to revise some of the basic, background articles. At the same time, the material about current events tends to be quite up-to-date.

If a choice must be made between this and the *Britannica,* the bow would go to the latter. Actually, the differences are not all that great, but the *Britannica* has the advantage of more scholarly articles —which, of course, can be a disadvantage where the library is serving adults with only a high school education. It is to be hoped the choice does not have to be made, and that the library will have both sets. Individuals making a selection between the two should consider first and foremost the desired educational level.

Supermarket sets

Funk & Wagnalls New Encyclopedia. New York: Funk & Wagnalls, 29 vols. $125.

There are numerous adult (and children's and young people's) encyclopedias sold in supermarkets and other such retail outlets. Usually there is a separate display with a notice that the first volume is a certain price (normally under $5 and often even free) and each additional volume another price. Many, too many, are the traditional "rip-off", in that the total price for a set may be well over $100 and the work itself dated, inaccurate, and often not even suitable for the audience it claims. Librarians are sometimes asked about such works, and the general warning is that, with the exception of *Funk & Wagnalls,* the supermarket set is probably a bad buy. The would-be purchaser is better off with a one- or two-volume work or even a second-hand standard set.

As one of the few sets not published by the major four encyclopedia publishers, *Funk & Wagnalls* has received the approval of the American Library Association and Kenneth Kister.

The set underwent an extensive revision in 1983, including both illustrations and text. It is prominently displayed in many supermarkets with usually one volume free, and subsequent volumes $3.99 to $4.50 each. For once, the value is there and no one can go wrong purchasing the set, either as individual volumes or in total.

There are now slightly over 9000 illustrations, of which about one-third are in color. Placed next to the relevant text, the pictures are up to date and, in terms of reproduction and subject matter, are good to excellent. The last volume is a detailed index, and in volume 28 one finds reading lists and subject outlines. The actual bibliography is both current and representative of the best material in the field. The result of the well-written articles and the carefully researched material is that the set is much above average. It is by far the best of the supermarket sets, and a viable alternative to more expensive encyclopedias. "The Reference Books Bulletin" (December 15, 1984, p. 570) rightfully says it "offers excellent value for its price . . . and is an excellent encyclopedia for homes, useful for both adults and older children."

Other Sets

There are at least two or three British and Canadian adult encyclopedias which are quite acceptable. *The Canadian Encyclopedia* (Edmonton: Hurtig Pbl. Ltd. 1985. $175) is a three-volume work which replaces the badly dated *Encyclopedia Canadiana.* Actually, with its 3 million words, it is the average size of the better one- and two-volume sets such as the *Random House Encyclopedia,* but it differs in that the total concentration is on Canada. There are some 1600 illustrations, primarily in color, and maps, as well as about 8000 articles. It covers the whole of Canadian history, as well as current artistic, social, political, and economic matters. It is an invaluable guide for Canadian libraries and for many libraries outside of that country.

In Great Britain, the best-selling *Everyman's Encyclopedia* (London: Dent) is a 12-volume, well-illustrated set directed to the average student and adult. Unfortunately, there is no consistent revision policy and the set, updated in 1978, is now somewhat out of date. *The New Caxton Encyclopedia* (London: Caxton) is much more ambitious. The 20 volumes are carefully illustrated, and the material is kept relatively current. The combination of excellent illustrations, meticulously written articles and well-balanced subject coverage makes this a leading set for any library—in or out of Great Britain. Unfortunately, for ready reference purposes, the index is not all that good and cross references are generally lacking.[9]

Popular adult and high school sets

Academic American Encyclopedia. Danbury, Connecticut: Grolier Incorporated, 21 vols. $750.

Collier's Encyclopedia. New York: Macmillan Educational Corporation. 24 vols. $1099.

Encyclopedia International. Danbury, Connecticut: Grolier Incorporated, 20 vols. $288.

There are at least three sets which claim to be of equal value to adults and to young people. The reader suitability level is from 12 to 18 years of age to adult. Here one should say that *Collier's* and the *Academic American* are better suited to adults than the *International*, albeit all may be used by teenagers.

All three differ from the *Americana* and *Britannica*, having as they do a particular emphasis on popular, concise writing. They are deliberately edited for the adult with a high school education, or for the high school or beginning college student. All are relatively accurate, but vary in regard to keeping material up-to-date. In terms of purchase, one would recommend *Collier's* first, followed by the *Academic*, with the *International* far, far in the rear.

Collier's deserves first place because it can be ranked good to excellent in almost all areas of evaluation. It has close to 5000 authorities as contributors, and most of the articles are signed. The publisher claims a good balance in coverage, e.g., about 20 percent in the humanities, 15 percent in science, 35 percent in geography and regional studies, and 20 percent given over to the social sciences. Also, there are useful, although at times oversimple, articles of a how-to-do-it, self-help nature.

The writing style may be too bland for some, but it has the advantage of clarity. The articles are extremely well organized and the set is unusual because it stresses the long, rather than the short, article. These are often accompanied by biographical sketches and glossaries of terms.

The total amount of revision is not satisfactory. If, for example, the editors supply information on the latest news events, this is not

[9]Reference Books Bulletin, *The Booklist*, September 1, 1983, pp. 55–57. This is a detailed review which was to be part of the original overall review of six major encyclopedias discussed earlier.

always the case in their coverage of individuals, smaller towns, and general economic and social trends in some countries. At the same time, the major stories are carefully updated.

Some complain that the articles in *Collier's* can be too long. They, in fact, can run over 40 or even 70 pages for a particular country. At the same time, there is a fine index which has over 400,000 entries—almost double those found in the rival sets. Another feature of the final volume is the section on bibliographies. About 12,000 titles are arranged under 31 broad subjects and subdivided. Most entries are current, and the reading lists offer adults and students a satisfactory supplement to material found in the set.

The illustrations remain a weak point. While about 20 percent of the set has black-and-white photographs or line drawings, few of them are either that clear or that relevent to the text. Thanks to a recent revision, the publisher is improving both the number and the quality of the color illustrations (now only about 2500 out of 17,000) and this is evident as each year of revision passes.

First published in 1980 by a Dutch firm, and then sold to Grolier, the *Academic American Encyclopedia* is equal to Collier's in many ways, but has only about one-half as many pages—9700 as compared to almost 20,000 in Collier's. At the same time the excellent black-and-white and color illustrations are equal in number and much superior to the rival set. Making up about one-third of the total space, they feature numerous cutaway models. Also, the maps (slightly over 1000) are by Rand McNally, and quite up to those in the rival sets. Not all of the towns pinpointed on the map are found in the index.

Grolier has adopted a thorough revision scheme, and the illustrations in the annual update are kept current. The major articles, and particularly those dealing with politics, science, and personalities, are revised regularly. Much of this revision may be due to the fact that the encyclopedia is available online and can easily be updated.

The emphasis, as in the other sets of this type, is fairly well divided: one-third sciences; one-third social sciences and related areas (places); and about one-third arts and humanities.

Although the index can't be trusted entirely for geographical points on the maps, it is generally good. There are, as well, numerous cross-references within the volumes.

When it comes to the writing style and the factual material, this set has few rivals in its price category. The writing, by over 2000 consultants, is particularly good, and most of the material can be easily understood. With its focus on being a truly popular set, there is considerable emphasis on individuals, with brief entries accounting for more than 35 percent of the total entries. The excellent index makes it easy to find what is needed.

Whereas *Collier's* and the *Academic American* are among the best choices for adults and young people, the *International* is only on the outskirts of acceptability. While it has about the same number of words as the *Academic American,* it has fewer illustrations and maps. When it comes to the index it is far behind both sets both in terms of number of entries and cross references in the set.

Directed more to young people than either of the other two sets, it at least has a clear idea of its audience. There is particular emphasis on how-to-do-it-type articles as well as the self-help variety. Actually, about 50 percent of the set is devoted to other popular areas such as famous people and geographical places of interest.

The writing style is less than sparkling, although generally the material is accurate enough. The catch seems to be that Grolier has lost interest in its revision, at least of the basic articles. Bibliographies, when present, make reference to books often not even found in libraries. Actually, there is little reason for a library to bother with this set, and it cannot be recommended to the public.

CHILDREN'S AND YOUNG ADULTS' ENCYCLOPEDIAS

Compton's Encyclopedia and Fact Index. Chicago: Encyclopedia Britannica, 26 vols. $599.

Merit Students Encyclopedia. New York: Macmillan Educational Corporation, 20 vols. $1099.

World Book Encyclopedia. Chicago: World Book, 22 vols. $499.

The New Book of Knowledge. Danbury, Connecticut: Grolier Incorporated, 21 vols. $650.

Among the children's and young adult encyclopedias, there is one clear favorite. The *World Book* really has no competitors. Still, in terms of excellence of presentation, at least *Merit Students Encyclopedia* is in the race. The problem here is that it is outrageously expensive— twice as much as *World Book.* Somewhat behind the two is *Compton's.* *The New Book of Knowledge,* written for much younger children, is in a different class.

Not only does the *World Book* stand alone, but it has the advantage of price. At close to $500 it is a bargain. (Even more so for libraries. The price to them in 1986: $403.) At $500 more, the *Merit* is a questionable purchase, although there are special price considerations for schools and libraries which make it more competitive.

The triumph of the *World Book* is not an accident but a careful combination of many elements, not the least of which is a nice balance between timely illustrations and text. The clarity of style and the massive number of excellent illustrations put it so far ahead of the other sets that it really has no competitors. Inevitably, it is ranked high by all critics and is a regular repurchase item by libraries. Its popularity, as noted earlier, makes it the best-selling single set in America.

The advertising for *World Book* may be faulted in indicating it is for younger children. Actually it is for someone at least 9, but probably closer to 10 or 12 in age.

In terms of difficulty of reading, the sets may be graded pretty much in this order with the easiest reading level first: (1) *New Book of Knowledge;* (2) *Compton's,* which is often preferred by younger grade school children; (3) *Merit Students;* and (4) *World Book.*

Compton's has more than 22,000 illustrations as contrasted with about 29,000 for *World Book,* but only about 20,000 for *Merit.* While adequate, neither the number nor the quality of the illustrations in the *Merit* set compete with those in the other two sets. Actually, even *Compton's* falls behind in terms of being as up-to-date as *World Book.*

All have indexes. The Fact-Index in *Compton's* is by far the most fascinating. A form of study guide and index, it is found at the back of each volume (it was deleted from several volumes in 1985). Many find this feature one of the strong points in the set. The *World Book* has many of the same index features, including a "Reading and Study Guide" for various topics. These include other books as well as specific subject headings in the *Readers' Guide.*

While the three are kept current, the degree of revision varies considerably. *World Book* is by far the best, particularly in that careful attention is given to current events, and biographical data is updated regularly. In the 1985 edition, for example, there are the results of the 1984 Olympics, a well-balanced article on Nicaragua, and a clear explanation of AIDS. Estimates are that about one-third of the set is revised each year. *Merit* has an acceptable policy on revision, but here *Compton's* appears to be quite vulnerable. It has failed to update material sufficiently.

None of the sets is likely to win applause for challenging the reader to consider controversial issues. *The World Book,* closely tied to the curriculum of the nation's schools, assiduously avoids anything which may be debatable. At the same time, it is quite objective in handling national arguments from abortion to the place of religion in education. It often fails to indicate that foreign affairs are controversial in much American policy. *Compton's* is no better, and, for example, when it comes to such problems as abortion, it stresses the medical aspects, while trying to side-step the moral and political issues. *Merit* comes close to following the *World Book* pattern.

The style of writing in the three is graded, i.e., the articles begin with relatively easy material and definitions and grow progressively more difficult. The coverage usually is brief, with particular emphasis on illustrations and cross references to related pieces.

As in any group of encyclopedias, one may have favorites. The division between *Merit* and *Compton's* is not all that great. At the same time, the writing style and the illustrations are better in *Compton's* than in the *Merit*. Above both, the *World Book* is really the best.[1]

Staking out a place of its own, *The New Book of Knowledge* is produced primarily for readers too young to appreciate the other two sets. The age group is from six, or even younger, to about 10 or 12. Fortunately, the set fulfills its objectives; however, the price is high in view of the fact that it has at least one-third fewer words than the sets for somewhat older children. At the same time, the numerous and excellent illustrations (half of which are in color) match anything found in the other sets.

The articles are well written, and, in fact, the writing style is better than that found in many of the pieces in *Merit* and *Compton's*. An effort is made to make everything clear, and most of the articles are short with precise definitions and explanations, usually punctuated with illustrations. There are numerous summary boxes of information. Coverage is quite even and the material is regularly updated.

The final volume is an index to the set, but there is a "Dictionary Index" in each volume. This is not only an access point, but similar to *Compton's* Fact-Index. There are brief explanations and summaries of some items not even found in the main set, particularly biographical sketches.

A cursory glance at the competitors will indicate that there really is little choice between the *New Book of Knowledge* and other sets directed to younger children. *The Britannica Junior Encyclopedia For Boys and Girls* (Chicago: Encyclopaedia Britannica, 15 vols. $250) is certainly much, much less expensive, but it is oppressively dull and the illustrations belong in a museum, not in a modern encyclopedia.[11] Even the prestigious Oxford University Press does not do complete

---

[10] This is the opinion of most librarians, including Kister and the "Reference Books Bulletin," e.g., see their 1984 review of the set in *Booklist*, February, 1984, pp. 791–794.

[11] Even the otherwise cautious "Reference and Books Bulletin" draws back from this work. While claiming it is "a good supplementary set" the evaluators go on to say "it cannot be recommended as a first choice encyclopedia." *Booklist*, May 15, 1983, p. 1235.

justice to young readers with its much better, yet dated *Oxford Junior Encyclopedia.* At $190, the 13-volume work is a bargain, but it is not often revised, and the slant is definitely English.

Encyclopedia supplements: Yearbooks

There are two basic purposes for the encyclopedia yearbooks, annuals, or supplements. They are published annually to: (1) keep the basic set up to date and (2) present a summary of the year's major events. A third, less obvious, purpose is to increase sales: it is comforting for the buyer to realize that the set will never be outdated (a questionable assumption, but one used by almost every encyclopedia salesperson).

The yearbooks are usually available only to purchasers of the initial sets. They are all attractively printed, and they generally feature numerous illustrations.

The supplements are not related to the complete set except in name. The arrangements are broad, with emphasis on large, current topics. Most of the material is not later incorporated into the revised basic sets—a positive and negative consideration. On the positive side, a run of the yearbooks does afford a fairly comprehensive view of the year's events. On the negative side, the library is wise to keep a run of the yearbooks because the revised complete set cannot be depended upon to contain the same material, or at any rate, not in such depth. Consequently, someone looking for more than basic facts on a given topic really should search not only the main encyclopedia, but a number of the yearbooks also.

Aside from the age of the audience for which each is prepared, significant differences between the various yearbooks are difficult to discover. In this, they resemble the daily newspaper. One reader may prefer the slant or emphasis of one newspaper over another, but both papers are drawing from the same general materials. Nor is the analogy as far-fetched as it may seem. In the annuals particularly, the predominantly newspaper-trained staffs of the larger encyclopedia firms have a holiday. Format, content, and the ever-important emphasis on up-to-date, often exciting events reflect more than scholars behind the final book; they reveal an emphasis on what makes the daily newspaper sell, at least from the standpoint of the ex-newspaper writer.

In libraries, it is sufficient to purchase yearbooks for encyclopedias not replaced that year. If more than a single adults' and children's yearbook is to be purchased, the nod will go to the work preferred by the librarian and the patrons of the library. As long as the preference is within the standards set for encyclopedias, it is a matter more of taste than of objective judgment, and any one of the accepted publishers will serve as well as another.

Encyclopedias online

As of this writing, there are three general encyclopedias available online in full text. Depending on the vendor's program, they may be searched by subject headings and/or from words in the text of the set. One may sit down at a computer and search the text (but not the illustrations) of: *Encyclopaedia Britannica,* via Mead Data Central;[12] *Academic American Encyclopedia* via BRS, CompuServe, Dow Jones, VuText, and DIALOG. The English general set, *Everyman's Encyclopedia,* is offered by DIALOG. There is at least one subject encyclopedia online: *Kirk-Othmer Encyclopedia of Chemical Technology* (3d ed. New York: John Wiley and Sons, 1983, 12 vols. via BRS).

The tremendous advantage of an online encyclopedia is that it can overcome the problem of the work going out of date. *Academic American,* for example, revises material every six months. The database claims to be from one year to six months more current than the revised annual printings. Also, of course, one may read the article, or parts of the article, at the terminal, and, if desired, have it printed out.

The disadvantages are numerous—so much so that one wonders whether or not the encyclopedias, at least by themselves, will ever be a viable success online. Three questions still have to be answered about the works online. (1) Isn't it just as quick to search an alphabetically arranged set, or, for that matter, use the index? The answer is yes.[13] (2) Isn't it much less expensive to purchase a set than use one online? Again, the answer is yes, at least if the set is used frequently. If, as in the case of *Kirk-Othmer Encyclopedia,* it is used only infrequently, then the online search might be more economical. (3) As of this writing, one cannot transmit pictures online. The result is that a good deal of the value of the general encyclopedias is lost. Understandably, librarians and, to a lesser extent, laypersons, are skeptical. There's

[12]As of this writing, the publisher will not allow libraries access to the set online.

[13]Personal experience with the *Academic American* online indicates a search actually can be much slower than a manual quest particularly if the person, place or subject appears in several places in the set. Also, at a computer trade show, a publisher "confessed that to read an entire encyclopedia entry about Thomas Jefferson required more than 100 screenfulls of information." This would take more than an hour to receive. "From 1,500 Miles, Professor Teaches His Class by Computer," *The New York Times,* November 20, 1983, p. 32.

definitely a place for online indexes and bibliographies, but encyclopedias, particularly the general type, still have to prove themselves.[14]

The probable future of the online encyclopedia will be to turn towards the use of optical disks which (1) allow use of pictures and (2) will be able to be sold to individuals and libraries for immediate access at home or in the library through a computer or video disk player, or both. This development is likely to take place soon.

A halfway step is suggested by Grolier's putting its *Academic American Encyclopedia* on a CD-ROM, 4 ¾-inch disk. Sold for $199, it requires a computer to use. (A package that includes a CD-ROM disk drive and the encyclopedia retails for about $1500.) One may search it as many times as one wishes without paying an online search fee. (The encyclopedia will remain available online.)

Still another "twist" is suggested by the Corporation for Entertainment and Learning. They offer what they term a "Video Encyclopedia" of the twentieth century. This consists of 75 one-hour video cassettes that cover major events from 1893 through the 1985 Presidential inauguration. Footage from news reels, television productions, movies, etc., are included. There is a five-volume index with a subject, author, and title approach and 2500 pages of printed reference material, including a list of 8 to 10 stories and books for every day of the 92 years covered. Aside from a VCR, the library needs a good budget. The cost, as of January, 1986: $8500.

ONE- AND TWO-VOLUME ENCYCLOPEDIAS

The New Columbia Encyclopedia, 4th ed. New York: Columbia University Press, 1975, 3052 pp. $79.50 (Distributed by J. B. Lippincott).

The Concise Columbia Encyclopedia. New York: Columbia University Press, 1983, 943 pp. hardcover, $29.95; paperback, $14.95.

The Random House Encyclopedia, rev. ed. New York: Random House, 1983, 2918 pp. $99.95.

The decline in favor of the general multivolume encyclopedia, rising production and advertising costs, and an effort to meet the challenge of a public which no longer has the patience to read detailed accounts of anything have resulted in an increasing emphasis

---

[14]Even some publishers are skeptical; e.g., *World Book* in 1982–83 tested putting their set online via CompuServe as the vendor, but decided "the electronic version was not equal to the printed one," *Time,* June 13, 1983, p. 76.

on one- or two-volume general encyclopedias. Typically, the one- or two-volume work is arranged alphabetically and lacks an index, which, in this case, is not needed. The information is stripped down to facts, and the specific-entry form is almost universal.

For home use, the one-volume works are economical and, compared with multivolume sets in the same general price range, a better buy. The information is exact, well presented, and more reliable than that in the similarly priced "supermarket" sets. Where cost is a factor, the librarian should always inform the prospective purchaser of these one-volume works, encouraging a personal comparison of reviews or of the encyclopedias themselves.

Depending on nuggets of information rather than exposition, the 10½ pound *New Columbia Encyclopedia* has more than 50,000 articles; 66,000 cross-references; some 400 integrated illustrations, including maps of all major countries; and approximately 6.5 million words. While the content is hardly up to the 14 million words and 102,000 entries in the Britannica's *Micropaedia,* it compares favorably with the content in almost all young adults' and children's sets.

Qualitatively, the *Columbia* is a valuable ready-reference aid. The fourth edition gives added attention to third-world countries, science, social sciences, and the humanities. The strongest area is biography. Biographical sketches will be found here for individuals not included, or at best only mentioned, in the standard multivolume sets.

The Concise Columbia Encyclopedia is a best buy, particularly in paperback for only $14.95. It has over one million words, or about one-ninth the number in many young people's full sets. The arrangement is alphabetical, and the some 15,000 entries cover the same topics as any standard work. The difference is that here the material is current (as of 1983), concise, and extremely well written. Most entries are short, but there are rather extensive subject surveys. The illustrations and maps are adequate, the numerous graphs and tables well placed. In terms of coverage, about one-third of the volume is given over to biography with the social sciences and the humanities somewhat stronger. Science is adequately covered.

The work, while original, does draw upon the parent encyclopedia, *The New Columbia Encyclopedia,* 4th ed., (New York: Columbia University Press, 1975, 3052 pp.) which is found in many libraries. It, too, is an excellent work, but it is now dated. There are promises that the 6.5 million-word encyclopedia will be issued in a new edition soon. Until then, one should refer here last, using the other more up-to-date one- and two-volume works first.

The first edition of the *Random House Encyclopedia* appeared in 1977 and was generally acclaimed as a fine work. The revision is equally good. The material is updated, and the three million-plus words, as in the previous edition, are complemented by excellent illustrations. In fact, the strong point of this work are the 11,000 color pictures and the over 2000 illustrations in black and white. It is by far the leader in terms of both the quality and number of pictures in the one-volume encyclopedia league. In addition, there is a separate atlas.[15] Unfortunately, at least for some, the work is in two parts. The first (Colorpedia) offers a thematic discussion of seven general categories from "The Universe" to "Man and Machines". The result is a type of National Geographic viewpoint which is instructive enough to read, but somewhat difficult to use for reference purposes.

Not content to leave well enough alone, Random House updated the original work in 1985 and gave it a new name—*The New Universal Family Encyclopedia*. While the publisher claims 30 percent of the material is revised, and the price is almost one-third less ($34.95), it is not as good as the 1983 title. Entries are too brief and many of them, despite the publisher's claim, are dated. The illustrations and maps are uneven in quality. The library is better off with the earlier *Random House Encyclopedia* and *The New Columbia*.

FOREIGN-PUBLISHED ENCYCLOPEDIAS

Most reference questions can be quickly and best answered by an American encyclopedia, but there are occasions when a foreign-language work is more suitable. Obviously, a foreign encyclopedia will cover its country of origin in much greater depth than an American work. The same will also be true for such items as biographies of nationals, statistics, places, and events.

Even for users with the most elementary knowledge of the language, several of the foreign works are useful for their fine illustrations and maps. For example, the *Enciclopedia Italiana* boasts some of the best illustrations of any encyclopedia, particularly in the area of the fine arts. A foreign encyclopedia is equally useful for viewpoint. Some American readers may be surprised to find how the Civil War, for example, is treated in the French and the German encyclopedias, and the evaluation of American writers and national heroes is sometimes equally revealing about the way Europeans judge the United States. More specifically, the foreign encyclopedia is helpful for information on less-known figures not found in American

---

[15]Earlier printings did not have changes in the Atlas index to reflect changes in the maps. This was, according to the publisher, subsequently corrected.

or British works, for foreign-language bibliographies, for detailed maps of cities and regions, and for other information ranging from plots of less-known novels and musicals to identification of place names.

French

> *Grand Dictionnaire Encyclopé*dique Larousse. Paris: Larousse, 1982–1985, 10 vols. $995. (Distributed in the United States by Pergamon Press Inc.)

The name Larousse is as familiar in France as the *Encyclopaedia Britannica* is in the United States. Pierre Larousse was the founder of a publishing house which continues to flourish and is responsible for the basic French encyclopedias. In fact, "Larousse" in France is often used as a synonym for "encyclopedia".

One problem, as with most European encyclopedias, is the alphabetical arrangement. Any student who has had a brush with a foreign language realizes that while the Latin alphabet is employed, there are variations in letters; Spanish, for example, has two letters not found in English, "ch" and "ll." There are also marked differences in common names. John turns up as Giovanni, Jan, Juan, Johannes, or Jehan. Consequently, before abandoning a foreign encyclopedia for lack of an entry, the user should be certain to look for the entry in terms of the language employed.

Larousse continues with the policy of short specific entries, but it does give some rather extensive treatment of major subjects. For example, the length of articles for countries and leading personalities often equals that found in American works. Returning to an older concept of encyclopedias, the *Grand Dictionnaire* is precisely what the title suggests in that it not only includes specific encyclopedia entries, but definitions of words as well. Over 1000 subject experts and language specialists assisted in the compilation, and the result is a work of unusual dimensions. As with previous editions (the last was in 1972–81), there is a strong emphasis on brilliant illustrations, usually in full color. Each page includes photographs, charts, maps, diagrams and the like. Regardless of one's command of French, everyone will enjoy the illustrations.

German

> *Brockhaus Enzyklopä*die, rev. 17th ed. Wiesbaden: Brockhaus, 1966–1975, 20 vols. $1200. *Supplement,* 1975–1976, 4 vols. Total: 24 vols.

First issued as *Frauenzimmer Lexikon* (between 1796 and 1808), an encyclopedia primarily for women, *Brockhaus* got off to a bad start. The original publisher, possibly because of his limited sales, gave up the financial ghost; in 1808, Friedrich Brockhaus purchased the set and issued the last volume. A wise man, Brockhaus continued to offer his volumes not as scholarly works, but as books guaranteed to give the average man (or woman) a solid education. In this respect, he was years ahead of the times—in fact, so far ahead of his American and English counterparts that they freely borrowed his text, if not his sales techniques. As noted earlier, the Brockhaus works were the basis for the early *Americana* and *Chambers's*.

Brockhaus extended his popular formula to cutting back articles to little more than dictionary length. In this respect, he followed the European form of specific entry. Consequently, all the Brockhaus encyclopedias—and there is a family of them—are an admixture of dictionary and encyclopedia. (The family includes the basic twenty-four-volume set, the revised twelve-volume set, and a one-volume work, among others.)

As might be expected, the longer articles, some of them over 100 pages, are on European countries. In many respects, the Brockhaus encyclopedia is considerably more provincial than the *Larousse;* and while it is an excellent source of material on German history and personalities, it can be passed up for other items.

Because of its scope, the *Brockhaus* is useful in large research libraries or where there is a German-speaking populace, but it is probably near the bottom among choices of all the foreign-language encyclopedias.

Italian

> *Enciclopedia Italiana di Scienze, Lettere ed Arti.* Rome: Instituto della Enciclopedia Italiana, 1929 to 1939, 36 vols., appendices I-III, 1938 to 1962, 5 vols. $2285.

Lavishly illustrated with black-and-white and superb color plates, the Italian encyclopedia is best known for its artwork. For this, it can be used profitably by anyone; and somewhat like the *National Geographic* magazine, it will afford hours of browsing time even for the person who does not understand a word of the language in which it is written.

At perhaps a more important level, it has an outstanding reputation for detailed articles in the humanities. All the entries are signed, and there are a number of bibliographies. One good example is the article on Rome, which runs to almost 300 pages and has close to

200 photogravure plates illustrating nearly every aspect of the city, present and past.

Grande Dizionario Enciclopedico UTET (Turin: Unione Tipografico-Editrice, 1966–1975, 20 vols.) is a more popular Italian set with short entries and massive numbers of colored illustrations. It is useful for ready reference because of the extensive index.

Japanese

> *Kodansha Encyclopedia of Japan.* New York: Kodansha International, 1983, 9 vols. $600.

This is an unusual and superior encyclopedia which analyzes, explains, and even critically assesses Japan, past and present. After 12 years of planning, and an estimated $15 million, the all English-Japanese encyclopedia represents the work of 1300 scholars from 27 countries, including Japan and the United States.[16] It is a landmark publication not only because of the approach, but because it is the only English-language encyclopedia to cover Japan and its multiple interests. The text was written with the average layperson in mind, although much of the material will interest the subject specialist. The style is much above average. There are about 10,000 entries and 4 million words. The largest single category of entries concerns Japanese history, followed by geography and art. There are slightly over 1000 articles covering Japanese economics and business. The articles are quite objective, and considerable effort was made to insure nothing about Japan's past was glossed over or ignored.

While the illustrations are not as numerous as those found in many encyclopedias, they are at least representative of the subject matter. Unfortunately, they are all in black and white. The final volume is the exhaustive index.

Russian

> *The Great Soviet Encyclopedia,* 3d ed. New York: Macmillan, 1973–1983, 32 vols. $1900. (Published in Russia from 1970–1980 as *Bol'shaia Sovetskaia Entisklopediia.*)

This set may be taken at two levels. It is passable, i.e., no better or worse, than most other works for factual material, particularly in the sciences. It is controversial when dealing with the social sciences,

---

[16]Edwin McDowell, "Major Encyclopedia on Japan Written in English," *The New York Times,* October 11, 1983, p. C13. See, too, the favorable review in Reference Books Bulletin, *Booklist,* May 1, 1984, pp. 1237–38.

and as one critic puts it, "it mirrors the intellectual sterility and political conformity of Soviet life" in its political, historical, and artistic viewpoints. It has numerous anti-Zionist and anti-Jewish views.

As most American readers will use the English translation, two points are worth making: (1) The index is necessary because of the unusual alphabetical arrangement of each volume, caused by differences between the Russian and Latin alphabets. For example, the first translated volume contains entries for "Aalen Stage" and the "Zulu War of 1879." (2) The quality of the translation is good. The American version differs from the Russian in that cost considerations made it necessary to delete the fine maps in the original Russian version.

The *BSE* is the basic encyclopedia for the Soviet schools and for families, being somewhat equivalent in scholarship to the older version of the *Britannica*. The entire set has more than 21 million words and over 100,000 articles. Including both the specific-entry and the broad-entry forms, the set is a combination of routine dictionary and gazetteer items, with detailed, many-paged articles covering every aspect of Soviet interest.

Spanish

> *Enciclopedia universal ilustrada Europeo-Americana (Espasa)*. Barcelona: Espasa, 1907 to 1933, 100 vols., including annual supplements, 1934 to date. (Distributed in the United States by Maxwell Scientific, Inc. $3250.)

Usually cited simply as *Espasa,* the *Enciclopedia* is a remarkable work. First, it never seems to end. Forgoing continuous revision or new editions, the publishers continue to augment the 80 volumes (actually 70 basic volumes with 10 appendixes) with annual supplements which are arranged in large subject categories and include an index. (The term "annual" must be taken advisedly, as the supplements generally are not issued until three to five years after the period covered. For example, the 1969–1970 volume came out in 1975.)

Second, *Espasa* has the largest number of entries—the publishers claim over 1 million. Since they evidently do not count on "authority," none of the articles is signed, although they are signed in the supplements after 1953. Again, as in the German and French encyclopedias, the emphasis is on short entries of the dictionary type. Still, there are a number of rather long articles, particularly those dealing with Spain, Latin America, and prominent writers, scientists, artists, and so on who claim Spanish as a native tongue. The longer articles are often accompanied by extensive bibliographies which can be used to find definitive studies usually not listed in other sources. The illustrations and paper are poor, and even the colored plates of paintings leave much to be desired.

SUBJECT ENCYCLOPEDIAS

Now that the general encyclopedia seems to be on the decline, the subject work is gaining added favor with both librarians and individual buyers. It is part of a media trend which has resulted in the increased development of specialized periodicals, recordings, and even radio and television programs for narrow segments of the population. The reasoning of publishers and producers is that it is no longer possible or profitable to reach out to everyone. The best approach is to prepare a work for a select group, normally a group with both a high interest in the subject and a medium-to-high income to purchase the book.

Publishers of subject encyclopedias follow the special audience philosophy. The result generally is encouraging for reference librarians, particularly when: (1) a ready-reference question is so specialized or esoteric it cannot be answered in a general encyclopedia or (2) a user needs a more detailed overview of a subject than that found in a single general-encyclopedia article. The more limited the library budget for both reference work and general titles, the more reason to turn to subject encyclopedias. The librarian may have a limited amount of material on, for example, modern China, but many questions can be readily answered with the one-volume *Encyclopedia of China Today* (3d ed. New York: Harper and Row, 1984).

Few months go by that another subject encyclopedia is not published, announced to be in preparation, or revised. Topics cover every conceivable interest. Today, one may find a one-volume or multiple-volume set in areas from archaeology to zoology. Less-traditional subjects are considered, too; e.g., in 1986 the University of North Carolina Press published a one volume *Encyclopedia of Southern Culture*. It covers "the mind and manners and mythology of the American South, from John C. Calhoun to the Dukes of Hazzard."[17] In the multi-volume category, *The Encyclopedia of Religion* (New York: Macmillan Publishing Co., 1986) is a sixteen-volume work with 2750

---

[17]William Schmidt, "Southern Culture Gets Its Own Encyclopedia," *The New York Times*, August 19, 1984, p. 20.

articles on a wide range of topics from leading figures of religions great and small, to both Western and non-Western gods and goddesses. The $1100 price is relatively modest considering the scope of the set. The American Library Association's list of outstanding reference books published each year inevitably includes subject encyclopedias such as: *Encyclopedia of American Political History, Encyclopedia of Drug Abuse, Encyclopedia of Historic Places, Encyclopedia of Mammals, Encyclopedia of Psychology,* and *The Encyclopedia of Visual Arts.*

Encyclopedias and handbooks

There is a thin line between the subject or specialized encyclopedia and the traditional handbook. The handbook, as discussed in a later section, is a collection of a miscellaneous group of facts centered on one central theme or subject area, e.g., *Handbook of Physics* and *Handbook of Insurance.* An encyclopedia tends to be more discursive, although the dictionary, specific-entry type may simply list brief facts. A handbook is usually a means of checking for bits of data to assist the user in work in progress. Also, a handbook presupposes some knowledge in the field. A subject encyclopedia normally assumes that interest, more than knowledge, is the point of departure. If one must draw distinctions, a handbook is a working tool, whereas a subject encyclopedia is more a source of background information which eventually may help the user to formulate a project or a work.

The differences between the traditional encyclopedia and the handbook are not always so evident. The title is not necessarily a clue. The distinction seems to be that a handbook is usually conceived in the old German *Handbuch* sense of being a compendious book or treatise providing guidance in any art, occupation, or study. The encyclopedia may supply equal guidance, but the information therein tends to be more general, less directly involved with use in an actual working situation. The encyclopedia, then, is primarily for retrospective research. The handbook is primarily for ongoing help or guidance.

Evaluation

Much the same evaluative techniques are used for subject encyclopedias as for general sets. Even with limited knowledge of the field covered, librarians may judge the set for themselves, although they are more likely to depend on reviews or subject experts for evaluation of the expensive works. Subject sets are evaluated in scholarly periodicals, which discuss them at greater length than standard reviews do.

Once it is determined that the encyclopedia is good, the librarian must ask which and how many readers will use the work. The subject encyclopedias will fill gaps in the collection of art, science, or more esoteric subjects. For this reason, a subject encyclopedia is often a better buy for small- and medium-sized libraries than multiple sets of general encyclopedias.

Examples

Space does not permit a full discussion of the numerous, many quite superior, subject encyclopedias. Here the focus is on works which are best known and likely to be found in many medium-to-large libraries. Most, although not all, have been published relatively recently. This rather arbitrary approach gives at least a cursory glance at the direction of subject-encyclopedia publishing.

Art[18]

> *Encyclopedia of World Art.* New York: McGraw-Hill Book Company, 1959–1968, 15 vols. $995. Supplement, vol. 16, 1983, 278 pp. $69.50.

The *Encyclopedia of World Art* is the finest set available among encyclopedias devoted entirely to art. It includes art of all periods and has exhaustive studies of art forms, history, artists, and allied subject interests. Arranged alphabetically, it contains many shorter articles which answer almost every conceivable question in the field. The fifteenth volume is a detailed index.

An outstanding feature is the illustrations. At the end of each volume, there are 400 to 600 black-and-white and color reproductions. They, as well as some color plates in the main volumes, are nicely tied to the articles by suitable cross references and identification numbers and letters.

The supplement, prepared by 20 American scholars, is a chronologically arranged work which traces new developments from prehistory to the present. Extensive bibliographies end each chapter, and there is a subject, artist, and title index. Unfortunately, the index is inconsistent, but the second half of the volume is a success. It consists of 48 pages of color and 295 pages of black-and-white reproductions.

---

[18]Alex Ross, "State of the Art Sources: Visual Arts Encyclopedias," *Reference Services Review,* Winter 1983, pp. 55–58. A critical and descriptive review of nine art encyclopedias, including the *Encyclopedia of World Art.*

History

Adams, James T. (ed.), *Dictionary of American History*, rev. ed. New York: Charles Scribner's Sons, 1976, 7 vols. and index. $370.

Concise Dictionary of American History. New York: Charles Scribner's Sons, 1983, 1140 pp. $60.

The standard overview of American history for the layperson and the expert is the *Dictionary of American History*. Revised in 1976, it now includes 6045 entries by over 1400 contributors. The revision carries the history through the early 1970s and has new or revised sections on American Indians, Afro-Americans, women, and so on. The title derives from the fact that a vast number of the articles are brief, but this is more a matter of editing than of depth or scope. Actually, major periods are simply broken down into much smaller parts than are normally found in an encyclopedia, and then treated as separate, specific entries. This approach is ideal for reference work. There are no biographical entries, although names mentioned in articles are in the index.

For libraries, or individuals who do not wish or cannot afford the multiple volume set, there is a one-volume *Concise Dictionary of American History* by the same publisher for $60. Published in 1983, it provides a summary of the articles in the main set. It also serves to update many of the entries in the main set, and it can be used as a supplement to that work.

While more a handbook than an encyclopedia, the typical historical chronology should be mentioned here. There are numerous reference works which offer an overview of the past, usually in tabular or outline form. Usually they are arranged chronologically from the early cave people through to the last Presidential election. The work may be general and cover the entire world. The classic example of this type is William Langer's *An Encyclopedia of World History* (5th ed. Boston: Houghton Mifflin Company, 1972) which is devoted primarily to political and military events. At the narrower end of such works is the *Encyclopedia of American Facts and Dates* (7th ed. New York: Crowell, 1979) which has parallel columns showing developments in everything from the arts to politics, but limited to the United States. *The Almanac of American History* (New York: Putnam Publishing Group, 1983) updates *The Encyclopedia* in that it covers the years from 1970 to 1980, and parallels *The Encyclopedia* with material before 1970.[19]

[19]Stephen Rogers, "Selected Historical Chronologies," *Reference Services Review,* Summer 1983, pp. 15–19. A good overview of world chronologies.

Library Science

The ALA Yearbook of Library and Information Services. Chicago: American Library Association, 1975 to date, annual. Price varies.

Encyclopedia of Library and Information Science. New York: Marcel Dekker, 1968–83, 35 vols. $45–$55 per vol. Supplements 1–4, 1983–1985, $55 per vol.

The ALA Yearbook is an indexed, close to 400-page double-columned overview of the past year's events. Articles, which vary in length from one column to many pages, are written by experts. After a series of special reports, including biographies and awards, the articles move from abstracting and indexing services to young adults and various state reports. While this is an annual, not an encyclopedia *per se,* it serves as such in that it is an informal update to the *ALA World Encyclopedia of Library and Information Services* (Chicago: American Library Association, 2nd ed. 1986. 802 pp.) This latter work remains a valuable overview, particularly in terms of fundamental principles and historical and biographical material.

While highly controversial, the *Encyclopedia of Library and Information Science* cannot be faulted for its wide coverage and its ambitious effort.[20] Some think there is too much material; others, that areas are not always covered as well as they might be, particularly by the contributors involved. The set is quite uneven. Some of the writing is excellent, but too much of it tends to be superficial and dated. The supplements, issued about every year, are an effort to keep the complete set current. Actually, the lengthy articles in the supplement tend to be better than in the primary set, and are a good source of information on major trends in library and information work.

Literature & Drama

The Cambridge Guide to English Literature. New York: Cambridge University Press, 1983, 993 pp. $29.95.

McGraw-Hill Encyclopedia of World Drama, 2d ed. New York: McGraw-Hill Book Company, 1984, 5 vols. $295.

There are numerous one- and two-volume guides and encyclo-pedias of literature, including those published by Oxford University press, e.g., *Oxford Companion to English Literature, Oxford Companion to*

---

[20]For a critical appraisal of the set and supplements see the 1985 edition of American Reference Books Annual.

French Literature, etc.[21] The *Cambridge Guide to English Literature* follows much the same pattern, yet is more current and somewhat wider in scope as it includes the literature of the entire English-speaking world from the United States to Nigeria. There are about 3000 entries of various length which cover ready-reference queries from names of characters in novels to authors and literary terms. There are a few, scattered illustrations.

All aspects of drama, both in the West and in other parts of the world, are considered in the *McGraw-Hill Encyclopedia of World Drama*. The focus is on writers, but there are excellent review articles of the forms (musical comedy to one person shows) and ethnic and regional theatre (from American to African). The articles on playwrights are typically divided into five sections, including not only a biography of the author, but (and this is most useful for readers) analyses and synopses of the major plays. There are numerous black-and-white illustrations, and almost all of them are current. The index is as comprehensive as the set.

Music

> *The New Grove Dictionary of Music and Musicians,* 6th ed. New York: Macmillan Company, 1980, 20 vols. $1900.

Compiled at a cost of over $7 million, the 20-volume *New Grove* is unquestionably the standard set in the field of music. Like its predecessors, it is extremely reliable, drawing on the experience and skills of over 2500 contributors.

While of value to reference librarians primarily for the detailed articles on pre-twentieth-century music and musicians, the latest edition now includes detailed information on modern musical life, covering not only the contemporary classical composers and performers, but also those from popular music, including the vast area of folk music.

There are some 22,500 articles with over 3000 illustrations, which, according to the publisher, occupy about 7 percent of the page space. In addition, there are several thousand musical examples.

---

[21]The Oxford Companion series are of extremely high quality, but tend to become dated. For example, the fifth edition of *The Oxford Companion to American Literature* (New York: Oxford University Press, 1983) was not published until 18 years after the fourth edition. For a detailed review of one of these companions, with notes on how it is compiled, see: Ian McGilchrist, "Summaries of Distinction", *Times Literary Supplement,* April 26, 1985, pp. 455–456. The review is of *The Oxford Companion to English Literature.* 5th ed, 1985.

Of particular value, in addition to the detailed material on music and the long biographical sketches, are the many bibliographies. Not only are these found at the end of articles but in numerous cases they are separate entries, e.g., "Germany and Austria: Bibliography of Music to 1600." There is equal emphasis on lists of works by various composers. Still, in many reviews of the set there is a consensus that the high points are the biographies. These are the best of their type to be found in any reference source, and a first choice for reference libraries.

The New Grove Dictionary of Musical Instruments (1984, 3 vols. $350) is a spin-off of the older set, i.e., most entries are extracted from the main set. At the same time almost all are revised, rewritten and expanded for this work. It includes information on over 12,000 musical instruments of every culture from almost every period of time. Each instrument is fully described and usually illustrated. All types of music are considered, including classical, rock, and computer composition. The 400 contributors write well, and it is hard to think of any set, aside from the parent work, that is more complete on the subject.

Psychology

Encyclopedia of Psychology. New York: Wiley-Interscience, 1984, 4 vols. $249.

Drawing upon the experience of some 500 international authorities, this set has about 2000 articles which consider in depth, or sometimes briefly, the various aspects of psychology and psychiatry. Some indication of the scope of its content may be gained by scanning the content page of an issue of *Psychological Abstracts.* The articles vary in length and difficulty. Some are easy enough to follow for the layperson, but others, such as those dealing with theoretical psychology, do require some training in the field. Possibly of most use to the average reader are the clear explanations of common mental disorders and various psychological tests. Also, there are over 650 biographies and current bibliographies. Subject/person indexes increase the usefulness of the work.

Where there is less scholarly interest in the subject, *The Encyclopedic Dictionary of Psychology* (Cambridge: MIT Press, 1983, 718 pp.) can be recommended. This has about 13,000 entries and serves both to define terms and to explain basic concepts. The bibliographies are current, and there is a detailed index. Most of the material is well within the understanding of the layperson.

Science[22]

> *McGraw-Hill Encyclopedia of Science and Technology,* 5th ed. New York: McGraw-Hill Book Company, 1982, 15 vols. $850.
>
> *Van Nostrand's Scientific Encyclopedia,* 6th ed. New York: Van Nostrand Reinhold, 1983, 2 vols. $129.50 (one vol. $95.50).

Thanks to its frequent revision (about every five years), the *McGraw-Hill Encyclopedia of Science and Technology* is considered a basic set for library or home. The 1982 edition has approximately 7700 articles of varying length, over 15,000 illustrations, and 64 color-plates. There are numerous charts, graphs and summaries which make it exceptionally easy to follow even the most detailed of the articles. Written with the layperson in mind, the encyclopedia can be read with ease by even the most scientifically naïve individual. The writing style is directed to teenagers and adults.

The set is ideal for an overview of a given topic, whether it be tube worms or artificial intelligence, and it has an excellent index which makes it suitable for ready-reference purposes. Also, one part of the index is called the "topical" index; it groups all of the articles under 75 major subject headings—this for the person who wants to see relationships between various subjects. There are numerous cross-references, for ease of use, and current bibliographies.

Issued each fall, *The McGraw-Hill Yearbook of Science and Technology* acts as an update for the basic set. Unlike many yearbooks, it has references from its pages to the encyclopedia, and it can be used in conjunction with the main encyclopedia. For libraries who either cannot afford the main set or do not have much call for such material, there is the useful and inexpensive ($89.50) one-volume edition of the McGraw-Hill set. This is: *McGraw-Hill Concise Encyclopedia of Science and Technology* (New York: McGraw-Hill Book Company, 1984). The 7300 brief articles, in 2000 pages, cover all of the subjects in the 15-volume work, but are cut back considerably. There are numerous illustrations, and a 30,000-plus entry index. All and all, this is a superior one-volume science encyclopedia, matched only by the Van Nostrand entry.

The Van Nostrand work is revised frequently and has two distinct advantages. First, the articles and briefer entries are written

---

[22]Larry A. Kimble, "The McGraw-Hill Encyclopedias and Dictionaries of Science: A Comparative Review," *Reference Services Review,* Summer 1982, pp. 15–18. This is a short yet thorough analysis and evaluation of some 10 scientific reference works by the publisher.

for the layperson. While the material can be quite technical, the explanations are exceptionally clear. Second, it has numerous illustrations which help to underscore and clarify the points made in the text. There are about 7000 entries, 3 million words, and over 2500 illustrations. Arranged in alphabetical order, the work includes numerous cross references. It is an ideal ready-reference source for busy librarians, and a first choice for the home where the McGraw-Hill multiple set is either too costly or too bulky. Actually, it would be useful to have both it and the one-volume McGraw-Hill encyclopedia side by side in the library.

Social sciences

International Encyclopedia of the Social Sciences. New York: The Macmillan Company, 1968, $935. *Biographical Supplement,* 1979, 820 pp. $75.

This is unquestionably the single-subject encyclopedia of most use and greatest interest in libraries; although it predates the 1977 cutoff, it is too important to exclude. Its coverage includes subjects most often central to reference questions and, more particularly, to those questions calling for a limited amount of research or requiring an unbiased overview of a given area. Some 1500 scholars from 30 countries have contributed lengthy, comparative, analytical articles on all aspects of the social sciences, including anthropology, economics, geography, history, law, political science, psychology, sociology, and statistics. In addition to articles on various subject matters, the work includes some 600 biographies.

The set is arranged alphabetically, and there are copious cross-references and a detailed index. All these features make it extremely easy to use for reference work. Of particular interest is the arrangement of related articles under a single heading; for example, there are 12 contributions under "Learning" with related articles on psychological aspects and sociological aspects.

In 1979 the set was supplemented with a volume containing 215 biographies of famous, primarily deceased, social scientists. In the biographies, the contributors have provided basic data on developments in the social sciences, so the work may be used as both a biographical reference and an update of sorts to the original set. While considerably less ambitious in scope, *The Social Science Encyclopedia* (London: Routledge and Kegan Paul, 1986) is a useful update for the major work. The close to 1000 pages cover most current trends in the social sciences.

SUGGESTED READING

Daub, Peggy. "Grove's Dictionary of Music and Musicians: From George Grove to the New Grove," *Reference Services Review,* Fall 1982, pp. 15–22. A delightful survey of the history of Grove and the people behind both the old and new sets. As well written as it is informative, it is an ideal model for this type of study.

Flagg, Gordon, "Online Encyclopedias: Are They Ready for Libraries? Are Libraries Ready for Them?" *American Libraries,* March 1983, pp. 134–136. A brief discussion of the pros and cons of the online encyclopedia, with most of the emphasis on the latter.

Mathisen, Tyler, "All About Encyclopedias," *Money,* October 1983, pp. 209–212. A popular survey of the basic encyclopedias available to American families, this is both descriptive and evaluative. Of particular value: the brief appraisal of encyclopedia sales practices and the arguments pro and con about purchasing a set.

Wellisch, M., "More On Indexes in Encyclopedias," *The Indexer,* April 1982, pp. 3–5. The author contrasts a good and a bad encyclopedia index. In so doing, he outlines the basic requirements for indexing a set.

CHAPTER EIGHT

Ready-Reference Sources: Almanacs, Yearbooks, Handbooks, Directories

W hen the librarian speaks of a ready-reference question, it is a query which may range from a batting average, astronomy, acid rain, to recipes and programming a computer. In the Albany (New York) Public Library, a librarian notes: "We've had people asking us how to fix their snowmobiles . . . or someone who wants to know how to go into the window-washing business."[1] While much of this may be dismissed as trivia, it is important to consider every question carefully. The Albany librarian adds "We treat each question very seriously, because it's probably very important to the person asking; every question is valid."[2] This contrasts sharply with the attitude of some large research libraries. For example, the Vatican Library guide carries a warning that any reader who asks more than three "senseless" questions will be expelled. Just who evaluates what is senseless is not explained.

What is one person's trivia is another's major concern. Looking up a fact about business may help someone decide on the course of an investment or the future of a career. Checking a trend in climate or spending for arms may trigger or settle a debate. On the turn of a rule of order or an interpretation of advice on etiquette may depend the course of a meeting or true love.

---

[1] "Pursuit of Trivia Keeps Answer Troops Busy at Albany Public Library," *Knickerbocker News*, February 27, 1984, pp. 1B–2B.
[2] *Ibid.*

The ready-reference question is one which normally can be answered with a fact or piece of evidence, usually from one source. It normally requires no more than a minute or two to answer. At the same time, it may develop into an involved question when: (a) one cannot immediately locate the source of the answer and must spend much time and effort seeking it out; or (b) the question becomes a search or research topic because the person asking it is really in need of more data than the query implies. For example, someone who wants the address of a corporation may actually want not only that address, but information on how to apply for a position with that firm, lodge a complaint, find data to prepare a paper, or make an investment. The ready-reference question may only be an opening gambit for the person who uses it to start the interview dialogue.

It is this latter development—the probability that a ready-reference question may become more complex—which supports the view that professional librarians should be on duty at the reference desk. While it is true that someone with a minimum of training is able to find a book to answer a question about a title or an address, it requires the expert to know when the query is really an opener for a complex series of other questions on the same or a related topic.

Facts approach infinity in number, and as any reference librarian will tell you, so do the reference titles which deal with the numberless facts. So do ready-reference questions, which, mercifully, can normally be answered with a half-dozen or so of the thousands of possibilities. Answers to fact or ready-reference queries are usually found in the forms to be discussed here and in the next chapter: almanacs, yearbooks, handbooks, and directories.

ALMANACS AND YEARBOOKS

Although almanacs and yearbooks are distinctive types or forms of reference work, they are closely enough related in both use and scope to be treated here as a single class of ready-reference aids. Aside from the general almanac, e.g., *World Almanac*, and the general yearbook, e.g., *Britannica Book of the Year*, the subject almanac and the yearbook are similar and often used for much the same purpose in reference.

Definitions

Almanac An almanac is a compendium of useful data and statistics relating to countries, personalities, events, subjects, and the like. It is a type of specific-entry encyclopedia stripped of adjectives and adverbs and limited to the skeleton of information.

As most special subject almanacs are published on an annual or biannual schedule, they are sometimes called yearbooks and annuals. Traditionally, the almanac per se was general in nature; the yearbook and the annual were more specific, that is, they were limited to a given area or subject. No more. There are now subject almanacs and encyclopedia yearbooks which are as broad in their coverage as the general almanac.

Yearbook/Annual   A yearbook is an annual compendium of data and statistics of a given year. An almanac will inevitably cover material of the previous year, too. The essential difference is that the almanac will also include considerable retrospective material—material which may or may not be in the average yearbook. The yearbook's fundamental purpose is to record the year's activities by country, subject, or specialized area. There are, to be sure, general yearbooks and, most notably, the yearbooks issued by encyclopedia companies. Still, in ready-reference work, the most often used type is usually confined to special areas of interest.

Compendium   A compendium is a brief summary of a larger work or of a field of knowledge. For example, the *Statistical Abstract of the United States* is a compendium in the sense that it is a summary of the massive data in the files of the U.S. Bureau of the Census. As almanacs and yearbooks have many common qualities, they are sometimes lumped together as "compendiums."

Purpose

Recency   Regardless of form and presentation, the user turns to a yearbook or an almanac for relatively recent information on a subject or personality. The purpose of many of these works is to update standard texts which may be issued or totally revised only infrequently. An encyclopedia yearbook, for example, is a compromise—even an excuse—for not rewriting all articles in the encyclopedia each year.

Although most almanacs and yearbooks are dated 1986, 1987, etc., the actual coverage is for the previous year. The 1987 almanac or yearbook probably has a cutoff date of late 1986. The built-in time lag must be understood, particularly when, in middle or late 1987, one is looking for data in a 1987 reference work which simply will not be there.

Brief Facts   Where a single figure or a fact is required, normally without benefit of explanation, the almanac is useful. A yearbook will be more useful if the reader wishes a limited amount of background information on a recent development or seeks a fact not found in a standard almanac.

Trends   Because of their recency, almanacs and yearbooks, either directly or by implication, indicate trends in the development or, if you will, the regression of civilization. Scientific advances are chronicled, as are the events, persons, and places of importance over the previous year. One reason for maintaining a run of certain almanacs and yearbooks is to indicate such trends. For example, in the 1908 *World Almanac,* there were 22 pages devoted to railroads. The 1986 issue contained about 2, while television performers rated close to 12 pages. The obvious shift in interest of Americans over the past 50 years is reflected in collections of yearbooks and almanacs.

Informal Index   Most of the reliable yearbooks and almanacs cite sources of information, and thus can be used as informal indexes. For example, a patron interested in retail sales will find general information in any good almanac or yearbook. These publications in turn will cite sources, such as *Fortune, Business Week,* or *Moody's Industrials,* which will provide additional keys to information. Specific citations to government sources of statistics may quickly guide the reader to primary material otherwise difficult to locate.

Directory and Biographical Information   Many yearbooks and almanacs include material normally found in a directory. For example, a yearbook in a special field may well include the names of the principal leaders in that field, with their addresses and perhaps short biographical sketches. The *World Almanac,* among others, lists associations and societies, with addresses.

Browsing   Crammed into the odd corners of almost any yearbook or almanac are masses of unrelated, frequently fascinating bits of information. The true lover of facts—and the United States is a country of such lovers—delights in merely thumbing through many of these works. From the point of view of the dedicated reference librarian, this purpose may seem inconsequential, but it is fascinating to observers of human behavior.

GENERAL ALMANACS AND YEARBOOKS

Canadian Almanac and Directory. Toronto: Copp Clark Pitman, 1847 to date. (Distributed in the United States by Gale Research Company, Detroit.) $48.

Information Please Almanac. Boston: Houghton Mifflin Company, 1974 to date. $9.95; paper, $5.95.

The People's Almanac. New York: William Morrow & Co. Inc., 1975 to date, irregular. Price varies ($14.95 to $19.95).

Reader's Digest Almanac and Yearbook. Pleasantville, New York: Reader's Digest Association, Inc., 1966 to date. $7.50.

Whitaker's Almanack. London: J. Whitaker & Sons Ltd., 1869 to date. $48 (Distributed in the United States by Gale Research Company.)

World Almanac and Book of Facts. New York: Newspaper Enterprise Association, 1868 to date. $11.95; paper, $4.95.

All the titles listed here are basic general almanacs found in most American libraries. For general use and importance, they might be ranked as follows: (1) *World Almanac* (2) *Information Please Almanac* (3) and *Whitaker's Almanac.* The order of preference is based on familiarity. Sales of the *World Almanac* (close to 2 million copies) now exceed the combined sales of its two principal competitors.

With the exception of *Whitaker's,* all are primarily concerned with data of interest to American readers. In varying degrees, they cover the same basic subject matter, and, while there is appreciable duplication, their low cost makes it possible to have at least two or three at the reference desk. The best one is the one which answers the specific question of the moment. Today, it may be the *World Almanac;* tomorrow, *Whitaker's.* In terms of searching, though, it is usually preferable to begin with the *World* and work through the order of preference stated in the previous paragraph.

All almanacs have several points in common: (1) They enjoy healthy sales and are to be found in many homes; (2) they depend heavily on government sources for statistics, and readers will frequently find the same sources (when given) quoted in all the almanacs; and (3) except for updating and revising, much of the same basic material is carried year after year.

Of the three works, *Whitaker's,* the English entry, is by far the most extensively indexed (25,000 entries), followed by the *World Almanac* (9000 entries). *Whitaker's* is distinctive in that, as might be expected, it places considerable emphasis on Great Britain and on European governments. For example, the 1985 edition has close to 95 pages of an almost complete directory of British royalty and peerage, with another 150 pages devoted to government and public offices. Other features include an education directory, lists of leading newspapers and periodicals, and legislative data. Each year the almanac includes special sections on items in the news, such as the Falkland Islands struggle, the coal strike, the Irish question, and current exhibitions. Usually from 60 to 75 pages are devoted to this "events of the year section." There are from 250 to 300 pages on Commonwealth nations and their activities, as well as major foreign countries. Other unique features include the only easy accessible list of salaries of the upper civil service, including Church of England stipends for dignitaries. There are charity advertisements which run year after year, and lists of charitable bequests. Unfortunately, the cost of the almanac is prohibitive for all but larger libraries, or those with a particular need for such information. No other almanac offers so much up-to-date, reliable data on Great Britain and Europe.

Whereas there is little real duplication between *Whitaker's* and the American works, the almanacs published on this side of the Atlantic are similar to one another in scope if not arrangement and emphasis. The cousins of the *World Almanac* feature discursive, larger units on such subjects as the lively arts, science, education, and medicine. *Information Please Almanac* expanded its contents to include medicine, the economy, political and world developments, and so on. It has several pages of colored maps. *Information Please* gravitates more to the methods of encyclopedia yearbooks than to the standard form set by traditional almanacs. The subtitle "yearbook" emphasizes this focus as does the advertising, which stresses that it is the "most complete, up-to-date, easiest-to-use reference book for home, school, and office." While "most" is questionable, it is certainly excellent. It is considerably more attractive in makeup (larger type and spacing) than the *World*.

By 1985, the *World Almanac* showed some inclination to provide brief, accurate essay pieces on topics of current interest. For example, there are now sections on diet and a part devoted to forecasting the future. Still, the real strength of the work is in facts, facts, and more facts.

In terms of eye appeal, the *Reader's Digest Almanac* is the best of the group. The makeup and layout are more inviting, as are the numerous illustrations. Current events are covered under major headings such as Women's Rights. In fact, the work is divided along lines similar to those in the *Information Please Almanac,* and has subject headings such as Language, History, Awards and Prizes, Cities, Energy, etc. As it is a relatively late member of the group, it does not include many of the statistics found in the standard works. Wisely, the editors concentrate more on summaries and standard yearbook materials.

Now over 130 years old, the *Canadian Almanac and Directory* is an authoritative work about Canada. There are four sections. The first is a directory of full names and addresses of a wide variety of public and political offices and organizations. Another section is a listing of Canadian law firms and lawyers, while a third is given over to statistics, and a fourth to more common type of almanac data. Actually, this work falls more in the directory category, although it is usually considered an almanac. Closer to the latter is *The Corpus Almanac of Canada* (Toronto: Corpus Publishers, 1966 to date). Here is excellent coverage of federal and local politics as well as data on everything from Canadian law to finance. There is good directory information here, too, although not as much as in the less current *Canadian Almanac and Directory.*

A distinction of *The People's Almanac* is that it is one of the few reference works which people enjoy reading, if not cover to cover, at least page after page. The reason is twofold. First, it is not a standard almanac, but a collection of odd, unusual, and fascinating facts about everything from sports and players to historical sites and famous people. It is a strange grouping of trivia and quite substantial data, a mixture of a first-rate encyclopedia and entertainment. Fortunately, there is an excellent index which pulls all of this together for ready-reference purposes. Another reason for the work's ongoing popularity is the style of presentation, nicely worked out by novelist Irving Wallace and his family. The prose, as it were, flows. This may be a bit too sticky for some, but it is vastly amusing and even informative for most.

Since 1975 there have been three different editions of *The People's Almanac* (in 1975, 1978, and 1981, with more promised). While there is some overlap, each tends to be a complete and separate work which requires individual searching. The authors are responsible, too, for a book of predictions (1980) and three books of lists (1980–1983). The prophecies and forecasts in the first work are about as accurate as today's economists, but much more fun.

The almanacs considered here are the basic ones found in many libraries. In addition, there are scores, if not hundreds, of specialized and subject almanacs published each year. For example there is *The Omni Future Almanac* (New York: Harmony Books, 1982 to date) which considers the future in space exploration, business, and all points east and west. The annual *Business Week Almanac* (New York: McGraw-Hill Book Company, 1982 to date) covers a wide field from advertising to women in business. The numerous summaries, lists, graphs, and tables make it an indispensable aid for the business library. A related work, with a self-explanatory title, is *The American Almanac of Jobs and Salaries* (New York: Avon Books, 1982 to date).

The Negro Almanac (New York: John Wiley and Sons, 1967 to date, irregular) makes the point that some almanacs are established to meet the needs of a particular group which is not well-represented in standard works. This often is the case. For example, see biographical reference works where there are separate volumes for women, blacks and various minorities.[3]

Published every six or seven years, *The Negro Almanac* offers both retrospective data (biographies, history, social commentary) as well as statistics and current information on such things as education, civil rights, income, etc. In fact, it is really closer to a one-volume encyclopedia than the general almanac. The 1983 edition suffers from lack of detailed indexing and cross-references, but it remains the best single source of current information on blacks now available.

REPRESENTATIVE YEARBOOKS

There are two types of yearbooks. The first, and probably best known, is the general work which covers, as the title suggests, the past year's activities. The type found in most libraries is the annual encyclopedia addition. These are used to check names, dates, statistics, events, and almost anything else which might have been noticed in the past year.

Newspaper indexes, from the *National Newspaper Index* to *The New York Times Index,* often serve the same purpose; as does the weekly *Facts on File.* The latter is the most up to date, and the most satisfying, because of the well-organized format and the brief annotated stories. The publisher, since 1940, has simplified matters for librarians by issuing what amounts to a cumulation in *Facts on File Yearbook* (New York: Facts on File, 1940 to date) which is divided into four or five large divisions. Most of the focus is on the American sector, although foreign events are covered when they are of interest to American policy. It is useful, too, for the objective summaries of everything from the year in crime and sports to what has been happening in the arts.

A related work, but published in Great Britain, is *The Annual Register of World Events* (London: publisher varies, 1761 to date. Distributed in United States by St. Martin's Press, Inc.). Essentially it follows the same approach as *Facts on File,* but the primary interest is the United Kingdom and Europe. There are some 16 sections which are adequately indexed. Americans find it of particular value for the statistical data on European politics and social developments.

[3]The obvious question is whether or not such works would be necessary if the groups were equally and fairly represented in standard works. As they are not, the specialized reference titles persist.

Subject yearbooks

Almost every area of human interest has its own subject compendium, or yearbook. In a text of this type it is pointless to enumerate the literally hundreds of titles. What follows, then, is a representative group and, more particularly, those "basic" or "classic" works which cross many disciplines and are used in some libraries as often as the familiar index, encyclopedia, or general almanac.

Government: International[4]

> *Europa Yearbook.* London: Europa Publications, Ltd., 1926 to date, 2 vols., annual. $210. (Distributed in the United States by Gale Research Company.)
>
> *Statesman's Year-Book.* New York: St. Martin's Press, Inc., 1864 to date, annual. $45.

It is somewhat arbitrary to separate most of these yearbooks from the "general" category, particularly as they all relate directly to the type of material found in encyclopedia annuals and, for example, *Facts on File Yearbook.* The major difference is in emphasis. The government titles stress the standard, statistical, and directory types of information, which change only in part each year. The aforementioned general yearbooks stress the events of the past year.

Published for over a century, the *Statesman's Year-Book* provides current background information on 166 nations. Along with a general encyclopedia and an almanac, it is a cornerstone for reference work in almost any type of library. It has a distinct advantage for ready-reference work—it is the most up-to-date of the group discussed here and can be relied on for currency. It has a superior index.

The *Year-Book,* grouping countries alphabetically, begins with comparative statistical tables and information on international organizations. With the 1978–1979 edition, more effort was made for balance of coverage, with the result that the third-world countries are now better represented than in earlier volumes. Still, the 1986 edition shows a heavy emphasis on England and Europe. The quantity of information varies in proportion not so much to the size of the country as to the definite Western slant of the reference work.

---

[4]For a comparison of the *Statesman's Yearbook* and *The Europa Year Book,* as well as fascinating notes on how they are compiled, see: Geoffrey Best, "The World of Facts," *The Times Literary Supplement,* April 26, 1985, pp. 471–472. For U.S. government yearbooks and ready-reference guides see the final chapter in this text on government documents.

The book arranges the information systematically. Typical sub-headings for almost every entry are: heads of government, area and population, constitution and government, religion, education, railways, aviation, and weights and measures. There are excellent brief bibliographies for locating further statistical and general information and numerous maps showing such things as time zones and distributions of natural resources.

The *Europa Yearbook* covers much of the same territory as its competitor, but it has several advantages. (1) Timeliness is a major factor. Not all the material is updated (an anticipated weakness in yearbooks), but most of it is relatively current, and both volumes begin with a page of late information on election results, cabinet changes, deaths, and the like. The work is almost as timely as the *Statesman's Year-Book*. (2) It leads in the number of words and amount of information. (3) The first volume covers the United Nations; special agencies, and international organizations, by subject and European countries. (4) The second volume covers non-European countries. There is a uniform format throughout. Each country begins with a short introductory survey, followed by a statistical profile, the constitution, government, political parties, diplomatic representatives, judicial system, religion, the press, publishers, radio and television, trade and industry, transportation, and higher education—as well as miscellaneous facts peculiar to that country. This wider coverage, particularly of the media, gives it a substantial lead for ready-reference queries over the other two works. The balance among countries is good.

Europa is far from perfect; the flaws continue despite its long publishing history. For example, the index in the first volume is only for the UN and international organizations. One must turn to the second-volume index for material on Europe. There is no composite index.

There are numerous titles which cover the same territory, although always with a bit of a difference. For example, *World Encyclopedia of Political Systems & Parties* (New York: Facts on File, 1983, 2 vols.) offers objective analysis of the political systems in over 170 countries. The work will be periodically updated. *The South American Handbook* (Chicago: Rand McNally, 1924 to date, annual) is an expanded version of the standard general work for one area of the world. There are similar guides for other parts, as well. Despite the numerous works, most libraries will function quite nicely with the two basic guides listed here, i.e., *Europa* and *Statesman's Yearbook*.

Libraries and publishing

The following are published by R. R. Bowker Company.

Bowker Annual of Library and Book Trade Information, 1965 to date. $79.95.

The Book Publishing Annual, 1983 to date. $60.

Many professions have their own yearbooks, and libraries and publishers are no exception. Actually, the works briefly noted here can be found, in other forms, of course, for everything from education to medicine and law.

The R. R. Bowker entries have self-explanatory titles, and while each is focused on publishing, each is of equal interest to librarians. The most general one is the *Bowker Annual* which has statistics and charts on everything from the types of libraries to statistics on research and the book trade. The first section is particularly useful as it gives well considered "reports from the field." The work ends with a directory of organizations of particular interest to librarians.

The Book Publishing Annual chronicles the past year's developments with articles and essays on everything from copyright to best sellers. The work is particularly good for the background on the industry's financial health, as well as federal legislation. It nicely supplements the *Bowker Annual* which, in recent years, has dropped most of the information about book publishing because it is now covered in the yearbook.

HANDBOOKS AND DIRECTORIES

The next large group of ready-reference sources consists of handbooks, manuals, and directories.

Because it is difficult to distinguish between the average handbook and the average manual, the terms are often used synonymously, or the confused writer solves the definition problem by again using the term "compendium" for either or both.

Purpose

The primary purpose of handbooks and manuals is as ready-reference sources for given fields of knowledge. Emphasis normally is on established knowledge rather than recent advances, although in the field of science, handbooks that are more than a few years old may be almost totally useless.

The scientific handbook in particular presupposes a basic knowledge of the subject field. A good part of the information is given in shorthand form, freely employing tables, graphs, symbols, equations, formulas, and downright jargon, which only the expert understands. Much the same, to be sure, can be said about the specialized manual.

Scope

With some exceptions, most handbooks and manuals have one thing in common—a limited scope. They zero in on a specific area of interest. In fact, their particular value is their depth of information in a narrow field.

There are countless manuals and handbooks. New ones appear each year, while some old ones disappear or undergo a name change. It is obviously impossible to remember them all. In practice, based on ease of arrangement, lack of substitute, or amount of use, librarians adopt favorites.

There are scores of general handbooks and manuals. There are thousands dedicated to specific subject areas and subsections of those areas. A cursory glance at *Guide to Reference Books* will make the point, and in the *American Reference Books Annual,* many of the subject areas include a section for handbooks. The following representative group was selected because of wide use in libraries.

General handbooks and manuals

> *Guinness Book of World Records.* New York: Sterling Publishing Company, 1955 to date, annual. $16.95; paper, $10.95.
>
> Kane, Joseph N. *Famous First Facts,* 4th ed. New York: The H. W. Wilson Company, 1981, 1350 pp. $70.

There are numerous fact books edited primarily to entertain, to settle arguments, to meet the insatiable needs of trivia collectors, and to provide people with the "first" to the "best" to the "worst" of everything. Most of these are at least accurate and provide the librarian with still another entrance into the sea of facts. Of the scores of such titles now available, the ones listed here are representative.

While *Guinness Book of World Records* needs no introduction—it is among the top ten best-selling books of all time, and known to almost everyone—it is worth reminding sport and game fans that it is a reliable place to check records. Divided into broad sections, it includes everything from winners of soccer and baseball to football and tennis.

There are, too, numerous illustrations, some of them in color. Also, it features much trivia from the fastest wedding to the record baby carriage pushing speed. For example, Bozo Miller ate 27 two-pound chickens at one sitting; while Alan Peterson holds the record for eating 20 standard hamburgers in 30 minutes. It is a good place to find information on almost any winner, and the quest is aided by an excellent index. Note: This is updated each year and past editions are useful for sometimes out-of-the-way facts.

Other related, spin-off titles by the same publisher, with self-explanatory titles, and updated frequently: *Guinness Sports Record Book, Guinness Book of Extraordinary Exploits,* and *Guinness Book of Surprising Accomplishments.* These are only a few. There are many, many more.

If Guinness is famous world-wide, *Kane's Famous First Facts* is equally well known in libraries. As the title suggests, it is a briefly annotated listing of over 9000 "firsts" in everything from the first toothbrush to a major discovery. It is arranged in such a way that one may find an umbrella subject area and either browse, or seek out the essential first fact. There are four excellent indexes which allow the reader to find an event by a year, or a month and a day, or by the name of the person involved, or the location where the first took place. Warning: Kane's firsts are only for American events and inventions. If it was a first in another part of the world, it is not included unless it has some American angle.

Literature

> Magill, Frank N. *Masterplots,* rev. ed. Englewood Cliffs, New Jersey: Salem Press, 1976, 12 vols. $320. Supplemented by *Survey of Contemporary Literature,* rev. ed., 1976, 12 vols. $320; and *Magill's Literary Annual,* 1977 to date, annual. $55.

As far back as the Middle Ages, there were so-called cribs to assist students studying for an examination or working on a paper. There is nothing new about the medium and, in its place, it is a worthwhile form of publishing. A reference librarian may have mixed views about the desirability of such works for students, but that is a problem which students, teachers, and parents must work out together. It is an error to deny a place on the reference shelf to valuable sources, regardless of how they may be used or misused.

Plot summaries and other shortcuts to reading are often requested by students. By far the most famous name in this area is Frank N. Magill's *Masterplots,* a condensation of almost every important classic in the English language. Not only are the main characters well explained, but there is also a critique of the plot highlighting its good and bad points. Somewhat over 2000 books are considered and there is easy reference to about 12,000 characters.

The basic set is supplemented by a whole series of direct and indirect sources. The direct line consists of: (a) *Survey of Contemporary Literature,* which includes additional plots for 2300 more books, published primarily between 1954 and 1976; (b) *Magill's Literary Annual* is a continuation of the basic *Survey* set, i.e., from where it leaves off in 1976 to the present. It contains sketches for 200 fiction and non-fiction titles published the previous year.

There are numerous versions of the plot/character shorthand approach to literature. Most bookstores, for example, have *Monarch Literature Notes* (New York: Monarch Press, various dates). The over 75 titles in this series are 35- to 75-page pamphlets outlining the plot, character and criticism of a particular work or the place of a writer in history. They are closely related to senior high school and college English courses. Teachers frown upon such cribs, and few libraries provide this type of service.

Occupations

> U.S. Department of Labor. *Occupational Outlook Handbook.* Washington, D.C.: Government Printing Office, 1949 to date, biennial. $13.
>
> *Current Careers and Occupational Literature.* New York: The H. W. Wilson Company, 1978 to date, biennial. $30.

Although vocational guidance is not usually a part of the reference service in larger libraries, it is very much so in medium-sized and small libraries, and certainly in schools. When occupational and professional advice is given to students by trained counselors, there inevitably is a fallout of young men and women seeking further materials—either for personal reasons or for preparing class papers. The rush has become so general that even the smallest library is likely to include a considerable amount of vocational material in the vertical file.

When working with students or, for that matter, with adults, a certain amount of probing and patience is normally required. Users may have only a vague notion of the type of information they desire, and may be quite uncertain about their particular interests and the possibility of turning those interests into a channel of work. Here the *Occupational Outlook Handbook* is especially useful. Close to 700 occupations are discussed in terms likely to be understood by anyone.

Each of the essays indicates what the job is likely to offer in advancement, employment, location, earnings, and working conditions. Trends and outlook are emphasized to give the reader some notion of the growth possibilities of a given line of work. Unfortunately, the writers are often no more accurate in their predictions than economists and racehorse touts. An effort to update the title is made through *Occupational Outlook Quarterly* (Washington, D.C.: Government Printing Office, 1957 to date, quarterly). The periodical contains current information on employment trends and opportunities.

A related work is the *Dictionary of Occupational Titles* (4th ed. Washington, D.C.: Government Printing Office, 1977), which classifies and briefly describes about 20,000 jobs. The 5-pound, 1300-page fourth edition is useful for people particularly high school and college students looking for ideas about employment. They may then turn to the *Occupational Outlook Handbook* for details on most, although not all, jobs. Nine-digit code numbers identify positions including such unusual ones as dog bather, bomb loader, and batperson—all unlikely to make the index of the handbook. Between editions, the basic work has irregular supplements, e.g., one was published in 1981 which is close to 500 pages long, while another, in 1982, is a 50-page pamphlet.

There are massive amounts of material published each year concerning occupations and professions. Much of this, in pamphlet and other ephemeral forms, is often difficult to locate. A great help is the biennial *Current Career and Occupational Literature,* ably edited by Leonard Goodman. The first part is an annotated listing of both books and pamphlets, with an asterisk denoting the recommended titles. The second part is a group of materials simply labeled "books and pamphlets describing more than one occupation." The last section gives the full names and addresses of many elusive publishers of this type of material. As a companion to *Occupation Outlook Handbook,* the bibliography is a required item in almost all libraries where vocational advice is a consideration.

Etiquette

> *Emily Post's Etiquette,* 14th ed. New York: Harper & Row, 1984. 1018 pp. $16.95.

In days past, strict codes of manners and dress bothered everyone except the upper classes who set their own rules, or the lower classes who had more to worry about than etiquette. The middle classes and those on the economic-social upswing did need guidance and a formal approach to everything from how to carry on a conversation to which spoon to use with soup. Emily Post became the standard guide, and even today is considered the judge of good manners. The last revision (1984) takes a much more liberal stand on such matters. This is particularly obvious in regard to what women may and may not do in social and business situations. The change comes, of course, from having at least 50% of women in the work force. Where an earlier edition warned of the hazards of dressing in the wrong fashion for an afternoon tea, the 1984 revision is considerably more concerned with the do's and don't's of women's clothing in the office. Elizabeth Post (who revised the 1922 Post volume) is no wilting flower. She asserts in the new edition that women must take a strong stand and not be afraid to be themselves.

Actually, the standard etiquette books now take much the same position, and it is difficult to say whether one is more liberal or conservative than the other. The *Amy Vanderbilt Complete Book of Etiquette* (rev. ed. Garden City, New York: Doubleday and Co., Inc., 1978) still seems more advanced than Emily. The latter, for example, believes "femininity is still more attractive in a woman than masculine capability. . . ."[5] Letitia Baldrige, who updated Amy, is more in tune with the women's liberation movement. At the same time, in her *Letitia Baldrige's Complete Guide to Executive Manners* (New York: Rawson Associates, 1985) she is a bit more conservative. Concerned with classic corporate protocol, she submits that only certain topics are suitable for small talk. Among these: landscape gardening, robots doing housework, Princess Diana, and the use of hypnotism to stop smoking.

Incidentally, men are dutifully considered throughout these works although one continues to have the distinct impression that good manners are the presumed territory of women, not men. The assumption is based on the amount of material addressed specifically to women.

Within the reference situation, books of etiquette serve the important purpose of answering ready-reference questions about standard items (forms of address, who sits where at a table, etc.) as well as less-usual queries. In the latter group, most books now explain how to handle weekend guests who are not married, and just about any aspect of sex often nicely skipped over in earlier editions.

Meanwhile, for the truly liberated—who have a sense of humor

[5] I am grateful to Jim Rettig of The Wilson Library Bulletin for bringing this quote to the attention of one and all. For a detailed, witty and perceptive review of basic books of etiquette, see Richard W. Grefrath, "Eating Clams with Your Fingers: A Survey of Contemporary Etiquette Books," *Collection Building*, Winter 1985, pp. 10–16.

and a sense of perspective about such matters—the best general book probably is Judith Martin's *Miss Manners' Guide to Excruciatingly Correct Behavior* (New York: Atheneum Publishers, 1982). While conservative in the sense of strongly maintaining the need for good taste, it is equally an impassioned plea for common sense. The author, for example, says it is perfectly acceptable to eat asparagus with one's fingers.

Science

> *Handbook of Chemistry and Physics.* Cleveland: Chemical Rubber Company, 1913 to date, annual. $59.95.

Considered the bible of chemists and physicists, the *Handbook of Chemistry and Physics* is, as the subtitle explains, "a ready-reference book of chemical and physical data." The data are readily accessible, as they are organized in a way that groups similar and related materials commonly needed in research. Much of the information is in tabular form and, like the rest of the annual, is constantly updated to include reference material in such developing areas as solar radiation and cryogenics. Although using it requires some basic knowledge of chemistry and physics, it is as familiar to beginning students as to experienced researchers.

ADVICE AND INFORMATION[6]

A common problem that arises in reference service is when to give information, when to give advice, and when to give neither. Normally, the emphasis is on information, not advice. The distinction is important, because in some librarians' minds, advice and information are confused when medicine, law, or consumer information is sought by the layperson. Most librarians are willing to give consumer data, even advice (as this author believes they should about reference books and related materials), but some hesitate to give out data on medicine and law.

[6]Bill Katz and Anne Clifford, *Reference and Online Services Handbook* (New York: Neal-Schuman Publishers, 1982, pp. 279–284). This section quotes the guidelines established by several public libraries concerning how to handle legal, medical and, to a lesser extent, consumer questions. See, also, entries in the index for treatment by other types of libraries. See, too, the second volume by the same publisher, *Reference and Online Services Handbook,* 1986, for additional information.

There is no reason not to give information about law or medicine. This does not mean the librarian is giving advice. The trend today is to welcome legal and medical queries. Still, doubts may arise in the following forms:

(1) "I may be practicing law (medicine) without a license." The answer is that there is no case of a library or a librarian being named as defendant in a legal suit on this ground. The librarian has no liability to fear. Of course, the librarian should not try to diagnose the situation or offer treatment (legal or medical), but simply provide the information required—no matter how much or in what form.

(2) "I don't know enough about law (medicine) to find required information." The answer is that there are now numerous books, articles, pamphlets, and television and radio tapes available for the layperson. These are reviewed in most of the standard reference review media. Furthermore, as with any subject area, the librarian soon becomes familiar with ways to evaluate a title for reliability, currency, style of writing, and the like. As for finding the data, again this is not difficult when one becomes accustomed to using a few basic reference works.

The sections which follow, on medicine, law, and consumer advice, point up specific problems and reference works. At the same time, it is good to remember that many basic questions about everything from medicine to law may be answered by consulting equally basic periodical indexes. The *Readers' Guide* and *Magazine Index* cover both general and some specialized magazines which touch most points of interest to laypersons concerning consumer, legal, and medical problems.[7] This equally is true when one turns to features in newspapers via, say, the *National Newspaper Index* or *NEXIS*. And, of course, one should never forget some quite excellent overviews offered in the encyclopedias.

How-To/Self Help

Katz, Bill and Linda S. Katz. *How-to: 1,400 Best Books on Doing Almost Everything.* New York: R. R. Bowker Company, 1985. $29.95.

————. *Self Help: 1,400 Best Books on Personal Growth.* New York: R. R. Bowker Company, 1985. $29.95.

---

[7]Trudy Gardner and Judy Siebert, "Consumer Health Information Needs and Access Through Existing Indexes," *RQ*, Summer 1981, pp. 366–1971. The article offers a good comparison of *Readers' Guide* and *Magazine Index.*

which give solid, clear definitions; and (3) purchasing or having access to technical information which is not beyond the understanding of the better-educated or the more involved layperson.

There are a number of standard medical dictionaries; among those most often found in libraries is *Dorland's Illustrated Medical Dictionary* (Philadelphia: W. B. Saunders Co., 1900 to date). Frequently revised, this is the work of over 80 consultants, who review all entries and the numerous illustrations. *Stedman's Medical Dictionary* (Baltimore: William & Wilkins: 1911 to date) is another often-revised work which has some of the more up-to-date entries.

By far the best dictionary for the layperson is Edward R. Brace's *A Popular Guide to Medical Language* (New York: Van Nostrand Reinhold, 1983). Some 1000 medical terms are defined and discussed in such a way that the average reader may understand the full implication of the word or phrase. Actually Brace goes beyond definition to consider variations, where necessary, on the term as well as such things as symptoms and possible treatments. The dictionary, then, is really more of a handy guide to common medical problems.

The best all-around title for libraries is Alan Rees, *The Consumer Health Information Source Book*. It has the advantage of currency (published in late 1984) and of being edited for librarians. After a brief introduction on consumers and health information, there follows an annotated listing of basic reference works as well as pamphlets, audiovisual, and other types of materials. There is a good title and subject index. A more selective annotated listing will be found in the "health and medicine" section of *Reference Sources for Small and Medium Sized Libraries* discussed in the second chapter of this text; and in various parts of the aforementioned *Self-Help: 1,400 Best Books on Personal Growth*. Both lists, too, are as current as Rees. See, too, the highly selective list, "General Consumer Health Reference Books," Reference Books Bulletin in *Booklist,* February 1, 1985, pp. 764–768.

The best-known and most often found pharmacology work in a library is the *Physicians' Desk Reference*. Frequently referred to as the PDR, it provides information on close to 3000 drug products. The publisher notes that "the information is supplied by the manufacturers." At the same time, the Food and Drug Administration has approved the material sent by the manufacturer.[8] Brand, generic, and chemical names are given, so, with a little experience, one can easily check the content of this or that drug. (A generic and chemical name

[8]I am grateful to Edward M. Brace for pointing out the full disclosure rule of the FDA. At the same time, he writes: "A manufacturer cannot, legally, omit any word of text that has been previously been approved by the FDA. If it is listed, it must reproduce the entire text as approved."

index is a major finding device.) For each item, the composition is given, as well as such data as side effects, dosage, and contraindications. One section pictures over 1000 tablets and capsules, with product identification. The neatly divided six sections are arranged for easy use.

Each annual volume may or may not have a supplement. According to the publisher, "the supplement is published when necessary during the year to provide . . . important revised information, as it becomes available, on products described in this volume." It is important to check to see whether a supplement has been issued. The obvious reason: between the annual volume and the supplement discoveries may have been made which will show side effects, even fatal dangers, in drugs otherwise approved in the main volume.

The PDR comes in another version, i.e., the *Physicians' Desk Reference For Nonprescription Drugs* (1980 to date, annual) which considers some 1000 over-the-counter products. Arrangement and content is much like the basic volume, including a section with photographs of actual tablets and packages. Updated each year, it is particularly useful for an objective analysis of not only what the drugs promise, but any bad side effects.

Another much-used basic work, equally technical, although suitable for certain library situations, is the *Merck Manual of Diagnosis and Therapy* (Rahway, New Jersey: Merck Sharp & Dohme, 1899 to date). Published for many years as a manual for physicians, it is equally clear to laypersons with patience and a medical dictionary at hand. Illnesses and diseases are described in relatively nontechnical language, symptoms and signs are indicated, and diagnoses and treatments are suggested. Beginning in 1986, this is online, with new material and revisions made every six months.

There is considerably more to health information than selecting the best books and having current reference works available. The whole process of the reference interview may be quite different from the usual question and answer encounter. In fact, many librarians feel slightly uncomfortable because they think the type of information required is more personal than usual. Then, too, there are other problems from offering "bad news" about a particular disease to the user who wishes to talk at great length about a personal difficulty. Nevertheless, the librarian is morally bound to remain objective, to give the right information, and to refrain from making judgments either about the patron or the advice given in a particular source.[9]

[9]Catherine Alloway and Linda Salisbury, "Issues in Consumer Health Information Services," *RQ*, Winter 1983, pp. 145–149. An excellent overview of current opinions about reference work and medical information. Note, too, the lengthy bibliography.

Law

> *Reader's Digest Family Legal Guide.* New York: Random House, 1981, 1268 pp. $23.50.
>
> *The Guide to American Law.* St. Paul, Minnesota: West Publishing Company, 1984–1985, 12 vols. $720.
>
> *Encyclopedia of Crime and Justice.* New York: Free Press, 1983. 4 vols. $300.

Librarians often are more reluctant to give out reference information about law than about medicine. Some believe they will be placed in legal jeopardy. A more prevailing view (for medical data as well) is that many people do not have the education to cope with technical legal data.

The librarian should not try to act as an attorney (any more than she should act as a doctor), but it is important to give information when requested. To do anything else is to be a censor, or so this author believes. Furthermore, not to give such information is to help keep many people who desperately need assistance in the dark about the law.

All librarians are likely to face both personal and ethical difficulties when asked for legal assistance. When people are trying to solve their own legal problems by using standard law books or popular titles, there is, as in medicine, the problem of the librarian's knowledge of the subject matter. Here, however, the problem is complicated, as there are few popular legal works and most people want the standard texts, statutes, interpretations, cases, and the like. This requires more than a passing familiarity with legal research. Also, lawyers are sometimes quick to take exception to anyone, even their peers, giving out legal help, and librarians are sometimes nervous about recriminations from attorneys.

The real question, however, concerns the practice of law. Is the librarian who gives legal information actually practicing the law? The answer is a categorical no. As with medical information, the response to a query, the location of the necessary data, is not practicing law. Even in a law library open to the public, the trained legal librarian is unlikely to be charged with unauthorized legal practice.

There are several helpful guides for the nonlawyer, but the best and by far the most consulted is Miles Price and Harry Bitner, *Effective Legal Research* (various publishers and dates). Often updated, it offers an easy-to-understand, jargon-free approach to the literature of law. Important sections on basic reference works are of particular value. Referred to as "Price and Bitner," it is both a starting point and a constant companion for the librarian.

Another somewhat more involved, yet equally useful guide is *Finding the Law: A Workbook on Legal Research for Laypersons* (Washington, D.C.: Government Printing Office, 1983). This close to 300-page government document opens with definitions and procedures and concentrates on explaining the various types of books and guides which may be employed by a person who wishes to become familiar primarily with federal laws. All of this is supported with illustrative pages of the texts being considered.

There is an annotated list of legal books suitable for the layperson in the aforementioned *Self-Help: 1,400 Best Books on Personal Growth*. These are under several subject headings. Also, see *Reference Sources for Small and Medium-Sized Libraries* (in the "political science and law" chapter) for suitable reference works from dictionaries to various guides. For an annotated, detailed list see Judith M. Nixon's "Legal Reference Service in the Public Library: a Guide to Primary Source Legal Material," *RQ,* Winter 1984, pp. 195–203.

Probably the best all-around legal guide for the librarian and layperson is the *Reader's Digest* entry. Prepared with the assistance of a leading legal publisher (West), it has basic information on all aspects of the law from divorce and wills to marriage and property sales. It is arranged under about 2000 topics. Particularly useful are the numerous charts and tables which summarize the various state laws on particular topics.

Considerably more detailed, and especially useful for detailed historical articles, *The Guide to American Law* may trace such a concept as "annulment" from the middle ages down through several state court decisions. The set is written for the layperson, and where legal terms are employed they are carefully defined. While this is more useful for background information than for current decisions about everyday legal matters, it is the best available work for someone seeking an authoritative and detailed view of American law.

Another work designed for a wide audience, the *Encyclopedia of Crime and Justice* narrows the scope to consider only criminal law. Law professors, social workers, and psychologists address current problems from street crime and overcrowded prisons to methods of improving the courts. Again, this is primarily an overview and does not necessarily answer specific questions about specific criminal charges.[10]

---

[10]Pamela Bradigan, "C.J.S. v. Am. Jur.2d: Amici Librarii," *Reference Services Review,* Spring 1984, pp. 35–42. This is a detailed discussion of the two general legal encyclopedias for professionals, i.e., *American Jurisprudence Second* and *Corpus Juris Secundum.* Larger libraries would have both of these sets, but because they require a knowledge of legal research neither competes with the layperson's encyclopedias.

The demystification of medicine for the layperson is closely followed by the law. More guides appear each year which help the individual make decisions, including whom to hire as an attorney. See, for example, Steven Naifeh's *The Best Lawyers in America* (New York: Putnam Publishing Group, 1983) which lists the leaders under five specializations from criminal law to civil rights. Choices were made by 2000 practicing attorneys.

While law librarians have several journals, the best general one, and useful for general reference librarians, is *Legal Reference Services Quarterly*. This usually has four to six articles and book reviews which touch on subjects of value to the non-law librarian as well as the person working in a law library.

Consumer aids

Consumer Index to Product Evaluations Ann Arbor: Pierian Press, 1973 to date. Quarterly with annual cumulations. $69.50.

Reader's Digest Consumer Adviser: An Action Guide to Your Rights. New York: Random House, 1984. 416 pp. $21.50.

Trade Names Dictionary, 5th ed. Detroit: Gale Research Co., 1986, 2 vols. $215. Trade Names Dictionary: Company Index. 1986, 2 vols. $285.

The reference librarian is usually asked one of three questions about products and consumer protection: (1) "What is the best product for my needs?" (2) "To whom can I complain, or to whom can I turn for information, about a product or service?" (3) "How can I protect myself from poor-quality products or services?" No one reference source answers all queries, although several are of particular value in locating possible sources. The best product answer may be found in numerous places, including articles indexed in *Reader's Guide* and *Magazine Index.*

The Consumer Index to Product Evaluations covers 100 magazines. Its advantage is twofold. It comes out quarterly and is well organized. Here, under 14 broad, and then narrower, related subject headings, one finds quick access to products, manufacturers and related areas. Many of the items include short descriptions and there is an excellent index. The wise reference librarian will look here first.

There are two basic periodicals, one of which is known to most quality-conscious Americans. This is *Consumer Reports* (Mount Vernon, New York: Consumer Union of the United States, 1936 to date, monthly) which has objective test reports on about 10 to 12 items each month. These may range from a deluxe automobile to an inexpensive toothbrush. An equally good, but not as well-known monthly is

Consumer Bulletin (Washington, New Jersey: Consumers' Research Inc., 1931 to date, monthly) with reports of the same type. Both magazines issue annual summaries in paperbacks which should be kept near the reference desk. The best known of these is *Consumer Reports Buying Guide,* issued by Consumer Reports since 1936.

The question "to whom can I complain" may be answered in many ways. At the local level, a call to the Better Business Bureau may serve the purpose. When one is trying to contact the manufacturer of the product, often a careful look at the container will give the address. If this fails, or if more information is needed, then the *Trade Names Dictionary* is most useful. In one alphabetical sequence one finds the trade names of over 200,000 different products. After the name is a one- to three-word description of the product, and the name of the company or distributor. Another section includes addresses of the manufacturers. An annual supplement, which provides about 20,000 new names, keeps the basic work current until it is revised about every three or four years. The Company Index volume is a reverse index in that one finds the name of the company and under it the trade name or names. Some 41,000 different firms are listed. The ins and outs of filing complaints are covered in considerable detail in Andrew Eiler's *The Consumer Protection Manual* (New York: Facts on File, 1984).

Protection from fraud is built into the just-discussed works, but if the user is seeking additional advice there are a great number of guides now available. Many of these are listed and annotated in the aforementioned, *How-to: 1,400 Best Books on Doing Almost Everything,* as well as in standard buying and reference guides such as *American Reference Books Annual.*

One example of many titles in this field is the *Reader's Digest* guide. It is written for the typical layperson who is involved in almost any kind of transaction where there may be trouble. Different sections and chapters analyze shopping, credit cards, business services, mail orders, and other major considerations from purchase of a car to a home. In each situation the reader is given sound advice on how to avoid fraud, and what to do when not satisfied with a service or a product. The guide is the best available as of 1986, and a copy should be in both the reference section and the general circulating collection.

DIRECTORIES

Directory-type information is among the most often called for in libraries, particularly public libraries. People are trying to locate other people, experts, and organizations through addresses, phone numbers, zip codes, correct titles, correct spelling of names, and so on.

Staff-produced directories can be found in almost all libraries, augmenting the standard reference works—from the city and telephone directory to the zip code directory. Here are such items as frequently requested phone numbers, the names of individuals and agencies in the community, sources of help for difficult questions, often-requested names of state and federal officials, and a wealth of other miscellany. The Chicago Public Library reference staff, for example, listed the staff-produced files as the most useful source of data for daily reference work—matched only by the *World Book Encyclopedia* and the *World Almanac*.

Definition

The *A.L.A. Glossary of Library Terms* defines a directory as "a list of persons or organizations, systematically arranged, usually in alphabetical or classed order, giving addresses, affiliations, etc., for individuals, and address, officers, functions, and similar data for organizations." The definition is clear enough for a directory in its "pure" form; but aside from the directory type of information found in biographical sources, it should be reiterated that many other ready-reference tools have sections devoted to directory information. Yearbooks and almanacs inevitably include abundant amounts of directory-type material.

Purpose

The purpose of directories is implicit in the definition, but among the most frequent uses is to find out (1) an individual's or a firm's address or telephone number; (2) the full name of an individual, a firm, or an organization; (3) a description of a particular manufacturer's product or a service; or (4) "Who is . . ." for example, the president of the firm, or the head of the school, or responsible for advertising, or in charge of buying manuscripts.

Less-obvious uses of directories include obtaining (1) limited, but up-to-date, biographical information on an individual—whether still president, chairperson, or with this or that company or organization; (2) historical and current data about an institution, a firm, or a political group—when it was founded, how many members it had; (3) data for commercial use, such as selecting a list of individuals, companies, or organizations for a mailing in a particular area; e.g., a directory of doctors and dentists serves as the basic list for a medical supply house or a dealer in medical books; and (4) random or selective samplings in a social or commercial survey, for which they are basic sources. Directories are frequently employed by social scientists to isolate certain desired groups for study. And so it goes. Because directories are intimately concerned with human beings and their organizations, they serve almost as many uses as the imagination can bring to bear on the data.

Scope

[handwritten: usually easier to use than a lot of reference sources]

Directories are easier to use than any other reference tool, chiefly because the scope is normally indicated in the title and the type of information is limited and usually presented in an orderly, clear fashion.

There are many ways to categorize directories, but they can be broadly divided as follows:

Local Directories   These are limited primarily to two types: telephone books and city directories. However, also included in this category may be all other types issued for a limited geographical audience—for example, directories of local schools, garden clubs, department stores, theaters, and social groups. The distinction is more academic than important.

Governmental Directories   This group includes guides to post offices, army and navy posts, and the thousand and one different services offered by federal, state, and city governments. These directories may also include guides to international agencies.

Institutional Directories   These are lists of schools, foundations, libraries, hospitals, museums, and similar organizations.

Investment Services   Closely related to trade and business directories, these services give detailed reports on public and private corporations and companies.

Professional Directories   These are largely lists of professional organizations such as those relating to law, medicine, and librarianship.

Trade and Business Directories   These are mainly lists of manufacturers' information about companies, industries, and personal services.

Additional directory-type sources

The almanac and the yearbook often include directory-type information, as do numerous other sources of directory information:

1. Encyclopedias frequently identify various organizations, particularly the more general ones which deal with political or fraternal activities.
2. Gazetteers, guidebooks, and atlases often give information on principal industries, historical sites, museums, and the like.
3. A wide variety of government publications either are entirely devoted to or include directory-type information. Also, some works are directories in name (*Ulrich's International Periodical Directory* and the *Ayer Directory of Publications,* for example) but are so closely associated with other forms (periodicals and newspapers) that they are usually thought of as guides rather than directories.

The basic listing of directories is the *Directory of Directories* (Detroit: Gale Research Company, 1977 to date). The annual publication lists more than 7000 new or revised titles under about 16 broad subject categories from business to professional and scientific. There is a detailed subject and a title index. Information for each entry includes the name of the directory, the publisher, address and phone number, and a full description of the work. The publication is updated twice a year by *Directory Information Service,* which follows the same pattern of arrangement and entry, listing new titles or basic changes.

As with other reference works, some of the same information can be found in another Gale publication, *Encyclopedia of Associations.* One simply turns to the subject index, locates associations in the subject area, and then goes to the entries to see whether or not the associations issue directories. The *Directory Information Service,* which describes nearly 1000 new services each year, also acts, in another way, to update the *Encyclopedia of Associations.* The two services are so interdependent that the library with one will want both.

City directories

The two most obvious, and probably the most-used, local directories are the telephone book and the city directory. The latter is particularly valuable for locating information about an individual when only the street name or the approximate street address is known. Part of the city directory includes an alphabetical list of streets and roads in the area, giving names of residents (unless it is an apartment building, when names may or may not be included). The resident usually is identified by occupation and whether or not she or he owns the home. Some city directories, but not all, have reverse telephone number services, i.e., a "Numerical Telephone Directory." If you know the phone number, you can trace the name and address of the person who has the phone.

The classified section of the directory is a complete list of businesses and professions, differing from the yellow pages of the telephone book in that the latter is a paid service which may not include all firms. Like the telephone book, city directories are usually issued yearly or twice yearly.

city directory good for getting complete listing of businesses

Most city directories are published by the R. L. Polk Company of Detroit, founded in 1870, which issues over 800 publications. In addition to its city directories, it publishes a directory for banks and direct-mail concerns.

A number of ethical questions arise regarding the compilation and use of the city directories. For example, bill collectors frequently call large public libraries for information which can be found only in the city directory, such as reverse phone numbers and addresses and names of "nearbys," that is, the telephone numbers of people living next door to the collector's target. Some librarians believe such information should not be given over the telephone. They argue that this helps the collectors in an antisocial activity and an invasion of privacy.

This policy may be commendable in spirit, although questionable in practice as it simply makes it more difficult, but not impossible, to use the directories. The author of this text would say the librarian is there to supply information, not to question how or by whom it is used. Several large urban libraries are currently examining their policy in this regard, and most now do give the information over the phone.

Telephone reference service

With enough telephone directories, many of the specialized directories might be short-circuited. A telephone book will give the address of a friend, business contact, hotel, and so on, in almost any community. The location of potential customers or services is a frequent purpose for using the familiar yellow pages. And from the point of view of a historian or genealogist, a long run of telephone books is a magic key to finding data on elusive individuals.

Most libraries have at least the local telephone directory and usually those for larger cities in the immediate area. As the library becomes bigger, so does the collection. One microphoto company, Bell & Howell, offers a solution to the space problem with a collection of microfiche cards for the 360 telephone books.

Another approach to phone numbers is, with a self-explanatory title, *The Young People's Yellow Pages: A National Sourcebook for Youth* (New York: Putnam Publishing Group, 1983). An annual since 1975, *Toll-Free Digest* (New York: Warner, 1975 to date) is a subject approach to company and services toll-free numbers. A related title of much use is Susan Osborn's *Dial An Expert* (New York: McGraw-Hill Book Co., distributors, 1986). This is a listing of government agencies, academic centers, and private groups staffed by people considered experts in various fields. Each entry describes the service and gives a phone number.

The telephone book is an integral part of ready-reference service, but requires little or no skill to use. A related area, and one of considerable importance to librarians, is telephone reference service.

Most libraries provide telephone reference service and use many types of reference works, including telephone books. Larger libraries have separate sections for phone reference, usually out of view of the public. The smaller and medium-sized libraries perform the service from the main desk.

There are specific procedures which are concerned with the telephone aspects of reference. For example, libraries differ in such matters as how to answer requests by a patron about whether or not the library has a book or periodical. (Some will look to see if the library owns the item; others will ask the user to come in and check.) Should one answer legal or medical questions over the phone? Should the librarian give out city directory information over the phone? These and countless other problems and questions must be solved if effective service is to be given.[11]

At the Enoch Pratt Free Library in Baltimore, the telephone reference service consists of answering ready-reference queries such as the number of liters in a gallon, the beginning of Lent in 1987, or a definition of a particular word. A second function of the service is to screen all incoming calls, and if not ready-reference, to pass them on to the appropriate department. "For example, a patron with a question about a book on retirement would be transferred to the Business, Science and Technology Department if the book dealt with

---

[11]For a sampling of various written policy statements about incoming and outgoing telephone calls see various sections of Bill Katz and Anne Clifford, *op. cit.*

the financial aspects of retirement. However, if the subject of the book was the locations of retirement communities the Social Science and History Department would be more helpful."[12]

At Enoch Pratt, as at all other libraries, there is a special group of reference works employed for telephone service. These vary from place to place, yet inevitably include local directories and telephone books, as well as national works such as *Facts on File* and *Books in Print.* Normally, too, a great deal of emphasis is placed on "how-to-do-it" types of manuals and handbooks from music and sports to first aid and gardening. The most often used reference sources tend to be a dictionary and the almanacs as well as local guides.

While the telephone service requires the same basic steps needed when dealing face to face with people at a reference desk, some particular skills are necessary. One must be able to ascertain the nature of the question quickly, and be sure it is clearly understood. Interviewing procedures tend to be somewhat less personal than at the desk, yet even more necessary to master. One must know when to terminate a query, when to call back, when the question should be referred to another section, etc. As more than one reference librarian has observed, telephone reference service can be a unique type of work which requires specific skills, and certainly much experience.

A model of its kind, the New York Public Library's telephone reference service draws upon 1500 reference works to answer some 1000 calls each day. Staffers can answer most questions without leaving the desk, but when an answer is not readily available they transfer the call to various subject areas within the library. The limitations to the service are those followed by many other libraries: (1) The question must be one which can be answered in about three minutes or less. (2) Questions will not be answered if they involve contests, crossword puzzles, or school homework. "When we can't answer a question within the alloted three minutes [a librarian explained] we tell the caller in what department or division of the library one can look for the answers or for more comprehensive research of the subject."[13]

---

[12]Kathleen Neumann and Gerald Weeks, "Reference Materials in a Telephone Reference Service: A Model for Telereference," *RQ,* Summer 1981, p. 395. This article is a detailed description of a large telephone reference service in an equally large public library. See, also: Brown, Diane, "Telephone Reference Questions . . ." *RQ,* Spring 1985, pp. 290–303 and Rochelle Yates' *A Librarian's Guide to Telephone Reference* (Hamden, Ct: Shoe String Press, 1986). This 126 page guide is a working manual which answers numerous questions. It's the best available, and can be used by both veterans and beginners.

[13]"For Library Reference Staff, It's A Question of Answers," *The New York Times,* January 3, 1982, p. 49.

Government directories

U.S. Congress Joint Committee on Printing, *Official Congressional Directory.* Washington, D.C.: Government Printing Office, 1809 to date, biennial. $15; pap. $11.

U.S. Postal Service, *National Five Digit Zip Code and Post Office Directory.* Washington, D.C.: Government Printing Office, 1979 to date, annual. $9.

A basic reference source for questions regarding government is the *United States Government Manual,* discussed earlier in this chapter. Equally important is the *Congressional Directory.* This is a who's who for Congress but includes a considerable amount of other information. In some 20 sections there are biographical sketches of the Supreme Court justices, items on members of congressional committees, names of foreign representatives and consular offices in the United States, members of the media who cover Congress, and the chief officers of departments and independent agencies. Used with the *United States Government Manual,* the *Directory* will answer virtually any question concerning individuals involved with the federal government at any major level.

Where does one find information on former members of Congress no longer listed in the *Congressional Directory?* If relatively well known, they will be listed in such sources as the *Dictionary of American Biography* (if deceased) or a good encyclopedia. But for short, objective sketches of all senators and representatives who served from 1774 to 1971, the best single source is *Biographical Directory of the American Congress,* 1774–1971 (Washington, D.C.: Government Printing Office). There is a handy first section which includes officers of the executive branch, i.e., the cabinets from George Washington through the first administration of Richard Nixon. There is also a chronological listing by state of members of the First through the Ninety-first Congress. This is somewhat updated by *Members of Congress Since 1789* (Washington, D.C.: Congressional Quarterly, 1981) which carries the information to about 1980. Among the most-used directories and biographical sources for members of government, at both the national and local levels, is *Who's Who in American Politics* (New York: R. R. Bowker Company, 1967 to date, biennial).

Related reference works include: *Congressional Staff Directory* (Indianapolis: Bobbs-Merrill, 1959 to date, annual), which includes biographies of members of Congress, as well as their major staff members. Other data covers committee assignments and a state-by-state listing of persons in Congress from cities with a population of over 1500. A companion volume by the same publisher, and issued each year since 1981, is the *Federal Staff Directory* which lists close to 30,000 people in various departments and agencies.

The post office and zip code directory offers a state by state, city by city, street by street answer to such questions as "What's my zip code?" or "Is there a post office in Zodunk, Your State?" Current postal regulations are included. Furthermore, zip code information can be found in many other reference works, including most almanacs, although not in such detail. *Note:* For those seeking more information on government directories, see Constance Gray's *U.S. Government Directories, 1970–1981* (Littleton, Colorado: Libraries Unlimited, 1984) There are descriptive annotations for about 600 directories.

Associations and foundations

Encyclopedia of Associations. Detroit: Gale Research Company, 1956 to date, annual, 4 vols. $190–210 ea. (DIALOG File 114, $45 per hour.)

The Foundation Directory. New York: Foundation Center, 1960 to date, irregular. $60. (DIALOG File 28, $45 per hour.)

One of the most useful and essential titles in any library's reference collection, the *Encyclopedia of Associations* is a single work in five volumes. The basic volume describes some 19,500 U.S. organizations under broad subject categories. Information for each entry includes the group's name, address, chief executive, phone number, purpose and activities, membership, and publications (which are often directories issued by the individual associations). There is a key word alphabetical index, but the second volume is really an index to the first in that it lists all the executives mentioned in the basic volume, again with complete addresses and phone numbers. A second section rearranges the associations by geographical location. The third volume is a periodical publication which is issued between editions and keeps the main set up to date by reporting, in two issues a year, on approximately 10,000 changes in the primary set. With this set, the librarian can easily retrieve information by subject, by the name of the association, and by the name of executives connected with the association, and generally can keep up with name changes as well as new organizations. Two other volumes were added in 1983, and, while useful, are not essential to the main set. *International Organizations* covers groups outside the United States not found in the first volume; and *Research Activities and Funding Programs,* which is issued twice a year, has news of about 1000 associations' research grants and research activities.[14]

Most Western countries have the equivalent type of directory. For example, in Canada there is the *Directory of Associations in Canada* (Toronto: Micromedia, 1978 to date, irregular) which includes data on over 10,000 organizations.

A number of associations are foundations, but the seeker of information on foundations and more particularly on their grants should turn to *The Foundation Directory*. The 1983 edition, the ninth, lists 4063 foundations by state, with their purpose and activities, administrators' names, and grants available. Only foundations having minimum assets of $1 million and making total grants of $100,000 in the last year of record are listed. (Individual grants are usually less than $100,000.) There is an index by subject, by cities, by donors, and by foundation name.

Grantsmanship is a full time occupation for many, and a necessity for some. The latter group may include undergraduate and graduate students seeking money from government agencies, foundations or business. There are scores of guides and directories in this field, and for an annotated listing of the major ones see "Grants, Scholarships and Financial Aid: A Guide to Selected Sources" in *Booklist* for June 15, 1983, pp. 1356–1360. There is information here about which of the services is online, and even basic periodicals covering the subject.[15]

Education[16]

American Council on Education. *American Universities and Colleges,* 12th ed. New York: Walter deGruyter, 1983, 2156 pp. $99.50.

---

[14]For an amusing, yet factual analysis of the types of associations listed, see: Margaret Wills, "Banana Club Meets Electrical Woman," *The New York Times,* August 11, 1986, p. A19.

[15]A related article, which is even more current: Ruth Dickstein and Robert Mitchell, "Grant Money and How to Get It", *Reference Services Review,* Summer 1984, pp. 12–21. It concludes with an annotated listing of online databases.

[16]Carolyn Mulac, "College Guides: A Crash Course," *Reference Services Review,* July/September 1981, pp. 23–28. A discursive view of the better guides. See, also, "College Directories: A 1985 Overview," *The Booklist,* September 15, 1985, pp. 116–120. This is an annotated listing in The Reference Books Bulletin section.

Comparative Guide to American Colleges, 12th rev. ed. New York: Harper and Row, 1985, 704 pp. $29.95; Pap. $14.95.

Lovejoy's College Guide. New York: Simon & Schuster, 1940 to date, biennial. pap. $14.95.

A standard work in the field, *American Universities and Colleges* is the first place to turn for detailed information on over 1700 institutions. One finds answers to questions ranging from what is taught by whom, to the number of students, to the shape of various graduate and professional education programs. Unfortunately, the much-awaited revision draws upon 1980 statistics, and, even at publication was somewhat dated.

A frequent query concerns how one school differs from another, which has the "best" this or that department, or social life, or football team, etc. Coming to the rescue, although the answers are sometimes admittedly subjective, is the *Comparative Guide to American Colleges.* Everything from admission requirements and the racial composition of the student body to the amount of social life is considered in a standard form for each institution. Often updated, it has proven to be remarkably accurate over the years.

There are several less-specialized, less-detailed directories, particularly of a popular type found in most bookstores and even on newsstands. The best-known is *Lovejoy's College Guide* which outlines, state by state, the various requirements, offerings, and so on, of American schools. There are also Lovejoy guides to vocational schools and prep schools. While uneven in presentation and arrangement, the various guides are at least as well known to many students as are those published by Barron and by Peterson.

The British-published *World of Learning* (London: Europa Publishing Company, 1947 to date, annual) gives data on educational institutions throughout the world, including the United States. The first volume begins with a discussion of international education and scientific and cultural organizations and continues with the country-by-country listing, completed in the second volume. There is a good index. Standard information (address, function, and so on) is given for each country and institution, here interpreted to mean not only universities and colleges but libraries, research centers, museums, art galleries, and even learned societies. There is a listing of professors at all major universities. This is more of a directory, not a discursive discussion of world education; but informative and considered "basic" in most larger libraries.

These are only examples in a field for which numerous publish-

Among handbooks and manuals certainly the most popular, the most read, have to do with "how-to-do-it" and self help. In fact, *The New York Times Book Review* now carries a special section of the best seller list which is dedicated specifically to this type of work. The problem for librarians is to find the best and the better volumes among the thousands published each year.

Arranged by subject headings, and with a subject, author, and title index, the *How-to* and *Self Help* guides suggest the "best" books available in everything from accounting and acrobatics to child care and sex. Most of the titles are current, i.e., published between 1980 and mid-1984. A descriptive and evaluative annotation is provided for each of the books listed. All are considered to be acceptable, so the annotations are favorable, although here and there one finds critical notes about specific areas.

Medicine

Physicians' Desk Reference to Pharmaceutical Specialties and Biologicals. Oradell, New Jersey: Medical Economics Company, 1947 to date, annual. $14.95.

Rees, Alan (ed.). *The Consumer Health Information Source Book,* 2d ed. New York: R. R. Bowker Company, 1984, 450 pp. $35.

The development of the consumer and health education movements in the United States has meant increased attention to medical information for the layperson. At one time, reference librarians hesitated to answer any type of medical question. That attitude is rapidly disappearing, although a few librarians still believe medical reference questions should not be answered, or only in a noncommittal way, such as sending the person to the card catalog or popular index or the shelf with the medical books. No other help is given, because the librarian fears possible complications.

Today, there is an active movement among public, school, and even some college and university libraries to develop community health information centers, health-lines, or whatever they may be called. At the same time, continuing education about various health sources and services is pursued by many librarians. While there is consensus that the librarian should neither interpret nor analyze medical advice, it is equally true that the library should be scrupulous about reference sources purchased.

The user must be able to understand the books concerning consumer health information. This can be ensured by: (1) purchasing books written for laypersons; (2) purchasing medical dictionaries

ers offer guides. There are no lack of choices, and the librarian should check with experts in education, including faculty where available, for ultimate selection. For example, Peterson offers some dozen different works which can be useful in particular library situations. These range from *Guide to Four-Year Colleges* to *Summer Opportunities for Kids and Teenagers.* Most are updated annually.

Libraries and publishing

The American Library Directory. New York: R. R. Bowker Company, 1923 to date, annual. 2 vols. $119.95.

Directory of Special Libraries and Information Centers. Detroit: Gale Research Company, 1963 to date, biennial. 3 vols. $265 to $320 ea.

The American Library Directory is included here to indicate that there are directories for virtually every profession. Published since 1923, it provides basic information on 32,000 public, academic, and special libraries in the United States and Canada. Arranged by state and city or town, the listings include names of personnel, library address and phone number, book budgets, number of volumes, special collections, salaries, subject interests, and so on. It has many uses, from seeking addresses for a survey or for potential book purchasers to providing necessary data for those seeking positions in a given library. (Information, for example, on the size of collections and salaries will sometimes tell the job seekers more than can be found in an advertisement.) There is a separate section on interlibrary loan and a bi-monthly updating service ($65) which keeps one current with changes in staff, funding etc.

Special libraries receive much more detailed treatment in the *Directory of Special Libraries and Information Centers.* This work lists over 17,000 units which are either special libraries or ones with special collections, including a number of public and university libraries. Arrangement is alphabetical by name, with a not-very-satisfactory subject index. (Subject headings are furnished by the libraries, and as this approach is uncontrolled, it tends to be erratic.) The second volume is the geographic-personnel index, and the third is a periodic supplement covering new material between editions. A spin-off of the basic set is the *Subject Directory of Special Libraries and Information Centers,* a five-volume work which simply rearranges the material in the basic set by subject area; e.g., volume one covers business and law libraries; volume four, social sciences and humanities libraries. Within each volume is the same material found in the basic set. The advantage is that the library may purchase a single volume for about $145 rather than invest about $625 in the whole work.

Three related directories from R. R. Bowker are more likely to be used by librarians and book people than by laypersons. These are: (1) *American Book Trade Directory* (1915 to date, annual) which lists booksellers, wholesalers, and publishers state by state and city by city, with added information on Canada and United Kingdom and Ireland. The 1985 edition included over 24,000 retail book dealers. (2) *Magazine Industry Market Place* (1980 to date, annual) lists the major magazine publishers with data on subject matter, personnel, and the like. There is other information and a concluding section of 20,000 addresses and telephone numbers of those listed in the main work. (3) *Literary Market Place* (1940 to date, annual), the standard in the field, gives directory-type information on over 10,000 firms directly or indirectly involved with publishing in the United States. It furnishes an answer to a frequently heard question at the reference desk: "Where can I get my novel [poem, biography, or other work] published?" Also, it is of considerable help to acquisitions librarians, as it gives fuller information on publishers than do bibliographies such as *Books in Print* or *Cumulative Book Index*. Among other things, it has a section, "Names and Numbers," which lists 17,000 executives and firms in publishing, with their addresses and phone numbers.

The *Literary Market Place* includes names of agents whom the writer might wish to contact. However, it presupposes some knowledge of the publisher and fails to answer directly the question: Does this publishing house publish fiction or poetry, or other things? For this, the beginner should turn to several much-used allied titles: *Writer's Market* (Cincinnati, Ohio: Writer's Digest, 1929 to date, annual), with a section on book publishers that includes not only directory-type information but paragraphs on types of materials wanted, royalties paid, and how copy is to be submitted. The remainder of the nearly 1000-page directory gives similar information for thousands of periodical publishers to whom free-lance writers may submit material. *The Writer's Handbook* (Boston: The Writer, Inc., 1936 to date, annual) gives some of the same information, but at least one-half of each annual volume is devoted to articles on how to write, and its listings are not as complete as those in *Writer's Market*. Writers who wish information on small presses should consult the *International Directory of Little Magazines and Small Presses* (Paradise, California: Dustbooks, 1965 to date, annual).

Directories online

An increasing number of directories are going online. The reason is twofold: (1) This is a rapid, easy way to keep the information current. (2) Esoteric directories may be accessed online without the necessity of the library purchasing the work which can be quite expensive and rarely used.

Examples range from the *Encyclopedia of Associations* and *Foundation Directory* to the still-to-be-discussed *Biography and Genealogy Master Index*. As of mid-1986, there are at least 60 to 75 directories online. These range from *D&B Million Dollar Directory* to the *U.S. Public School Directory*.

The *Electronic Yellow Pages*, for example, divided by types of services from financial to professional, is produced from the yellow pages of over 4800 telephone books and special directories throughout the United States. The directory is updated twice a year and may be accessed through DIALOG for about $60 per hour.

CD-ROM is another upcoming form for directories, and in the next few years it is estimated that 50 percent or more of such reference works will be available on CD-ROM.

SUGGESTED READING

Brcic, Visnja, et al., "Public Libraries as Sources of Occupational Health Information," *Ontario Library Review,* June 1982, pp. 23–28. The authors show how the library serves to help workers and employers concerned with conditions which affect the health of employees. Steps on how to set up such a service are explained in detail.

Christie, D. Elizabeth, "A Role for the Medical Library in Consumer Health Information," *Canadian Library Journal,* April, 1986, pp. 105–109. Although this is a study limited to Montreal libraries, most of the findings are applicable elsewhere. Of primary interest is the emphasis on giving health information to experts, not to laypersons. Here the respondents believe the public libraries should serve a major role.

Fecher, Ellen, "Consumer Health Information: A Prognosis," *Wilson Library Bulletin,* February 1985, pp. 389–391. The present health information policies of libraries is examined and the author then goes on to predict that the service will be expanded and modified. She calls for improved levels of service based upon a better understanding of health information needs.

Groen, Frances, "Provision of Health Information Has Legal and Ethical Aspects," *Canadian Library Journal,* December 1983, pp. 359–362. The author is primarily concerned with medicine, but most of the discussion would be equally true for the reference librarian offering information about the law and consumer data.

"Manners Count on the Corporate Ladder," *The New York Times,* April 24, 1985, p. C12. "In board rooms across the country, corporate etiquette has become increasingly important . . ." says the author. The remainder of the article is a justification for etiquette books and courses. An example of the latter is a "weekend package for 10 executives at $54,000."

McDowell, Edwin, "World Almanac Fact: It's a No. 1 Best Seller," *The New York Times,* December 27, 1984, p. C13. Both a popular description of how the almanac is edited and a brief history, this is a good overview of almanacs in general.

Nixon, Judith M., "Law and the Undergraduate," *Reference Services Review,* Spring 1984, pp. 77–87. This is an excellent, annotated listing of basic federal law works. The most important books are starred.

Rees, Alan (ed.), *Developing Consumer Health Information Services.* New York: R. R. Bowker, 1982. Several experts contribute essays on how the library may establish, operate and develop various types of consumer health information services.

Segesta, Jim, "Printed Sources for American Weather Records," *Reference Services Review,* Fall 1982, pp. 65–71. Many ready-reference questions concern the weather, and here are some of the sources of answers. More important, the author demonstrates how one may take a narrow subject area and develop a comprehensive bibliography of reference sources. It is a model for those seeking to prepare their own work in other areas.

Tesich, Steve, "Facing Facts Factually," *The New York Times Magazine,* May 11, 1986, p. 14. A humorous piece on the curious habit of gathering facts. The article indicates to the librarian why so many people are enamored of ready reference aids. According to the author, it is an affliction which only can be overcome by careful attention to opinion rather than fact.

Webster, David, "Jack Gourman's Rankings of Colleges and Universities: A Guide for the Perplexed," *RQ,* Spring, 1986, pp. 323–331. This is a superior example of evaluation of a reference work. The professor closely examines a standard guide to education, i.e., ten books published from 1977 to 1985 in various editions. Although these are widely cited and often recommended by reference librarians (but not in this text), Webster charges that most of the information in the books is less than reliable. "Gourman's books, individually and as a group, are virtually without merit." Students may employ the techniques to evaluate other ready reference aids.

Yellott, Lynn, and Robert Barrier, "Evaluation of a Public Library's Health Information Service," *Medical Reference Quarterly,* Summer 1983, pp. 31–49. A county library (Syracuse, NY) conducted a survey to ascertain the degree of satisfaction with their health information program. The article explains how the survey was carried out and, more important, the type of people who ask questions, as well as the methods of answering.

CHAPTER NINE

Biographical Sources

The writer Edmund Gosse once described biography as "a study sharply defined by two definite events, birth and death." Commenting on this observation, another author explains the problem concerning biography. It "will always remain an imprecise form: by means of some peculiar alchemy a jumble of facts and impressions is transformed into a life, resurrecting the dead".[1]

The quest for information about the living and dead has made numerous publishers, compilers, and biographers (not to mention those quite lively celebrities penning their autobiographies) the richer. Whether or not the massive numbers of biographies issued each year has made the reader or the librarian the richer is another question.

Even a cursory glance at a standard bibliography such as Sheehy's *Guide to Reference Books* will indicate the wide universe of biographical possibilities. In attempting to trim these back to manageable proportions, the Reference Books Bulletin committee first came up with an essential number of 450, but later decided on only 200 titles.[2] Actually, many small- to medium-sized libraries might get

---

[1]Stanley Olson, "On Biography," *Antaeus*, Autumn 1982, p. 168.

[2]"Biographical Reference Sources: A Selective Checklist," *Booklist*, May 15, 1984, pp. 1314–1327; Part 2, June 15, 1984, pp. 1447–1461. Additions, May 15, 1985, pp. 1309–1311. See, too; *Biographical Books, 1876–1949* (New York: R. R. Bowker Company, 1983) and a supplement covering 1950–1980. Some 75,000 biographies are listed by personal name and subject headings.

along with even fewer reference works in this area, while large libraries would number their collection in the thousands.

EVALUATION

How does the librarian know whether a biographical source is reliable? There are a number of tests.

Selection Why is a name selected (or rejected) for the various biographical reference aids? The method for the several who's who entries is discussed later, but the process is relatively easy to establish for biographical aids limited to a given subject or profession: the compiler includes all the names that qualify for the scope of the work, as in *American Men and Women of Science* or *World Authors.* In both cases, the widest net is cast to include figures and authors likely to be of interest. There are limitations, but they are so broad as to cause little difficulty for the compiler. As one moves from subject and profession to the famous, eminent, or renowned on a national or international scale, the choices become increasingly difficult.

All the editors of reputable works do, however, establish some objective guidelines for inclusion; e.g., *Who's Who in America* features many people "arbitrarily on account of official position." This means that a member of Congress, a governor, an admiral, a general, a Nobel Prize winner, or a foreign head of government is automatically included; and numerous other categories, as well, ensure a place in the volume. The *International Who's Who* is certain to give data on members of all reigning royal families. The *Dictionary of American Biography* takes a more negative approach—one must first be dead to be included; after that requirement is met, the editor begins making selections.

Then, too, there are some automatic exclusions. In the case of subject biographical reference works, the exclusion is usually evident in the title: one does not look for poets in *Who's Who in American Art* or *American Men and Women of Science.*

There are levels of exclusiveness; it may be somewhat more difficult to get into *Who's Who in America* than *Who's Who in American Art.* For the former listing, it is a matter of "Don't call us, we'll call you" and depends on some public achievement. Others depend only on membership in a group or profession; it is difficult to stay out of such titles as *Who's Who in the United Nations* if one happens to work there, or *Who's Who in Golf* should one be a professional or a well-known amateur. A listing depends upon one's filling out forms for a given title. Failure to do so may mean failure to be included unless one is such a famous U.N. employee or golfer that the editor digs out the information.

There are automatic methods of selection or rejection which may be applied by a publisher to a biographical source. Briefly: (a) the person must be living, or dead; (b) the individual must be a citizen of a given country, region, or even a city; (c) the person must be employed in a specific profession or type of work; (d) the individual must be a given sex or age. One or more of these measurements may be employed in any given reference work.

Audience   The majority of reference works in biography are for adults, although there are some (particularly concerning books and writers) for younger people. Given the adult category, they can then be divided by interests, education level of the user, etc. Obviously, the lines here are not all that clear, and an adult may well refer to a child's reference work (such as the *World Book* biographies).

Length of Entry   Once a name is selected, another question presents itself: How much space does the figure warrant? five or six lines? a page? The purpose and scope of the work may dictate at least a partial answer. The who's who data calls for a relatively brief outline or collection of facts. The biographical dictionary may be more discursive; the essay type of work will approach the same entry in a way peculiar to its form. Regardless of approach, the editor still has to make decisions about balance and length.

Authority   Biography began as an accepted form of approbation; e.g., *Ecclesiastes* has the famous line, "Let us now praise famous men"; and this was the purpose of biography until well into the seventeenth century. After a period of relative candor, including Boswell's famous *Life of Johnson* and Johnson's own *Lives of the Poets*, the form returned to uniform panegyric in the Victorian nineteenth century. With the Freudian spirit of the twentieth century, praise once more gave way to reality. Truth now so much guides biographers that many famous people have stipulated that no biography should be written about them.

The development of authoritative biography is relatively recent, and the librarian must beware (1) Victorian, i.e., nineteenth and early twentieth century, standard biographical works which took more pride in painting everything with rosy colors than in delivering the truth and (2) modern biographical outlines or even essays where the author is so devoted to the subject that the evaluation is suspect.

Today the question about authority must begin with another question: Who wrote the biographical entry—an editor, the subject, an authority in the field, a secretary? In preparing almost any material except statistical information, the person who penned the entry will have had either conscious or subconscious biases. Even in a straightforward presentation of data, if the biographical subject supplied the information (the usual case with most current biographies), there may be slight understatements or exaggerations concerning age (men more often than women lie about this), education, or experience. Biographical sources relying almost entirely on individual honesty cannot be completely trusted. This leads to the next query: Have sources of information other than the subjects' own questionnaires been cited? The preface should make these two points clear.

Equally, it is useful to know if the biography was prepared by the publisher's editorial staff, or was simply slightly edited by that same staff from information received from the subject. At the other extreme, there may be a sketch written by an outside expert. This is the usual procedure for essay-length biographies.

When the source is questionable, the information should be verified in one or more other works. If a serious conflict remains which cannot be resolved, what should be done? The only solution is to attempt to trace the information through primary source material: newspapers, contemporary biographies, or articles about the individual or his or her family or friends. This undertaking involves historical research. An excellent example can be found in the recurrent arguments concerning details of Shakespeare's life and times or the famous attempt to straighten out the facts in the life of Sir Thomas Malory, author of the stories of King Arthur and his knights.

How does the librarian know if a work is truly legitimate, i.e., authoritative and based on an accurate, relatively objective selection policy? A rule of thumb will do in most cases: If the title is not listed (or minimally praised) in any of the basic bibliographies, such as Sheehy, Walford, *American Reference Books Annual,* or the current reviewing services, then there is the possibility it is a worthless volume.

The publisher's name is another indication of authority. In their study of biography, the Reference Books Bulletin committee reports "five publishers are responsible for a large number of available (biography) titles."[3] They are the Gale Research Company, The H. W. Wilson Company, St. Martin's Press, Marquis Who's Who Inc., and R.

[3]"Biographical Reference Sources," *op. cit.* p. 1315.

R. Bowker Company. It is no surprise that most of these are major publishers of other standard reference works. Trade publishers, from Random House to Harper & Row, publish biographical sources, but they tend to be more popular. At any rate, if the librarian does not recognize the publisher, and particularly if it is not one of the major five, then the warning flag is out for further checking.

Frequency Most biographical reference sources are on a regular publishing schedule. Some are issued each year, or even every month, while others are regularly updated every three or four years. With celebrities coming and going rapidly, it is obviously important to know the range of time covered by the parent work and its supplements. If there is no updating procedure, many (although not all) biographical reference books are less than satisfactory.

Other Points Are there photographs? Are there bibliographies containing material both by and about the subject? Is the work adequately indexed or furnished with sufficient cross-references? (This is important when seeking individuals connected with a major figure who may only be mentioned as part of a larger biographical sketch.) Is the work arranged logically? The alphabetical approach is usual, although some works may be arranged chronologically by events, birth dates, periods, or areas of subject interest.

In practice, few of these evaluative tests are actually employed. If a person is well known, the problem normally is not one of locating a source but of screening out the many sources for pertinent details. If the individual is obscure, usually any source is welcome.

SEARCHING BIOGRAPHIC SOURCES

The first problem, with all but the very well known, is to locate a biography of the individual. Fortunately, this is now relatively easy. One need only turn to *Biography and Genealogy Master Index* for an alphabetical listing of names and some 6 million citations where information can be located. This is not to suggest that *all* names one is searching for will be found in this index, but it is at least a major point of departure.

In determining what biographical source to search, the librarian will work from two basic beginning queries: How much of the history of an individual life does the user require, and what type of data is required? (This query is usually appropriate for a ready-reference question about address, profession, and so on.) At what depth and sophistication should the answer be to a more involved question? This can be determined by the age, education, and needs of the individual user. The quantitative question will require either (1) a silhouette or simple data or (2) an essay form of answer.

This data type of question is by far the most common in the ready-reference situation. Typical queries: "What is the address and phone number of X?" "How does one spell Y's name?" "What is the age of R?" "When did Beethoven die?" Answers will be found in the familiar who's who directory-biographical dictionary sources. Approach varies with each title, but they are consistent in listing names alphabetically and, at a minimum, giving the profession and position (with or without claim-to-fame attributes) of the individual. At a maximum, these sources will give full background on the entry from birth and death dates to publications, names of children, and so on. The information is usually, although not necessarily, in outline form. It is rarely discursive or critical. The data are all.

The second major type of biographical question comes from the person who wants partial or relatively complete information on an individual. The questioner may be writing a paper, preparing a speech, or seeking critical background material. Typical queries: "How can I write a paper on Herman Melville?" "What do you have on [X], a prominent American scientist?" "Is there a book about George Washington and the cherry tree?" Answers will be found in reference sources with an emphasis on essays (300 words to several pages in length).

INDEXES TO BIOGRAPHY

Biography and Genealogy Master Index, 2d ed. Detroit: Gale Research Company, 1980, 8 vols. $950. 1981–85 Cumulations, 1985, 5 vols. $750; Annual supplements, 1986 to date, $180 ea. (Online DIALOG File 88 $55 per hour.)

BioBase 1984: Master Cumulation, 1984, Microfiche, $975. Annual supplements. 1985–86, $175.

Biography Almanac, 2d ed., 1983, 2 vols., $85; Supplement, 1986, 200 pp. $42.

Biography Index. New York: The H. W. Wilson Company, 1947 to date, quarterly with annual cumulations. $70. (Online, Wilsonline $25–$45 per hour.)

There are two types of indexes to biography. The first, represented by *Biography and Genealogy Master Index,* is a key to some 6 million entries found in biographical dictionaries and directories such as *Who's Who in America.* The purpose is to reduce tedious searching of basic, generally current guides.

The second type of index, represented by *Biography Index* includes citations to biographies appearing in periodicals and selected books. The purpose is to offer a key to biographical information about persons living and dead in a wide variety of general sources.

The first type would be employed for ready reference when the data type of information is required. The second would more likely be used to seek detailed information for a paper, research project, speech, or other presentation.

For example, a user who wished to find the address of Mary Doe would turn to the *Master Index* for sources of short data entries in the various biographical dictionaries indexed. The user who wished to write a paper on the achievements of Doe would need a fuller entry and would turn to biographical information in periodicals as indicated in *Biography Index.*

In an opening search, where not much is known about an individual, the *Master Index* would be preferable. If the person is well known to the searcher, and the essential facts are in hand, then one would go first to *Biography Index.* All of which is to say, the two basic reference works may be used separately or together, but they are the first steps in any biographical search.

With its annual supplements, the *Master Index* offers a key to about 5.5 million individuals. There are some 6 million citations found in approximately 600 biographical reference works. Beginning in 1985, the publisher has issued a new volume each year, and cumulates the annual volumes every five years. The work is arranged in a single alphabet by the last name of the individual. After the name come the birth and death dates, and then a key to one or more sources in which there is a short entry or essay about the individual. Famous people may have up to a dozen or more citations, but for the most part the citations usually number no more than two to three. Given a source for John Oaks, say, in *Who's Who In America* and/or *World Authors: 1970–1975,* one simply turns to that book for the needed information.

Among the some 565 biographical works indexed are both data type (Who's Who variety) and essay type (*Dictionary of American Biography*). In the early years the focus was almost entirely on the data variety, but this changed as the publisher indexed more and more biographical sources. Most of the standard works published by the five largest biographical reference publishers are indexed in the *Master Index.*

There are several variations on the main set: (1) *Biography Almanac* is a cut-down version, at a much lower price, for smaller libraries. It indexes only about one-half the number of sources and concentrates on about 25,000 quite well known figures from times present and past. In addition to the alphabetical arrangement with birth and death dates, there is an indication of nationality, occupation, and the reason for the individual's claim to fame. The second volume of the main set is a chronological arrangement by year of the subjects, as well as by place of birth. While no substitute for the *Master Index,* it is at least better than nothing. (2) Bio-Base is the other extreme. Here all of the entries found in the *Master Index* are included in microfiche. In fact, it is really nothing but a different form of the primary work. It is preferred in some libraries because it saves space and includes all entries in one alphabet, thus eliminating the need to check the supplements.

(3) Online, DIALOG provides the full work. If only a few searches are to be made each year, it is obviously preferable to the printed version. It's also somewhat more convenient, although one probably can find what is needed as fast, if not faster, in the Bio-Base. (4) Duplicating entirely what is found in the main set, the publisher offers six spin-offs. These are *not* needed when the main set is available, but may be useful for particular subject areas. They range from *Children's Authors and Illustrators* to *Historical Biographical Dictionaries Master Index.*

As useful as all of this may be for the librarian, the index is far from perfect. The publisher simply prints names as found in the sources. If, for example, Joe Doaks uses this form in Who's Who In America, but prefers Joe Vincent Doaks in Who's Who In American Rat Catchers and Joseph V. P. Doaks in American Businesspersons, his name will be alphabetically arranged in three different ways. Of course, it could be three different Doakses, but the date of birth indicates it is probably the same person. Just to make things confusing, the date of birth for the same person may vary, depending on which source was indexed. Also, there may be a simple listing of the same name, albeit with reference to different sources, four or five times.[4]

Where periodical articles are required, *Biography Index* is the first choice. More than 2600 different magazines are analyzed for biographical material. This gives the user an extremely wide range of sources, which move from the extremely popular to the esoteric. The

---

[4]Bruce Bonta and Frances Cable, "The Gale Biography Series," *Reference Services Review,* Spring 1982, pp. 25–33. A careful analysis of the good and bad points about the service.

end result is rarely disappointing. Given a search over several years, and the *Index* goes back to 1947, inevitably something turns up, and often that "something" may be quite detailed. Arrangement is by name of the person. An added bonus—birth and death dates, nationality, profession and, of course, the citation to the periodical. Another most useful feature is the index by profession or occupation. Someone looking for material on an architect, not Frank Lloyd Wright, simply turns here, as would another individual looking for biographical data about dentists or zoo keepers.

True, the index does cover some books, and particularly makes note of individual biographies and autobiographies, as well as collections. A nice touch is the inclusion of some, but certainly not all, fiction which has a well-known figure at the center of the novel. The same is true of poetry, drama, etc.

Obituaries are indexed, including those from *The New York Times* up to 1947. Anyone looking for earlier obits from that same newspaper is advised to consult *The New York Times Obituaries Index, 1858–1968* (Sanford, North Carolina: Microfilming Corporation, 1970. Supplement covers 1969–1978). Here are over 400,000 names, but one must turn first to *The New York Times Index* to find the precise citation.[5]

There are a total of over 400,000 names, with reference to the notices, often of essay length, in *The New York Times*. Thanks to the worldwide coverage of the *Times*, the list is not limited to Americans and includes almost every prominent world figure who died during the period covered by the *Index*. Its secondary advantages (primary to many) are: (1) It does include less-known personalities not often found in standard biographical works; (2) the obituary often presents a summation of the reputation of the figure at the time; and (3) as each entry includes not only page and issue number but death date, it can serve as a ready-reference aid. The cutoff date is 1978, but the *Times Biographical Service* (discussed in the next section) fills the gap from 1978 on.

UNIVERSAL AND CURRENT BIOGRAPHICAL SOURCES

Universal biographical sources include those from all parts of the world, or at least those parts selected by the editors, and normally

[5]A related index: *Personal Name Index to the New York Times Index, 1851–1974,* plus Supplement for 1975–79. (Verdi, Nevada: Roxbury Data Interface, 1976–in progress). This is over 22 volumes which includes more than 3 million names of people mentioned in the newspaper, not simply in the obituaries. Many of these, particularly in the earlier years, are not found in the main index to the paper.

include both living and dead personalities. The result is a compendium of relatively well-known individuals.

Current sources may cover the same geographical area but narrow the scope by concentrating on people who are still active or only recently dead.

Biographical dictionaries

Webster's Biographical Dictionary, rev. ed. Springfield, Massachusetts: G. & C. Merriam Company, 1985. $17.50.

Before the advent of the *Biography and Genealogy Master Index,* the biographical dictionary was a first place to turn to identify, qualify, and generally discover basic facts about an individual. With that, one might go on to other works, or, if nothing more was needed than a birth or death date, occupation, claim to fame, etc., the biographical dictionary might be quite enough. Today, in order to quickly find information about an individual, it is much faster to consult the Master Index first. Lacking that reference work, then one might return to the dictionary, or it can still be used for ready reference facts about famous people who are almost sure to be included.

By far the best known and most used of the biographical dictionaries, *Webster's* gives brief biographies for about 40,000 people from the beginning of history through the early 1970s. The individual's primary contribution is noted, along with nationality, birth (and death) dates and pronunciation. The majority, well over 80 percent of the listings, are deceased and its primary, if not almost exclusive value, is for checking on persons who are dead. American and British subjects receive most space, with appropriate attention given to major international and historical figures.

Other reference works of this type found in larger ready reference sections: *Chamber's Biographical Dictionary* (rev. ed., London: Chambers, 1978) which lists 15,000 prominent people, with particular emphasis on British and American personalities. *The New Century Cyclopedia of Names* (New York: Appleton, 1954) is a three-volume work of some 100,000 names, including fictional and mythological characters.

Pseudonyms

Pseudonyms and Nicknames Dictionary, 2d ed. Detroit: Gale Research Company, 1982. 995 pp. $180.

Covering all periods and most of the world, here is a listing of about 50,000 pseudonyms and nicknames from Johnny Appleseed (John Chapman) to Mark Twain (Samuel Clemens). Information includes birth and death dates, nationality and occupation. When one looks up the pseudonym or nickname there is a reference to the original name and the primary information. Cited sources are included, and these amount to over 200 basic biographical works. Arranged in a single alphabet, the guide is extremely easy to use. It is updated by two supplements which are issued between editions of the primary work.

Directory: Who's who form

Who's Who in America. Chicago: Marquis Who's Who, 1889 to date, biennial, 2 vols. $135. (DIALOG file 234, $95 per hour.)

Who's Who. London: Black, 1849 to date, annual (distributed in the United States by St. Martin's Press, Inc.). $115.

International Who's Who. London: Europa Publications Ltd., 1935 to date, annual (distributed in the United States by Gale Research Company). $130.

While the biographical dictionaries are primarily concerned with dead celebrities, the who's who directory forms list only the living, and, for that matter, only those in some outstanding position. Again, most of the who's who are indexed in the *Biography and Genealogy Master Index.*

The directories are among the most frequently used of the biographical sources, and top the list when it comes to ready reference data. Common questions they answer: (1) Where does X live, or receive his or her mail? (2) What is X's age and position? (3) What has X written? (4) What honors does X claim? These are just a few of the typical queries.

The who's who directories vary in scope, and often in accuracy and timeliness, but their essential purpose is the same: to present objective, usually noncontroversial facts about an individual. The approach and style are monotonously the same; most are arranged alphabetically by the name of the person, with a following paragraph of vital statistics which normally concludes with the person's address and phone number.

The who's who aids may be classified by scope as international, national, local, professional or business, religious or racial, and so on, as is usually indicated by the title.

Information is normally compiled by sending a questionnaire to the candidate, who is then free to provide as much or as little of the requested information as he or she wishes. The better publishers check the returns for flaws or downright lies. Other publishers may be content to rely on the honesty of the individual, who normally has little reason not to tell the truth, although—and this is a large "although"—some candidates for entry may construct complete fabrications.

The American *Who's Who in America* has a long history of reliability. It is a source for about 75,000 names of prominent American men and women, as well as a few foreigners with some influence in the United States. As the nation's current population is over 226 million, how do the editors determine who is, or who is not, to be included? The answer is complex, usually based on the person's outstanding achievement or excellence.

The inclusion-exclusion process is of more interest when the reputation and fame of a work, such as *Who's Who in America*, is purposely built upon selectivity of a high order. The natural question is one of legitimacy. Is the selection of Y based on Y's desire to be included (supported by willingness to buy the volume in question or, in a few cases, literally to pay for a place in the volume), or is it based on the editor's notion of eminence, where no amount of persuasion or cash will ensure selection? All works listed here are indeed legitimate; in them, one's way to fame cannot be bought. This is not to say there is no room for criticism. No one will entirely agree on all names selected or rejected in, say, *Who's Who in America*.

On balance the selection is adequate, if not brilliant. The data for entrants varies in length but not in style, as each fills out a standard form requesting basic information, including date of birth, education, achievements, and address. The form is used to compose the entry, and a proof of the entry is sent to the individual for double-checking.

The set also includes a list of those who died since the last edition, those who retired, and a feature "thoughts on my life" which is included in some entries. Here the notable figures are asked to reflect on principles and philosophies which have guided them through life. This can be inspirational, or downright disturbing, but it is always a fascinating facet to otherwise straight directory type information.

A third index volume is now available (from 1982 at $50), which lists the entries in *Who's Who in America* geographically by state, and then by city. A similar arrangement is found for those from Canada and Mexico. In the "professional area index" there are 16 broad subject headings (arts to unclassified specialities) which lists entries by occupation. Unfortunately, the subject headings are much too broad, but this may improve with time.

Updated quarterly, the online *Who's Who in America* consists of the 75,000 records in *Who's Who in America* and the 15,000 records in *Frontier Science and Technology*. In time, the publisher will expand the database to include more of the who's who files. The online version, except for the cost, has several advantages over the printed works. First and foremost, there are over 40 different points of entry, from the person's name to his or her address, company or other affiliation. The geographic possibilities are even more rewarding. For example, how many prominent Americans are women living in Chicago; or what is the ratio of successful attorneys in Los Angeles and San Francisco (as compared with the total number and those not found in the guide). Another advantage is that new names may be added each quarter, so one does not have to wait for the annual or the bi-annual printed volumes.

After a subject's death, membership in *Who's Who in America* continues in *Who Was Who in America* (Chicago: Marquis Who's Who, Inc. 1942 to date, irregular). A historical volume covers 1607–1896, then there are volumes for 1897–1942, 1943–1950, 1951–1960, 1961–1968, 1969–1973, 1974–1978, 1978–1982 and 1982–1985. Now the retrospective volumes appear about every four years. In 1985 the publisher issued an index which covers the eight volumes. The benefit of this set for reference work is that many people originally listed no longer are famous enough to be listed in the standard biographical dictionaries. *Who Was Who* may be used to trace difficult-to-find individuals who have virtually sunk out of sight.

One work which would be unnecessary if women were not treated as the second sex is *Who's Who of American Women* (Chicago: Marquis Who's Who, Inc., 1959 to date). A biennial dictionary of notable living American females, it follows the same general pattern as all the Marquis works. The tenth edition includes 20,000 women's names. The editor's breakdown of 1000 sketches indicated that, according to occupation, a woman's chances to earn an entry were best if she was a club, civic, or religious leader (9.6 percent of all biographies). Broadening the scope of this basic volume, Marquis now issues *Directory of Women in Marquis Who's Who Publications,* (1983 to date, biennial) which is a listing of 30,000 entries from nine of their publications. Women are listed alphabetically by name and then geographically by state.

Minorities fare no better than women in the standard who's who. As a result there are separate directories. One example is *Who's Who Among Black Americans,* (Northbrook, Illinois: 1976 to date, about every three years). This lists 15,500 people from all fields of endeavor, and is standard.

Who's Who was first published in Britain on January 15, 1849, some 50 years before there were enough prominent Americans to make a volume possible here. During its first 47 years, *Who's Who* was a slim book of some 250 pages which listed members of the titled and official classes. In 1897, it became a biographical dictionary, and the 1972–1973 edition is close to 4000 pages. Selection is no longer based on nobility but on "personal achievement or prominence." Most entries are English, but it does include some notables from other countries. And in the past decade, it has put more and more emphasis on prominent scholars and professional people as well as political and industrial leaders among its 27,500 entries (1986).

Depending on size and type of audience served, most American public, university, and college libraries will have *Who's Who in America* and possibly *Who's Who*—"possibly" because the better-known figures apt to be objects of inquiry in *Who's Who* are covered in the *International Who's Who*, which opens with a section of names of "reigning royal families," then moves to the alphabetic listing of some 12,000 to 15,000 brief biographies of the outstanding men and women of our time. The range is wide and takes in those who are prominent in international affairs, government, administration, diplomacy, science, medicine, law, finance, business, education, religion, literature, music, art, and entertainment.

Marquis issues *Who's Who in the World* (1970 to date, biennial) which lists about 25,000 names, or about 10,000 more than in the *International*. Interestingly enough, the amount of duplication is minimal, although the form and type of information is much the same in both.

Almost every country in the world has a similar set of "who's who" directories, that is, a basic work for the living famous and a set for the famous who have died. Most of these are published by reputable firms listed in the standard bibliographies such as *Guide to Reference Books* and *Guide to Reference Materials*. For example, there is *Canadian Who's Who* (Toronto: University of Toronto Press, 1910 to date, every three years). This includes a wide variety of biographical sketches from all walks of life, including businesspeople, authors, performers and teachers. While more current, *Who's Who in Canada* (Toronto: International, 1911 to date, biennial) concentrates primarily on the business community.

Among the latest is *Who's Who in Poland*. Issued in 1984 by a government publishing house, it takes a hard line on who is included or excluded. While it does include Lech Walesa, noting he is an "electrician" and winner of the Nobel Prize, it mentions little about his other activities. "Among those missing from the volume are some of

Poland's best known personalities, people whose curricula vitae were ordered excised by Government censors as being politically unacceptable. Other citations were trimmed."[6]

Essay form of biographical sources

Current Biography. New York: The H. W. Wilson Company, 1940 to date, monthly except August. $42.

The New York Times Biographical Service: A Compilation of Current Biographical Information of General Interest. Sanford, North Carolina: Microfilming Corporation of America, 1970 to date, monthly. Loose leaf, $85.

Current Biography is the single most popular current essay-length biographical aid in almost all types of libraries. Issued monthly, it is cumulated, often with revised sketches, into annual volumes with excellent cumulative indexing. Annual emphasis is on some 200 international personalities, primarily those in some way influencing the American scene. Articles are long enough to include all vital information about the person and are usually relatively objective. The sketches are prepared by a special staff which draws information from other biographical sources and from the person covered in the article. Subjects are given the opportunity to check the copy before it is published and, presumably, to approve the photograph which accompanies each sketch. Source references are cited. Obituary notices, with due reference to *The New York Times Obituaries Index,* are listed for those who at one time have appeared in the work.

Thanks to the format and rather "catchy" photographs on the cover, *Current Biography* resembles a magazine which, literally, can be read cover to cover.

Each issue includes a cumulative index to past issues of the year, and with the twelfth number, the title is published as a hard-bound yearbook. The yearbook adds a subject index by profession, useful for looking for leaders in various fields. A cumulative index to the yearbooks is issued every 10 years, with paperback cumulative indexes issued between; e.g., as of 1986 there is a hardbound index for 1940–1985. Another feature in the annual is a list of current "biographical references." This serves as a convenient up-to-date checklist for purchases.

The New York Times Biographical Service serves the same purpose,

---

[6]Michael Kaufman, "A New Who's Who Tells What's What in Warsaw," *The New York Times,* August 14, 1984, p. A2.

and usually the same audience, as *Current Biography*. The essential difference is that *Current Biography* is staff-written with source references. The *New York Times* biographies are usually written by individuals who do not cite sources. Published each month in loose-leaf form, it is a first choice for any medium-sized or large library. It includes obituaries and the "man in the news," and features stories from the drama, book, sports, and Sunday magazine sections. Each sheet is a reprint of biographical material which has appeared in the *Times*. The monthly section has its own index, cumulated every six months and annually. The sketches are often reports on controversial, less-than-admirable, individuals. Most of the reporting is objective.

No matter how large the cast of characters in these various biographical sources, there is always someone missing. Counting on that, as well as a new approach to the famous found in all sources, Gale Research Company launched a rival to the two standards in 1985. This is *Contemporary Newsmakers* (1985 to date, quarterly) which considers about 30 to 40 people in each issue. All are presented in a uniform style, including numerous photographs. Among the "newsmakers" in the first edition is Christie Hefner. She is quoted as saying "Playboy has been more supportive of feminist politics and philosophies than most other companies I know of . . ." There is no indication of her grasp of other companies.

Retrospective essay form

> *Dictionary of American Biography*. New York: Charles Scribner's Sons, 1974, 11 vols. Supplements, 1977 to date, irregular. The set, $695.
>
> *Dictionary of National Biography*. Edited by Leslie Stephen and Sidney Lee, 1885 to 1901; reissue, London: Oxford University Press, 1938, 21 vols. and supplement; 2d to 8th supplements, 1912–1986. Base set, $550; Supplements 2–8, $90. each.
>
> *Notable American Women 1607–1950. A Biographical Dictionary*. Edited by Edward T. James. Cambridge, Massachusetts: Harvard University Press, 1971, 3 vols. $75; paper, $35; supplement, 1980, $35.

The proper use of these national, retrospective biographical aids depends on the librarian's or user's recognizing the nationality of the figure in question and the fact that all entrants are deceased. When the nationality is not known, it will save time to first check *Biography and Genealogy Master Index* and its companion for historical figures *Historical Biographical Dictionaries Master Index.* Where neither is available, one might turn first to a biographical dictionary, encyclopedia, or *Biography Index.* The latter may prove particularly productive when the name cannot be found in any of the sources noted.

The listing in either the DAB or DNB is a way of making certain a person's reputation lives forever. The judgement of the works is the yardstick whereby everyone from historians to art curators measure the importance of an individual. Posthumous celebrity is the final accolade, although it often is bestowed on somewhat obscure, dimly remembered politicians and sports figures.

The *Dictionary of American Biography* (or the *DAB*, as it is usually called), with its supplements, covers some 17,084 figures who have made a major contribution to American life. Almost all are Americans, but there are a few foreigners who significantly contributed to our history. (In this case, they had to have lived in the United States for some considerable length of time.) Furthermore, no British officers "serving in America after the colonies declared their independence" are included. A separate index gives a subject, contributor, birthplace, topic, and occupations entry to the set and its supplements.

Some 3000 scholarly contributors add their distinctive styles and viewpoints to the compilation. As a consequence, most of the entries —which vary from several paragraphs to several pages—can be read as essays rather than as a list of connected, dry facts.[7]

As of 1985 there were six supplements to the main set. Fortunately, there is an index in the sixth volume which covers all the supplements.

The *Dictionary of National Biography* (or *DNB*) is the model for the *DAB;* and having learned one set, the librarian can handle the other without difficulty. The *DNB,* approximately twice the size of the *DAB,* includes entries on over 32,000 deceased "men and women of British or Irish race who have achieved any reasonable measure of distinction in any walk of life." It also includes early settlers in America and "persons of foreign birth who have gained eminence in this country." The original set, edited by Leslie Stephen, Virginia Woolf's father,

---

[7]Smaller libraries will find the *Concise Dictionary of American Biography* (3d ed., New York: Charles Scribner's Sons, 1980) a substitute for the large set. However, it reduces the primary essays to little more than sketches of highlights of a person's life and is more properly suited to ready-reference work than to research. There are some medium-to-long essay entries which are almost the same as in the master set, but the selection is limited to better-known figures who usually can be found in numerous other sources.

includes short to long signed articles with bibliographies. Aside from the scope, it can be used in much the same way and for many of the same reasons as the *DAB*.

In the 1961–1970 supplement (issued in 1981), there are 745 biographies of people who died between 1961 and 1970. Few of these are women, although Vita Sackville-West, Vivien Leigh, and Dame Myra Hess are included. Here, too, for the first time the matter of sex is considered, e.g., E. M. Forster's homosexuality "is straightforwardly but delicately touched on. . . . Without this adjustment it would have been impossible to have included Joe Orton," whose plays focus almost completely on homosexuality.[8] A useful feature in each supplement is a retrospective index of all entries from 1901.

A Chronological and Occupational Index to the Dictionary of National Biography (New York: Oxford University Press, 1985) is primarily an index which divides the entries into 20 basic professional and occupational categories. There is a separate chronological listing for each category. This is a massive index (close to 1000 pages) to both the basic set and the supplements.

Notable American Women includes 1359 biographies of subjects who died prior to 1950, and the supplement adds 442 who died between 1951 and 1975. Inclusion is based on their "lives and careers (having) had significant impact on American life in all fields of thought and action." The long, signed biographies are similar to those in the DAB and DNB, and the author of each entry has special knowledge of the subject. In explaining who was included or excluded, the editors noted that the usual test of inclusion—being the wife of a famous man—was not considered. (The only exception is the inclusion of the wives of American Presidents.) Once more, the domestic skills of a woman were seldom considered, and no moral judgments as to a female's being a criminal or an adventuress were used to exclude a name. There is an excellent 33-page introduction, which gives a historical survey of the role of women in American life; there is also an index of individuals grouped by occupations.

The dictionary for women once again emphasizes the lack of proper coverage in the DAB, as does the *Dictionary of American Negro Biography* (New York: Norton, 1982) for blacks. Here one finds more

---

[8]Alan Bell, *The Times Literary Supplement,* October 2, 1981, pp. 1116–1117. Bell makes the good point about evaluating such books. "With so wide a range of subject matter, it is virtually impossible for a single reviewer to gauge the amount of major error of fact or emphasis." See, also, the same periodical for a tribute to 100 years of the DNB, i.e., A.O.J. Cockshut, "The Century of the DNB," *The Times Literary Supplement,* April 26, 1985, p. 466.

than 600 detailed essays about individuals who died before 1970. The highly readable essays cover almost every interest from photography to explorers and cowboys.

PROFESSIONAL AND SUBJECT BIOGRAPHIES

The importance of biography to almost everyone from the researcher to the layperson has not escaped publishers. Consequently, almost every publisher's list will include biographical works, from individual biographies to collective works to special listings for individuals engaged in a profession. The increase in the number of professions (almost every American claims to be a professional of sorts), coupled with the growth in education, has resulted in a proliferation of specialized biographical sources.

The reliability of some works is questionable, primarily because almost all (and sometimes all) the information is supplied directly to the editor or publisher by the subject. Little or no checking is involved except when there is a definite question or the biographical sketch is evaluative. Entries tend to be brief, normally giving the name, birth date, place of birth, education, particular "claim to fame," and address. There are rare exceptions to this brief form. The H. W. Wilson Company series on authors features rather long, discursive essays. Most biographical works devoted to a subject or profession have mercifully short entries, however.

The primary value of the specialized biographical work is as a:

1. Source of address.
2. Source of correct spelling of names and titles.
3. Source of miscellaneous information for those considering the person for employment or as an employer or as a guest speaker, or for a number of other reasons.
4. Valuable aid to the historian or genealogist seeking retrospective information, if maintained for a number of years.

When one turns from the standard Marquis titles to other who's who titles, the list is as imposing as it is indicative of numerous professions. For example, there is a *Who's Who in American Music: Classical* (New York: R. R. Bowker, 1983); *Who's Who in Real Estate* and *Who's Who in Aviation and Aerospace,* both published by Warren, Borham & Lamont of New York and London.

While all of these are legitimate, Clarke points out that "there are nearly five hundred biographical directories of a questionable

reference value that are published irregularly in the United States."
He then goes on to explore the various facets of what constitutes a less
than reputable directory.[9] The directory form has reached a point
where almost everyone can qualify for at least one, or even a dozen
such listings. *The New Yorker* ran a cartoon in 1983 which shows a
cowboy taking a letter out of a mail box. The letter begins: "You've
been selected to appear in the forthcoming edition of *Who's Who on the
Lone Prairie.*" It is too close to the truth to be funny.

Following are only representative examples of professional and
subject sources. There are hundreds more. When conducting a
search for a specific individual, it is usually much faster to begin with
Biography and Genealogy Master Index or one of its spin-offs. The
exception is when the profession of the individual is known and it is
obvious he or she will be listed in one of the basic professional and
subject biographical sources.

Beginning in 1985 an English publisher, Chadwyck-Healey Inc.,
began publication of *British and Irish Biographies, 1840–1940* which is
an index to four million names from biographical dictionaries. The
index is on microfiche as are the indexed dictionaries. The whole will
be in six parts to be published over a period of years. The cost for the
first part, as of 1985, was $6950.

Business

> *Biographical Dictionary of American Business Leaders.* Westport,
> Connecticut: Greenwood Press, 1983, 4 vols. $195.
>
> *Standard and Poor's Register of Corporations, Directors, and
> Executives.* New York: Standard & Poor's, 1928 to date, annual, 3
> vols. $270. (Online, DIALOG Files 527 & 526.)

Businesspersons are heavily represented in the standard who's
who series, if not in the various dictionaries of national biography.
Still, there is constant call for current information on individuals and
their associations. The works listed here are among the best, particularly as they offer details not found in the general biographical
directories.

For day-to-day reference, the Standard and Poor's is a much-
used work. It lists over 75,000 directors and executives for close to
40,000 companies in the United States and Canada. The first volume
is arranged by companies with a listing of the executives, as well as

---

[9]Jack A. Clarke, "Biographical Directories, the Fine Line Between Vanity and Pride,"
RQ, Fall 1982, pp. 76–78.

outline information about the corporation. The second volume rearranges the names of executives alphabetically and gives brief information about each. The last volume is a Standard Industrial Classification Index, as well as a breakdown by geographical area. There are, also, obituaries.

The biographical directory includes brief to long essays on 1100 individuals from all periods of American history and from almost as many types of firms. Both the living and the dead are included, and the primary focus is on the person's business activities, not personal life. Unfortunately, only 53 women are included. The appendixes divide the biographies by company, birthplace, and even year of birth.

Librarianship

Who's Who In Library and Information Services. Chicago: American Library Association, 1982, 559 pp. $150.

The librarian interested in the career, background, education, or just the age of a colleague will turn to what is, admittedly, a rather limited who's who for most public use. Still, it can be of great interest to librarians and, to be sure, people dealing with them. The majority of the 12,000 short listings are from Americans who were asked to fill out a questionnaire. The initial mailing went to some 55,000 people, but only relatively few considered it of enough importance to reply. As more than one reviewer points out, the majority of entries are from public libraries, library schools, and from college and university libraries. There are few from special or school libraries. Meanwhile, the *American Library Directory* is at least a good way of checking who works where, although it does not give specific biographical information.

The directory is supplemented by the Who's Who *Directory of Online Professionals* (Chicago: Marquis, 1984 to date). This is a listing, with emphasis on the online activities of the entry, of some 6000 people, many of whom are librarians. It has the advantage of being kept current, and is available online—DIALOG File 235.

Literature

World Authors, 1950–1970. New York: The H. W. Wilson Company, 1975, 1594 pp. $75. Supplement: *World Authors 1970–1975,* 1979, 893 pp. $52. *World Authors 1975–1980,* 1985, 829 pp. $65.

Contemporary Authors. Detroit: Gale Research Company, 1962 to date, annual. $88.

There are biographical essay collections for many subject areas. One of the most often consulted concerns writers and writing. Students use the library often for information on specific authors for class reports. When the author is well known, there is little difficulty. A good encyclopedia will give information, which can be supplemented by literature handbooks and periodical articles.

Another place to check where to find information on a dead or a living author is the *Author Biographies Master Index,* 2d ed. (Detroit: Gale Research Company, 1984) which alphabetically lists 300,000 different authors found in about 225 different sources. A supplement (1986) adds another 200,000 citations to the main work. The same publisher's *Biography and Genealogy Master Index* is as useful. In fact, if the latter is available, the former really is not necessary because the larger index includes all of the material found in the *Author Biographies Master Index.*

World Authors, issued by the Wilson Company, is one of the best-known series on authors. The series is useful because it includes not only the essential biographical information but also bibliographies of works by and about the author. The source of much of the material is the author, if living, or careful research if the author is deceased. Some of the entries are printed almost verbatim as written by the author and are entertaining reading in their own right.

An example of the series is *World Authors 1950–1970,* edited by John Wakeman, with Stanley Kunitz as a consultant. International in scope, the alphabetically arranged volume includes material on 959 authors, most of whom came to prominence between 1950 and 1970 or, for one reason or another, were not included in previous volumes. Entries run from 800 to 1600 words, with a picture of the writer and a listing of published works as well as major bio-bibliographies. The style is informative, and about half the biographies include autobiographical essays. The work periodically is updated, e.g., *World Authors 1975–1980* appeared in 1985.

The latest edition, edited by Vineta Colby, follows the style of the other volumes. Close to 400 biographical sketches are included of poets, novelists, dramatists, as well as philosophers, historians, and educators. Unlike earlier volumes, about one-third of the profiles here are prepared by the authors. The rest of the sketches are by experts.

Related titles in the H. W. Wilson series are *Twentieth Century Authors,* 1942, and the *Supplement,* 1955. Until publication of *World Authors,* these two titles were the basic sources of "current" information on writers. They now may be used to supplement *World Authors*. For deceased writers, Wilson has five author titles: *Greek and Latin Authors, 800 B.C.–A.D. 1000*, 1980; *American Authors, 1600–1900*, 1938; *European Authors, 1000–1900*, 1967; *British Authors before 1800*, 1952; *British Authors of the Nineteenth Century*, 1936. All these follow the style of *World Authors*.

The Wilson series leaves a serious gap, in that the volumes are revised infrequently and do not offer access to newer writers. Also, the Wilson works disregard authors of more ephemeral titles. Here *Contemporary Authors* is of assistance.

Almost any published American writer is included in the *Contemporary Authors* volumes; the qualifications according to a publicity release by the publisher are:

> *The author must have had at least one book published by a commercial, risk publisher, or a university press within the last three or four years . . . Novelists, poets, dramatists, juvenile writers, writers of nonfiction in the social sciences or the humanities are all covered.*

In fact, just about anyone who has published anything (this side of a vanity or a technical book) is listed. Newspaper and television reporters, columnists, editors, syndicated cartoonists, and screenwriters, are included.

The information is gathered from questionnaires sent to the authors and arranged in data form—personal facts; career data; writings; and "sidelights," which includes discursive remarks about the author and his or her work.

As of 1986, the various volumes included about 84,000 contemporary writers. This makes *Contemporary Authors* the most comprehensive biographical source of its type. Each volume has a cumulative index to the whole set. Unfortunately, the numbering system is totally confusing, and understood, if at all, only by the publisher. Fortunately, the indexes can be followed, after a bit of study, without too much difficulty.

Adding to the confusion, the publisher is revising the main set as *Contemporary Authors: New Revision Series*. In 1986 there were 17 volumes in print, and more promised. This serves to update the biographical material in the earlier volumes.

There are scores of other reference sources which help trace the activities of an author. See, for example, the *Masterplots* series listed earlier, as well as *European Writers* (New York: Charles Scribner's Sons, 1984 to date. To be 11 vols.). For each year's production see the *American Reference Books Annual* and, of course, *Guide to Reference Books*.

Science

Dictionary of Scientific Biography. New York: Charles Scribner's Sons, 1970–1980, 16 vols. $695.

International in scope, the *Dictionary of Scientific Biography* concentrates on famous scientists, now deceased, from all periods and countries. The work is called monumental by many. It took 17 years to complete, and not only are some 6000 notables covered, but the reader is given a history of science from antiquity to the mid-twentieth century. Most entries are two or three pages long, take a critical perspective, and highlight the individual's contributions. Several entries (Louis Pasteur, Isaac Newton) run over 50 pages. Fortunately, the material is written with the educated layperson in mind, and most of it is comprehensible to the general reader.

The last two volumes are of particular interest to reference librarians. Volume 15 features a series of essays on aspects of the history of science in non-Western countries. (A criticism of the set is its concentration on western science, and the editors tried to offset this with the fifteenth volume.) The index volume has more than 75,000 topics. Each topic has reference to one or more biographies. The result is a sweeping view of anatomy, blood, fermentation, radiation, and so on as seen through the eyes of the scientists discussed.

A one-volume edition is available from the same publisher, *Concise Dictionary of Scientific Biography* (1981, $60) which follows the same format, but reduces the amount of information for each entry substantially.

SUGGESTED READING

Bockstruck, Lloyd, "Four Centuries of Genealogy: A Historical Overview," *RQ*, Winter 1983, pp. 162–170. A scholarly view of reference works essential to the study of family history, this is equally a good overview of the whole subject of genealogy and reference services.

DeBruhl, Marshall, "Publishing the Dictionary of Scientific Biography," *Scholarly Publishing*, July 1982, pp. 309–315. The founder of the *Dictionary* traces the history of its development and publication, comparing it to building a Gothic cathedral. See, too, Charles Scribner, Jr., "Publishing the Dictionary of Scientific Biography," *Reference Services Review*, April/June 1981, pp. 7–13.

"Feast of Stephen—in 63 vols," *Manchester Guardian Weekly*, February 3, 1985, p. 21. An entertaining and informative sketch of the history of the *Dictionary of National Biography*. The entry ends with a note that the 1971–80 volume is planned for 1987, and a compact edition is expected in 1990.

Goldsmith, Barbara, "The Meaning of Celebrity," *The New York Times Magazine*,

December 4, 1983, p. 75+. The author shows that the line between fame and notoriety is no longer visible, that immutable standards for determining who is, or who is not, worthy of biographical notice are difficult to isolate. The article demonstrates the problems of selection and rejection faced by biographical reference work publishers.

Haley, William, "Permanently Prominent," *The Times Literary Supplement,* June 4, 1982, p. 606. While this is a review of a biographical work which has essays on about 7000 people from all places and periods, its primary interest is the critical analysis of what constitutes selection of names. See, too, letters to the editor, July 2, 1982, p. 726 for further comments on selection.

Hast, Adele, and Jennie Farley *American Leaders Past and Present: The View from Who's Who in America* (Chicago: Marquis Who's Who Inc., 1985). A 36-page paper-bound monograph which shows how various professions and leaders have been concentrated in *Who's Who in America* from its earliest beginnings until the present. The well-documented study is apparently free for the asking from the publisher.

McCoy, W. Keith, "Dictionary of American Biography," *Reference Services Review,* Fall 1983, p. 17–20. A short history of the DAB, as well as an equally brief evaluation. See the bibliography which lists other articles on the same subject.

Nadel, Ira, *Biography, Fiction, Fact and Form,* New York: St. Martin's Press, 1984. Here the focus is on biography as literature, but the introductory chapters serve as a good overview of biography in general. The author is concerned with "how biographies are written and what form they have assumed in the last century and a half."

Reinhart, M. Ann, "The Challenge of Genealogical Reference Services: Introduction," *RQ,* Winter 1983, pp. 159–210. The author is editor of a special issue of *RQ* devoted to genealogy. There are six articles on aspects of the subject as they involve reference librarians.

CHAPTER TEN

Dictionaries[1]

I f nothing else, the dictionary indicates the reader's own, sometimes deplorable, knowledge of his or her native language. "Dictionaries are far more effective instruments for inculcating linguistic humility than prayer-books are for inculcating the spiritual variety."[2] Beyond that, one may turn to the dictionary for the last word on spelling, pronunciation, meaning, syllabication (word division), and definitions. Hardly a day goes by that the average person does not have need of a dictionary, only to check the meaning of this or that word, or to assist (on the sly) with a crossword puzzle.

Not all spelling can be checked in a dictionary. For example, how does one track down the spelling of the Callippe Silverspot butterfly, an endangered species in California. This question was put to the librarian at the magazine *U.S. News and World Report*. "She made eight phone calls, but experts at the Agriculture Department, universities in Maryland and California and country agricultural agents could not

---

[1]Totally unconnected items in alphabetical order make up the dictionary. Where there is a "connection," the publisher may use the term "dictionary" in the title. *The Dictionary of National Biography*, for example, is in alphabetical order but has the connection of listing only the dead who are, to be sure, famous. Hence, "dictionary" in the title of a reference book does not necessarily refer to a language dictionary, but only to alphabetical order, and a central theme.

[2]Roy Harris, "The History Men," *The Times Literary Supplement*, September 3, 1982, p. 935.

tell her until she could identify the genus—or subfamily—of the butterfly. Finally, she got both from the National Museum of Natural History."[3]

What are the most common usage and grammar types of questions? If the experience of a grammar hotline (REWRITE) is any indication, "the standard queries include ones on hyphenation; which-versus-that; getting rid of legalese (using 'about' instead of 'with respect to', for instance, and eliminating words like 'therein'), and spelling." The hotline staff members do much to deflate jargon. "The other day someone called about the wisdom of using the word 'ongoing.' One of the New York grammarians replied, 'Aaarrrggghhh.' "[4]

Scope[5]

The public is apt to think of dictionaries in only one category, but they cover almost every interest. Categorization usually is reduced to: (1) general English-language dictionaries, which include unabridged titles (i.e., those with over 265,000 entries) and desk or collegiate dictionaries (from 130,000 to 180,000 entries); these are for both adults and children. (2) Paperback dictionaries which may have no more than 30,000 to 55,000 words and are often used because they are inexpensive and convenient to carry; (3) historical dictionaries which show the history of a word from date of introduction to the present; (5) period or scholarly specialized titles which focus on a given time period or place such as a dictionary of Old English; (4) etymological dictionaries which are like historical titles, but tend to put more emphasis on analysis of components and cognates in other languages; (5) foreign-language titles, which are bilingual in that they give the meanings of the words of one language in another language; (6) subject works which concentrate on the definition of words in a given area, such as science and technology; (7) "other" dictionaries

[handwritten margin note: types of dictionaries]

[3]"A Memo to Our Readers," *U.S. News & World Report*, April 9, 1984, p. 4. The librarian spends most of her time double-checking the spelling of hundreds of words and proper names. One of the most frequently misspelled names is Weyerhaeuser.

[4]"Dialing for Scholars," *The New York Times*, July 25, 1984, p. B5. This is a grammar hotline operated by two New York English professors. People phone for help with grammatical problems.

[5]Annie Brewer, *Dictionaries, Encyclopedias, and Other Word Related Books*, 3d ed. (Detroit: Gale, 1982, 3 vols.) includes more than 28,000 titles. The compilation indicates the number of both English- and non-English-language dictionaries and related titles. See, too: *World Dictionaries in Print* (New York: R. R. Bowker, 1983) which is a bibliography of dictionaries, glossaries, word books, and thesauri in 238 languages and from almost as many subject areas.

which includes almost everything from abbreviations to slang and proper usage.

Most libraries have sections devoted exclusively to dictionaries and related works, but this side of the Library of Congress, the largest collection of dictionaries is at Indiana State University. Here 7000 titles are available to students specializing in lexicography. It is the home, too, of the Dictionary Society of North America, which issues papers on "semantics, etymology, vernaculars and other heavy stuff that pop grammarians crave."[6]

A curious feature of the second edition of *Webster's Unabridged* was the inclusion of a "ghost word". The word "dord" was simply an error on the part of an overzealous clerk, which resulted in its inclusion as a loose synonym for density. After the error was discovered, the publishers decided to keep it in the dictionary for a few years in the hope that another publisher might pick it up and be caught as a plagiarist. The word was later eliminated, and there is no record of whether or not it served its purpose.[7]

The larger dictionary publishers offer a wide line of their products. Not only are there specialized works, but there are different versions of the basic dictionary. For example, Merriam-Webster not only has the popular *Webster's Ninth New College Dictionary* but three editions for younger people, as well as the related *Webster's Concise Family Dictionary* and a paperback, *Webster's Vest Pocket Dictionary.*

Compilation

How is a dictionary compiled from the written and spoken words that are its source? Today the larger publishers, from Merriam-Webster to Houghton Mifflin, have substantial staffs and free-lance lexicographers. The staff at *American Heritage Dictionary* offices was over 40 people when the new edition of the desk dictionary was in preparation. *The Oxford English Dictionary* has an even larger part- and full-time staff.

The process differs from firm to firm, but essentially it is in two stages. The free-lance readers send in words taken from magazines, newspapers, and other sources. The newly-coined words, or the variations on an older word (as for example the use of "hardware" in relationship to computers) are dutifully recorded on 3 x 5 cards, or,

[6]William Safire, "On Language," *The New York Times Magazine,* July 31, 1983, p. 10. The Society is open to anyone and, as of 1983, costs $15 a year. Membership application to Edward Gates, Office of Continuing Education, Indiana State University, Terre Haute, IN 47809.

[7]Philip Gove, "The History of Dord," *American Speech,* vol. 29, 1954, pp. 136–138. My thanks to Dusan Gabrovsek for this reference.

these days, in a computer. The precise citation is noted, and often one finds not only the word and its definition, but how it is used in a sentence, as well as where it was used—sometimes for the first time.

The second step occurs when it is time to define a new word, or add to or modify definitions. Here the full-time lexicographers choose the various senses of the word, and write definitions. These, in turn, are usually checked by their peers and by the editors. Where there is any real conflict, the definition may be thoroughly discussed and rewritten. Often, too, the definitions are supported by pictures. This is particularly the case when dealing with objects and animal life.

A major concern about new words is whether or not they really are part of the language, or simply a flash in the verbal pan. A word which has been in use only a few months generally is not included. It must demonstrate staying power of at least a year, although at one time the span was seven years. Also, the word must be in general use, and not one limited to a single magazine or small region.

In addition to deciding what is to be included, as well as deleted, other staff members determine the proper spelling, pronunciation and usage. Someone is responsible for etymology, and this may often be the person who is a careful reader of *The Oxford English Dictionary* which specializes in such matters. Considerable research goes into how words are being pronounced. This is not always as easy as it may sound, according to a researcher.

> *"I was doing a phonology (pronunciation study) in the South," she says, "and I asked one lady what's the metal that cans are made of, and she said 'tin.' And I asked what's the number after nine? And she said 'tin.' And I said, 'So, you pronounce them exactly the same?' And she said, 'I do NOT.' "*

> *"This is the problem when you are doing phonetics," DeVinne says. "Is there really a distinction that, because of your own mind-set or dialect, you are missing? This happens very often in fieldwork."*[8]

EVALUATION

For those who seek to evaluate dictionaries, the first rule is not to expect any dictionary to be perfect. Dr. Johnson said, "Dictionaries are like watches: the worst is better than none, and the best cannot be

---

[8]Daniel Wood, "Scholars Labor Mightily Over Revised Edition (of *American Heritage Dictionary*)." *Los Angeles Times,* August 18, 1983, p. 9 (1-B).

expected to go quite true." There is no perfect dictionary and there never will be until such time as the language of a country has become completely static—an event as unlikely as the discovery of a perpetual-motion mechanism. Language is always evolving because of the addition of new words and the change in meaning of older words. No single dictionary is sufficient. Each has its good points, each its defects.

The second rule should be self-evident, but rarely is it followed: Consult the preface and explanatory notes at the beginning of a dictionary. The art of successfully using a dictionary, or any other reference book, requires an understanding of how it is put together. This is important because of the dictionary's constant use of shortcuts in the form of abbreviations, various methods of indicating pronunciation, and grammatical notations.

A good source of evaluation for dictionaries is Kenneth Kister's *Dictionary Buying Guide* (New York: R. R. Bowker Company, 1977, 358 pp.) Following the same general style as his *Encyclopedia Buying Guide,* it gives data on some 58 general English-language dictionaries; evaluates 60 children's works; and has briefer notes on 225 special-purpose titles, such as rhyming and slang dictionaries. The work begins with an intelligent and lucid guide to evaluation, i.e., an essay on "Choosing the Right Dictionary." Although now dated, the work does offer a good overview and most of the titles are still basically the same as described by Kister.[9]

[good source for evaluation]

The best reviews of current dictionaries will be found in the Reference Books Bulletin section of *Booklist.* For example, in the July 1982 issue (pages 1469–1477) there is a detailed discussion of dictionaries for children and young adults;[10] and in the December 1, 1983 (pages 538–544) number there is a consideration of desk dictionaries, reprinted by A.L.A. in 1986 as *Desk Dictionaries.*

[current reviews-Booklist]

Authority   As in the case of encyclopedias there are only a limited number of publishers of dictionaries. The reputable ones include Merriam-Webster, Oxford University Press, Random House, Macmillan, Simon & Schuster and Houghton Mifflin—to name the larger, better-known publishers. In specialized fields and other areas where dictionaries are employed, there are almost as many reputable

[always check for authority]

[9]The author reports his work will be updated in 1987. It will be expanded to include not only English-language dictionaries, but specialized works, including subject dictionaries.

[10]Reprinted as *Dictionaries for Children and Young Adults,* (Chicago: American Library Association, 1983). The reviews are somewhat updated in this 38-page pamphlet.

publishers as there are works. No particular monopoly of either quality or quantity exists outside the standard unabridged and desk dictionary fields.

Often, the name "Webster" is the sign of reassurance, and it frequently is found as the principal name of a number of dictionaries. The original claim to use the name is held by Merriam-Webster Company, which bought out the unsold copies of Noah Webster's dictionary at the time of his death. For years, the use of Webster's name was the subject of litigation. Merriam-Webster finally lost its case when the copyright on the name lapsed. It is now common property and may be used by any publisher. Hence the name "Webster's" in the title may or may not have anything to do with the original work which bore the name. Unless the publisher's name is recognized, "Webster" per se means nothing.

Vocabulary Vocabulary can be considered in terms of the period of the language covered and the number of words or entries. These terms may be extended to include special features such as slang, dialect, obsolete forms, and scientific or technical terms. Still, the primary consideration comes down to the question of how many words or definitions will be found.

In the United States the field is divided between the "unabridged" (over 265,000 words) and the "abridged" (from 130,000 to 265,000 words) type of dictionary. Most dictionaries are abridged or limited to a given subject or topic. The two unabridged ones vary from about 460,000 entries for *Webster's* to 260,000 for *Random House.* The *Oxford English Dictionary* has some 500,000 words but is not considered a general dictionary.

Most desk dictionaries, such as the much-used *Webster's Ninth New Collegiate* or the *American Heritage,* have about 150,000 to 165,000 words, considered more than sufficient for average use. How important is it to have a volume which includes more than 100,000 words? There are many paperback dictionaries of from 50,000 to 85,000 words which serve the purpose of millions of people. Of course nothing is to prevent a dictionary from using the term "unabridged", e.g., *Webster's New Twentieth Century Dictionary of the English Language Unabridged* (New York: Simon & Schuster, 1983). The publisher claims 320,000 entries, but the actual number of words is about 156,000. Lesson: don't believe everything you read in a title.[11]

In counting words in a dictionary, the distinction must be made between headwords and entries. Headwords are those at the start of

---

[11]For a less-than-favorable review of this work, see Reference Books Bulletin, *Booklist,* September 1, 1984, pp. 44–45.

each paragraph, and usually in boldface. Word entries are headwords plus the derivatives and variants. Some dictionaries simply number the word entries and make them all headwords. This is much easier to follow, and preferable, at least in desk dictionaries.

Currency　All of the reputable dictionary publishers, and particularly those of the common desk or college dictionary, update their works thoroughly every three or four years, and often make minor revisions with each printing. Thanks to the computer, this task is made considerably easier in that it is now possible to add or revise the basic database of words with a minimum of difficulty. Conversely, almost as many publishers continue to rely on the familiar 3 × 5 card, at least for keeping the basic work up to date.

One need only look up a new, familiar word to ascertain whether or not the dictionary is current. For example, today some relatively new words and terms might include acid rain, robotics, Moonie, and a wide number of scientific and technological terms which seem to creep into the language daily. Failing to find a new word, or a definition which takes into account the ways a word may have changed (e.g., sting for not only what a bee does, but for an undercover operation; plastic not only as a material, but as an indicator of poor taste or quality), one may assume the dictionary is not current. Also, to be sure, the same test might be applied to illustrations.

litmus test for currency ↓ look up new word or one that may have new meaning

Both what is included and what is excluded are strong indications of certain passing preoccupations and attitudes. For example, the following words were added to the 1982 *American Heritage Dictionary,* but were not in the 1969 edition: upmanship, fed up, last ditch, ground zero and breast beating, to name only a few of the 15,000 additions. At the same time, what is to be said about a culture that no longer, at least according to the editors, is likely to look up words which were dropped from the latest edition. These include Marx Brother, bread line and carpenter moth.

Format　A major aspect of format is binding. Both individuals and libraries should purchase hardcover editions. Another major aspect of format is how the words are distributed. Most dictionaries now divide the words among a great number of separate headwords, although some may have excessively long passages for common words with different meanings. The worst offender is the dictionary which crams many items under a single entry, such as lay. One must look for lay before finding such words as laid-back or lay-by.

A noticeable factor is the print size and how its readability is affected by spacing between words, the use of boldface type, and the differences in type families. With the exception of some colored plates, most dictionary illustrations are black-and-white line drawings. Where appropriate, the actual size of the object illustrated should be indicated, for example, in the case of an animal or a plant. The average desk dictionary has from 600 to 1500 illustrations, the unabridged from 7000 to 12,000.

Usage   Although traditional books have regularly prescribed rules for correct usage by most Americans, the ultimate authority is the dictionary. But which dictionary? Up until the publication of *Webster's Third*, it was *Webster's Second*. With the advent of the later title, the editors broke with tradition. The third made little or no effort to prescribe correct usage. Critics contend that it opened the floodgate of permissiveness, providing no rule other than popularity. This laxity, it is argued, not only removes *Webster's* as a source of proper usage, but in so doing, clears the road for the progressive deterioration of the language.

Prescriptive versus Descriptive Approach   Arguments for the descriptive and the prescriptive schools can be summarized briefly.

Advocates of the *descriptive* approach, who now govern the compilation of almost every major dictionary, claim:

(1) The people dictate the proper usage of the language. Language is in a natural process of change. In time, the new word, the altered definition or pronunciation, becomes the standard. Anyone who wishes to return to the original meaning stands in the way of understanding.

(2) The guardians of the language are guarding a myth, in that language has never been stable, is always changing; e.g., try reading any middle-English text without a dictionary or, conversely, attempt to use Dr. Johnson's dictionary to decipher a government memorandum.

(3) The language reflects the common culture in which it is used. To tamper with the language is to deny the culture.

Advocates of the *prescriptive* approach assert that the major role of a dictionary is to set standards.

(1) Word definitions and approved usage should adhere to tradition and authority based on correct historic usage.

(2) Support of this philosophy is essential to prevent the contamination of the pure language by slang, lingo, and fashionable jargon. Here scores of examples are given, from the refusal of

Webster's to categorically outlaw "ain't" to creeping misuses of the language, from "hopefully" used as a synonym for "it is to be hoped" to "due to" for "because of" to the use of buzzwords to hide real meaning, e.g., "pacification" for "killing."

(3) Failure to maintain these principles is virtually an agreement to debase the language.

A former editor of *The New York Times* puts the prescriptive case succinctly and well: "The intent is to give preference to that which safeguards the language from debasement: to maintain, for instance, distinctions like that between 'imply' and 'infer'; to avoid faddish neologisms like the verbs 'host' and 'author', while also avoiding the timeworn and the trite; to shun slang and colloquialisms in inappropriate contexts, but to use them without self-consciousness when the context is appropriate."[12]

In a somewhat less formal, yet equally serious way the Unicorn Hunters International, at Lake Superior State College, Michigan each year issues a list of "dumb words and phrases" in an effort to improve the language. The mid-1983 list includes "gut feeling"; "state of the art" (applied to everything from plastic garbage cans to the Mona Lisa); and "political reality" (used extensively to justify not doing anything). In previous years the group has tried to curb the wild use of "dialogue", "at this point in time", "hopefully" and "maturation" (meaning "getting old").[13]

The real problem is that whether one has a board of experts or an editor or two, there is no certainty about who is really able to be prescriptive. "It is difficult enough to determine whether a particular expression is frequent or not, but how do you verify and grade its acceptability by different speakers? Thus actual usage, observed usage, preferred usage and received usage . . . remains only partly tackled by the usage notes."[14]

After the heat of argument, most desk dictionaries today compromise, or lean in the direction of the prescriptive school. This is true of *The American Heritage Dictionary* and *Webster's New World Dictionary*. With the ninth edition of the Merriam-Webster desk dictionary, the total reliance on the unabridged work faded, and now usage notes, as well as helpful paragraphs explaining proper use, are included. The prescriptive advocates are closer to winning in the

---

[12]"Ongoing Language Barrier Build-up Situation," *The Guardian,* May 31, 1983, p. P6.

[13]"Lewis Jordan Is Dead," *The New York Times,* November 18, 1983, p. D 19. The quote in the obituary is from the editing manual used by the Times's staff.

[14]R. R. K. Hartman, "Advancing Definitions," *Times Literary Supplement,* September 3, 1982, p. 953.

1980s than their descriptive counterparts. Even though indication of proper usage is the most debated aspect of word treatment in a dictionary, other elements are of equal concern.

Spelling   Where there are several forms of spelling, they should be clearly indicated. *Webster's* identifies the English spelling by the label "Brit."; other dictionaries normally indicate this variant by simply giving the American spelling first, e.g., "analyze, analyse" or "theater, theatre." Frequently two different spellings are given, either of which is acceptable. The user must determine the form to use. For example, "addable" or "addible," "lollipop" or "lollypop".

✓   *Etymologies*   All large dictionaries indicate the etymology of a word by a shorthand system in brackets. The normal procedure is to show the root word in Latin, Greek, French, German, Old English, or some other language. Useful as this feature is, the student of etymology will be satisfied only with historical studies, such as Mencken's *The American Language,* to trace properly the history of a word and how it developed.

Definitions   Dictionaries usually give the modern meaning of words first. Exceptions include most older English-based dictionaries as well as the Merriam-Webster publications and *Webster's New World.* Without understanding the definition ladder, an unsuspecting reader will leave the dictionary with an antiquated meaning.

The quality of the definition depends on several factors. Separate and distinct meaning of words should be indicated clearly, and this usually is done by numbering the various definitions. The perfect definition is precise and clear, but in more technical, more abstract situations this is not always possible. What, for example, is the true definition of "love"? Purists tend to use words which are not easily understood by laypersons. The meaning may be precise, but it can lead to "circularity" in which words of similar difficulty and meaning are employed to define each other.

Pronunciation   There are several different methods of indicating pronunciation, but most American publishers employ the diacritical one. In *Webster's Ninth New Collegiate* the pronunciation system tends to be quite detailed, and except for the expert, quite confusing. In the *American Heritage Dictionary* the process is much easier to understand.

All dictionaries employ the simple phonetic use of the familiar, that is, a person looking up "lark" finds the "r" is pronounced like "park." Regardless of what the person's accent may be, the transferred sound will be the same as that in "park." Regional accents do make a difference in that "park" may be pronounced as "pock," "pawk," or even "pack." At the same time, the phoneticists consider variations such as the pronouncing of "tomato," "potato," and "economics" which differ from region to region, even person to person. In these cases, more than one pronunciation is noted as correct.

Variations can be difficult, even for those who compile dictionaries. Few indicate true Midwestern pronunciations of certain basic words.

> These days Mr. Wall, a 51-year-old English language consultant to 28 school districts around Sioux City (Soo Siddy) is filling up the notebook for a new dictionary.
>
> Among the rules:
>
> Whenever possible, substitute "un" for "ing" as in, go-un, workun and bringun.
>
> "T" sounds within words become "d" sounds, as in "See ya layder" or "budder", the yellow stuff one spreads on bread.
>
> Run words together to save time. "Awrite, I hurja the furs time," or "S'worse'nigh thought" or "Wire you do-un that?"
>
> But many nouns can be broken into two or more words as in "am blunts" (a murrn'cy vickul), "bild ins" such as barns and farmhouses, or "lug jurys" such as fur coats and Cadillacs.[15]

Synonyms   The average user does not turn to a general dictionary for synonyms, but their inclusion helps to differentiate between similar words. Some desk dictionaries indicate the differentiation and shades of meaning by short essays at the conclusion of many definitions.

doesn't turn to for this

Syllabication   All dictionaries indicate usually by a centered period or hyphen, how a word is to be divided into syllables. The information is mainly to help writers and editors, not to mention secretaries, divide words at the ends of lines. There are special short desk dictionaries which simply indicate syllabication of more common words without benefit of definition or pronunciation.

Grammatical Information   The most generally useful grammatical help a dictionary renders is to indicate parts of speech. All single

---

[15]Andrew Malcolm, "A Region That Takes Its Freedom of Speech Literally," _The New York Times_, February 26, 1984, p. 2E.

entries are classified as nouns, adjectives, verbs, and so on. Aside from this major division, dictionaries vary in method of showing adverbs, adjectives, plurals, and principal parts of a verb, particularly the past tenses of irregular verbs. Usually the method is clearly ascertainable; but, again, the prefatory remarks should be studied in order to understand any particular presentation.

Bias   Most dictionaries are quick to point out that certain terms or words are not socially acceptable because they are vulgar or have insulting ethnic overtones. This type of label is found even in the most descriptive work. The interesting point is noting when the editor and the editorial board come to recognize what is or is not acceptable. Cultural prejudices against women in such words as "girl" for a grown woman took many years to overcome in dictionaries. No one seemed to question sexist attitudes. Although this has changed, at least in part, dictionaries continue to err.

A political form of bias is reported by the editors of the seventh edition of the *Oxford Advanced Learner's Dictionary of Current English*. The Oxford University Press says the work—a standard teaching aid in English language courses—gave publishers in the Soviet Union in 1984 the right to change certain definitions. These are considered sensitive in the U.S.S.R., and include such words as "capitalism", "communism" and "socialism". Capitalism is redefined by the Russians as a social system "based on the exploitation of man by man, replacing feudalism and preceding communism."

UNABRIDGED DICTIONARIES

advantages and disadvantages

Webster's Third New International Dictionary. Springfield, Massachusetts: Merriam-Webster Inc., 1961. 2752 pp. (450,000 entries). $69.95. *6,000 Words, A Supplement to Webster's Third New International Dictionary*, 1976, 220 pp. $10.95.

The Random House Dictionary of the English Language. New York: Random House, 1966, 2059 pp. (260,000 entries). $49.95.

Today there is only one unabridged dictionary of the English language. This is *Webster's Third New International*. One may count *The Oxford English Dictionary* in this category, but it really is more concerned with etymology than definitions, and is not meant to be an everyday working dictionary. *The Random House Dictionary* may come close to being unabridged, but 260,000 entries puts it somewhere between Webster's with 450,000 words and the typical 150,000-word desk dictionary.

As there is no choice, the library buys the *Webster's* and supports it with the *OED*, several desk dictionaries, and special dictionaries. Despite the publishing date (1961), the *Webster's* is essential. Each new printing includes some new words, or variations on definitions of older words. See, for example, recent computer, political and sociological terms. Most will be included, if not in the main work, at least in the 6000-word supplement.

Webster's was first published in 1909. (Actually Noah Webster had been involved with publishing dictionaries through the early nineteenth century, so it is important to stress 1909 is the date of the first current series of *unabridged* titles.)[16] A second edition came out in 1934 and a third in 1961. A 1985 dictionary has several copyright dates: 1961, the date of the original revision, and later dates—usually every five years—which imply some revisions since 1961. However, the work is primarily the original 1961 edition. While the 1909 edition is rarely found in libraries, the second is commonly stocked.

The third edition, at least when it appeared, was compared less than favorably with the second of 1934. The primary complaint, as indicated, was the change in policy from prescriptive (second edition) to descriptive (third edition). Another major difference between the two, and why many libraries still maintain the second edition, is the number of words. The present edition has 450,000 entries, while the earlier work had over 600,000 words. Also, the third edition dropped many proper names and geographical entries found in the second. Because many obsolete and rare words have been deleted, the older work is a necessity for historical purposes.

Most of the definitions are supported with quotations which show how the word is employed and how it developed over time. Most of the quotations are drawn from contemporary sources.

As in all Merriam-Webster works, the historical meaning is given first. Pronunciation is indicated by methods unique to the publisher. All proper names and adjectives are in lower case. For example, "Christmas", "French" and "English" are noted in lower-case but marked "use cap" or "often cap". The only words capitalized are "God" and trade names. Fortunately, this approach is not followed in the desk dictionaries.

---

[16]In the nineteenth century, Webster published his own unabridged work in 1828, *American Dictionary of the English Language*. The 1909 edition is the first in the New International Series.

Turning to the *Random House Dictionary*, this has only 260,000 entries, but several advantages. It is updated with each new printing, and while in need of a total revision, it does include most of the new, often used words.

Many critics were disenchanted with *The Random House Dictionary* because it is divided between the descriptive and prescriptive philosophy. The editor calls the dictionary purely descriptive, but it does include definite indications of how the average person (if not the expert) is likely to react to the use of certain words and expressions. This is done by the liberal employment of usage labels ("nonstandard," "informal," "slang," and so on) to guide readers to appropriate speech.

[margin handwritten: Seems to be divided b/t prescriptive & descriptive]

Definitions are supported by quotations—the majority composed by the editors, not taken from literature and current magazines and newspapers as is the custom with other dictionaries. The editors claim the made-up quotations illustrate meaning better than those taken from actual works. That is questionable. For example, nearly a full column is devoted to variations of "lay". Among the quotations: "They laid themselves out to see the reception would be a success," to illustrate the meaning of "lay out" as "to try one's best." One wonders how a foreign language student would take it. Or what a nonbricklayer would make of this: "The masons laid the outer walls up in Flemish bond." And then, what is one to say about confusing English construction?—"She was glad to be told what a fine cook she was, but they didn't have to lay it on so much." (This, by the way, is labeled "informal" English.)

As more than one critic has observed, the dictionary is sometimes less than a model of lucidity. The definition of "door," for example, reads: "A movable piece of firm material or a structure supported usu. along one side and swinging on pivots or hinges, sliding along a groove, rolling up and down, revolving as one of four leaves, or folding like an accordion, by means of which an opening may be closed or kept open for passage into or out of a building, room or other covered enclosure of a car, airplane, elevator or other vehicle."[17]

Frequently one finds various "unabridged" Webster dictionaries being advertised by bookstores at discount prices. Supermarkets feature similar works. None of these is reliable. All are out of date, and none is recommended. It comes down to the librarian recommending with confidence only one unabridged dictionary, and that is

---

[17]In the much-improved Ninth edition of the desk version, "door" is simply defined as "swinging or sliding barrier by which an entry is closed and opened."

the one published by Merriam-Webster. A substitute, although smaller, is the perfectly acceptable *Random House Dictionary.*

DESK (COLLEGE) DICTIONARIES

The American Heritage Dictionary of the English Language, 2d
College Edition. Boston: Houghton Mifflin Company, 1982,
1568 pp. $15.95.
Webster's New World Dictionary of the American Language, 2d ed.
New York: Simon & Schuster, 1984, 1642 pp. $15.95.
Webster's Ninth New Collegiate Dictionary, 9th ed. Springfield,
Massachusetts: Merriam-Webster, Inc., 1983, 1693 pp. $15.95.

These are the three desk dictionaries found in most libraries and
millions of homes.

The standard publishers' dictionaries are periodically revised
and all are authoritative. Differences are essentially of format, arrangement, systems of indicating pronunciation, and length of definitions. All include synonyms, antonyms, etymologies, and limited
biographical and gazetteer information. Price variations are minimal.

The natural question is which is best, and the answer depends
primarily on personal need. All have about the same number of
words, and all meet the evaluative tests of excellence.

Which one is best? Kenneth Kister votes for the *Webster's Ninth
New Collegiate* and *Webster's New World. The New York Times* recommends
the *New World* for its staff, and the author now favors *Webster's Ninth.*
The Reference Books Bulletin (December 1, 1983) give a "highly
recommended" to *Webster's New World* and *Webster's Ninth.* Considering
the similarities among the three, including price and number of
words, there is not all that much difference. The wise librarian will
have all three.

When first published in 1969, the *American Heritage* was hailed
by critics for its excellent layout (type which was large enough to read,
among other things) and numerous illustrations. Unfortunately, with
the 1982 revision the publisher reduced the size of the type, and in
the process equally reduced the size of the numerous illustrations
which are found in the margins of almost every page. While there are
still more illustrations here (about 4000) than in any other desk
dictionary, the revision's additions and deletions did little to improve
the work.

At the same time, more space seems to have been conserved by
cutting back on the length of the otherwise excellent definitions.

Some do not think this is a great loss, and in that it allows the addition of at least 15,000 new entries, it may not be considered more than an inconvenience.

prescriptive

The new edition continues to stress prescriptive entries, and the usage notes are useful to help guide the average person seeking to find whether this or that word may be used in polite society. This is determined by a panel, and while the individual members may argue, the result is a valuable guide for laypersons. The notes summarize the views of the panel and are well worth reading.

Definitions remain clear and are particularly good in using simple, easy-to-understand words. The revised edition has about 15,000 new words (25,000, if one counts the new geographical and biographical entries), and the 160,000 entries represent an excellent selection.

In the first edition, editor William Morris took pride in the fact that this was one of the first desk dictionaries to include slang and four-letter words. Since then, it has been a regular policy of almost all other desk dictionary publishers as well. While the revised edition follows the same guidelines, there is a special school edition of the work which eliminates the four-letter words. In explaining this situation, Michael Rybarski, vice-president at Houghton Mifflin's Reference Division, told reporter Nat Hentoff that "There is a high school edition of the AHD. It's actually the same book as the regular AHD, but with all the vulgar slang removed."[18]

descriptive

Now in its ninth edition, *Webster's New Collegiate Dictionary* is based on the unabridged Third. It reflects the philosophy of the larger work and places considerable emphasis on contemporary pronunciation and definitions. As in the larger work, the philosophy is descriptive, although with the ninth edition there is more emphasis on usage notes (fully explained in the explanatory preface). "Substandard" is the warning for the use of "ain't", and this is followed by a short paragraph which discusses the current use of the word.[19] In this case it is noted that "although disapproved by many and more common in less educated speech, ain't is used orally in most parts of the U.S." When the four-letter words are explained, and major ones are included, the usage note is "considered obscene" or "considered vulgar".

[18]Nat Hentoff, "The Deflowering of the American Heritage Dictionary," *The Village Voice,* October 11, 1983, p. 6. See, too, the same writer's "Selling the American Heritage for Texas Big Bucks," *The Village Voice* October 4, 1983, p. 6.

[19]This essay feature is new to the Ninth and, according to the editors, is based on "over 13,000,000 examples of usage by educated speakers and writers." As the editors note, it is "a feature whose depth no other dictionary can match." The question remains, though, whether one has to agree with the paragraph's conclusions.

There are passable line drawings, although in number they do not come close to those found in the *American Heritage Dictionary.* The history of words is usually shown, and, in fact, now includes dates when it appears the word first entered the language.

The pronunciation system remains a problem.

The symbols employed are listed in full inside the back cover, and a shorter version appears at the bottom of each right hand page. The problem is that the whole is extremely complicated and it takes a special section, "guide to pronunciation," to try to explain the process to readers. The result is less than satisfactory.

Although the maze of pronunciation symbols may be puzzling, the definitions are improved. While derived from the unabridged version, the definitions are considerably more lucid and simplified. They are still given in chronological order, with the modern meaning last. For example, "explode" begins with the labelled archaic definition "to drive from the stage by noisy disapproval." Still, they show signs of revision and they are models of clarity.

Geographical and personal names are not included in the main alphabet, but are separate features in the appendixes, a habit now taken on by other dictionaries. The appendixes include foreign words and phrases, as well as colleges and universities.[20]

Webster's New World Dictionary of the American Language is not from Merriam-Webster, and often the two works are confused. The *New World* is aptly named because its primary focus is on American English as it is spoken and written. There are particularly good definitions which are closely related to current speech. The definitions are in historical order, not by the most common current understanding of the word. Of the three, it is by now the most prescriptive, even more so than the *American Heritage.* The problem, at least for some, is that it does not include common Anglo-Saxon four-letter words.[21] Be that as it may, it is favored by *The New York Times,* as well as Associated Press and United Press International. Given this type of recommendation, it has won many readers. The difference between it and the Merriam-Webster is not great; it is really a matter of personal taste.

---

[20]Edwin McDowell, "Webster's Ninth Published," *The New York Times,* June 29, 1983, p. C21. This is not only a review, but a history of the work in relation to the unabridged versions.

[21]In the foreword to the volume the editors explain that the decision to eliminate such words was made "on the practical grounds that there is still objection in many quarters to the appearance of these terms in print and that to risk keeping this dictionary out of the hands of some students by introducing several terms that require little if any elucidation would be unwise."

Other Desk Dictionaries

While these are the three primary adult desk dictionaries, there are several others which are as acceptable. The Reference Books Bulletin (December 1, 1983) recommends the *Oxford American Dictionary* (New York: Oxford University Press, 1980) although this has only 70,000 entries; and the quite excellent *Random House College Dictionary* (rev. ed. New York: Random House, 1982). They also take note of eight other smaller works.

Three fine desk dictionaries are published in England, and available in America. They are: *The Concise Oxford Dictionary of Current English,* 7th edition (New York: Oxford University Press, 1982); *Longman New Universal Dictionary* (London: Longman, 1982) and *The New Collins Dictionary of the English Language* (London: Collins, 1983). Most follow the conventional patterns of the American dictionaries, and Longman is particularly good for pronunciation.

Many people are content with paperbacks, and these can be useful when space is a problem, or when one only wants to spend a few dollars. The best of these include: *The New York Times Everyday Dictionary* (New York: Times Books, 1982, $9.95); *The Oxford American Dictionary* (New York: Avon Books, 1982, $3.95) and *The Random House Dictionary* (concise ed. New York: Ballentine Books, 1983, $3.50). These contain from 70,000 to 85,000 entries, or about half what is found in the standard desk dictionary. Most have larger, bolder type than in the desk versions and what they lack in special features is made up by being current and concise.

Children's Dictionaries[22]

> *The World Book Dictionary.* Chicago: World Book, 1983. 2 vols. (225,000 entries), $89.

There are children's dictionaries for various age levels. For example, *My First Dictionary* (Boston: Houghton Mifflin, 1980) is taken from the American Heritage Dictionary and lists and defines 1700 words used by children at the primary level. At the other extreme is the same publisher's *The American Heritage School Dictionary* (1977) for grades 4 through 11. By high school, it is expected that the student be capable of using an adult dictionary.

The World Book Dictionary with 225,000 entries is "highly recom-

---

[22]For a detailed discussion of the methods of evaluating children's dictionaries, as well as criticism of specific titles see Reference Books Bulletin, *Booklist,* July 1982, pp. 1469–1477.

mended" by the Reference Books Bulletin (December 1, 1983) and by many others who consider it an excellent work for both children and adults. Be that as it may, it is edited to be used with the encyclopedia, and it does not include biographical and geographical entries. Nor, as one can understand, does it include the four-letter words found in most adult dictionaries. At the same time it does have useful usage notes for more common, less obscene language.

The definitions are models of clarity, although a sophisticated adult is likely to find many of them much too simple. The format is good, and the illustrations, while not up to the number in the *American Heritage,* are at least clear and placed properly. While this author cannot share the enthusiasm of others for this work—if nothing else, the two-volume format is so clumsy that it begs not to be used—there is no denying that it is a good dictionary. The problem is the price. One may buy an excellent desk dictionary for about $15, and *Webster's Third New International,* with almost twice the number of words is only $69.95, even less expensive than the *World Book* entry. With all of that, the dictionary is a good buy for children and young adults—in fact a first choice. Adults, however, should look elsewhere.

Scott Foresman publishes a series of dictionaries which include beginning through high school. The beginning version for elementary grades (3 through 5) has about 25,000 entries and some 1000 illustrations. Among other reputable publishers of children's dictionaries are Merriam-Webster, Macmillan, Simon & Schuster, and Houghton Mifflin.

HISTORICAL DICTIONARIES

Murray, James, et al. *New English Dictionary on Historical Principles.* Oxford: Clarendon Press, 1888 to 1933, 10 vols. and supplement; reissued in 1933 as 13 vols. under the title *The Oxford English Dictionary.* $850.

————.*A Supplement to the Oxford English Dictionary.* Edited by R. W. Burchfield. New York: Oxford University Press, 1972–1986, 4 vols. $125 to $150 each.

Of all the dictionaries of the English language, the *Oxford English Dictionary* (begun as the *New English Dictionary on Historical Principles*) is the most magnificent, and it is with some justification that H. L. Mencken called it "the emperor of dictionaries." The purpose of the dictionary is to trace the history of the English language. This is done through definitions and quotations which illustrate the variations in the meaning and use of words.

The dictionary defines over 500,000 words and supports the definitions and usage with some 2 million quotations. In *Webster's New World Dictionary* the etymology of "black" takes 5 lines, whereas in the OED it takes 23 lines. The word "point" in the OED consumes 18 columns; "put," 30.

No dictionary of this type is ever finished, although in 1986, the complete four-volume supplement is available. The Oxford Word and Language Service (OWLS) offers solutions to any language problem, and particularly answers to things not in the OED.[23] Many of the questions and answers considered by the publisher of the OED are incorporated later into the main set, or supplements. In addition, the publisher is working on a $10 million dollar program to put the dictionary online. This would offer immediate access to new words, as well as speed up the new editions and supplements.[24]

The OED does not employ usage labels, but it does indicate whether or not a word or a phrase is "slang", or "coarse". Both labels are found in the supplements because a decision was taken in 1970 to at long last print, define, and explore the history of four-letter Anglo-Saxon words. Volume 1 of the supplement, for example, now not only defines the four-letter word for sexual intercourse, but offers citations dating from 1680.

It was more than the use of four-letter words which brought about the use of labels. As it now stands, the OED is neither purely prescriptive or descriptive. There is, as one critic puts it, "a confusion between value judgements and descriptive categorizations, providing no clear criteria for any of them.[25]

Almost every western country has something equivalent to the OED, e.g., see the next section on American regional dictionaries. In addition, there are related works. For example, in 1982 Oxford University Press published the *Oxford Latin Dictionary* which took 50 years to compile. The over 2000-page volume is not only the familiar Latin-English dictionary, but it is much more. It examines classical Latin from its earliest beginnings until about 300 A.D. Each word or phrase is followed in the same loving way it is in the OED.

---

[23]Robert Burchfield, "The OWLS of the O.E.D.," *The New York Times Magazine*, September 11, 1983, pp. 32–33.

[24]"An Electronic O.E.D. Edition," *The New York Times*, July 3, 1984, p. D2. "Oxford Turns to High Tech," *The Albany Times Union*, March 9, 1986, pp G5. The process is hardly new. Houghton Mifflin and G. & C. Merriam Company use computers to update their works and stripped-down versions of dictionaries are software programs for correcting spelling on home computers.

[25]Harris, *op. cit.* p. 936.

American regional dictionaries

Dictionary of American Regional English (DARE). Cambridge, Massachusetts: Harvard University Press, 5 vols. Vol. 1, 1985, $60. Vol. 2–5, date of publication to be announced.

While the OED remains the "bible" of the linguist or the layperson tracing the history and various meanings of a word, it is not the best place to go for correct usage, at least for Americans. In fact, according to its current editor, Robert Burchfield, English-speaking Americans and English-speaking Britons actually come close to using two different languages, the latter, of course, being recorded in the OED. Mr. Burchfield believes that at some point within the next 200 years, the two nations will no longer be able to understand each other. *[handwritten: OED not best place to go for current usage]*

A decision was made that in the OED supplements more attention would be paid to American words, particularly as most of these are now familiar to foreign viewers of television and films and readers of American magazines. In fact, since 1970, the OED supplements are equal to, if not better than, many American dictionaries at careful definitions and the history of new and slang American words.

In any discussion of the history of the American language, there is one outstanding work which many have enjoyed reading, literally from cover to cover. This is Henry Mencken's *The American Language* (New York: Alfred A. Knopf, Inc., 1919 to 1948). In three volumes, the sage of Baltimore examines a very large proportion of all American words in a style and manner that are extremely pleasing, always entertaining, and informative. The initial one-volume work of 1919 was supplemented with two volumes. All are easy to use as each volume has a detailed index. *[handwritten: one American Language excellent]*

Planned for completion in the mid-1990s, the *Dictionary of American Regional English* will assemble colloquial expressions and their meanings from all 50 states. The monumental project began in 1965, and specially trained workers spent five years interviewing nearly 3000 native Americans in over 1000 communities. In addition to the interviews, material for the *Dictionary of American Regional English,* often referred to as DARE, has been gathered from countless printed sources including regional novels, folklore journals, newspapers, and diaries.

SPECIALIZED DICTIONARIES

There are numerous forms and types of dictionaries. Among the most common found in libraries: slang, synonyms and antonyms, usage, abbreviations, subject, and foreign language.

Slang

Wentworth, Harold, and Stuart Flexner. *Dictionary of American Slang*, 2d supplemented ed. New York: Thomas Y. Crowell Company, 1975, 766 pp. $14.95.

Freedom of expression in films, television, books, magazines, and conversation has resulted in the use of many slang, four-letter words which several decades ago would have not been recognized as even existing. Of course they did exist, but were not given a place in dictionaries. The attitude was that if one waited long enough they would disappear. They did not, and as a result of this and a relaxed attitude toward censorship, dictionary editors now include the forbidden words of a generation or so ago. The *Oxford English Dictionary* supplements, as well as most desk dictionaries, define the so-called sexually slanted vulgarisms as well as words and terms used to refer to ethnic minorities in a less-than-favorable way.

Today the committee of the Reference Books Bulletin considers a dictionary remiss if it refuses to include such terms—carefully labeled, to be sure, as vulgarisms or unacceptable. Other reviewers, aside from those evaluating children's works, take much the same attitude.

The library needs dictionaries of slang. Why? There are several answers: (1) Most dictionaries do not indicate the variations of meaning of given slang terms or words, and few trace their history, which is as much a part of the history of a nation's popular culture as are its primary figures and events. (2) Readers often come across expressions which are not defined well in an ordinary dictionary. (3) Authors often look for words which will convey the background, class, or occupation of a given character, and the slang dictionary is a fine place to double-check such words. (4) Finally, just plain curiosity and interest in the language will lead anyone to pause and enjoy the wild imagination of people able to conceive of the 22,000 different slang words in Wentworth and Flexner.

Then, too, up-to-date slang dictionaries are a great help in deciphering what young people are talking about. For example, in Brooklyn a common expression is "chill out." This expression for "relax" and "be cool" is usually employed with friends, frequently called "homeboys." Just as popular is "word," which should be said slowly and used only when the person speaking says something with deep meaning. This is another version of "I hear you." If it's really meaningful, "Word, man, word" should be used.[26]

[26]Rosemary Breslin, "City Teen-Agers Talking Up a "Say What? Storm," *The New York Times*, August 29, 1983, p. B2.

General in scope, Wentworth and Flexner's *Dictionary of American Slang* gives definitions which are supplemented by sources and one or more illustrative quotations. It is accepted in libraries, and certainly by all scholars. The particular merit of the work is its broad general approach to all aspects of the culture, from the slang of space scientists and FBI men to the jargon of stripteasers and Madison Avenue advertising tycoons. Where possible, the history of the term is given, with the approximate date when the slang entered the written (not the oral) language. In 1986 the basic work is updated by Robert L. Chapman's *New Dictionary of American Slang* (New York: Harper & Row, 1986). This gives the meaning of more than 15,000 words and phrases. There are examples of usage and explanations of word origins.

The name in this field remains Eric Partridge. He was a one-man operation who during a long lifetime prepared numerous dictionaries. Probably his most famous is *A Dictionary of Slang and Unconventional English* (8th ed. New York: Macmillan Publishing Company, 1984.) As William Safire has said in discussing Partridge's lifework, he taught the English-speaking world to treat slang with respect. Many consider him to be the modern Samuel Johnson, and his is a name every self-respecting librarian should know.

The eighth edition is the final Partridge (edited by Paul Beale) and it contains numerous American expressions as well as those employed in England, and the Commonwealth. While accuracy, particularly in terms of the history of a word or expression, is much lower than in the OED Supplements, there are words here which are found nowhere else. It is, as one reviewer puts it, an "all-embracing, humorous, energetic, speculative, unsnobby, celebratory guide to the demotic."[27]

Finally, there is a journal devoted completely to what the editor terms "verbal aggression." This is *Maledicta* (1976 to date, semiannual). The 160 to 200 pages contain scholarly articles on slang.

Synonyms and antonyms

Roget's International Thesaurus, 4th ed. New York: Thomas Y. Crowell Company, 1977, 1455 pp. $12.50.

Webster's Collegiate Thesaurus, Springfield, Massachusetts: Merriam-Webster, 1976, 944 pp. $11.95.

Webster's New Dictionary of Synonyms, rev. ed., Springfield, Massachusetts: Merriam-Webster, 1980, 942 pp. $12.95.

[27]Julian Barnes, "Off-Street, Up a Gum-Tree." *The Times Literary Supplement*, August 3, 1984, p. 860.

A book of synonyms often is among the most popular books in the private or public library. It offers a key to crossword puzzles, and it serves almost everyone who wishes to increase his or her command of English. There are several dictionaries giving both synonyms and antonyms in English, but the titles listed above appear more often in libraries. Certainly, the most popular and best known is the work of Peter Mark Roget (1779–1869), inventor of the slide rule and a doctor in an English mental asylum. He began the work at age seventy-one and by his ninetieth birthday had seen it through 20 editions. (The term "thesaurus" means a treasury, a store, a hoard; and Roget's is precisely that.) His optimisitic aim was to classify all human thought under a series of verbal categories, and his book is so arranged. There are approximately 1000 classifications; within each section, headed by a key word, there are listed by parts of speech the words and phrases from which the reader may select the proper synonym. Antonyms are usually placed immediately after the main listing. Thus: "possibility/impossibility"; "pride/humility."

The advantage of this grouping is that like ideas are placed together. The distinct disadvantage is that *Roget* offers no guidance or annotations; and an overzealous user may select a synonym or an antonym which looks and sounds good but is far from expressing what is meant. Sean O'Faolain, the Irish short story writer, recalls giving a copy of Roget's to a Dutch-born journalist to improve his English, but the effect was appalling. For example, the journalist might wish to know the synonym for "sad." He would consult the index and find four or five alternatives, such as "painful"; "gray"; "bad"; "dejected"; and, surprisingly, "great." When he turned to the proper section, he would find two or three hundred synonyms. Unless the user has a clear understanding of the language, *Roget's* can be a difficult work. One method of overcoming the problem is to provide definitions and then offer the synonyms, e.g., *Roget's II: The New Thesaurus* (Boston: Houghton Mifflin Company, 1980).

There are at least a dozen titles which freely use Roget's name. (Like "Webster", the name "Roget" cannot be copyrighted and is free to any publisher. Many of the dozen titles are little more than poor, dated copies of the master's original work.) Of this group, the Crowell is the best, certainly the most frequently updated, and maintained in the spirit of Peter Mark Roget. The 1977 edition, for example, added synonyms and antonyms from the 1960s and 1970s. The next edition will be due in about 1992.

Meanwhile, there is an even later edition published in England. This is *Roget's Thesaurus of English Words and Phrases* (London: Longmans Inc., 1982). The advantage of later editions is that new words and changes in meaning are included. As one critic puts it, "The accumulation of many editorial hands over a hundred and thirty years, a resolve to pursue the greatest possible comprehensiveness . . . has not only continued to the great increase in the book's size, it has also somewhat blurred the conceptual integrity of the sections. But Roget is not a dinner party where one talks to one's immediate neighbours; it is a large drinks party where one does not have any idea who one is going to end up with."[28] Another aspect of the new edition is that sexist categories are eliminated. "Mankind" becomes "humankind", a "countryman" is a "country dweller", and a "rich man" is a "rich person".

Aside from *Roget's International,* the most popular book of synonyms is *Webster's Collegiate Thesaurus.* Here the 100,000 entries (as contrasted with about 250,000 in the *International*) are arranged alphabetically. After each main entry there is a definition (a useful device) and then a list of synonyms. This is followed by related words and, finally, a list of antonyms. Sometimes quotations are employed to make it clear how words should be used.

Webster's is updated with each edition and the work is as current as almost any now in print. However, its primary claim to popularity is its ease of use. Some would say it is too easy and totally escapes the purpose of the original **Roget's** but nevertheless the *Webster's* should be found in libraries.

Webster's New Dictionary of Synonyms is another version of the Collegiate. It has fewer words, but the arrangement and the approach is much the same. The work is particularly helpful in discriminating between what, at first sight, appear to be similar words. There are scores of other books of synonyms, although the average library or individual would do quite well with only those listed here.

Usage and manuscript style

Fowler, Henry Watson, *Dictionary of Modern English Usage,* 2d ed. rev. by Sir Ernest Gowers. New York: Oxford University Press, 1965, 725 pp. $16.95; pap., (1983), $8.95.

Turabian, Kate. *A Manual for Writers of Term Papers, Theses, and Dissertations.* 4th ed. Chicago: University of Chicago Press, 1973, 216 pp. $12; pap., $3.95 (Note: an updated English version of this, prepared by John E. Spink, was published in 1982 by Heinemann.)

[28]Anthony Quinton, "Articles of Association," *The Times Literary Supplement,* June 4, 1982, p. 605.

"Even in the era of computers, word processors, video cassettes and data banks, the urge to put a sentence together sensibly, even lovingly, still engages the attention of students, teachers and professional wordsmiths. . . . To scholars, Fowler's has been the standard that other books on usage have had to look up to."[29] Found in every library, Fowler's guide to good English continues to sell at a steady clip of about 5000 copies a year, and the paperback version more than doubles the number.

One of the classics in the field is Fowler, who deals extensively with grammar and syntax, analyzes how words should be used, distinguishes cliches and common errors, and settles almost any question that might arise concerning the English language. The dictionary, and the revision by Sir Ernest Gowers, has a special flavor treasured by all readers. Fowler commented on practically anything that interested him, and the hundreds of general articles can be savored for their literary quality, aside from their instructional value. He and subsequent editors have inspired several other books and countless articles.[30]

In a moving message, Admiral Wesley L. McDonald fired this off from the Pentagon on October 28, 1983: "We were not micromanaging Grenada intelligencewise until about that time frame."[31] It is such rhetoric which inspires one to turn to manuals that explain ways to write clearly and well. The Admiral might have done well to consult Fowler.

A *Manual for Writers,* or "Turabian" as many librarians call it, is the bible of both trade and scholarly book editors as well as writers. It is not a book on word usage, although many of the rules and examples are useful in determining which word or style to employ. It does answer questions on how to prepare footnotes and how to edit a manuscript; it also discusses rules concerning punctuation, spacing, and indexing. There are explanations of how to cite nonprint material, the meaning of cataloging in publication, and even how an author should phrase a letter when sending a publisher a manuscript.

The Chicago Manual of Style (13th ed. Chicago: University of Chicago Press, 1982) is a longer version of "Turabian" and the place

---

[29] Herbert Mitgang, "Fowler Classic on Language Translates to Paper," *The New York Times,* September 6, 1983, p. C 12.

[30] "Usage Survey . . ." *The Quill,* March 1979 to date, annual. This is a survey by the journalism magazine and the Indiana University School of Journalism to determine what some 100 editors think of current usage of common phrases and words. The offending examples change each year.

[31] Translation by Bruce L. Felknor, director of yearbooks for the Encyclopaedia Britannica: "Up to then, we hadn't paid much attention to spying on Grenada."

to turn when one cannot find precisely what is needed in Turabian's guide. Here is everything from quite detailed discussions of copyright and technological aspects of printing to more guidance on footnotes and style. It is the basic guide for writers.[32]

There are many other guides, and each year new ones appear. For example, the *Harper Dictionary of Contemporary Usage* (New York: Harper & Row, 1985) is in its second edition. Questionable words and phrases are listed in alphabetical order from "a/an" to "zip/Zip codes" and experts give their opinion as to proper or improper usage.

Abbreviations and acronyms

Acronyms, Initialisms, and Abbreviations Dictionary, 10th ed. Detroit: Gale Research Company, 1985, 3 vols. $515.

The basic guide in this field is the Gale publication. It is in three volumes. The first volume has over 340,000 entries for acronyms, initialisms and related matters. These are listed alphabetically and the full meaning of the term is then given. Most of the focus is on the United States, but basic acronyms from Western Europe are included. The second volume is really two softbound supplements issued between editions. They provide about 25,000 new acronyms in two sequences, by acronym and by meaning. The third volume is a "backwards" companion to the first volume, i.e., here one looks up the 340,000-plus entries to find the acronym. For example, one would turn here to find the acronym for the American Library Association . . . ALA. Concentrating solely on international acronyms, Gale brought out the first edition of *International Acronyms, Initialisms and Abbreviations Dictionary* in 1985. This has about 80,000 entries, some of which are found in the main work, although most are not so included.

A less ambitious effort, but one which "meets the needs of the general public" is *Webster's Guide to Abbreviations* (Springfield, Massachusetts: Merriam-Webster Inc., 1985). First issued in 1985, the work is limited to 7700 abbreviations and is arranged by abbreviation, and by words and phrases followed by their abbreviations.

Subject dictionaries

Dictionaries devoted to specialized subject fields, occupations, or professions make up an important part of any reference collection.

[32]Few professionals agree on which is the "best" style manual. There are now about 200 such manuals available, and for a guided evaluative and descriptive tour see John Howell's *Style Manuals of the English-Speaking World,* (Phoenix, Arizona: Oryx Press, 1983).

This is especially true in the sciences. General dictionaries tend to be stronger in the humanities, weaker in the fast-changing scientific fields. Consequently, there are a vast number of scientific dictionaries, but relatively few in the humanities.

In the computer field alone, for example, there are now dozens of dictionaries. These range from *Webster's New World Dictionary of Computer Terms* (New York: Simon & Schuster, 1983) to *Computer Dictionary & Handbook*, 4th ed. (Indianapolis: Howard W. Sams, 1985). The first gives concise definitions, while the second concentrates on what are basically essay-length explanations as well as definitions.

Library and information science, too, has its own dictionary. This is *The ALA Glossary of Library and Information Science* (Chicago: American Library Association, 1983). Here one finds 4700 briefly defined terms. There are numerous cross references which help tie together the various subject areas (from printing and publishing to archives administration). The definitions vary from those found in regular dictionaries in that the focus is on the utilitarian. The explanations are considerably different in emphasis from those found in a standard dictionary for laypersons.

The emphasis on the particular meanings a word or term may have for a profession, occupation, or subject interest explains the wide interest in such dictionaries. Otherwise, of course, most of the material might be found in the unabridged dictionary, or those desk dictionaries such as *The American Heritage* which are regularly updated and take a particular interest in adding new terms.

The major question to ask when determining selection is: Does this dictionary offer anything that cannot be found in a standard work now in the library? A careful answer may result in bypassing a special dictionary. It is surprising, particularly in the humanities and social sciences, how much of the information is readily available in a general English dictionary.

While all evaluative checks for other dictionaries apply, there are also some special points to watch:

1. Are the illustrations pertinent and helpful to either the specialist or the layperson? Where a technical work is directed to a lay audience, there should be a number of diagrams, photographs, or other forms of graphic art, which frequently make it easier for the uninitiated to understand the terms.
2. Are the definitions simply brief word equivalents, or is some effort made to give a real explanation of the word in the context of the subject?

3. Is the dictionary international in scope or limited chiefly to an American audience? This is a particularly valuable question when the sciences are being considered. Several publishers have met the need by offering bilingual scientific dictionaries.
4. Are the terms up to date? Again, this is a necessity in a scientific work, somewhat less so in a social science dictionary, and perhaps of relatively little importance in a humanistic study.

Many of the subject dictionaries are virtually encyclopedic in terms of information and presentation. They use the specific-entry form, but the entry may run to much more than a simple definition.

Foreign-language dictionaries (bilingual)

The Cassell's series, all published by The Macmillan Company, different editions and dates, various pagination, e.g., *Cassell's French Dictionary; Cassell's German Dictionary; Cassell's Italian-English, English-Italian Dictionary;* etc. Price range $13.50 to $14.95.

Guinagh, Kevin. *Dictionary of Foreign Phrases and Abbreviations,* 3d ed. New York: The H.W. Wilson Company, 1982. 288 pp. $30.

Most readers are familiar with the typical bilingual dictionary which offers the foreign word and the equivalent English word. The process is then reversed with the English word first, followed by the equivalent foreign word. For other than large public, academic, and special libraries, the bilingual dictionary is usually quite enough, particularly as the number is limited to European languages. For that purpose the Cassell's entries are standard, familiar desk dictionaries (issued in England under the Cassell imprint, here by Macmillan). Most have gone through numerous editions and revisions by many editors. Pronunciation is given clearly enough for even the amateur to follow, and the equivalent words are accurate. Definitions, of course, are not given. All the dictionaries usually include slang words, colloquialisms, idioms, and more common terms from various subject areas. The number of main entries varies from 120,000 to 130,000.

There are several other reputable publishers of basic foreign language dictionaries. Collins of England (distributed here by Rand McNally), Scribner Book Company, Simon and Schuster, and Oxford University Press, as well as Cambridge University Press, are only a few of the better-known, reliable publishers of works which range from Arabic to Swahili.

For the person who simply seeks a common foreign word or phrase the answer is likely to be found in almost any desk dictionary. These are either part of the main dictionary, or set off in a special section. When it comes to more sophisticated, specialized words, then the choice is either to turn to a bilingual dictionary, or a work such as Guinagh's. Here one finds definitions for more than 5000 abbreviations, words, phrases, quotations, proverbs, etc. All of the entries are in a single alphabet, with cross references when appropriate, to other languages. The languages covered include French, Italian, Greek, German, Spanish and Latin.

In the next decade or so, translation from a foreign language to English may be a routine reference process. The dictionaries will remain, but for rapid translation, say of a business letter, one will simply turn to a computer. Computers will be able to translate, if only roughly, not only individual pages of material, but individual words. In fact, today "computerized dictionaries (which are available) can be quicker than books in providing the translation for an occasional word that the translator does not know."[33]

(In conclusion I wish to give special thanks to Dusan Gabrovsek [Titova 85, 61000 Ljubljana, Yugoslavia] who took the time to send me detailed suggested revisions of this chapter. Its improvement is due in no small way to his contribution.)

SUGGESTED READING

The Barnhart Dictionary Companion. 1982 to date, quarterly, (P.O. Box 247, Cold Spring, New York 10516). A 32-page newsletter by the well-known dictionary expert, Clarence Barnhart, this follows developments in words, usage, and the like. Every issue contains about 200 brand new words and meanings, with full quotations. The newsletter is $50 per year.

Brooks, Andree, "Battle of Sexes, War of Words," *The New York Times,* January 13, 1986, p. B5. "After more than a decade of taking a defensive posture against feminist allegations that English usage is biased in favor of the male, men are launching a counterattack." Various groups and individuals are cited who are trying, for example, to have lowly jobs (such as doorman) made neutral so as to indicate women, too, can open doors. The success of the movement is not predicted.

Burchfield, Robert. *The English Language.* New York: Oxford University Press, 1985. The chief editor of the *Oxford English Dictionary* offers a prescriptive analysis of the language and the role of the dictionary editor in keeping that language in order. As a pontiff, some may take exception with the author. None can fault him for his wit and style. A good companion volume to Landau.

[33]Andrew Pollack, "The Computer as Translator," *The New York Times,* April 28, 1983, p. D2. The process is far from perfect, and, while possible, is still a difficult task.

Harris, Roy, "The History Men," *Times Literary Supplement,* September 3, 1982, p. 935. (See, also, "To the editor", letters about this article on September 10, 1982 and September 24, 1982.) In Harris's review of the OED supplement (third volume) he traces the history of the dictionary and how the new editor has changed the course, but not enough for what Harris terms "new techniques of investigation and description."

Landau, Sidney, *Dictionaries: The Art and Craft of Lexicography.* New York: Charles Scribner's Sons, 1984. The former editor of *Webster's Third* gives a history of the dictionary, but of more interest, points out the problems associated with the modern compilation of dictionaries. An excellent book on the subject, particularly as the author has a marvelous writing style. An excerpt from the book ("Webster and Worcester: The War of the Dictionaries") was printed in *The Wilson Library Bulletin,* April 1984, pp. 545–549.

Maleska, Eugene, "The Clue's The Thing," *The New York Times Magazine,* November 25, 1984, pp. 120–121, 133. A history and short explanation of the crossword puzzle, this amusing essay goes a long way to explain how the puzzle is constructed and the "evolution of definitions." The process of definition is applicable, if only as a bad example, to regular dictionary construction.

Miller, Elizabeth, "Five English-Spanish/Spanish-English Dictionaries," *Reference Services Review,* Summer 1983, pp. 35–38. While this is a specific comparison of Spanish dictionaries, it serves to show how all types of foreign language dictionaries might be evaluated. The author covers points sometimes not considered in more general evaluative listings.

Pierson, Robert, "Offensive Epithets in Six Dictionaries," *Reference Services Review,* Fall 1984, pp. 41–48. The author uses six popular dictionaries to determine "how even handedly, dictionaries present and label potentially offensive designations." Dictionaries far from pass the test.

Safire, William, "On Language," *The New York Times Magazine.* In every weekly issue of this publication, the columnist offers a two-page discussion of some current phrase, word, or usage. These short essays range from jargon used by politicians and marines to proper usage.

Shepard, Richard, "Oxford Dictionary Yields to Wimmin, Yuppies and Yuck," *The New York Times,* May 9, 1986, p. 1, C29. Celebrating the publication of the last volume of the OED supplement, the reporter gives a brief history of the four-volume supplement and the primary set. There is an interview with the editor who observes: "When we reached zilch and zillionaire, it was like having the finishing tape in sight in a marathon run and we were entering the stadium." Work began on the supplement in 1957, and it was not completed until 1986.

Weiner, Edmund, "Computerizing the Oxford English Dictionary," *Scholarly Publishing,* April 1985, pp. 239–254. The decision in 1984 to computerize the OED will result in an expected total automation of the work. The database will allow the editor to keep the OED up to date. Precisely how this will be done and what it will mean is explained by the author.

CHAPTER ELEVEN

Geographical Sources

G eographical sources may be used at the mundane (where is it?) level or in a more sophisticated way to help clarify linkages between human societies. Reference librarians are familiar with both approaches. The first, and the more common, is the typical question about where this or that town is located, the distance between points X and Y, and what type of clothing will be needed to travel in Italy in December. Moving away from the ready-reference query, one becomes involved with relationships concerning climate, environment, commodities, political boundaries, history, and everything else with which geographers are deeply interested.

When she is asked to quickly identify a city or a country, the reference librarian has little difficulty matching the question with a source. The correct answer usually is in an atlas, individual map, or compilation of geographical data. Asked to establish the common elements of the Philippines and Ethiopia, she must turn to both geographical sources and related works which, in this case, might range from the *Statesman's Yearbook* and an encyclopedia to the periodical and newspaper indexes for current events. Then, too, one would wish to search the geographical texts and individual economic and political historical studies.

Once one embarks on trips which go beyond the ready-reference desk, the geographical sources become more complex. This chapter is not concerned with that aspect of the subject. Due to space limitations and the scope of the text, it is limited to basic geographical sources. These must be mastered before one may advance to the key role of geography in international knowledge.

Compared with other industrialized nations, the level of geographical literacy in the United States has been found "appallingly low." Tests revealed that high school students have trouble finding Chicago or assigning north and south to Florida, and 20 percent of American students cannot find the United States on a world map. There seems to be widespread ignorance about other nations, their languages, their cultures, and even where they are located. This may be explained by the fact that few people any longer take courses in geography. In a test of geographical knowledge, some 3000 college and university students averaged only 43 percent "correct answers on a global understanding."[1]

Given this situation, the reference librarian should be willing and anxious to assist with geographical questions. Furthermore, a strenuous effort should be made to keep the geographical sources current, easily available to users (they are not, too often, because of their awkward size), and a major part of reference services.

Definition and scope

A primary characteristic of geographical sources is that they are generally graphic representations which allow the imagination full reign. Indeed, many of them are works of art, and they provide a type of satisfaction rarely found in the purely textual approach to knowledge.

Geographical sources used in ready-reference work may be subdivided into three large categories: maps and atlases, gazetteers, and guidebooks.

Maps and Atlases   Everyone understands that a map is, among other things, a representation on a flat surface of certain boundaries of the earth (or the moon and planets as well). Maps may be divided into flat maps, charts, collections of maps in atlas form, globes, etc. Cartographers refer to these as "general" maps, i.e., for general reference purposes.

A physical map traces the various features of the land, from the

---

[1]Theodore Shabad, "Americans Get a Failing Grade on Geography," *The New York Times,* May 27, 1982, p. A7. The score was repeated in 1984, e.g., see "Geography Illiteracy Is Assailed by 2 Groups," *The New York Times,* December 14, 1984, p. A28.

rivers and valleys to the mountains and hills. A route map shows roads, railroads, bridges, and the like. A political map normally limits itself to political boundaries (e.g., towns, cities, counties, states) but may include topographical and route features. Either separately or together, these three types make up a large number of maps found in general atlases.

Cartography is the art of mapmaking, and a major headache of cartographers has been achieving an accurate representation of the features of the earth on maps. This task has resulted in various projections, i.e., the effort to display the surface of a sphere upon a plane without undue distortion. Mercator or his forerunners devised a system, still the best known today, which is based on parallel lines, that is, latitude (the lines measuring the "width" of the globe, i.e., the angular distance north or south from the equator) and longitude (the lines measuring the "length" of the globe, i.e., the angular distance east or west on the earth's surface). This system works well enough except at the polar regions, where it distorts the facts. Hence on any Mercator projection, Greenland is completely out of proportion to the United States. Since Mercator, hundreds of projections have been designed; but distortion is always evident—if not in one section, in another. For example, the much-praised azimuthal equidistant projection, with the North Pole at the center of the map, indicates directions and distances more accurately, but in other respects it gives a peculiar stretched and pulled appearance to much of the globe.

The only relatively accurate representation of the earth is a globe. The need for a globe in a reference situation is probably questionable. It is certainly desirable to have one; however, the reference librarian who has had occasion to use a globe instead of a map to answer particular reference questions is rare indeed.

The average general map gives a wide amount of information for the area(s) covered. Cities, roads, railroads, political boundaries, and other cultural elements are indicated. The physical features, from mountain ranges to lakes, are considered. There is usually an indication of relief.

Libraries will primarily purchase atlases, or collections of maps. Larger holdings will include flat or sheet maps such as those distributed by the National Geographic Society or the traditional state and regional road maps.

Automation is bound to play an increasing role in library map reference use. For example, the Denver Public Library now offers an electronic approach to the state of Colorado. One types in the key coordinates and then adds the type of demographic and business information required. The system displays the tailor-made 8×11-inch map, and if one wants a full color printout, one only presses another key to print it—and gives $5 to the library.

The focus in this chapter is on the atlas. Details on other types of maps may be found in a number of textbooks concerned with map librarianship. See, for example, the second edition of Harold Nichols' *Map Librarianship* (London: Bingley, 1982), or the somewhat dated, yet still-useful Mary Larsgaard's *Map Librarianship* (Littleton, Colorado: Libraries Unlimited, 1978). For those seeking information on specific map collections, turn to David Cobb's *Guide to U.S. Map Resources* (Chicago: American Library Association, 1986). This describes more than 900 library holdings of maps.

Another large group of maps are termed "thematic," in that they usually focus on a particular aspect of geographical interest. Reference here is usually to historical, economic, political, and related matters which may be shown graphically on a map. An example: *The Times Atlas of World History.*

Often grouped with the thematic map is the "topographic" map which gives details on geologic, soil, forest and other basic features of the earth. *The Times Atlas of the Oceans* is a map of this type.

Gazetteers are geographical dictionaries, usually of place names. Here one turns to find out where a city, mountain, river, or other physical feature is located. Detailed gazetteers will give additional information on population and possibly leading economic characteristics of the area.

Guidebooks hardly need a definition or introduction. These furnish information on everything from the price of a motel room in Paris or Kansas to the primary sights of interest in New York or London.

EVALUATION

Maps and atlases are a mysterious area for the average librarian or patron. They depend primarily on the graphic arts and mathematics for presentation and compilation. Skill in determining the best map or atlas draws upon a type of knowledge not normally employed in evaluating a book.

Buying guides

Kenneth Kister, the authoritative guide to encyclopedias and dictionaries, offers similar assistance with atlases. This is *Kister's Atlas Buying*

Guide: General English-Language World Atlases Available in North America
(Phoenix, Arizona: Oryx Press, 1984). After a lucid discussion on
evaluating atlases, Kister offers descriptive and evaluative comments
on 105 titles. This is followed by a handy set of charts which compare
the various works. Each section considers the same basic points and it
is easy to see where one atlas is better (or worse) than another. As a
highly objective and witty guide to a mysterious field, it is required in
all libraries. Not only will it assist users, but it will be of even greater
benefit to librarians seeking advice on what to buy and what to avoid.

From time to time, the Reference Books Bulletin in *Booklist*
offers reviews of just-published atlases. In addition, the group has an
excellent survey of basic works in the September 1, 1983 *Booklist* (pp.
40–50). The Geography and Map Division, Special Libraries Association, issues the *Bulletin* which frequently has articles of interest to
librarians. Contributors cover new atlases, books, and related material
in each issue. See, for example, "Draft Standards for University Map
Collections" in the March 1986 number. The detailed standards are
not only a guide to developing and maintaining a map collection, but
may be used in judging such collections.

Where the librarian wishes to evaluate a map or atlas there are
several major points to consider.

Publisher

Map printing is a specialized department of the graphic arts; while
simple maps can be prepared by an artist or draftsperson, more
complicated works require a high degree of skill. More important,
their proper reproduction necessitates expensive processes which the
average printer of reference works is not equipped to handle. As with
dictionaries and encyclopedias, the inherent expenses and skills of
the field narrow the competent cartographic firms down to a half-
dozen or so. In the United States, the leading publishers are Rand
McNally & Company, C. S. Hammond & Company, and the National
Geographic Society. In Great Britain, the leaders are John G. Bartholomew (Edinburgh) and the cartographic department of the Oxford
University Press.

There are several hundred other publishers. Most of these are
small, specialized, and of limited interest to librarians. A few, such as
the H. M. Gousha Company, are large, but generally do not make
their maps available to retail outlets.

When the cartographic firm is not known, it is advisable to check
on its reputation and integrity through other works it may have
issued, or in a buying guide. The mapmaker may differ from the
publisher and, in the case of an atlas, both should be checked.

Scope and audience

As with all reference works, the geography section must represent a wide variety of titles for many purposes and, in a public or school library, for different age groups. Essentially it is a matter of scope. Some atlases are universal, others limited to a single country, or even a region. Other maps, even within a general work, may be unevenly distributed so that 50 percent or more of the work may give undue attention to the United States or Canada, ignoring the weight of the rest of the world. Kister points out that "Asia covers approximately 30 percent of the earth's land surface and has about 60 percent of its people, yet some world atlases practically ignore that part of the world."[2]

It may be argued, justifiably in some cases, that the atlas is primarily for nationals who are more interested in particulars of North America than in the remainder of the world. European atlases frequently are guilty of the same fault, with emphasis on Europe at the expense of the remainder of the world.

Scale

Maps often are classed according to scale. One unit on a map equals a certain number of units on the ground, i.e., one inch on the map may equal 10 or 100 miles on the map. The detailed map will have a larger scale. The scale is indicated, usually at the bottom of the map, by a line or bar which shows distances in kilometers or miles or both.

Geographers use map scale to refer to the size of the representation on the map. A scale of 1:63,360 is one inch to the mile (63,360 inches).[3] The larger the second figure (scale denominator), the smaller the scale of the map. For example, on a map which shows the whole United States, the scale may be 1:16,000,000 (one inch is equal to about 250 miles). This is a small-scale map. A large-scale map of a section of the United States, say the Northwest, would have a scale of 1:4,000,000. In the same atlas, the scale for Europe (and part of Russia) is 1:16,000,000; but for France (and the Alps) it is 1:4,000,000.

Within an atlas, the scale from map to map may vary considerably, although better atlases attempt to standardize their work. The standardization is based as much on the size of the page on which the

[2]*Kister's Atlas Buying Guide* (Phoenix, Arizona: Oryx Press, 1984), p. 9.

[3]While miles to the inch is the familiar scale concept, a more precise measurement is expressed as RF, i.e., *representative fraction.* This is a constant whether the measuring unit be an inch or centimeter.

map appears as on any effort of the publisher to use the same basic scales throughout.

American atlases are often faulted for failure to maintain the same relative scales throughout their works. This is true when the United States and Canada are given emphasis and the remainder of the world is pushed into a small section of the atlas. For example, in the basic *Rand McNally Cosmopolitan World Atlas,* the scale for the United States and Europe is larger than for the rest of the world. In the same company's *Pictorial World Atlas* (published in 1980), scales vary so that a map of Australia is at 1:13,200,000 while the New Zealand map is at 1:3,300,000. The difference would make some believe the two countries are approximately the same size.

One way out of the problem is to show regional maps in the same scale; the *Cosmopolitan,* for example, does have double-page, full-color global sections which use the same scale. Thus the innocent viewer gets a fair comparison of sizes and distances between different parts of the world.

Lewis Carroll in *"Sylvia and Bruno Concluded"* has the last word on scale, and in so doing explains it quite nicely, thank you.

> *"What do you consider the largest map that would be really useful?"*
> *"About six inches to the mile."*
> *"Only six inches!" exclaimed Mein Herr. "We very soon got to six yards to the mile. Then we tried a hundred yards to the mile. And then came the grandest idea of all! We actually made a map of the country, on the scale of a mile to the mile!"*
> *"Have you used it much?" I inquired.*
> *"It has never been spread out, yet," said Mein Herr. "The farmers objected: they said it would cover the whole country and shut out the sunlight! So we now use the country itself, as its own map, and I assure you it does nearly as well."*[4]

Currency and standardization

Slow yet constant changes in names, as well as spelling of established place names, can be difficult for cartographers. For example is it Rome or Roma? Peking or Beijing? Nicolet Bay or Shanty Bay? In an effort to resolve these problems, the United States Board on Geographic Names was established about 100 years ago. While originally the purpose was to establish names for settlements, mountains and

[4]Quoted in an equally delightful article on "A Philosophic Look at Maps Old and New," by Adan Nicolson, *The New York Times,* September 29, 1982, (Travel Section) p. 14, 28.

other geographical features in the United States, as the years passed the board's mandate was extended. It now includes standardizing all foreign and domestic names for use by Federal agencies on maps and in periodicals. By extension, the board influences the commercial map makers. In seeking to standardize foreign names, the board works with similar groups in other Western countries.

The work of the foreign names committee of the board is the most arduous, precipitated in no small way by China's decision several years ago to render Chinese words in the Roman alphabet. Today, for example, it is Sichuan instead of Szechwan, but it is up to individual cartographers whether to use Peking, the conventional name of the Chinese capital, or Beijing, the new form.

Many rules are fixed; others, subject to change. For example, living persons cannot be used for place names; a feature can be named for a deceased person, but only when in the public interest; and no derogatory names may be used. "Some years ago, the board provided a less salacious name for an Oregon site known as Whorehouse Meadow by renaming it Naughty Girl Meadow. But now, a move is afoot in that community to regain the old name."[5]

Reputable mapmakers follow a revision policy similar to that of encyclopedias. They are continually revising as they reprint. Normally, this is clearly indicated by: (1) the copyright date on the verso of the title page; and (2) revision date, with some indications of revision. Much of this is an act of faith because the publisher may offer a new copyright and/or revision date, yet leave most of the maps untouched. The wise librarian will go beyond the publisher's date and check to see if the name, say, of the major third world city or town actually has been changed; or if the new preferred spelling for a Chinese river is used.

There is some historic value to older atlases and maps, and, to be sure, if they are old enough (measured by centuries) they are collector's items. In the average library, the emphasis is on the current, and as a rule of acquisitions, a new atlas should be purchased every year or so. Older ones may be retired every five to eight years.

Format

When one considers format, the basic question is simply: Can I find what I want easily on the map, and is it as clear as it is legible? The obvious problem is to print a map in such a way that it is easy to read a

[5]Marjorie Hunter, "Rome or Roma? China or Zhongguo?" *The New York Times,* January 5, 1984, p. B10.

mass of names which cover a densely populated area. It is one thing to clearly print maps of the north and south polar regions, quite another to be able to arrange type and symbols so that one can find a path from point to point in a map of the areas around New York City, Paris, and London.

The less that has to be shown, the more likely the map will be clear and easy to read. The actual number of points represented on the map is a major editorial decision.

The detail will, to a great extent, depend upon the scale and page size. Other aspects may range from the purpose of the map (if it is thematic it may not have to indicate as many features) to the area or areas covered or not covered. A major consideration is how well the map will reduce from the initially drawn base map. Usually the reduction is done photographically, and is at least 50 percent.

Other considerations include:

Color   Color's chief value is to enable different classes of data to be related to one another and to show distinctions among details. On physical maps, color clarifies approximate height by hatch lines, hill shading, and special cross sections.

The success or failure of color depends on careful consideration in printing. Most multicolor maps are printed on two- or three-color lithographic offset presses, the latter allowing six-color reproduction. This is delicate work, and where it is not successful, there is a lack of perfect registration. In a word, where colors slop over, where the color for a town does not correspond with the outline of the town, the librarian can be sure that the map was poorly printed. The secret is to have colors which make the printing legible. Contrasts are sometimes so severe as to make it nearly impossible to read the maps. A poorly printed work is indicative of the publisher's whole attitude toward the map.

Symbols   As important as the choice of colors is the selection of symbols. A standard set of symbols for roads, streams, villages, cities, airports, historical sites, parks, and the like is shown on most maps. While these legends are fairly well standardized in American maps, they vary in European ones. Consequently, the symbols should be clearly explained on individual maps, or in an atlas, at some convenient place in the preface or introductory remarks.

Thematic mapmakers have a considerable problem with symbols, and here the variation from map to map and country to country will be significant. The problem becomes complicated when a number of different subjects are to be displayed on a single map. Frequently, the task is so complex that the map becomes illegible. Hence, in the case of thematic maps, it is best to have different maps indicating different items, such as population, rainfall, or industry, rather than a single map.

Projections All maps are distorted, and with any single method employed to indicate surface, numerous distortions are possible. Normally, an atlas will use a number of projections to overcome distortions and to indicate the degree of distortion in a map. These may range from global views of continents as seen from space to the world as seen from an airplane crossing the North Pole. The projections should be clearly indicated, although the technique may be of more interest to the professional cartographer than to the casual reader.

Grid Systems Latitude and longitude are the essentials of any map, and are particularly helpful for locating a special place on the map. These are further subdivided by degrees, minutes, and seconds —45°12′18″N, 1°15′E, for example, is the location of a certain French town. The advantage of this system is its ultimate accuracy, but it has the distinct disadvantage of being a number of such length as to be difficult to remember from index to map. Consequently, most maps also are divided into grids, or key reference squares. Index references are then made to these squares, usually by letter and number—E5, D6, and so on, with the page number of the map.

The usefulness of a map may be evaluated by the size of the grid system. Obviously, the larger the squares, the more difficult it is to pinpoint a place.

Type There is clearly scope for considerable improvement in the design of lettering on most maps. Even the best of them often use typefaces developed for display or book texts, and not specifically for maps. Sans serif is used as the basic face for many maps, variation being shown more in the size of the type than in the different kinds of faces. The normal procedure is to use a scale whereby large places are indicated by large type, medium ones by medium-sized type, and so on.

Binding The need for a sturdy binding is evident, but in addition to strength it must allow the atlas to be opened easily. When the book is lying flat, the entire map should be visible and not hidden in part of the binding. Oddly enough, this latter fault is more frequent than the relatively high prices of some atlases would indicate.

Marginal Information   Each map should give certain basic information, usually in the margin. A quick way of ascertaining the worth of a map is to check for this type of information. It should include, at minimum, the scale (inclusion of both a bar and natural scale is desirable), the type of projection, and where thematic maps are employed, the symbols and significance of the colors. In an atlas, the meaning of the general symbols may be given in the preface or introduction, which should include as well as the date of printing, the dates of revision, and other such data. Normally, the directions are not given in an atlas, it being understood that north is at the top of the map. On single sheets, there should be a compass rose indicating direction.

The index

A comprehensive index is as important in reference work as the maps themselves. A good index is in alphabetical sequence and clearly lists all place names which appear on the map. In addition, there should be reference to the exact page, the exact map, and latitude, longitude, and grid information. A page number alone is never enough, as anyone who has sought an elusive town or city on a map lacking such information will testify.

The index in many atlases is really an excellent gazetteer; that is, in addition to basic information, each entry includes data on population and country. When an index becomes a gazetteer, it should include not only place names shown on the map, but places so small or inconsequential as not to be located on the maps. The difference may be indicated by some type of marking or special column. But the difference must be apparent or the user may be searching in vain for something not in the atlas proper.

Other useful index information will include pronunciation, standard transliteration of non-Romanized place names, and sufficient cross-references from spellings used in a foreign country to those employed by the country issuing the atlas or map; e.g., Wien, Austria, should be cross-referenced to Vienna, as well as an entry from Vienna to "*see* Wien."

A check: Try to find four or five names listed in the index on the maps. How long did it take, and how difficult was the task? Reverse this test by finding names on the maps and trying to locate them in the index. Failure of either test spells trouble.

WORLD ATLASES

Medallion World Atlas. rev. ed. Maplewood, New Jersey: Hammond Incorporated, 1984. 672 pp. $65.

National Geographic Atlas of the World, 5th ed. Washington, D.C.: National Geographic, 1981. 386 pp. $44.95.

The New International Atlas. Chicago: Rand McNally Company, 1982. 568 pp. $125.

Times Atlas of the World: Comprehensive Edition. London: Times Newspapers Limited, 7th rev. ed. 1985, 512 pp. $139.95 (distributed in U.S. by Times Books).

How many world atlases does the average library need? In his buying guide, Kister considers over 100 general English-language atlases. The American Library Association's *Reference Sources for Small and Medium Sized Libraries* lists a half-dozen, with an added nod to atlases for specific countries. While there is no fixed number, it is safe to recommend current world atlases published by the three or four major publishers. A base number would be from 10 to 15, with at least one to two new atlases purchased each year, if they are updated. Larger collections will number world atlases closer to the 100s, and here Kister, and Sheehy's *Guide to Reference Books* is a reminder of the wide, wide world of such atlases.

Many publishers update their atlases about every five to six years, and inevitably after each census. The next round of new editions should be in 1987. Still, the basic configuration for the atlases does not change much, and what is outlined here will be much the same for the next editions.

This side of overall quality, atlases may be divided in several ways. Kister does it by size, i.e., "large adult atlases," "intermediate (medium-sized) adult atlases," etc. That procedure is followed here, with the largest ones considered first.

The *Times Atlas of the World* is the best single-volume atlas available. That it happens to be the most expensive is chiefly because such meticulous care has been taken, with emphasis on large-scale, multiple maps for several countries and attention to detail and color rarely rivaled by other American atlases.

The volume consists of three basic parts. The first 40-page section is a conspectus of world minerals, sources of energy and food, and a variety of diagrams and star charts. The atlas proper comprises 124 double-page eight-color maps, the work of the Edinburgh house of Bartholomew. This is the vital part, and it is perfect in both typography and color. The clear typeface enables the reader to make out each of the enormous number of names. A variety of colors is used with skill and taste to show physical features, railways, rivers, political boundaries, and so on. A remarkable thing about this atlas is that it shows almost every noteworthy geographical feature from lighthouses and tunnels to mangrove swamps—all by symbols which are carefully explained.

The Times Atlas is suited for American libraries because, unlike many other atlases, it gives a large amount of space to non-European countries. No other atlas matches it for the detailed coverage of the Soviet Union, China, Africa, and Southeast Asia—lands hardly overlooked in other atlases, but usually covered in much less detail. A uniform scale of 1:2,500,000 is employed for most maps, but is changed to 1:850,000 for the United Kingdom. Maps of the larger land masses are supplemented with smaller, detailed maps which range from maps of urban centers to maps of the environs of Mt. Everest.

The final section is a 210,000-name index, which, for most purposes, serves as an excellent gazetteer. After each name, the country is given with an exact reference to a map.

The Times Atlas comes in a shorter version: *The New York Times Atlas of the World,* 2nd rev. ed. (New York: Times Books, 1985, various paging, $49.95). This has many of the same features, certainly the same maps, as the more expensive, larger edition. However, it is a smaller work and instead of 200,000 names in the index, it has half as many, about 90,000. It weighs only 5 pounds.

The cartographer for the two *Times* atlases is John Bartholomew who publishes the excellent English-based *Bartholomew World Atlas* (12th ed. Edinburgh: John Bartholomew & Sons Ltd, 1982). However, this is a much smaller work with only about 24,000 index entries and 112 pages of excellent maps, many of which are thematic and stress the interests of English readers. While it is not in the same category as the other maps in this section and, indeed, might better be termed an "intermediate-sized" atlas, it is worth mentioning here because of its close connection with the two better-known Times entries.

The second choice of atlases, although in need of revision, is *The New International.* This has 160,000 entries in the index and close to 300 good to excellent maps. A team effort of international cartographers, the atlas strikes a good balance between the needs of American readers and those in other countries. The scales are large with most countries at 1:6,000,000 to 1:3,000,000. The maps tend to be double-paged and are models of legibility. The birthday-cake-type material (from essays on the climate to thematic maps) is mercifully missing.

Almost the whole concentration is on maps of extraordinary quality. By far the best American atlas available, the only drawback as of this writing is the need to update information, and particularly the new Chinese approach to place names.

Another Rand McNally entry is *The Great Geographical Atlas,* published in 1982. It, too, represents an international collaboration, and the 67 major maps are the work of an Italian cartographer. These are quite up to those in the *International* with excellent color separations which stress physical features. These are followed by maps of the United States and Canada produced by Rand McNally. The two sections have separate indexes with 75,000 entries in the international part and 25,000 for the United States and Canada. So far so good, but a strong objection to the work is the 112-page encyclopedia section which, in no small way, accounts for the high price of $75. Here are sections on astronomy, earth sciences, etc. The graphics are excellent, and the explanations are clear. The real question, though, is whether one wishes to combine an atlas with an encyclopedia. For most libraries the answer is "No." The money is better spent on other atlases devoted to maps.

The National Geographic Atlas has much added material, but it is quite attractive, at least to many people and school children. Here one finds numerous thematic maps and discussions of world resources, although fewer than those found in previous editions which go back to 1963. Divided by continent, the maps are introduced in each section by an encyclopedic-like article on the various countries. The maps, while clear and easy enough to read, fail to indicate more than rudimentary aspects of relief. Another negative is found in the 155,000-entry index where there are no coordinates of latitude and longitude. Finally, there is much too much emphasis on American interests, sometimes to the lack of proper attention to the third world countries. Having said all of that, the atlas has its strong points including large scales, good-sized pages and the aforementioned extensive index. It is favored by many who want something more than just an atlas.

The Medallion World Atlas is the largest of the numerous atlases issued by Hammond. (Kister annotates 16; Rand McNally has 11 entries.) The atlas is the work horse of the line with some 400 maps and over 100,000 entries in the index. The maps are heavily biased in favor of the United States and Canada, but here the energy is well spent in that the scale, features, legibility, etc., demonstrate a solid command of the art of cartography. Critics sometimes are hard on the aesthetic qualities of the maps. True, they are not up to Bartholomew, yet they certainly are clear and easy to follow. Also, thanks to the

American bias, they often give details, at least state by state and province by province, not found in other atlases. There are maps of states, for example, which show everything from the topography to distribution of agriculture and population. Another excellent feature: each map has its own gazetteer, including state, county and city population figures.

Of somewhat dubious value is the added material. In this case there is a 42-page atlas of the Bible, a 48-page world history atlas and a 62-page United States history atlas—each with an index. A library with thematic atlases hardly needs this added, costly feature and a better buy would be the same publisher's Ambassador atlas discussed below.

Intermediate-sized atlases

Citation World Atlas. Rev. ed. Maplewood, New Jersey: Hammond, Incorporated, 1984. 376 pp. $22.95.

Rand McNally Cosmopolitan World Atlas. Rev. ed. Chicago: Rand McNally Company, 1984. 392 pp. $45.

Hammond, like Rand McNally and numerous other cartographers, builds atlases around a basic set of maps. The more expensive volumes include more items in the index, and inevitably more thematic and sometimes less than necessary encyclopedic material. At the other end of the price scale one finds precisely the same maps, but shorn of the extras. This is pretty much what separates the "intermediate-sized" atlases from their big brothers.

A case in point is the *Citation World Atlas.* This is an abbreviated version of the *Medallion,* but at $22.95 as contrasted with $65. The *Citation* has 26,000 entries in the index as compared with 100,000 in the more expensive edition. And there are other differences, yet the maps are precisely the same. Again, the United States is emphasized with individual maps for most states, and there are a number of thematic maps, although it lacks the 160 pages of historical mapping found in the *Citation.* Given the general excellence of the maps, if not the balance of coverage, and the lack of extraneous materials, this is a "best buy" for the average librarian or home.

Another version of the basic three, i.e., *Medallion* and *Citation,* is the *Ambassador.* Actually, of the three it is preferable in that it is precisely like the *Citation* (even to the number of index entries) but lacks the added maps at the back, and costs $34.95 as compared to $65 for the *Medallion.*

As one goes down the price scale, Hammond (like Rand Mc-

Nally) has atlases in the $5 to $10 range, but these are too small for the library, and are less than adequate for the home. A rule of thumb for a workable atlas might be not only the publisher, but the price. An atlas selling under about $15 is not going to be suitable for a library: Conversely, there are many between $15 and $35 which are more than sufficient.

As one goes up the price scale, beyond $20 to $35, there comes the real question whether or not it might not be better simply to buy the basic, larger works. In the case of libraries one comes up with an affirmative answer, although one might fill in with the intermediate atlases, such as the *Rand McNally Cosmopolitan*. There are approximately 300 maps on a scale of from 1:300,000 (1 inch equals about 4.75 miles) to 1:16,000,000 (1 inch equals about 250 miles). For the 12 largest metropolitan areas in the United States, the scale is jumped to 1:300,000. Heaviest emphasis, as might be expected, is on American maps. About 82,000 entries are in the general index, and these help to locate political names and physical features. The facts and text material found in the nonmap sections are in another index. Most of these sections are given over to descriptions of the United States, including many travel maps.

The *Cosmopolitan* is part of a group which, like the Hammond atlases, are much the same except for the number of index entries and added thematic maps and descriptions. Among the quite acceptable Rand McNally atlases in this series belongs the *Premier World Atlas*, 1981, $35; *Family World Atlas*, 1981, $16.95; *Worldmaster World Atlas*, 1981, $14.95. In a class by itself is the Rand McNally *Goode's World Atlas* which is frequently updated and is considered a basic purchase for most schools teaching geography. It can be recommended, too, for library reference collections.

GOVERNMENT MAPS

U.S. Geological Survey. *National Atlas of the United States*. Washington, D.C.: Government Printing Office, 1970. 417 pp.

It is a conservative estimate that of the majority of maps published each year, at least 90 percent originate from government sources. These include a wide variety of materials and when examined provide detailed mapping of almost every area of the world, with particular emphasis on the United States. Many of the items are available to the public and are found in libraries.

Although by now out-of-print and in need of revision, the

National Atlas of the United States remains an impressive and still much-used reference work. The oversized 14-pound volume has over 335 pages of maps and a 41,000-entry index. "General Reference Maps" make up the first part, and these are on a scale of 1:200,000,000 with urban areas at 1:500,000 and certain other areas at 1:1,000,000. In addition, there are a great number of "Special Subject Maps" which cover the thematic aspects of the country. These range from economics to demography and are some of the best available. Again, they are in need of revision. There's a valuable section on administration maps which show various districts and regions.

While this atlas is no longer available, the U.S. Geological Survey has a continuing publishing program whereby many libraries routinely receive maps as issued. These are detailed, covering elevation, vegetation, cultural features, etc. The National Mapping Division of the USGS provides mapping information to the library as does National Cartographic Information Center of the USGS. Libraries may learn about these various publications through the USGS'S *New Publications of the Geological Survey* and *A Guide to Obtaining Information from the USGS. The Monthly Catalog of United States Government Publications* is another source, and, from time to time, maps appear in *U.S. Government Books,* a quarterly listing of more popular publications.

The best single work, which is revised every four or five years, is *Maps for America: Cartographic Products of the U.S. Geological Survey and Others,* 2d ed. (Washington, D.C.: Government Printing Office, 1981). Beyond the listing of maps, there is considerable background information on cartography and related matters.[6]

Of all the USGS series, the topographic maps are the best known, the most often used.[7] The maps, which show in detail the physical features of an area—from streams and mountains to the works of man—are of particular value to the growing number of hikers and those who enjoy outdoor activities. Libraries have a separate collection of these maps, and take particular pride in offering them to the public. They are sold by map dealers throughout the United States and are available directly from the USGS, National Mapping Program at Reston, Virginia.

[6]The Canadian equivalent of *Maps for America* is N. L. Nicholson, *The Maps of Canada: A Guide to Official Canadian Maps, Charts, Atlases and Gazetteers* (Hamden, Connecticut: Shoestring, 1982).

[7]Most of these are large-scale maps at 1:24,000, and are for sale at about $2 each. For a discussion of these and other related maps see Barbara Shupe, "Maps for Business," *Special Libraries,* April 1982, pp. 118–134.

Beyond the work of the USGS, the National Oceanic and Atmospheric Administration offers maps for ocean navigation. The Bureau of Land Management distributes maps of wilderness areas, and the Department of Defense sells a set of navigational charts.[8]

Local and regional

When one turns to the local map, the requirements are usually threefold. First, the map should be truly local and show the area in detail. Second, it should be large scale. Third, it should be recent. While all of these requirements may be difficult to meet, at least an effort should be made to keep the local collection as current and as thorough as possible.

The United States Geological Survey topographic maps, mentioned in the previous section, are ideal local maps. There are thousands of these covering every region and area in the United States. Among the series, one will inevitably find the detailed map needed for either an urban or rural area.

Local state and city government departments are a good source of maps. State and provincial offices issue them, usually to encourage tourists. Chambers of Commerce usually have detailed city maps as well as considerable information on the city itself. The most direct way for a library to get such material is to send a request to the Chamber of Commerce in the desired city or town. If an exact address is required see the phone book for that community, or consult *World Wide Chamber of Commerce Directory* (Loveland, Colorado: Johnson Publishing Company, 1976 to date, annual).

THEMATIC MAPS AND ATLASES

The Times Atlas of the Ocean. New York: Van Nostrand Reinhold, 1983. 272 pp. $90.50.

The Times Concise Atlas of World History. Maplewood, New Jersey: Hammond Incorporated, 1982, 184 pp. $40.

Rand McNally Commercial Atlas and Marketing Guide. Chicago: Rand McNally & Company, 1976 to date, annual. $135.

The thematic or subject map is usually limited to a specific topic

---

[8]Shupe, *op. cit.* pp. 125–131. This is a detailed listing of maps published by government agencies arranged by type of map.

or related topics. Almost anything with a locational focus may be the subject of such a map. Conversely, thematic mapping is not always available. "Anyone with the expectation of finding a map showing the exact topic for the exact area, and often for an exact time-period, is frequently doomed to disappointment. There are so many possibilities that at best only a fraction are ever mapped."[9] At the same time, for the average library there are a suitable number of thematic maps and atlases available. Those listed here are representative of a much larger number which can be located by consulting Sheehy's *Guide to Reference Books, American Reference Books Annual,* and, of course, geographical bibliographies.

While the thematic items listed are separate publications, many general atlases include thematic maps. These may range from climatic and primary-industry-type maps to those concerned with soil and mining. Unfortunately, they are rarely detailed enough for more than superficial overviews. For details and more current data, one should turn to a specific thematic work.

Both of the Times entries are edited in England, but both have wide readership in the United States and are, by now, standard thematic titles found in most libraries. *The Times Atlas of the Ocean* was called by reviewers everything from "a rare book" to "an incomparable work." It covers every aspect of the oceans from physical oceanography to history. Whether the reader is interested in finding a particular resource of the sea, or is interested in the politics of fishing, this is the first place to turn. There are 17 thematic chapters, 11 appendixes, and an excellent index. The maps and other illustrations are examples of map making at its very best. By count there are 284 maps as well as 320 charts and close to 150 full color photographs.

The *Times Concise Atlas of World History* follows the same path of excellence. Based on the much larger and earlier *The Times Atlas of World History* (Maplewood, New Jersey: Hammond Incorporated, 1978), the smaller version has two advantages. First, it is updated; 70 of the 320 maps found in both editions are revised. Second, recent history (i.e., from approximately 1975 to 1980) is included. A third advantage, at least for some, is that the entries are much shorter than those in the parent work although they cover essential facts and events. The work is arranged chronologically, and maps follow that order. Both in terms of the writing style—which is as clear as it is well written—and the balance of presentation, this is by far the best of

[9]Muriel Strickland, "Which Map to Use for What," Geography and Map Division, Special Libraries Association, *Bulletin*, March, 1984, p. 10.

numerous world history atlases now available. The exception: the larger, earlier edition, although libraries will wish to have both.

Of historical atlases there are scores. The best known, at least in past years, was William Shepherd's *Historical Atlas* (9th ed. New York: Barnes & Noble, 1964). A rival of later vintage is the *Rand McNally Historical Atlas of the World* (Chicago: Rand McNally & Company, 1981). Both cover world history, Shepherd from about 3000 B.C., and the Rand McNally title from about 40,000 B.C. Outline maps indicate developments. There are 240 in Shepherd, although they are not all the full-page size of the 115 in the Rand McNally work. The latter has essays and is designed for the general audience; Shepherd has no essays and is prepared for students. In terms of ready reference, Shepherd is preferable, not only because of the additional maps, but because there are far more place names in the index—a ratio of about seven to one.

There are numerous variations on the theme of an historical atlas. For example, there is the *Atlas of the Roman World* (New York: Facts on File, 1982); the *Atlas of the Greek and Roman World in Antiquity* (Park Ridge, New Jersey: Noyes Data Corp., 1982); *Reader's Digest Atlas of the Bible* (New York: Random House, 1981); and many more which focus on a particular period of history or a country or region. All of these are useful, although the first choice will be the more general historical atlas.

The value of the *Rand McNally Commercial Atlas* is that it is revised every year, and for the library which can afford to rent it (it is rented, not purchased), the *Atlas* not only solves the problem of adequate United States and Canadian coverage, but solves it in the best form possible.

The *Commercial Atlas* accurately records changes on a year-by-year basis. All information is the most up to date of any single atlas or, for that matter, any reference work of this type. It is an excellent source for current statistical data, and the first 120 pages or so offer (a) regional and metropolitan area maps, (b) transportation and communication data, (c) economic data, and (d) population data. Most of this is listed by state and then by major cities with codes which clearly indicate the figures.

The largest single section is turned over to "State maps and United States index of statistics and places by states." Here one finds the state maps. The statistical data, arranged by state, follows. This includes such things as principle cities and towns in order of population, counties, basic business data, transportation, banks, post offices by town, etc. The section, which includes pages 126 to 580 in the 1985 edition, is the heart of the work. It is followed by briefer data for Canada and the world.

Astronomy and air photos

The Cambridge Photographic Atlas of the Planets. New York: Cambridge University Press, 1982. 224 pp. $24.95.

Now that space is a regular part of our world view, it is necessary to have atlases and maps which clearly show aspects of astronomy of interest to both laypersons and experts. There are several good to excellent guides, of which the Cambridge entry is one of the best. Here one finds detailed maps of the planets, satellites, and related areas of the universe. In addition, the publisher provides over 200 excellent photographs, many taken in space. The text is clear, nontechnical, and current. It is an ideal place to start for any imaginary (or, for that matter, real) trip to the stars.

Much satellite imagery is now available in single maps or in atlases. As Strickland points out, this type of map is a prime source of information.

Whereas a map is the result of editing and contains only clearly defined facts, photography is unedited; everything seen by the camera or sensor is recorded, nothing is identified. Mapping routinely is based on air photos, and recently imagery has augmented these views of the earth, so the use of them could be compared to getting information from a prime rather than from a secondary source. Experience and skill are needed to get more than superficial information from imagery, but used in conjunction with maps of the same area, it can reveal interesting facts not always shown on maps; agriculture is particularly noticeable.[10]

Gazetteers

Webster's New Geographical Dictionary, rev. ed. Springfield, Massachusetts: Merriam-Webster, 1985, 1,408 pp. $19.95.

In one sense, the index in any atlas is a gazetteer—that is, it is a geographical dictionary or finding list of cities, mountains, rivers, population, and the features in the atlas. A separate gazetteer is precisely the same, usually without maps. Why, then, bother with a separate volume? There are three reasons: (1) The gazetteers tend to

[10]Strickland, *op. cit.* p. 13.

list more names; (2) the information is usually detailed; and (3) a single, easily-managed volume is often welcomed. Having made these points, one can argue, with some justification, that many atlas indexes have more entries, are more up to date, and contain a larger amount of information than one finds in a gazetteer. The wise librarian will first consider what is to be found in atlases before purchasing any gazetteer.

The number of gazetteers and indexes found in good atlases, the expense of preparation, and the limited sales probably account for the lack of interest by many publishers in gazetteers as a separate group. The fact that most information sought by the layperson can be found in even greater detail in a general or geographical encyclopedia does not increase the use of gazetteers. Their primary value is as a source for locating places possibly overlooked by a standard atlas and as informal indexes.

There are two American gazetteers found in almost every reference section. The first, most current and, for that reason, most used is *Webster's New Geographical Dictionary*. This has 47,000 entries and over 200 maps. The work is easy to consult, and the information, while quite basic, gives specifics on where a given place is located. It can be used for many other purposes, including checking the spelling and pronunciation of place names. More detailed information is given on states, such as date of entry into the United States, motto, chief products, etc. The entries for countries follow the same detailed presentation, but for most place names, the entry is short and primarily useful for location.

Unfortunately, the second work is now so far out of date that it is of limited use. This is the *Columbia Lippincott Gazetteer of the World* (New York: Columbia University Press, 1952, 1962). The initial work and the 1962 supplement have over 130,000 entries, or almost seven times the number found in Webster's. Whereas the latter constantly revises their dictionary, Columbia has not chosen to do so, and it must be used with that in mind.

The aforementioned United States Board on Geographic Names makes its decisions known in the quarterly publication *Decisions on Geographic Names in the United States,* and this serves to update gazetteers. Also, since 1955 the Board has been the issuing agency for an irregular series of international gazetteers. Each volume covers a different country or group of countries. The series includes the seven-volume U.S.S.R. and Certain Neighboring Areas as well as the more modest gazetteers on Greece, Algeria, Australia, and so on. Approved names and cross references from variant names are given, as is the latitude and longitude on specified official maps.

The Board is in the process of producing a state-by-state gazetteer under the general name *National Gazetteer of the United States*. This will be a detailed account of new names, corrections, formal name changes, etc. A typical example is the 220-page list of New Jersey place names. Issued in 1983, this book "contains the names of more than 10,000 airports, arches, areas, arroyos, bars, basins, bays, beaches, and other places in New Jersey. . . . For each entry, it lists information including the place name, a description of what the feature is, its county, its latitude and longitude and its elevation." Commenting on the project, one of the compilers observes that "It seems that every country in the world has gazetteer coverage but us. It gets to be a little embarrassing when you travel to conventions."[11]

TRAVEL GUIDES[12]

American Automobile Association. *Tour Book*. Washington, D.C.: American Automobile Association, various dates, titles. Free to members.
Hotel and Motel Red Book. New York: American Hotel and Motel Association Directory Corp., 1886 to date, annual. $16.50.

The purpose of the general guidebook is to inform the traveler about what to see, where to stay, where to dine, and the best way of getting there. It is the type of book best carried in the car or in one's pocket. Librarians frequently find these works useful for the vast amount of details about specific places. Atlases and gazetteers are specific enough about pinpointing locations, yet rarely deal with the down-to-earth facts travelers require.

The American Automobile Association numbers its members in the millions, and it is estimated at least 45 to 50 percent of middle-class American drivers belong to the Association. It issues regular tour books which cover the states, either state by state or in groups. For example one book is devoted to Florida, while another considers Georgia, North Carolina and South Carolina. The books are divided into two primary sections. One part, alphabetically by city or town, points out the primary points of interest. The second section, arranged in the same fashion, lists motels and hotels and restaurants

[11]"Official Jersey Gazetteer is Completed by U.S.," *The New York Times*, March 20, 1983, p. 42.
[12]Gale Research Company publishes a series of annotated bibliographies which include travel guides: *Travel in Asia*, 1983; *Travel in Canada*, 1984; *Travel in Oceania. . . .*, 1980; *Travel in the United States*, 1981. See, too, Jon Heise, *The Travel Book: Guide to the Travel Guides* (New York: R. R. Bowker Company, 1981).

with price ranges. The Association has similar books for Europe and other parts of the world, and makes available single maps for states and countries. All of these are free to members, and may be obtained by libraries.

Of all the guides, the single most useful work for reference is unquestionably the *American Guide Series*. Originally produced during the Depression by writers for the Federal Writers' Project of the Works Progress Administration, the series includes over 150 volumes. Either private publishers or historical groups working within the various states have managed to update many of these works and to keep them in print. The guides include basic, usually accurate, historical, social, and economic information for almost every place in the state from the smallest unmarked hamlet to the largest cities. Maps, illustrations, and highway distances add to their usefulness, and most also have excellent indexes. For the reference desk, they are particularly helpful for locating information on communities, either entirely overlooked or only mentioned in standard reference books.

Putting more emphasis on comfort than on courage, the *Mobil Travel Guides* (Chicago: Rand McNally & Company, 1958 to date, annual) are a typical example of annual guides organized to inform the traveler about the best motels, hotels, restaurants, and resorts. The work is divided into seven regional volumes, each organized by state and town. There are a number of city maps, and the usual data on each place are covered. Some 21,000 different spots are graded with the star system—one for good, five for the best.

If the more adventuresome American traveler wants a simple listing of hotels and motels without ratings but including prices, the old standby is the *Hotel and Motel Red Book*. Revised annually, it is arranged by state and city and gives basic information about each accommodation. Since it lists only association members, facilities in small towns are often not included. There are advertisements that further indicate features.

The Places Rated Almanac (2d ed. Chicago: Rand McNally, 1985) is an accurate, enjoyable guide to 329 urban centers in the United States. The idea is simple. Each center is graded according to some quality of life, whether that be the availability of a major league ball club or an opera house. Weather, crime, housing, health care and the like are other concerns which help the reader add up the pros and cons of a particular city. The book is arranged by topic of interest within each city, then rated under that given topic in numerical order from best to worse. A related guide by the same publisher is *Places Rated Retirement Guide*. This is a slightly revised version of the first title, but cut back to 107 sites in the United States.[13] Another work, with a self-explanatory title is *Book of World City Rankings.* (New York: The Free Press, 1986) This lists and ranks 105 major cities on the basis of 82 factors affecting quality of life.

Beyond these basic guides, the library will have a number of series. Among the standards are *Fielding's Travel Guide to Europe* (New York: Sloane, 1948 to date, annual) and the *Fodor's* modern guides (New York: McKay, 1953 to date, annual) which cover much the same material found in *Fielding's,* although in a different fashion. The famous French Michelin guides (dist. in U.S. by Michelin Guides, New Hyde Park, New York) date back to 1900, and are in two parts. The separate red guide rates restaurants and lodgings in almost every part of the world. The green-covered guide concentrates on what to see at various points. Here the descriptions are as concise as they are historically accurate. The guides are periodically revised and recommendations are considered by seasoned travelers to be excellent. They are particularly useful for people who are driving, e.g., see *The 54-City Michelin Guide* which covers restaurants and lodgings in large European urban centers as well as Japan.

SUGGESTED READING

Brouwer, Onno, "The Cartographer's Role and Requirements," *Scholarly Publishing,* April 1983, pp. 231–242. The combination art and science of cartography is explained as it relates to the editor and cartographer working together, primarily on thematic maps. Of particular interest is the section on evaluation, "Recognizing quality in cartography", p. 237+.

Cobb, David, "Map Librarianship in the U.S.: An Overview," *Wilson Library Bulletin,* October, 1985, pp. 14–16. A report on an ALA project which eventually will offer a "comprehensive and current guide to the map collections of the United States." Over 3,000 libraries were surveyed and close to 1,000 are listed in *Guide to Map Resources* (Chicago: American Library Association, 1986). There are five other articles in this same issue, all dealing with maps and their use in libraries.

Cobb, David, "Reference Service and Map Librarianship," *RQ,* Winter 1984, pp. 204–209. A map and geography librarian offers practical advice on how to use maps in reference service. There is a good definition and explanation of the service, as well.

Eder, Richard "Guidebooks to Almost Everywhere," *The New York Times,* April 18, 1982,

---

[13]Mary Ellen Huls, "Choosing a Place to Live: A Comparison of Information Sources," *Reference Services Review,* Summer 1985, pp. 21–24. A valuable checklist of points covered, or not covered in other places to live guides.

(Travel Section) p. 9+. A thorough discussion of the classical guidebooks which continue to be used. The article divides the books by countries.

"Government Mapping," *Government Publications Review,* July/August 1983. This special issue is devoted exclusively to government mapping, including federal, state and local efforts. The seven contributors offer a survey of cartography, as well as several historical studies. A required issue for anyone interested in the subject.

Grimes, Paul, "Practical Traveler: When Events Overtake Guidebooks," *The New York Times,* January 12, 1986, p. 3, travel section. From natural disasters to political changes, the travel guides are always in danger of being overtaken by events. Along the way the author explains the problems of editing a guide, and offers suggestions on better guides.

Hannah, Kerry et al., "Mastering the Map Muddle," *Emergency Librarian,* January–February 1984, pp. 10–11. Public librarians explain a relatively simple method of organizing a map collection for daily use. "No longer do we face the prospect of a long, sometimes fruitless search through a disorganized array of maps."

Koepp, Donna, "Maps in Public Libraries," *Public Library Quarterly,* Winter 1985/86, pp. 13–26. This is a practical approach to the use of geographical sources in the average library. The author offers guidelines for establishing, organizing and developing a map collection.

Lang, Elizabeth, "Travel Guides," *Reference Services Review,* Winter 1985, pp. 71–75. A critical, evaluative look at about a dozen well-known travel guides from Fodor's to Mobil, this makes recommendations about the best reference work for particular needs. "The significance of travel guides in a library's (reference) collection cannot be overstated," the author says—and she more than makes her point.

Neville, Ellen, "A New Golden Age in Map and Atlas Publishing," Geography and Map Division, Special Libraries Association, *Bulletin,* September 1983, pp. 17–22. A brief discussion of the technological advances of the past few years which has made it possible to update maps and make them more reliable. There is a useful and relatively current bibliography.

"Role of Maps in Sci-Tech Libraries," *Science & Technology Libraries,* Spring 1985. The complete issue is turned over to map collection development. Much of the material is applicable to other types of libraries.

Shupe, Barbara and Colette O'Connell, *Mapping Your Business,* New York: Special Libraries Association, 1983. This is a thorough discussion of how maps may be used by business and other professional people. There are descriptions of a wide variety of maps, with most of the focus on thematic works.

Southworth, Michael and Susan Southworth, *Maps: A Visual Survey and Design Guide.* New York: New York Graphic Society, 1983. A heavily and well-illustrated guide which gives a history of cartography and then explains the various uses of maps. It is useful for anyone with the slightest interest in maps.

Wolf, Eric, "Cartobibliography: Whither and Why," *SLA Bulletin, Geography and Map Division,* June 1986, pp. 28–34. A specialized form of bibliography is explained, particularly in terms of how it differs from the standard approach. The author asks for an international effort "to compile an annotated bibliography of all cartobibliographies, past and present."

CHAPTER TWELVE

Government Documents

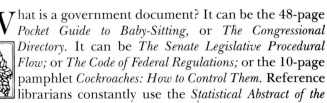

What is a government document? It can be the 48-page *Pocket Guide to Baby-Sitting,* or *The Congressional Directory.* It can be *The Senate Legislative Procedural Flow;* or *The Code of Federal Regulations;* or the 10-page pamphlet *Cockroaches: How to Control Them.* **Reference** librarians constantly use the *Statistical Abstract of the United States,* and turn to various sources for business statistics generated by the government and its many agencies. To answer the question, "What is a government document?" is to reply, almost anything in print.[1] Name the subject and the chances are there is a government document in the area.

Specifically, a government document is any publication that is printed at government expense or published by authority of a governmental body. Documents may be considered in terms of issuing agencies: the congressional, judiciary, and executive branches, which include many departments and agencies. In terms of use, the documents may be classified as: (1) records of government administration; (2) research documents for specialists, including a considerable number of statistics and data of value to science and business; and (3) popular sources of information. The physical form may be a book, pamphlet, magazine, report monograph, or microform.

---

[1]Since it was established in 1865 as the sole printer of documents, the Government Printing Office has catalogued and published 2.3 million works. About 20,000 are still in print.

While this discussion mainly concerns federal documents, state, county, and municipal publications are also a major concern of any library.

Some of the mystery surrounding government documents will be dispelled if one compares the government with the average private publisher. The latter may well issue a record of government action, although normally the commercial publication will be in somewhat more felicitous prose and with editorial comments. The transcendent purpose of the government is to publish documents that may be considered useful for research, while the substantial returns are realized by popular works.

What, then, is the difference between using the government document and the average work issued by one of the publishers whose items appear in *Books in Print?* The source, the retrieval, and the organization puzzle most people.

One may freely admit that the bibliographical control and daily use of documents in reference work often are difficult and require expertise beyond the average experience of the reference librarian. Nevertheless, there are certain basic guides and approaches to government documents which should be familiar to all librarians.

GUIDES

Morehead, Joe. *Introduction to United States Public Documents,* 3d ed. Littleton, Colorado: Libraries Unlimited, Inc., 1983, 309 pp. $28.50.

Schwarzkopf, Lehey. *Government Reference Books,* Littleton, Colorado: Libraries Unlimited, Inc., 1972 to date, biennial $47.50.

The basic textbook in the field is the Morehead volume, which is revised about every four years. It is a nice combination of facts about individual reference works and a clear, concise explanation of how the government manages to publish documents. Thanks to the superior organization and fine writing style, the textbook is easy to read. Both the beginner and the expert will find considerable assistance here, and it is a first place to turn when puzzled about some mysterious aspect of the acquisition, organization, and selection of government documents. It should be noted that the author is a frequent contributor to periodicals and for a number of years has been the editor of the government documents column in *The Serials Librarian.*

Government Reference Books is a two-year roundup of basic reference books, many of which are not familiar to either the layperson or the expert. Here they are arranged by broad subject, i.e., general, social sciences, science and technology, and humanities. The documents are then indexed by author, title, and subject. Each is fully described. About 1500 to 2000 titles are annotated every two years, and it has become a habit to star those which the editor believes of particular importance to smaller and medium-sized libraries. Carefully edited and easy to use, the Schwartzkopf bibliography augments the standard sources and now stands as the Sheehy-Walford of the government documents field.

Larger, usually depository, libraries rely on John Andriot, *Guide to U.S. Government Publications* (McLean, Virginia: Documents Index, 1959 to date, irregular). Now issued in microfiche, this is a three-volume work which lists all of the government agencies and organizations in the first volume with their regular publications such as yearbooks and reports. The second volume consists of Superintendent of Documents publications, arranged by class number, abolished prior to the last edition of the guide. The third volume is an index to the two others. Supplements are issued to update the work until it is completely revised.

From time to time popular guides are offered to government documents. The latest is Matthew Lesko's *Information U.S.A.* (New York: Viking Press, 1983). Directed to the layperson, not the librarian, it explains how one can obtain information from the government. The first 100 pages give sources, and this section is followed by what may be obtained from specific agencies. There is an indifferent index, but the book may be used without too much difficulty.[2]

The American Library Association publishes a number of guides. Gladys Sachse's *U.S. Government Publications for Small and Medium-Sized Public Libraries* (1981) is an easy-to-follow manual on selection and acquisition of documents. The publications likely to be found in most small libraries are described in detail. Turning to larger libraries, Charles R. McClure and Peter Hernon demonstrate how to augment reference service using government documents. The emphasis is on integrating documents with references services. This is *Improving the Quality of Reference Service for Government Publications* (1983). The two teachers are the authors of *Public Access to Government Information* (Norwood, New Jersey: Ablex Publishing Corp., 1984) which is an aid for people who have some background in the subject.

Betsy McIlvaine's *A Consumers' Researchers' and Students' Guide to Government Publications* (New York: The H. W. Wilson Company,

---

[2]At $19.95 the paperback book is one of the highest priced trade paperbacks ever to appear on the best seller list, which it did for a brief time in 1983.

1983) concentrates on the typical reference question and how it may be answered with a document. Her look at the broad problems of working with government sources is quite useful.

A somewhat similar approach is suggested in the two-volume *Using Government Publications* (Phoenix, Arizona: Oryx Press, 1985, 1986). Edited by Jean Sears and Marilyn Moody, it offers a subject approach in the first volume and an explanation of statistical searches in the second.

A *Subject Guide to U.S. Government Reference Sources* (Littleton, Colorado: Libraries Unlimited, 1985) offers a selective approach to more popular titles. It is arranged under four broad subject headings with numerous subheadings. Enough information is given to indicate the scope and purpose of the document.

There are also retrospective guides for in-depth research. These are discussed in detail by Morehead in his sixth chapter, "Selected Information Sources for Federal Government Publications." The ongoing guides are considered below.

Current information sources

Almost all of the periodicals which carry reviews of books from time to time consider government periodicals. *Booklist,* for example, has a regular annotated selection section. *Library Journal* and *Choice,* as well as the *Wilson Library Bulletin* and *American Libraries,* feature articles and reviews. Particularly useful is the "Notable Documents List." The May 15, 1986 issue of *Library Journal* devotes six pages to this critical, annotated listing which covers both American and international documents.

As mentioned, Joe Morehead has a regular column on documents in *Serials Librarian* and *RQ* has different experts. *Government Publications Review* (New York: Pergamon Press, 1973 to date, bimonthly) considers federal, state, and local materials, and each issue normally has three to five scholarly articles about government documents. There's a major section, too, which is turned over to reviewing the major documents. The last number of each year is devoted entirely to reviews.

Documents to the People (Chicago: American Library Association, 1972 to date, bimonthly) is a newsletter and watchdog for the Freedom of Information Act. It includes news on government documents, abstracts of ERIC titles, notices of new commercial indexes, and much material of value to reference librarians.

Government organizations

> *United States Government Manual.* Washington, D.C.: Government Printing Office, 1935 to date, annual. $9.50.

The basic purpose of the *Manual* is to give in detail the organization, activities, and chief officers of all government agencies within the legislative, judicial, and executive branches. Each of the agencies is discussed separately, and the units within each organizational pattern are clearly defined. Occasionally, charts and diagrams are employed to make matters a bit clearer. The style is factual, yet discursive enough to hold the interest of anyone remotely involved with such matters.

A useful feature of each year's issue is the list of agencies transferred, terminated, or abolished. Full particulars are given. This, by the way, is a justification for holding several years of the *Manual* on the shelves. All too often, someone will want information on a certain agency which can be found only in earlier editions.

One drawback to the *Government Manual* is its lack of adequate background material on the various agencies. For this, turn to Donald Whitnah's *Government Agencies* (Westport, Connecticut: Greenwood, 1983). Here are long, historical profiles of both existing and former government bodies. Each is signed and written by an expert. Each is followed by a detailed bibliography, and there are numerous chronologies in the appendixes. The index is adequate. Not only does the author chart the past of the agencies, but as of the early 1980s he explains, usually in more detail, what they are about. Compare, for example, the entries on the CIA in this guide and the *Government Manual.*

CATALOGS

> U.S. Superintendent of Documents. *Monthly Catalog of United States Government Publications.* Washington, D.C.: U.S. Government Printing Office. 1895 to date, monthly, $125. (DIALOG file 66, $35 per hour.)
> ———. *U.S. Government Books.* 1982 to date, quarterly. Free.
> ———. *New Books.* 1982 to date, bi-monthly. Free.
> ———. *Subject Bibliographies.* 1975 to date, irregular. Free.

Government documents take numerous forms, from reports on arms to studies of tulip growing, but they do have one thing in common, and that is numbers. In 1980, the Superintendent of Documents sold over 75 million publications. Government documents are not all legal, technical, or how-to-do-it approaches to existence. They touch on almost every human activity. Even a cursory glance at any of the above bibliographies will make the point. An issue of *U.S. Government Books,* for example, opens with a $2 pamphlet on camping on public lands, moves on to an $11 title on careers and ends with a $6 study on aging.

There are a few bibliographies on government documents used in almost all libraries. Large institutions tend to rely on the *Monthly Catalog of United States Government Publications* both as a finding device and catalog as well as a source of information for purchase. Arrangement in the *Monthly Catalog* is by Superintendent of Documents classification number which amounts to an index by issuing agency; that is, most documents issued by the Library of Congress will be listed under that agency name—most, but not all. Special classification situations arise when documents are arranged under a main entry other than the organization that issued the document. Hence, it is always wise to check the indexes and not to rely on the document being under the likely agency, department, and so on. The index to the *Monthly Catalog* is cumulated every six months and combined once a year.

Full cataloging information is given for each entry, so the user can generally tell much about the contents from the descriptors. There are four major indexes: author, title, subject, and series and reports. For reference, the subject and title indexes are the most useful. The subject and author indexes list the documents by their full title.

Most government documents are listed under a corporate entry in the card catalog, rarely by title or by subject. A corporate entry is a listing under the name of the government body responsible for its issue. For example, a corporate government entry will be under the country (United States), state (Minnesota), city (St. Paul), or other official unit that sponsored publication. Thus someone requesting a publication about foreign affairs would probably first look under the U.S. Department of State. Since there are vast numbers of government agencies, it is frequently difficult to remember the proper point of entry.

Another problem is that usually people ask for a government document by its popular name, not by the Superintendent of Documents classification or its official title. For example, The Senate Nutrition Subcommittee released a report, "Dietary Goals for the United States." How does the librarian locate it by its popular name or, for that matter, the follow-up report on the same subject by the Surgeon General's Office?

Popular names are now used in the title index of the *Monthly Catalog*, either with cross-references or by themselves. However, there never seem to be enough of them, so when this fails, *Popular Names of U.S. Government Reports* (Washington, D.C.: The Library of Congress, various dates) should be tried. This is frequently updated and contains reports listed alphabetically by popular name. There is a valuable subject index. Despite the popular-name approach, there still is no single all-inclusive source which will give entry in this fashion.

Although it is a basic finding tool for government documents, the *Monthly Catalog* does not index the majority of them. Estimates vary, but only about two or three out of every 10 documents come from the Government Printing Office. The remainder, therefore, are not in the *Catalog*. Neither does it index periodicals and the material therein.

Documents are not included in the *Monthly Catalog* for a number of reasons, although the most common one is that they are issued outside of the Government Printing Office, and printed or otherwise made available somewhere besides the GPO. This may include everything from a local report on weather or crops to top secret documents. While almost 98 percent of classified information is generated from the CIA and the Department of Defense, some documents, which seem harmless, may be, if only temporarily, removed from circulation. "During the war between Britain and Argentina over the Falkland Islands, the Pentagon classified weather information secret even though it was obtained from the United States Weather Service and was available to anyone, including the Soviet Union."[3] Both the United States and the Soviet Union profit from government documents. Various officials from both countries monitor the documents for information on everything from helicopters to agricultural data.[4]

Consider a government publication which reaches 15,000 government and military personnel each day, but is virtually unknown to the general public. This is "Current News," which is printed not at the Government Printing Office, but at the Pentagon each morning. It consists of readings and clippings from America's major daily news-

[3]Richard Halloran, "The Number of Secrets is Up, But Not by So Much," *The New York Times,* August 9, 1983, p. A18.

[4]Knut Royce, "Soviet Publication's Technology Leaks Aid U.S. Spy Effort," *The Sunday Times Union* (Albany, New York), January 9, 1983, p. 1, 7.

papers. "More than any one newspaper, 'Current News' (published since 1950) offers its readership the latest and most varied coverage of military analysis and news from large newspapers as well as small ones."[5] This is only one example of thousands of such publications which are rarely listed in the *Monthly Catalog.* How can they be found? Here one must turn to other indexes and services enumerated in this chapter, such as the *Index to U.S. Government Periodicals.*

The lack of total coverage must be stressed. For one reason or another, including the desire to be secret, not all government documents are available in a bibliography or index, much less in the *Monthly Catalog.*

In 1985–86 Auto-Graphics introduced a cumulative system similar to the by now familiar *Magazine Index* and *Business Index* approaches. A full ten years of the *Monthly Catalog* is mounted in a reader. Each month the film is replaced as it is updated. One may search June 1976 to June 1986 in one place, at one machine. The cumulation is in two main parts: alphabetical by author-title; and alphabetical by subject. In addition there is a Sudoc Number and a Report Number index. The service eliminates a major problem of going through ten separate annual indexes.

There are numerous other systems such as this, as for example one by Brodart Inc. The problem is cost. Most run from $2,000 and up for the machine and the service.

In smaller libraries, the documents and periodicals are integrated into the general collection or are variously classified like other ephemera in the vertical file. Little or no effort is made to consider them unique. Small and medium sized libraries may have no more than *U.S. Government Books* as a buying aid. This annotates selected publications from the *Monthly Catalog.*

Other bibliographies

Another catalog of interest to large libraries is the *Publications Reference File* (Washington, D.C.: U.S. Government Printing Office, 1977 to date, bimonthly).[6] This is a microfiche version of *Books in Print* for libraries. It lists up to 30,000 government publications which are available for sale. The publication is issued every two months, and, in format, resembles the *National Union Catalog* microfiche edition. There is also a monthly supplement. While primarily for large

---

[5]"A Pentagon Newspaper Consisting of Clippings," *The New York Times,* July 6, 1983, p. B5.

[6]This is free to depository libraries. Nondepository libraries may purchase the identical item, but with another name, i.e., *GPO Sales Publications Reference File.*

research libraries, the PRF can be a useful tool for someone who does not want to carry on correspondence with the Government Printing Office about what is, or is not, in print.

Turning to a more manageable type of bibliography, *U.S. Government Books* is an annotated listing of about 1000 popular and semi-popular documents for laypersons and professionals. The bibliography, of some 60 pages, is composed like a magazine and almost every one of the entries includes a picture, often in color. It is a persuasive sales tool as well as a source of information. For small to medium-sized libraries, it is an ideal buying guide. Also, thanks to its pleasing format, it will be of interest to many laypersons and it should be made available for easy inspection.[7]

A related free government document selection aid: *Consumer Information Catalog* (Pueblo, Colorado: Consumer Information Center, 1970 to date, quarterly. Free). This lists and annotates pamphlets and booklets concerned with everything from automobiles (the first subject heading) to travel and hobbies.

New Books, by comparison, is a drab, matter-of-fact listing of new titles put on sale during the previous two months. There are no annotations, no pictures and the assumption is that it is primarily for the government's document person in the library.

Subject Bibliographies, as the title indicates, stress documents in a specific subject area. There are now close to 300 of these, and they cover material on everything from air pollution to zoology. Many of the entries are annotated. The guides cover a wide variety of interests and levels of interests. A listing is available from the Government Printing Office.

For the library seeking information on government periodicals, the best single source is *Price List 36,* Government Periodicals and Subscription Services, (Washington, D.C.: Government Printing Office, 1974 to date, quarterly. Free). This is an annotated listing of over 500 publications, the majority of which can be classified as periodicals.

Other governments follow much the same bibliographic control.[8] For example, Canada offers *Government of Canada Publications Catalogue* (Ottawa: Canadian Government Publishing Center, 1953 to

---

[7]Due to the austerity program, it is necessary to order an item from one catalog in order to stay on the mailing list. Otherwise, one has to write for each issue of the free publication.

[8]For those seeking information on government documents of other countries, the best series of guides are: *Official Publications of Western Europe* (New York: The H. W. Wilson Company & Mansell, 1984, 1985). The first volume, covering Western Europe, deals with official publications and practices of that area. A second volume covers other European countries.

date. Weekly & quarterly). This is a listing of Canadian departmental and parliamentary documents which range from the esoteric to the popular.

ORGANIZATION AND SELECTION

The organization and selection of government documents in all but the largest of libraries are relatively simple. Librarians purchase a limited number of documents, usually in terms of subjects of interest to users or standard titles, such as the *Statistical Abstract of the United States.* If pamphlets, they are usually deposited by subject in a vertical file. If books, they are cataloged and shelved as such.

The reference librarian normally will be responsible for the acquisition of documents. Confusion is minimal because government documents are rightly treated like any other information source and shelved, filed, or clipped like other media.

When one moves to the large or specialized libraries, the organizational pattern is either a separate government documents collection or an integration of the documents into the general collection. Even the large libraries tend to partially integrate government documents with the collection, although complete integration is rare. About one-third of large libraries have totally separate collections.

Where there is a major collection, an average of two or three people are in charge. Almost 60 percent of the libraries organize the material by the standard Superintendent of Documents classification.

The justification for separate collections is that the volume of publications swamps the library and necessitates special considerations of organization and classification. There are other reasons; but on the whole, it is a matter of the librarian's seeking to find the simplest and best method of making the documents available. Some argue that separation tends to limit use, and they try to compromise by separating the administrative and official works while integrating the more popular and highly specialized subject documents into the general collection.

A distinct disadvantage of a separate documents collection is that it isolates the materials from the main reference collection. The reference librarians are inclined to think of it as a thing apart and may answer questions with materials at hand rather than attempt to fathom the holdings of the documents department. If patrons are referred to the documents section, the librarian there may attempt to answer questions that might be better handled by the reference librarian.

For most librarians, the matter of organization is not a problem, chiefly because they are coming to rely more and more on the large research and depository libraries for help in answering questions which call for specialized documents. The two major factors determining the selection and use of government documents are similar to those governing the selection and use of all forms of communication: the size of the library and its purpose.

The majority of large libraries are depository libraries for government documents. Since the Printing Act of 1895, modified by the Depository Act of 1962, approximately 1313 libraries have been designated as depositories for government documents. The law was modified in 1972 and 1978 to include law school libraries and court libraries. They are entitled to receive publications free of charge from the Superintendent of Documents. While few of them take all the government documents (the average is about 54 percent of what is published), they at least have a larger-than-average collection. The purpose is to have centers with relatively complete runs of government documents located throughout the country. They are likely to be state, regional, and large-city public libraries and the major college and university libraries.[9]

Evaluation

The essential problem with evaluation of government documents is simple: There is no choice. One either accepts or rejects, say, *The Statistical Abstract of the United States*. The government has no competitors, and to speak of evaluating such a document in terms of acquisitions is analogous to commanding the seas to dry up. Conversely, one may object about this or that feature, and sometimes the government actually listens and makes the required revisions. The choice is made even more narrow by the fact that many government documents are unique and that no one, but no one, is going to challenge them with another publication of, say, the *Congressional Record* where the words and actions of Congress are more or less dutifully recorded each day.

[9]Thomas Kleis, "Politics and Publishing," *Special Libraries*, January 1984, pp. 14–16. A discussion of the Joint Committee on Printing and its influence on the depository system, as well as a consideration of the new pricing system for government documents. The depository system is discussed in detail by Morehead in his guide, *Introduction to United States Public Documents, op. cit.* pp. 71–88.

Still, there are some matters which are under one's own control. The librarian and the layperson may consider the following:

Cost When the government first began its massive publishing program it was considered a service, done either at cost or even below cost. Since 1978 that is no longer the case. Now, thanks to appropriation cuts and a new philosophy of budgeting, the documents are supposed to pay for themselves. This does not always happen, but it is reflected in the individual prices of items.

Government documents formerly distributed free or at low cost have been eliminated or given to a private publisher. In 1982, for example, the Government Printing Office "initiated a policy of offering for sale only those publications with an anticipated sale value of $1000 or more. . . . *News Digest,* a publication of the Securities and Exchange Commission, is no longer available on subscription . . . but must now be purchased from a private firm at a 50% increase in price. . . . The price of a subscription to the *Federal Register* and the *Congressional Record* increased from $75 to $300 and from $75 to $208 respectively, in 1981."[10]

The all-time best seller, *Infant Care,* not too long ago cost 20 cents. By 1986 the 67-page document, which sold over 18 million copies since 1919, is slightly less than $5. Another best seller, consistently in the Government's top 10, gives details on septic tanks. This, too, went from a few cents to several dollars.

Currency Currency is another valuable feature, particularly in the statistical reports and with the present methods of keeping up with scientific and technological advancement. Many publications are issued daily or weekly. Still the problem remains of the frequency of indexing or abstracting; e.g., the *Monthly Catalog* has been almost five months behind the material published.

Range of Interest The range of interest is all-encompassing. No publisher except the government has such a varied list.

Indexes and Bibliographies Indexes and bibliographies are improving, not only in the documents themselves, but in works intended as finding devices for those documents.

Other aspects, such as arrangement, treatment, and format, may not be perfect, but the reference librarian hardly has any choice. There is, after all, only one *Congressional Record;* it is judged not for its

[10]Jean Smith, "Information: Public or Private," *Special Libraries,* October 1984, p. 278.

intrinsic value, but in terms of whether it can be used in a particular library.

Acquisition

Once a document has been selected for purchase, its acquisition is no more difficult—indeed, often somewhat easier—than that of a book or periodical. Depository libraries have a peculiar set of problems, but for the average library, the process may be as follows:

1. Full information is given in the *Monthly Catalog* and *U.S. Government Books* on methods of purchase from the Superintendent of Documents. Payment may be made in advance by purchase of coupons from the Superintendent of Documents. In the case of extensive purchases, deposit accounts may be established.
2. Some documents may be obtained free from members of Congress. However, as the supply of some documents is limited, the specific member should be warned in advance. It is particularly advisable to get on the regular mailing list of one's representative or senator to receive such publications as the *Yearbook of Agriculture.*

    Issuing agencies often have a stock of publications which must be ordered directly from the agency. These are noted by a plus sign in the *Monthly Catalog* and frequently include valuable specialized materials, from ERIC documents to scientific reports.
3. There are now 26 government bookstores across the country which sell documents. In addition, some larger private bookstores sell the documents, or at least the books dealing with popular subjects from space to gardening.
4. A growing number of private firms now publish government documents; for example, the *CIS/Index* offers a complete collection of the working papers of Congress on microfiche. Most of the publications are highly specialized, expensive, and reviewed in a number of the reviewing services mentioned earlier.

INDEXES[11]

CIS Index to Publications of the United States Congress. Washington, D.C.: Congressional Information Service, 1970 to date, month-

[11]See, also, the section on "Statistics" in this chapter where there is a discussion of indexes to government statistics.

ly. Service: $600 to $2200 per year. (DIALOG file 101, $90 per hour.)

Turning to the indexes, one of the most frequently used is the *Index to Publications of the United States Congress,* usually called the *CIS/Index.* The *Monthly Catalog* lists only complete congressional documents; the *CIS/Index* analyzes what is *in* those documents, covering nearly 875,000 pages of special studies, bills, hearings, and so on each year.

Published by a private concern, the *Index* averages between 100 and 200 pages a month in loose-leaf form. It is in two parts: (1) The index section offers access by subject, author, and title. This section is cumulated quarterly and there is an annual. (2) The summary section gives the full title of the document and includes an abstract of most of the items indexed.

There is a complete system for the library that can afford to purchase all the indexed materials. These are made available by Congressional Information Service (CIS) on microfiche. The user locates the desired item in the index and through a simple key system finds the microfiche copy.

As one of the most comprehensive of document indexes, although limited to the activities of Congress, the *CIS/Index* is a blessing for the reference librarian seeking information on the progress of a bill through Congress. Popular names of bills, laws, and reports are given, as well as the subject matter of those materials. In addition, an index covers the same material by bill number, report number, and so on. Hearings are covered as well as the names of witnesses, committees, and the like, so the librarian can easily keep up with the development of legislation.

The comprehensive quality of the *CIS/Index* is such that, with a little practice, the reference librarian will feel fully capable of tracking down even the most elusive material. It is an exemplary index and abstracting service for current materials. (In time, of course, it will be equally useful for retrospective searching.)

Weekly summaries of congressional action

CQ Weekly Report: Washington Congressional Quargerly 1945 to date, weekly. Libraries: rates on request. Summarized in *Congressional Quarterly Almanac,* 1945 to date, annual. $115. (Online: Congressional Quarterly, rate per hour varies.)

The *CQ Weekly Report,* a much-used reference aid similar in some ways to a congressional version of *Facts on File,* was mentioned earlier in the text. It is *not* an index but a summary of the week's past events—a summary which is often sufficient either to identify a government document to be later found in a specialized work or to answer in one step a reference query.

Each issue analyzes in detail both congressional and general political activity of the week. The major bills are followed from the time they are introduced until they are passed and enacted into law (or killed along the way). A handy table of legislation shows at a glance where bills are in the Congress. Cross-references to previous weekly reports allow easy access to material until the quarterly index is issued and cumulated throughout the year.

Periodical indexes

> *Index to U.S. Government Periodicals.* Chicago: Infordata International, 1974 to date, quarterly. $300.

There are a number of practical indexes which make some effort to index government periodicals and documents selectively. The best known, most often used, is the *Public Affairs Information Service Bulletin,* followed by *Resources in Education,* published by the U.S. Educational Resources Information Center (ERIC).

The librarian looking for material should turn to the *Index of U.S. Government Periodicals,* which indexes close to 200 titles. Comparatively, there are about 2000 periodicals and serials currently available from the federal government and probably several times that number from agencies and sections not found in Washington, D.C.

The limitation of numbers imposed by the index is a blessing, in that many of the 2000-plus government periodicals and serials are so specialized as to be of little use to more than a few people and, except in a depository library, not likely to be readily available. While primarily used by subject, the index does provide an author index which is useful to check for what has been published by an agency, bureau, or department. The index has proved particularly useful for searches involved with the sciences and social sciences.

STATISTICS

> U.S. Bureau of the Census. *Statistical Abstract of the United States.* Washington, D.C.: Government Printing Office, 1879 to date, annual. $27; paper $22.
>
> *Historical Statistics of the United States, Colonial Times to 1970.*

Washington, D.C.: Government Printing Office, 1975, 1979, 2 vols. $35.

United Nations Statistical Office. *Statistical Yearbook.* New York: United Nations Publications, 1949 to date, annual. $60.

Statistics are concerned with the collection, classification, analysis, and interpretation of numerical facts or data. The reference librarian meets a statistical question when the user opens a query with "How much?" or "How many?" Depending on whether the query is motivated by simple curiosity or by a serious research problem, the sources of possible answers are as numerous as the hundreds of reference works dealing peripherally or exclusively with statistical data.

The reference librarian's most difficult problem remains one of identifying a source for an answer to the esoteric, specialized statistical query; almost as hard is translating the query into the terminology of the statistical source. Given the numerous sources and the specialized terminology, it is no wonder that in larger libraries the expert in statistics is as important as the subject bibliographer. Normally, this librarian is located in the government documents or the business section. Statistical reference work is highly specialized; all that can be done here is to indicate the basic general sources with which the beginner should be familiar.

The federal government, followed by states and local governments, accounts for the greatest number of statistical documents. A number of agencies issue these regularly and they are an important part of planning in the private sector. It is a vast undertaking; for details see *Statistics Sources* (Detroit: Gale Research Company, 1962 to date). The 1986 edition lists more than 40,000 sources of statistics under 12,000 subject headings. To be sure not all of these are government, but the major American government sources are dutifully listed—as are sources for 186 nations of the world.

There are a number of general guides and indexes which will help even the most statistically unaware librarian through the maze. While not all of these are published by the government, the majority rely on government statistics.

How reliable is the statistical data? If it comes from standard federal and major state agencies, it is likely to be quite reliable, although there are always exceptions. Most of the errors are caught, at least when it is in the interests of any given group to pay that much attention to the data. This is not always the case with international data because, among other things, "legal constraints imposed on the agencies that collect and disseminate international statistics by their own parent organizations heavily influence the accuracy and validity of the data presented for consumption".[12]

By and large if only one statistical source were available in a library, it would be the *Statistical Abstract of the United States*. In reviewing the 1981 edition the Reference Books Bulletin termed it "venerable" and "virtually indispensable for any library."[13] Few will disagree.

The data is favored by newspaper reporters who delight in summarizing its contents. The work is a mirror of American habits. In considering the 1982–83 editions of over one thousand pages, Marjorie Hunter writes:

> *Americans are eating more beef but fewer eggs. Church membership is up, but so is the divorce rate. About 98 percent of all American households own at least one television set. American women spend nearly $4 billion a year on cosmetics. . . . A treasure trove for sociologists, economists and mere trivia collectors, the book is crammed with charts and tables that can tell you much that you may want to know, as well as a great deal you may not want to know.*
>
> *Says James A. Michener, the novelist: "For half a century I have used the abstract to clarify and to fortify my thinking. I use it in three distinct ways: to explain my homeland, to make comparisons with other nations and to amuse myself in idle exploration."*[14]

The Statistical Abstract of the United States is the basic source of American statistical data in any library. Filled with 1500 tables and charts, but less data than many might wish, the work serves to summarize social and economic trends. The work is divided into 34 major sections—from education and population to public lands—with a detailed 40- to 50-page index which takes the reader from abortion to zoology.

Despite the good index, the 500,000-plus statistics are not always easy to understand. The massive number of figures can be quite baffling, particularly for the layperson. There is a need to formulate the statistics in such a way that they are much easier to understand,

---

[12]John Ratcliffe, "International Statistics: Pitfalls and Problems," *Reference Services Review*, Fall 1982, p. 93. The article stresses the fact that national statistics often serve the interest of the nation-state and "nation-states can and do lie about statistics in order to serve such interests" (p. 95). Of course, various United States agencies are not always free of such problems, and all statistical data is worth questioning.

[13]*Booklist*, May 1, 1983, p. 1163.

[14]Marjorie Hunter, "Prized Abstract Paints U.S. Portrait in Statistics," *The New York Times*, March 28, 1983, p. B6.

and as more than one critic has observed, there is even more need for explanations of the figures.[15] Reference librarians should study each edition with care.

Historical Statistics of the United States, is revised over the years. The present edition includes data for more than 12,500 time series grouped in tabular form. It gives comparative figures on statistics, ranging from the average wage over the years to the number of residents in a given state or territory. Most material is on the national level but a few sections cover regions and smaller areas.

The majority of Western nations follow the pattern established by the American government in issuing equivalents of the *Statistical Abstract* and specialized statistical information. For example, England has *Annual Abstracts of Statistics* (London: Her Majesty's Stationery Office: 1854 to date). On an international level the best-known equivalent is the United Nations *Statistical Yearbook,* which covers basic data from over 150 areas of the world. The information is broken down under broad subject headings ranging from population to transportation, and no effort is made to single out units of government smaller than national.

Indexes

The three indexes to statistics are published by the Washington-based Congressional Information Services. Price depends on institutional budget, but it averages about $1200 a year.

American Statistics Index, 1973 to date, monthly. (DIALOG file 102, $90.)

Statistical Reference Index, 1980 to date, monthly.

Index to International Statistics, 1983 to date, monthly.

These indexes follow a basic pattern: (1) Issued monthly, they have a quarterly index and are cumulated, with an index, annually. When searching, generally one should begin with the annual index to get a sense of subject headings and general arrangement. (2) The index, a separate section or volume, refers the user to the document in the main work. Material is indexed by subject, title, issuing agency, primary individuals involved with the document, etc. Each document or series is abstracted, and there is complete information about the issuing agency and the necessary background about the statistics. The entries in the main section are arranged by accession number. Each

[15]Christopher Jencks, "How We Live Now," *The New York Times Book Review,* April 10, 1983, pp. 7, 36–37.

document is within a particular issuing agency. (3) Almost all of the documents are available, as with ERIC and similar services, in microfiche. Each abstract is keyed to the proper microfiche item. In addition there is a Superintendent of Documents classification number to help locate the hard copy.

Given this type of detailed support system, the librarian has a marvelous set of tools for answering almost any statistical question. The indexes are extremely easy to use, particularly as they have such detailed abstracts. There is no problem in locating the documents themselves. Actually, the abstracts often are enough to answer more than an involved research question.

The three works cover three equally distinct areas. *American Statistics Index* indexes and abstracts almost every statistical source issued by the federal government. This includes the contents of over 800 periodicals. It is entry to close to 10,000 different reports, studies, articles, and the like.

Its twin, *Statistical Reference Index,* indexes and abstracts state documents. It does *not* include federal material. It *does* include many nongovernmental statistics, as well. These range from those issued by private concerns and business to nonprofit organizations and associations.

The *Index to International Statistics* includes major governmental statistics from around the world. There is particular emphasis on Western European countries, including the European community. It is an excellent source of United Nations statistical data. As in the other indexes, periodicals are analyzed (in this case about 100). Almost all of the publications are in English, albeit there are some in Spanish and other languages when there is no English equivalent.

Statistical information is hardly limited to these three indexes. One may wish to consult the previously discussed *CIS Index.* Other valuable data will be found in the basic indexes such as *Public Affairs Information Service Bulletin; Business Index; Business Periodicals Index;* and any service which regularly reports on the activities of government and business such as *Predicasts.*

STATE AND LOCAL DOCUMENTS

Book of the States. Chicago: Council of State Governments, 1935 to date, biennial. $35.

Index to Current Urban Documents. Westport, Connecticut: Greenwood Press, 1972 to date, quarterly. $215.

Parish, David, *State Government Reference Publications,* 2d ed.

Littleton, Colorado: Libraries Unlimited, 1981. 355 pp. $27.50.

U.S. Bureau Of the Census. *County and City Data Book*. Washington, D.C.: Government Printing Office, 1952 to date, every 5 years. 1984 ed. 996 pp. $24.

————. *State and Metropolitan Area Data Book*. Washington, D.C.: Government Printing Office, 1979 to date, biennial. 1982 ed. $15.

U.S. Library of Congress. *Monthly Checklist of State Publications*, 1910 to date, monthly. $25.

In examining how state documents are used (or not used) in public libraries in 10 states, Purcell found the most persistent calls for such titles come from businesspeople, followed by college students, professional persons and those in local or state government, with the most frequent users in the latter category.

He asked, too, "What types of state documents are perceived by librarians as having the greatest reference value?" The answer comes as no surprise, particularly as in studies of federal documents the order is pretty much the same. The most used are those concerned with statistical information, legislative publications and government structure. Maps and recreational information are high on the list, but at the bottom are reports concerning regulatory agencies and judicial reports.[16]

At the state level, there is no entirely satisfactory bibliographical tool that lists the majority of publications. Of considerable help is the *Monthly Checklist of State Publications*. Prepared by the Library of Congress, it represents only those state publications received by the Library. Arrangement is alphabetical by state and then, as in the *Monthly Catalog*, by issuing agency. Entries are usually complete enough for ordering, although prices are not always given. There is an annual, but not a monthly, subject and author index. The indexes are not cumulative. Since 1963, periodicals have been listed in the June and December issues.

The single best guide to state government documents is the Parish work. Parish offers a retrospective listing of 1756 basic state publications. These are annotated and placed under various categories, and then under state. Primarily the annotated items can be considered reference works and these vary from the standard legisla-

---

[16]Gary Purcell, "Reference Use of State Government Information in Public Libraries," *Government Publications Review*, March/April 1983, pp. 173–187.

tive manuals and directories to specialized bibliographies and statistics. The guide is updated every four or five years.[17]

For those seeking a textbook guide to state publications, the best one is Margaret Lane's *State Publications and Depository Libraries* (Westport, Connecticut: Greenwood Press, 1981). The first section explains the depository system. The second part, of most interest to the general reference librarian, is concerned with various types of state publications, as well as a detailed bibliography. Most of the basic titles are annotated.

The most comprehensive index and bibliography of local publications will be found in the *Index to Current Urban Documents.* This covers a wide variety of material from pamphlets issued by the various city agencies to annual audits and reports. It is supported by a microfiche collection which is tied to the main index.

The County and City Data Book is a mass of statistical information. Here one finds data for each county in the United States, as well as for close to 1000 cities with populations of over 25,000. Page after page provides information on everything from income levels to weather and types of jobs in various communities.[18] A related work is Joseph Kane's *The American Counties* (4th ed. Metuchen, New Jersey: Scarecrow Press, 1983) which draws upon the federal work, but is arranged state by state, county by county. Here, though, there is more emphasis on place names (including information about the base of the county name) than on statistics.

The Bureau of the Census publishes another similar work in the *State and Metropolitan Area Data Book.* Under more than 2000 different subjects one can trace statistical data for each state and major metropolitan area. This ranges from education and housing to employment and crime.

The aptly named *Book of the States* is valuable on three counts. First, there are standard articles on issues such as reapportionment, consumer protection, rights for women, and the like. These are updated with each new volume. Second, there are reviews of trends, statistics and developments at both the local and federal level which have, or will have, a strong influence on state government. Third, it has relatively current information on names of principal state officers.

[17]Parish updates the work in his column on "State Publications" in each issue of *Government Publications Review.* For a short article on his book see John Richardson, "State Government Reference Publications," *Reference Services Review,* Spring 1983, p. 7–8.

[18]This work always enjoys news coverage when it is released, e.g., see "Anyplace U.S.A.? It's Listed Somewhere in the 996 Pages," *The New York Times,* April 8, 1984, p. 58.

The wealth of data makes it an invaluable reference work for almost any type or size of library.

U.S. Census[19]

A word about the census. Data collected by the Bureau of the Census is the statistical backbone of most of the works considered in this section. Where specific census data is required there are three basic approaches. First, one should turn to *American Statistics Index*. Second, other business and related indexes (from *Predicasts* to the *CIS/Index*) will analyze census material. Third, for a detailed description of the various files and reports there is the *Bureau of the Census Catalog* (Washington, D.C.: Government Printing Office, 1946 to date, annual). While this has changed in form and format, essentially it arranges news and information about statistical data by subjects from agriculture to trade. There is a detailed index which allows one to locate material by a specific area.

The ten-year census, as well as the ongoing collection of statistical data by federal agencies, provides a portrait of Americans which cannot be rivaled. The most complete compendium of the 1980 census, however, comes not from the Government but from the National Decisions Systems, a San Diego market research firm. Their work, *1980 U.S. Census,* issued in 1983, consists of five paperbound volumes of statistical data. Expertly edited and produced, the set offers a quick, easy approach to the 1980 census. The drawback: the cost which is $395 for the set, or as one reviewer puts it, "On a per-page basis, this comes to about 10 times what the Government Printing Office charges for documents."[20] Nevertheless, it is a marvelous guide for the layperson who can't be bothered to try to fathom the official census report.

SUGGESTED READINGS

Durrance, Joan, "Spanning the Local Government Information Gap," *RQ,* Fall 1985. How can the reference librarian keep up with local government documents? First, an appreciation of local government organization is required, and it is with this that the author primarily is concerned. There is specific advice on equally specific guides such as LOGIC.

---

[19]For a clear discussion of the various census publications, see Morehead, *op. cit.,* pp. 217–231.

[20]Andrew Hacker, "Census Figures for Corporate Use," *The New York Times Book Review*, August 21, 1983, p. 7.

Eidelman, Diane et al. "Documents to the People: Long Island," *Reference Services Review,* Winter 1982, pp. 97–98. Three librarians explain how, as a group, they established government document service which serves a large community. Furthermore, there is an enthusiastic discussion of how such a group may be organized.

Heckman, Lucy, "Statistical Sources in Business and Economics," *Reference Services Review,* Summer 1983, pp. 72–76. An annotated listing of "the leading sources of business and economic statistics." The listing is based upon the most common types of questions asked at the average reference desk.

McClure, Charles and Peter Hernon, *Improving the Quality of Reference Service for Government Publications.* Chicago: American Library Association, 1983. This gives the results of an unobtrusive testing of reference librarians who work with government documents. The results of the study of the 17 academic depository libraries is far from satisfactory, and the authors suggest how reference services with government documents might be improved. The major recommendation is that government documents be integrated into regular reference services.

Morehead, Joe, "Abridging Government Information: The Reagan Administration's War on Waste," *Dartmouth College Library Bulletin,* April 1985, pp. 58–71. The well-known author and writer on government documents considers what has happened to the publication of documents since the Reagan administration took power. It is primarily negative in that prices have gone up and many services previously offered have been diminished or dismissed. For another view of this see Diane Smith, "The Commercialization and Privatization of Government Information," *Government Publications Review,* vol. 12, 1985, pp. 45–63.

Mourey, Deborah, "Conquering the Fear of Searching for Statistical Information," *Online,* March, 1986, pp. 59–64. "The very mention of statistics can send even a competent searcher into a panic." It need not be so, and the author explains how to overcome the fear through knowledge. She concentrates on databases, but much of what she writes is a applicable to the manual search.

Samuelson, Robert, "The Joy of Statistics," *Newsweek,* November 4, 1985, p. 55. A single-page justification for the use and love of statistics; this is witty and even useful in that it explains the imperfections of data. The author opens with a short note on the *Statistical Abstract of the U.S.*

Shiflett, Orvin, "The Government as Publisher: An Historical Review," *Library Research,* no. 4, 1982, pp. 115–135. A brief yet thorough article on the history of government printing. There is good coverage of how documents are printed and who is involved.

Willard, Robert and Donna Demac and Allan Adler, "Whose Information Is It Anyway?" *Government Publications Review,* vol 13, 1986, pp. 323–335. A three-way discussion of the privatization of government produced information. Willard justifies the publication of government documents by private companies. Ms. Demac takes the stand that government documents are public and should be for the public good. The third speaker "places government information and the people's right to know within the context of principles laid down by the founding fathers."

Zink, Steven (ed.), "Statistical Abstracts for Reference," *Reference Services Review,* October/December 1981, pp. 71–84. This is an annotated listing, by several experts, of statistical data published by major federal agencies from Agriculture to Transportation. Each publication is examined critically from the point of view of the average reference situation.

Index

Index